THE RIGHTS OF THE ACCUSED

In Law and Action

Volume I. Sage Criminal Justice System Annuals

THE RIGHTS
OF THE ACCUSED

IN LAW AND ACTION

STUART S. NAGEL, *Editor*

SAGE Publications
Beverly Hills · London

212709

For information address:

SAGE PUBLICATIONS, INC.
275 South Beverly Drive
Beverly Hills, California 90212

SAGE PUBLICATIONS LTD
St George's House / 44 Hatton Garden
London E C 1

Printed in the United States of America

International Standard Book Number 0-8039-0131-3

Library of Congress Catalog Card No. 72-84052

FIRST PRINTING

This book is dedicated
to protecting the innocent
whether they be suspects
or victims

PUBLISHER'S PREFACE

This volume inaugurates a new series, *The Sage Criminal Justice System Annuals.* Each volume will focus on a theme or topic of current concern to professionals interested in the study and improved operation of criminal justice systems throughout the world—social scientists, law professors, public officials at both the research administration and policy-drafting levels, professionally oriented police officials and police science faculties, and a certain segment of the bar and the judiciary.

We are pleased that the first volume in this series should represent a significant interdisciplinary contribution to the literature on civil liberties, criminal procedure, constitutional law, judicial process and criminal law. Future volumes are planned on Drugs and the Criminal Justice System (1973), Proposals for Criminal Justice System Reform, the Judiciary System, and so on. Suggestions for future volumes will, of course, be welcomed from our readers.

Sara Miller McCune
Publisher and President
SAGE PUBLICATIONS, Inc.

Beverly Hills, California
October, 1972

CONTENTS

Publisher's Preface   7

Part I.
INTRODUCTION

1. The Rights of the Accused: Overview, Effects, and Causes   13
   STUART S. NAGEL

Part II.
PRIOR TO FIRST COURT APPEARANCE

2. Search and Seizure   27
   JACOB W. LANDYNSKI

3. Confessions and Self-Incrimination   59
   O. JOHN ROGGE

Part III.
FROM FIRST COURT APPEARANCE TO TRIAL

4. Justice in the Accusation   111
   DELMAR KARLEN and J. LAWRENCE SCHULTZ

5. The Right to Counsel   145
   WILLIAM M. BEANEY

6. The Right to Bail Revisited: A Decade of Promise
   without Fulfillment   175
   PATRICIA M. WALD

Part IV.
THE TRIAL STAGE

7. The Jury System   209
    RITA JAMES SIMON and PRENTICE MARSHALL

8. Trial, Testimony, and Truth   235
    JAMES MARSHALL

Part V.
POST-TRIAL

9. The Sentencing and Correctional Process   259
    ROBERT O. DAWSON

10. The New Broom: The Federalization of Double Jeopardy 281
    JAY A. SIGLER

    Index of Cases   299
    Index of Names   309
    Subject Index   317

PART I.

INTRODUCTION

Chapter 1

THE RIGHTS OF THE ACCUSED:
OVERVIEW, EFFECTS, AND CAUSES

nor shall any person be . . . deprived of life, liberty, or property,
without due process of law

From the Fifth and Fourteenth Amendments
to the U.S. Constitution

STUART S. NAGEL is Professor of Political Science at the University of Illinois and a member of the Illinois bar. He is the author of *The Legal Process from a Behavioral Perspective* (1969) and the forthcoming *Effects of Alternative Legal Policies,* as well as numerous journal articles and chapters in books. He has been a Yale Russell Sage Fellow in Law and Social Science and a Fellow of the Center for Advanced Study in the Behavioral Sciences. For three years he was the attorney-director of the OEO Legal Services Agency of Champaign County.

Chapter 1

THE RIGHTS OF THE ACCUSED:
OVERVIEW, EFFECTS, AND CAUSES

STUART S. NAGEL

I. PURPOSES OF THIS VOLUME

The rights of the accused refer to various aspects of criminal procedure designed to safeguard the innocent from harassment and conviction. Basically, these rights are nine in number, starting from the original arrest to the final appeal. They may be listed as follows in the order in which they usually occur:

I. Rights Prior to First Court Appearance
  (1) Arrest or search only where there is substantial likelihood of guilt;
  (2) No involuntary confessions or self-incrimination.

II. Rights from First Court Appearance to Trial
  (3) Release pending speedy trial;
  (4) Right to hired or provided counsel at trial and before;
  (5) Formal notice of charges.

III. The Trial Stage
  (6) Impartial jury trial;
  (7) Right to cross-examine and subpoena witnesses.

IV. Post-Trial
  (8) No excessive fines or punishment;
  (9) No double jeopardy and right to appeal.

The main purpose of this volume is to bring together a set of interdisciplinary perspectives by established scholars on each of the nine rights mentioned above. We were fortunate in obtaining an available person who has published an important book in at least one of the nine areas.[1] The total list of authors combines the perspectives of (1) law teaching (Beaney, Karlen, P. Marshall, Dawson, and Sigler); (2) active law practice (Rogge, Wald, P. Marshall, and J. Marshall); (3) political science (Landynski, Beaney, and Sigler); (4) sociology (Simon); and (5) psychology (J. Marshall). Each individual author also combines to some extent, a legal, empirical, and philosophical perspective in writing his chapter. As such, this volume hopefully will be valuable to students, teachers, researchers, lawyers, and laymen both American and non-American. Perhaps some judges, legislators, and administrators might also find helpful some of the ideas presented. No technical knowledge is presumed although the chapters often discuss more complex matters after providing the basic background. Historical and cross-cultural materials are also occasionally presented.

Earlier literature in the field for the most part lacked the breadth of perspective which this group of authors brings to the subject. The leading works from a legal teaching perspective include casebooks like William Lockhart, Yale Kamisar, and Jesse Choper, *Constitutional Rights and Liberties* (West, 1970) and Lloyd Weinreb, *Cases on Criminal Process* (Foundation, 1970). An excellent practicing lawyers' manual is Robert Cipes, *Criminal Defense Techniques* (Matthew Bender, 1969). Insightful empirical perspectives are provided in William Chambliss and Robert Seidman, *Law, Order, and Power* (Addison-Wesley, 1971) and Abraham Blumberg, *Criminal Justice* (Quadrangle Books, 1967). One book which attempts to combine interdisciplinary perspectives is David Fellman, *The Defendant's Rights* (Rinehart, 1958), but it is rapidly becoming dated in this ever-changing field. A recently attempted combination is Stephen Gillers, *Getting Justice: The Rights of People* (Basic Books, 1971), but it deals primarily with search, counsel, and confessions rather than all nine of the above-mentioned rights of the accused.

The sub-title of this volume (i.e., "in law and action") emphasizes the fact that the rights of the accused may differ as stated in the legal norms from what they are in empirical practice. Some rights are embodied only in law, but often not in action—such as counsel for the indigent at the police interrogation stage (Milner, 1971; Wald, 1967; Robinson, 1968; Medalie, 1968). On the other hand, some rights are embodied only in action, but not in law—such as the aid which prosecutors and police often give to middle class defendants and which such defendants tend to expect (LaFave, 1965; Miller, 1969). Likewise some rights are generally embodied in both law and action—such as counsel for the indigent at the trial stage (Silverstein, 1965).

Each chapter, with regard to the right discussed attempts to cover: (1) the basic law, (2) justifications for, and arguments against, the law in view of the law's consequences, (3) empirical research already done, (4) legal trends and reasons for those trends, (5) new research needed, and (6) new laws needed—although not necessarily in that order. The remainder of this introduction will attempt a partial tying together of the portions of the individual chapters dealing with empirical research on the consequences of the rights of the accused (points 2, 3, and 5 above), as well as the empirical research which helps to explain the legal trends and causal forces behind those rights (points 3, 4, and 6).

II. EFFECTS OF THE RIGHTS OF THE ACCUSED

Those responsible for legislating the nine rights of the accused mainly intend to achieve the effect of lessening the likelihood that an innocent person will be convicted or harassed. This effect can be endorsed by people who are unlikely to commit crimes, but who recognize the possibility that they (or other innocent persons) might find themselves in a situation or business practice where they could be falsely suspected or accused of wrongdoing. These rights also decrease the likelihood that a guilty person will be convicted of a greater crime than he committed, or that he will receive punishment (or treatment) disproportionate to his crime. That effect too can be endorsed by most people who recognize that if the guilty are overconvicted or oversentenced, the end result may well be unnecessary bitterness and general disrespect for the law rather than rehabilitation or deterrence. The rights of the accused also make it more difficult to convict the guilty, but most people probably recognize that it is more detrimental to their self-interest and the orderly functioning of society for one innocent person to be convicted, than for one or even a few guilty persons to go uncaught for a specific crime. In general there would be no need to have these rights if there were some accurate automatic way of separating the innocent from the guilty.[2]

With regard to the nine specific rights, the right to a lawyer (whether hired or provided) is probably the most important for preventing wrongful convictions and harassment.[3] Having a lawyer aids investigation of the facts, negotiation with the prosecutor, examination of witnesses, presentation of legal and factual arguments to the judge and jury, and preparation of an appeal. A lawyer also provides psychological support to the defendant and an air of objectivity which the defendant himself could not provide. All the other procedural rights become less meaningful without an attorney to inform the defendant of his rights and to call violations to the attention of the courts, including violations that might occur at the police interrogation stage. Of the basic legal rights, only free speech may be more important, because without free speech violations of rights could not be readily called to the attention of a larger public.

Besides protecting the innocent, the right to counsel has some important effects on the legal system. The American adversary system presumes that both sides will be vigorously represented so that the neutral judge can arrive at the truth (which presumably lies somewhere between the adverse positions); but if only one side is represented, the system may not function effectively. If the poor lack lawyers when prosecuted, their respect for the law is likely to decrease. Counsel for the poor and other alienated groups can also help to bring about orderly reform of the law as an alternative to disorderly or violent change. In addition, widespread availability of counsel can serve to educate through counseling those who otherwise would be without counsel, and such education may prevent them from getting into legal trouble.

While it is generally agreed that arrests, searches, and confession-obtaining techniques that are brutal or random have adverse social effects (by creating an unduly fearful population as well as widespread disrespect for the police), there has been some controversy over how to deter such police tactics. One cannot expect the prosecutor to be very vigorous in prosecuting police who have been zealously (although perhaps overzealously) trying to help him. Similarly private damage suits are costly, time-consuming, embarrassing to the plaintiff, unlikely to result in victory (because of police leeway to make mistakes and generally unsympathetic juries), and if victorious unlikely to result in a deterring damage judgment (because of the officer's lack of money, the difficulty of assessing damages, and the likelihood the city—and hence the taxpayers—will pay the judgment). Internal police administration in these matters tends to be more protective than disciplinary. The lack of more effective alternatives has resulted in a choice by the courts to exclude illegally obtained evidence from the courtroom, hoping thereby to encourage a more lawful approach by the police in the processes of arrest, search, and obtaining confessions. Studies by behavioral scientists have shown this exclusionary rule has in fact changed some police behavior.[4]

Some important behavioral research has recently shown that regardless of the nature of the crime or the defendant's prior record, he is more likely to be convicted if he is not released pending trial (Rankin, 1964). His conviction chances are increased (1) because being in jail awaiting trial decreases his ability to investigate and prepare his defense, and (2) because he makes a relatively bad impression on the judge and jury when he is brought for each trial session from the prisoner's lockup area, rather than on his own through the regular courtroom entrance. Denying pretrial release for want of bail money also has the effect of discriminating against the poor, increasing jail costs, promoting loss of jobs, and increasing the likelihood that the innocent will spend time in jail and that the guilty will spend more time than their sentence or the law provides. Studies have shown that careful screening of defendants to determine their roots in the community followed by reminders of their court dates has the effect of producing a higher percentage of pretrial releases and a lower percentage of those who do not show up in court than the traditional money-bond system does (Ares, 1963). Other studies have provided useful information with regard to how court congestion can be reduced so that both released and jailed defendants can be tried and convicted or acquitted sooner (Zeisel et al., 1959; Navarro and Taylor, 1967).

There has been solid behavioral research on the consequences of some other criminal procedure rights. The effect of criminal jury trials rather than bench trials has been well researched and reveals that juries are more likely to acquit in 17 percent of the cases; there is agreement in 75 percent; the judge is more likely to acquit in 2 percent; and the jury is undecided in 6 percent (Kalven and Zeisel, 1966). The unanimity requirement, the multiple decision makers, and the less upper-class composition of juries probably account for their lower propensity to convict compared to judges. Studies have also been made of the effect of various punishments (especially capital punishment—Bedau, 1967), although the right to be free from the threat of capital punishment has not yet been established as an American legal right except in a few states.

Although to date little behavioral research has been done on the effects of the other procedural rights (like double jeopardy, formal accusation, and confrontation), the effects of the presence or absence of these rights can be hypothesized. It seems apparent that if a prosecutor could repeatedly prosecute a defendant for the same matter, he might eventually get a conviction of an innocent person or an overconviction of a guilty person, to say nothing of the obvious harassment involved. Likewise, without clear notice of the charges against him and the right to call his own witnesses (as well as to question opposition witnesses), an innocent defendant would clearly tend to have a much more difficult time establishing his innocence.

III. CAUSAL FORCES BEHIND THE RIGHTS OF THE ACCUSED

In discussing the causal forces behind the rights of the accused, one can distinguish between two important kinds of causation. First, what explains why constitutional rights are more recognized in some situations than in others? Second, why are the general constitutional rights of the accused expanding, at least in the long run?

Much short-run differential treatment can be explained in terms of the characteristics of the accused, the victims, the decision makers, and the crime. Certain studies, for instance, have revealed differential treatment at various stages of the criminal justice process depending on the economic class, sex, race, age, education, urbanism, or region of the accused (Nagel, 1967; Martin, 1970). The stages studied include arrest and police interrogation, release on bail, having counsel, formal notice of charges, jury trial, and sentencing.

The general findings are that there are three patterns of differential treatment based on the characteristics of the accused. One pattern might be called the disadvantaged pattern. It particularly applies to indigents, blacks, and the less educated. It involves a tendency to receive relatively unfavorable treatment with regard to all the rights of the accused in comparison to nonindigents, whites, and the more educated, who in general represent the more favored dominant groups in American society.

A second pattern might be called the paternalized pattern. It particularly applies to juveniles and women. It involves a tendency to receive relatively unfavorable treatment with regard to certain formal procedural safeguards for the innocent like having a jury trial or being represented by a lawyer, but favorable treatment with regard to being kept in jail before or after conviction in comparison to adults and men. This pattern is in conformity with the notion that juveniles and women, being relatively weak, should be treated in a fatherly way and therefore not be so readily subjected to cold legalistic formality or to lengthy pre- or posttrial imprisonment.

A third pattern might be called the industrialized pattern. It applies to situations arising in urban or in northern areas as contrasted to rural or southern areas. It involves unfavorable treatment with regard to formal accusation and delay pending trial while in jail, but favorable treatment with regard to being provided with a lawyer. Crimes against persons seem to be dealt with more harshly in industrialized areas where organized police rather than personal violence is the relatively more favored way of settling severe disputes, as contrasted to nonindustrialized areas. On the other hand, crimes against property seem to be dealt with more harshly in nonindustrialized places, where property is more likely to be individually owned than in industrialized places.

Some differential treatment can be explained by the nature of the victim of the accused. Thus, blacks seem to receive relatively less favorable treatment with regard to the rights of the accused in crimes against persons which tend to be within-race crimes, than they tend to receive in crimes against property, which tend to be between-race crimes (Bullock, 1961; Nagel, 1967). Likewise, if a man sexually assaults a woman, he is more likely to receive unfavorable treatment with regard to his rights than if a woman sexually assaults a man. In fact, most states do not provide for actual or statutory rape of men by women (Kanowitz, 1967).

Some differential treatment can also be explained by the characteristics of the decision makers. For example, judges with attributes associated with having greater sympathy for less privileged persons in American society do have a greater propensity to decide for defendant in appellate criminal cases (many of which involve constitutional rights issues), than judges having the opposite characteristics (Nagel, 1962). Somewhat pro-defendant characteristics of appellate judges include being a Democrat; being a nonmember of the ABA or of a nativist group, not having been a former prosecutor, being a Catholic rather than a Protestant, and receiving a relatively high score on a general liberalism and a criminal liberalism attitude questionnaire.

The nature or severity of the crime (as well as the nature of the accused, the victim, or the decision makers) can also help explain why the rights of the accused are sometimes more exercised in some situations than in others. For example, suspects are less likely to be released on bail for more severe crimes than for less severe ones (Ares, 1963), on the theory that one suspected of a more severe crime has more incentive to skip out. Likewise defendants are more likely to request and be awarded jury trials for more severe crimes (Broeder, 1959) on the theory that there is more at stake to merit the extra system effort to prevent wrongful convictions.

In the long run, civil liberties including the rights of the accused seem to be expanding (Roche, 1956; Konvitz, 1967). For example, an analysis of annual reports of the American Civil Liberties Union over the last fifty years reveals a decreased concern with third-degree forced confessions and an increased concern with the relatively milder problem of lack of provided counsel in police interrogation. Likewise, one can readily observe the expansion of constitutional rights at the United States Supreme Court level by noting that it was not until the 1930s that the states were obligated to comply with any of the provisions in the Bill of Rights, and by the 1970s they were legally obligated to comply with virtually all of them, with the exception of relatively minor provisions like grand jury indictment (Fellman, 1970).

Most of this expansion can be explained in terms of (1) pressures from below by those who are discriminated against and those who empathize with their problems, and by (2) concessions from above made by elite decision makers.

Pressures from below take various forms. They include formal pressure groups like the American Civil Liberties Union which has engineered a number of expansive Supreme Court decisions, including Mapp v. Ohio requiring the state courts to exclude illegally seized evidence. The NAACP has been particularly important in expansive decisions involving racial issues, such as those which require the states to provide black representation on criminal juries. Law firms with a public interest orientation have functioned almost like pressure groups, as when Abe Fortas' firm fought the right-to-counsel case of Gideon v. Wainwright.

Probably more important than the role of pressure groups or public interest law firms is the role of mass movement activities on the part of those who have been especially discriminated against. Thus, the recent prison riots have been especially important in pressuring the decision makers to grant more rights to prison inmates. Likewise, the ghetto riots of 1966 through 1968 may have done more to change discriminatory abusive behavior by the police than court decisions excluding illegally obtained evidence or confessions. Black and poor whites may become especially vigorous and effective in pressing for an expansion of the rights of the accused as they move upward toward middle class status and develop rising expectations.

Concessions have also been made from above by legislators, judges, and administrators, partly because the characteristics of those decision makers have been changing so that they are possibly more willing to yield to the pressures from below. One changing characteristic is the increasing affluence and economic security which has become present in most of American society. Material well-being may allow one to be relatively more liberal with regard to granting rights to less privileged segments of society than if one's material status is highly precarious. In other words, the rights of the accused may in a sense be a societal luxury which presupposes that more basic material needs be met first. There is support for such a hypothesis relating at least moderate affluence to tolerance of civil liberties in both the public opinion literature (Stouffer, 1955) and in cross-cultural studies (Nagel, 1971: 308). Improved education is also a factor in that it may better enable the poor to manipulate the system and better enable decision makers and their middle-class constituents to learn of the societal benefits with regard to protection of the innocent which are provided by the rights of the accused. Furthermore, prior concessions tend to lead to subsequent concessions, particularly in a precedent-following legal system.

In general, both short-run differential treatment and long-run expansion of the rights of the accused can be largely explained in terms of class conflict and related phenomena (Chambliss and Seidman, 1971; Heinz et al., 1969). To the extent that America is becoming a more middle-class society, there will be less relevant differences among people to serve as a basis for discrimination. Likewise, there will be more middle-class security, education, and rising expectations, to serve as a basis for a more equal and effective system of rights for the accused.

NOTES

1. The list of authors and their most relevant prior publication is as follows:
   (a) Arrest and search: Jacob Landynski, *Search and Seizure and the Supreme Court* (Johns Hopkins Press, 1966).
   (b) Confessions and self-incrimination: O. John Rogge, *Why Men Confess* (T. Nelson, 1959); and *The First and the Fifth, with Some Excursions into Others* (T. Nelson, 1960).
   (c) Bail: Patricia Wald, *Bail in the United States: 1964* (Justice Dept. & Vera Foundation, 1964).
   (d) Counsel: William Beaney, *The Right to Counsel in American Courts* (University of Michigan Press, 1955).
   (e) Accusation: Delmar Karlen, *Anglo-American Criminal Justice* (Oxford, 1967).
   (f) Jury: Rita James Simon, *The Jury and the Defense of Insanity* (Little, Brown, 1967).
   (g) Testimony: James Marshall, *Law and Psychology in Conflict* (Bobbs-Merrill, 1966).
   (h) Punishment: Robert O. Dawson, *Sentencing: the Decision as to Type, Length, and Condition of Sentence* (Little, Brown, 1969).
   (i) Double jeopardy: Jay Sigler, *Double Jeopardy: The Development of a Legal and Social Policy* (Cornell University Press, 1969).

2. For empirical research dealing with the effects of various rights of the accused, see Stephen Wasby (1970: 146-148) and Donald McIntyre (1967).

3. Behavioral studies of the consequences of having counsel include L. Silverstein (1966); N. Lefstein and V. Stapleton (1967); and D. Wenger and C. Fletcher (1969).

4. Empirical research on protecting the right to be free from unreasonable arrests, searches, and interrogation techniques include E. Green (1970), S. Nagel (1965), and R. Medalie et al. (1968).

REFERENCES

Ares, C. (1963) "The Manhattan bail project: an interim report on the use of pretrial parole." New York University Law Rev. 38 (January): 67-95.

Bedau, H. (1967) *The Death Penalty in America.* New York: Anchor.

Broeder, D. (1959) "The University of Chicago jury project." Nebraska Law Rev. 38 (May): 744-760.

Bullock, H. (1961) "Significance of the racial factor in the length of prison sentences." J. of Criminal Law, Criminology, and Police Science 52 (November-December): 411-417.

Chambliss, W. and R. Seidman (1971) *Law, Order, and Power.* Reading, Mass.: Addison-Wesley.

Fellman, D. (1970) "The Supreme Court's changing views of the criminal defendant's rights," pp. 93-123 in B. McLennan (ed.) *Crime in Urban Society.* New York: Dunellen.

Green, E. (1970) "Race, social status, and criminal arrest." Amer. Soc. Rev. 35 (June): 476-490.

Heinz, J. et al. (1969) "Legislative politics and the criminal law." Northwestern University Law Rev. 64 (August): 277-358.

Kalven, H. and H. Zeisel (1966) *The American Jury.* Boston: Little, Brown.

Kanowitz, M. (1967) *Women and the Law: The Unfinished Revolution.* Albuquerque: University of New Mexico Press.

Konvitz, M. (1967) *Expanding Liberties: The Emergence of New Civil Liberties and Civil Rights in Postwar America.* New York: Viking Press.

La Fave, W. (1965) *Arrest: The Decision to Take a Suspect into Custody.* Boston: Little, Brown.

Lefstein, N. and V. Stapleton (1967) *Counsel in Juvenile Courts.* Chicago: National Council of Juvenile Court Judges.

Martin, G. (1970) "Judicial administration and racial discrimination: fifteen years of literature." Chicago: American Judicature Society.

McIntyre, D., Jr. (1967) *Law Enforcement in the Metropolis.* Chicago: American Bar Foundation.

Medalie, R. et al. (1968) "Custodial police interrogation in our nation's capital: the attempt to implement Miranda." Michigan Law Rev. 66 (May): 1347-1422.

Miller, F. (1969) *Prosecution: The Decision to Charge a Suspect with a Crime.* Boston: Little, Brown.

Milner, N. (1971) *The Court and Local Law Enforcement: The Impact of Miranda.* Beverly Hills, Calif.: Sage Publications.

Nagel, S. (1971) "The social consequences of basic legal rights," pp. 306-320 in E. Pollack (ed.), *Human Rights.* Buffalo: William Hein.

——— (1967) "Disparities in criminal procedure." UCLA Law Rev. 14 (August): 1272-1305.

——— (1965) "Testing the effects of excluding illegally seized evidence." Wisconsin Law Rev. 1965 (Spring): 283-310.

——— (1962) "Judicial backgrounds and criminal cases." J. of Criminal Law, Criminology, and Police Science 53 (September): 333-339.

Navarro, J. and J. Taylor (1967) *Data Analysis and Simulation of a Court System for the Processing of Criminal Cases.* Arlington, Virginia: Institute for Defense Analyses.

Rankin, A. (1964) "The effect of pretrial detention." New York University Law Rev. 39 (June): 641-655.

Robinson, C. (1968) "Police and prosecutor practices and attitudes relating to interrogation as revealed by pre- and post-Miranda questionnaires: a construct of police capacity to comply." Duke Law J. 1968 (June): 425-524.

Roche, J. (1956) "We've never had more freedom." New Republic 134 (January 23): 12-15 (January 30): 13-16 (February 6): 13-15.

Stouffer, S. (1955) *Communism, Conformity, and Civil Liberties.* New York: Doubleday.

Wald, M. et al. (1967) "Interrogations in New Haven: the impact of Miranda." Yale Law J. 76 (July): 1521-1648.

Wasby, S. (1970) *The Impact of the United States Supreme Court: Some Perspectives.* Homewood, Ill.: Dorsey Press.

Wenger, D. and C. Fletcher (1969) "The effect of legal counsel on admissions to a state mental hospital: a confrontation of professions." J. of Health and Social Behavior 10 (March): 66-72.

Zeisel, H. et al. (1959) *Delay in the Court.* Boston: Little, Brown.

PART II.

PRIOR TO FIRST COURT

APPEARANCE

Chapter 2

SEARCH AND SEIZURE

The right of the people to be secure in their persons, houses, papers, and effects, against unreasonable searches and seizures, shall not be violated

From the Fourth Amendment
to the U.S. Constitution

JACOB W. LANDYNSKI received his B.A. summa cum laude at Brooklyn College, 1958, his M.A. at Johns Hopkins University the following year, and his Ph.D. with honors at Johns Hopkins in 1963, receiving awards at both institutions. He has taught at Johns Hopkins, City University of New York, Douglass College (Rutgers), and New School for Social Research, where he is presently an Associate Professor on the graduate faculty. In 1968-1969 he was awarded a faculty research fellowship in social sciences from the Ford Foundation. He has published *Search and Seizure and the Supreme Court: A Study in Constitutional Interpretation* (1966) and numerous articles.

Chapter 2

SEARCH AND SEIZURE

JACOB W. LANDYNSKI

More than any other branch of constitutional law, the law of search and seizure has undergone dramatic change in recent years, and continues in a state of flux. Several landmark decisions, each overruling a deeply rooted precedent, indicate the extent of innovation: (1) Mapp v. Ohio[1] required the exclusion of unconstitutionally seized evidence from state trials; (2) Berger v. New York[2] and Katz v. United States[3] brought to a successful conclusion the struggle begun forty years earlier by Justice Brandeis to place technological eavesdropping under constitutional restrictions; (3) Chimel v. California[4] drastically limited the area in which police may conduct a warrantless search "incidental" to a valid arrest on premises. This essay focuses essentially on the law of search and seizure as it has undergone judicial development during the last decade or so, incorporating such earlier materials as are necessary to put the contemporary period in perspective.

I. THE FOURTH AMENDMENT

The constitutional law of search and seizure is governed by the Fourth Amendment, which states: "The right of the people to be secure in their persons, houses, papers and effects, against unreasonable searches and seizures, shall not be violated, and no Warrants shall issue, but upon probable cause, supported by Oath or affirmation, and particularly describing the place to be searched, and the persons or things to be seized." The amendment was adopted in response to deep resentment against the general warrant (known as the writ of assistance) used by British customs officials to search for goods smuggled into the Colonies in violation of the trade and navigation acts, which severely restricted the ability of the colonies to trade with areas outside the Empire. So widely shared was the indignation, and so determined were Americans to prevent a recurrence of these abuses, that each of the state constitutions adopted prior to the formation of the federal union contained a "little Fourth Amendment" limiting the authority of government agents to conduct searches.

The key to the protection granted by the Fourth Amendment is the warrant, which interposes an impartial magistrate between the policeman and the individual, so that the policeman cannot act as judge in his own cause. In contrast to a general warrant, which permitted search to be made on unverified suspicion, which placed no limits on the scope of search, and which was, in effect, a permanent license in the hands of the officer to search wheresoever he pleased, a warrant authorized by the Fourth Amendment puts a number of important restrictions on the ability of officers to invade the privacy of a dwelling. Chief among these are: (1) the standard determining the issuance of warrants is probable cause, an elusive concept difficult to define precisely, but which, in general terms, requires reasonable grounds to believe that the dwelling contains the things to be searched for; (2) particularity to the extent possible in the description of persons, premises, and things.

It may be recalled that the Fourth Amendment is divided into two clauses, the first forbidding "unreasonable" searches, the second stating the conditions to be met for issuance of a valid warrant. Since only unreasonable searches are forbidden, the question arises as to what is a reasonable search. A common sense interpretation, which is supported by the antecedent history of the amendment, would consider the two clauses in conjunction so that the second clause becomes determinative of the first: a reasonable search is one that meets the warrant requirement, and conversely, an unreasonable search is one that does not do so. Nevertheless, this issue, above any other in search and seizure law, has badly divided the Court for a quarter of a century. Several of the Justices, more often than not constituting a majority of the Court, have taken the position that the clauses are separable and that the reasonableness of a search does not necessarily depend on the issuance of a warrant, but "on the facts and circumstances—the total atmosphere of the case."[5] According to this view, the determination of reasonableness would, in the first instance, be at the discretion of the police,

with judicial review taking place retrospectively, and only if the search produced evidence which the government sought to use at the trial.

II. JUDICIAL APPROACHES

The construction that the Justices place on the Fourth Amendment depends to some extent on their reading of the text, for instance, the relationship of its two clauses, and ultimately, on the importance they attach to the values it safeguards. Justice Frankfurter accorded the amendment "a place second to none in the Bill of Rights,"[6] and this attitude is reflected in the positions he took. Justice Black, on the other hand, once expressed the view to the writer of this article that "the method of getting him [the suspect] is not the supreme thing; what happens *after that* is supreme,"[7] and his opinions tend to mirror this approach.

A crucial complicating factor in assessing judicial performance is the variety of search and seizure law. In contrast to single-topic constitutional provisions (for instance, right to counsel) this field encompasses not only the physical search of the dwelling, but such diverse matters as arrest law, stop-and-frisk, mechanical eavesdropping, administrative searches, search incidental to arrest, compulsory blood tests in criminal cases, and automobile searches. It would be difficult to find more than a handful of Justices who have been either consistently lenient or strict in approach to all of the Fourth Amendment issues on which they have voted.

For these reasons, the usual designation of Justices as "conservative" or "liberal," "activist" or "restraintist," in civil liberties cases generally, has little meaning in connection with the Fourth Amendment. Even a Justice who is conservative in other contexts may confound expectations and develop a deep respect for a constitutional provision rooted in the maxim, "A man's house is his castle." Justices Frankfurter and Harlan, who were invariably regarded as conservative (more accurately, restraintist) judges usually advocated more stringent constitutional search standards than did most of their colleagues, while Justice Clark, with a lifelong background in law enforcement positions, wrote the Mapp and Berger opinions for the Court. Conversely, Justices Black and Douglas, who were akin in their approach to most other civil liberties issues, were markedly divergent in their handling of Fourth Amendment issues. Black, who took an absolutist approach to the interpretation of the First Amendment, construed the Fourth Amendment in as restrictive a manner as any other Justice in the history of the Court: Black believed electronic eavesdropping to be constitutional, favored granting the police wide latitude in conducting "incidental" searches, and continually excoriated the Court for being insensitive to the requirements of law enforcement in this field. Douglas, who until 1948 took a very lenient view of the Fourth Amendment's protection,[8] dramatically changed course afterwards, yet he joined the Court in extending the authority of the police to search an automobile without a warrant, leaving Justice Harlan as the lone dissenter in that case.[9]

III. THE WARRANTLESS SEARCH

Even when the Court has taken the position that the reasonableness of a search is measured by all the circumstances rather than by the ability to secure a warrant, it has never sanctioned the warrantless search of a dwelling on probable cause alone. Rather, the conflict over the relationship of the amendment's clauses has come to a head in issues of search incidental to arrest, which has for half a century been judicially recognized as an "emergency" exception to the warrant requirement. Where police enter a home in order to make a valid arrest, it is necessary to conduct an immediate search of the arrestee so as to remove from his control weapons which he might use to escape or endanger the lives of the police, and evidence which he might destroy. Similarly a warrant is not required for the search of a moving vehicle, since the delay involved in obtaining one might defeat the purpose of the search. As a result, probable cause rather than a warrant has been held sufficient for the search of a moving vehicle, while in the case of search incidental to arrest, the arrest itself furnishes, in a sense, probable cause for the search.

In consonance with this rationale, search incidental to arrest, in its original conception, was confined to the person of the arrestee and the area within his reach. Beginning, however, with Harris v. United States[10] in 1947, the Court moved to the position that the entire premises could be searched,[11] on the theory that once privacy had been lawfully invaded by entry of the police to make an arrest, the accompanying search was only a minor and reasonable additional incursion on privacy. Thus when the arrest was made in the dwelling (and if additional evidence was needed the police were usually careful not to make the arrest elsewhere) the Fourth Amendment's warrant requirement was in effect bypassed. Yet probable cause to arrest does not, as many believe, automatically establish probable cause to search. If probable cause to search did indeed follow from probable cause to arrest, there would be no reason to allow a search of the home only when the arrest is made in it, yet the Court has consistently forbidden search of the home "incidental" to an arrest made elsewhere. In a typical situation, there may be reason to believe that a person has committed a crime, but none that his home contains evidence relating to the offense. Moreover, since the warrant allows the magistrate to put concrete limits on the search (not every warrant allows a search of the entire premises), this theory had the striking effect of allowing incidental searches a broader scope than searches under warrant.

The transition to the new doctrine was far from smooth. For two decades the Court was almost continuously divided, with majority and minority of nearly equal strength. To make matters worse, the cases followed a see-saw pattern, with first one view, then the other prevailing, depending on changes in the Court's composition. To illustrate, the permissive Harris decision was, in effect, discarded one year later by Trupiano v. United States,[12] which was, in turn, explicitly overruled shortly afterwards in United States v. Rabinowitz.[13]

To be sure, the Court did place certain restrictions on incidental searches: the arrest must not serve as a pretext for the search; the search must not be exploratory, but limited to evidence of the crime for which the arrest was made; the closeness of the search must be proportionate to the character of the things sought, thus forbidding a search for large objects in small spaces. These limitations are, however, easily circumvented, and therefore of doubtful usefulness.

An indication of how the leeway granted to the police has caused the warrant requirement to fall into virtual disuse may be secured from the following figures: "In 1966 the New York police obtained 3,897 [search] warrants and made 171,288 arrests. It is reliably reported that in San Francisco in 1966 there were 29,084 serious crimes reported to the police, who during the same year obtained only 19 search warrants."[14] In an attempt to reverse this trend, the Court in the 1969 case of Chimel v. California[15] overruled the Harris and Rabinowitz decisions and limited the scope of incidental search to the person of the arrestee and his immediate environs, thus bringing the concept once again into harmony with the need that gave rise to it.

The Chimel opinion appeared to have the stamp of finality on it. The majority was 6-2, and almost certainly would have been 7-2 but for the recent resignation of Justice Fortas. The long and acrimonious debate on the Court over the relationship of the two clauses of the Fourth Amendment seemed to be at an end. But appearances are deceiving in this ever-changing field of constitutional law. The Chimel majority has now been depleted by the loss of two of its members (Chief Justice Warren and Justice Harlan), and so the future scope of incidental searches must again be regarded as uncertain until the new Court appointees, Justices Powell and Rehnquist, have an opportunity to express their views. Chief Justice Burger and Justice Blackmun, named to the Court since the Chimel decision, have clearly shown themselves antagonistic to the new doctrine.

Even assuming that the Chimel rule will survive, a number of matters still require clarification. In the Chimel case the police had sufficient opportunity to obtain a warrant in advance of the search, and this consideration was crucial to the reasoning of the Court. The question arises whether, if no such opportunity presents itself, the Court would permit a search without a warrant. For instance, a patrolman comes upon a narcotics transaction on the street, and arrests one of the culprits on the sidewalk in front of his house, and his family is aware of what has happened and therefore may dispose of evidence within the home. Narcotics in the home poses a particular problem to the police, since unlike most types of evidence or contraband, they can easily be flushed down a toilet and disappear without trace.

In this connection it is worth noting that in 1967, in Warden v. Hayden,[16] the Court upheld the thorough search of a suspected robber's apartment by police, who, upon being tipped off that he had fled there, entered in "hot pursuit." Even though the search preceded the arrest, it was sanctioned as necessary for the confiscation of weapons which might endanger the police. Nevertheless, the parallel should not be overdrawn. Narcotics searches account for a large proportion of warrants issued (in New York County the figure is 95 percent),[17] and if the Court were to regard searches for narcotics as emergency searches, the search warrant might become an historic relic and the object of the Chimel decision, to infuse life into the warrant requirement, would be defeated.

Another significant issue, also unresolved, concerns arrests for minor traffic offenses and the like, where it is improbable that the arrestee is armed and a search seldom yields evidence related to the crime. To allow such arrests to be followed by searches seems clearly inconsistent with the rule that warrantless searches can only be justified by exigent circumstances. Several state courts have held that evidence so obtained is inadmissible, yet this type of search continues to be routine police practice, the opportunity to conduct a search often being the real motivation for the arrest.

Even while the Court was limiting the authority of the police to conduct incidental searches, it was, strangely enough, almost simultaneously expanding their authority to conduct warrantless searches of automobiles. Chambers v. Maroney,[18] decided in 1970, permitted the search in a police station of an automobile which had been stopped on the road for probable cause and then removed to the station. Even though the emergency which attends a search on the road no longer exists once the automobile is in police custody, the Court pointed to the "convenience" of the owner in having the search expedited and the car released without the delay the issuance of a warrant would entail. This reasoning seems odd, since the best judge of what serves his convenience is surely the owner himself, who, if he wishes, can expedite matters by simply consenting to a search.

Also seizable without a warrant, although for a different reason, is evidence exposed to the "plain view" of an officer. Even though the owner may merely be careless and has not (as where something is abandoned) consciously relinquished his right to privacy in the article, it is nevertheless seizable since no search—and hence no intrusion on privacy—is necessary in order to achieve the seizure. Thus when police enter premises to make an arrest, their ability to seize evidence is not limited by the Chimel doctrine if the articles sought are in plain view from the place of arrest. However, in an innovating 1971 decision the Court held that a plain view of the interior of a house obtained through, say, a window or open door, does not allow a warrantless entry, any more than does probable cause, and that, furthermore, the plain view discovery must be fortuitous: even a legitimate entry on to premises to make an arrest does not negate the requirement for a warrant where police anticipate finding the object because they have foreknowledge of its location.[19]

IV. THE LAW OF ARREST

By its coupling of the words "persons" and things to be "seized," the Fourth Amendment makes it clear that arbitrary arrest, no less than arbitrary search, falls under its ban. However, while the common law, upon which the Fourth Amendment was largely patterned, had an overriding requirement of a warrant for the search of a dwelling, it permitted a felony arrest within as well as outside a home on probable cause alone, and American legal practice has conformed to this distinction. The danger that a felon might flee before a warrant could be obtained has been regarded as creating an emergency situation justifying immediate action. As a result, the arrest warrant is (except in Federal Bureau of Investigation cases) a rarity in this country today.

This "law of arrest" has become so deeply rooted in both federal and state arrest statutes and judicial decisions as to appear scarcely open to challenge. Yet, considering that the seizure of a person is, quite clearly, a greater transgression on his liberty than is a search of his dwelling (it is in fact the ultimate deprivation of liberty), it seems anomalous that even a meager showing of exigent circumstances does not need to be made; such circumstances are simply assumed to be invariably present. In 1971, however, the Court strongly hinted that this ambivalent approach to the problem of warrantless arrest on the one hand, and warrantless search on the other, might be in for rough sledding, when it observed in a dictum that "the notion that the warrantless entry of a man's house to arrest him on probable cause is per se legitimate is in fundamental conflict with the basic principle of Fourth Amendment law that searches and seizures inside a man's house without warrant are per se unreasonable. . . ."[20]

V. STOP-AND-FRISK

Probable cause, the point at which the interest of the government in securing evidence constitutionally supersedes the individual's interest in privacy, has traditionally been the standard for issuance of warrants and for permissible warrantless searches. Yet even more vital than the solving of crime is its prevention. Thus the more important function of the policeman is to intimidate potential criminals. The interest of society clearly requires that, where possible, the culprit be stopped before he commits a crime, particularly one that may involve violence and endanger life and limb. An officer observing the suspicious conduct of an individual, for instance, his "casing" of a store, will apprehend danger even though no crime has yet been committed and there is no probable cause to justify an arrest. What action may he take?

The careful officer who encounters a suspicious individual will usually put a question to him. If it is freely answered and dispels his doubts, there is of course no constitutional problem. If, however, he meets with a refusal to answer, or the answer is evasive or false, may he briefly detain this individual while he attempts to get to the bottom of the matter? When there is a good chance that the suspect is armed, may he "frisk" him for concealed weapons? A head-to-toe frisk, even when circumspectly carried out, is a far more humiliating experience than a "stop" for questioning which, if it is done expertly and politely, is not likely to attract any undue attention.

Stop-and-frisk is regarded by police as an indispensable instrument of crime prevention, and regardless of formal authorization (which has been granted by a number of state legislatures, and in several other states by judicial decision), it is common police practice, both in this country and elsewhere. Opposition centers largely around the possibilities of abuse, especially of minority groups, by policemen who may be tempted to exercise this authority on mere pretext.

In Terry v. Ohio[21] and Sibron v. New York[22] the first cases to be decided by the Court in this gray area of law enforcement, a limited authority to frisk was sustained. The Court took a stance midway between those who contended that the interventionary power of the police should be limited by the probable cause standard, and those who argued that a detention short of a formal arrest is not a "seizure" in Fourth Amendment terms, and that a frisk of outer clothing is not a "search." The first position, said the Court, made light of the potentialities for violence lurking in suspicious conduct, while the second "torture[d] the English language,"[23] and would remove stop-and-frisk from all Fourth Amendment restraints. Instead, where circumstances are such as entitle an officer to believe that his safety and that of others is in jeopardy, and speedy action is imperative, he may, consistently with the reasonableness clause, "conduct a carefully limited search of the outer clothing of such [suspicious] persons in an attempt to discover weapons which might be used to assault him."[24] Since the justification lies in the need for self-protection, a frisk, unlike a search incidental to arrest, may not extend beyond outer garments to a more thorough search for evidence. In the Terry case, this limit was observed and the conviction was allowed to stand. In the Sibron case, where the officer thrust his hand into the suspect's pocket, the conviction was overturned.

Although the Court did not, in so many words, authorize the stopping of a suspect for investigation it is reasonable to assume that the decision implied as much. Even Justice Douglas, the lone dissenter in Terry, while maintaining that the probable cause standard must govern on-the-street encounters, would nevertheless move probable cause ahead in time to allow anticipation of criminal conduct. Where there is probable cause to believe that "a criminal venture . . . is about to be launched," said Douglas, the suspect may be arrested.[25] "Police officers need not wait until they see a person actually commit a crime before they are able to 'seize' that person."[26] If the suspect is arrested (not merely stopped) before the commission of a crime, with what can he be charged? The answer appears to be that he could not be charged at all, and that the "arrest" would serve as a form of preventive detention. Douglas did not say how long a suspect might be held. In Canadian law, belief that a suspect is about to commit a crime empowers the police to arrest and hold him for twenty-four hours.

It remains to be seen whether a suspect's refusal to answer questions when stopped by an officer will permit suspicion to be elevated to probable cause; it is arguable that exercise of the constitutional right against self-incrimination cannot be regarded as a circumstance of suspicion. It is also uncertain whether the Court will require that the Miranda[27] warnings be given routinely, since on-the-street questioning is usually far less distinct with coercion than custodial interrogation. A clear limit on the length of detention (possibly half an hour) seems an obvious necessity, even though it carries the risk that police may be tempted to hold suspects for the maximum period allowed. Above all, the standard of reasonable suspicion will need to be developed on a case-by-case basis.[28] The difficulty of the task may be gauged by the fact that, after nearly two centuries of definition by the Court, probable cause itself is still far from being an explicit standard.

VI. THE PROBLEM OF CONSENT

The problem of consent is a particularly annoying one in the law of search and seizure. When the householder consents to a search, he in effect waives his Fourth Amendment rights and makes it unnecessary for the police to obtain a warrant. However, when such a search yields evidence, and the validity of the consent is contested at trial, it is frequently difficult for the court to determine whether the consent was indeed voluntary or mere acquiescence to a show of uniformed authority. The kind of explicit warning concerning constitutional rights which Miranda v. Arizona[29] made mandatory for custodial interrogation, shows no sign of being required in consent cases.

When one entrusts one's possession to the care of another person, and that person consents to a search which implicates the owner, the evidence is admissible on the theory that the owner has assumed the risk that the other person might consent to a search.[30] But why, in this situation, must the owner be presumed to have surrendered his privacy to the intrusions of other individuals, and particularly of the police? The law appears to be inconsistent with the recently enunciated principle that a justifiable expectation of privacy is the criterion which determines the scope of Fourth Amendment protections.[31]

May a wife legally consent to a search of the home which is directed against her husband, and thereby waive his constitutional rights? The Court has never answered this question directly, but different aspects of the problem may be distinguished. If she is motivated by malice it is arguable that the consent is in disharmony with the marital relationship from which her joint control is derived,[32] and that her consent is therefore as worthless as that given by a hotel clerk to search the room of a guest.[33] However, when in the course of a police visit to the home she voluntarily turns over some of her husband's things in an effort to establish his innocence, but succeeds only in implicating him further, the evidence is admissible[34] —apparently because a husband in trouble may expect his wife to act in this way, and is therefore presumed to have tacitly consented to a search.

VII. MECHANICAL EAVESDROPPING

The invention of mechanical eavesdropping devices and their frequent use by law enforcement agents have posed a grave threat to individual privacy. Unlike the human eavesdropper against whose presence it is usually possible to be on guard, a mechanical device can from a distance maintain surveillance of an office, a kitchen, or a bedroom without the victim being aware of the intrusion on his privacy. This is a development which the framers could scarcely have foreseen, and to which the Fourth Amendment does not, of course, clearly address itself.

When the issue of evidence obtained by wiretap first came before the Court, in the 1928 case of Olmstead v. United States,[35] the 5-4 decision was based on an excessively literal rendering of the amendment. Wiretapping was not a search in Fourth Amendment terms, said the Court, unless it involved a trespass on to premises, nor a seizure, since the "seized" words were not tangible items. Justice Brandeis protested that a flexible interpretation of the language, which would place greater emphasis on underlying purpose than on textual exegesis, was required; it was an insufficient reason to remove the search from the control of the Fourth Amendment merely because the *method* of search was of recent vintage and unknown to the eighteenth century.[36] In 1937, following changes in the personnel of the Court, the Olmstead decision was effectively circumvented without being overruled; in a remarkable piece of statutory construction, the Court held that Section 605 of the Federal Communications Act of 1934 (which was drafted to forbid the unauthorized interception of telegraph messages) banned wiretapping.[37] In subsequent decisions, the Court in effect attributed to Congress the intention to grant the privacy of telephone messages protection equivalent in extent to that which the Constitution would have supplied had the Olmstead case been decided the other way.

So long as mechanical eavesdropping was limited to the tapping of telephone wires, Section 605 served the Court well; but technological advance soon began to outstrip the Court's ability to use the statute as a substitute for reinterpretation of constitutional doctrine. The employment by police of sophisticated electronic gadgets capable of picking up sounds through walls and independent of telephone systems, made a reexamination of the Olmstead rule urgent. At first the Court refused to alter its course; for example, evidence obtained by agents using a sensitive device to eavesdrop on the conversation of a suspect in an adjoining office was ruled admissible.[38] But the wind of doctrinal change began to blow in 1961, when the Court declared unconstitutional the use of a "spike mike," a listening device whose tip was placed under the floor of a gambling headquarters by police stationed in an adjoining house, although technically no trespass had taken place.[39] Finally, in two 1967 cases, Berger v. New York[40] and Katz v. United States,[41] the wind of change became a hurricane. In Berger, the Court ruled invalid a New York law which permitted eavesdropping by law enforcement officials on the grounds, among others, that the warrant application required neither a showing of probable cause for the commission of a specific crime, nor a particular description of the conversation sought to be "seized," and that the length of the authorization (two months) was excessive. This implicit overruling of the Olmstead doctrine was made explicit in Katz, where the Court overturned a conviction based on evidence obtained through the placing of an electronic device on the outside of a public telephone booth. Thus protection of the Fourth Amendment, said the Court, was no longer dependent on such considerations as whether there had been a physical intrusion on to premises, or whether the privacy of a "constitutionally protected area" had been invaded. "For the Fourth Amendment protects people not places."[42] Since the user of a public phone booth is entitled to assume the privacy of his conversations, the booth, no less than his home, may serve as his castle.

This new approach is not without limitations. The designation of certain places—homes, hotel rooms, offices, automobiles, and the like—as constitutionally protected areas has at least the advantage of drawing clear lines for the guidance of police and citizens alike. Whether persons engaging in conversation in a public park, or in a visitors' room in a prison (which the Court in 1962 held not to be a constitutionally protected area)[43] are justified in an expectation of privacy, is the sort of question which the Court may eventually be called upon to answer.

While the Court has on the one hand placed eavesdropping under the restraint of the Fourth Amendment, it has on the other made it plain that, at least under certain conditions, an eavesdropping warrant can meet constitutional standards. Until 1967 this was debatable. The sole purpose of eavesdropping is, of course, to discover evidence, yet under a rule stemming from common law property concepts a search warrant might be issued only for contraband (goods which are legally prohibited to their possessor) and instruments of crime (articles helpful in facilitating the commission of the crime), but not for "mere evidence."[44] Courts striving to overcome this restriction gave the term "instruments of crime" a flexibility which justified a great variety of seizures. In the Supreme Court's continuing effort to dissociate Fourth Amendment interpretation from the property law principles with which it had become encrusted, the "mere evidence" rule was formally abandoned as "wholly irrational" in Warden v. Hayden.[45]

Eavesdropping of the kind thus far discussed is accomplished by a third party who intrudes a mechanical ear on a private conversation involving other persons. A different situation arises in the case of participant monitoring (or consensual surveillance) where one party to a conversation records or transmits what is being said, without the approval of the other party. In three cases widely separated in time, On Lee v. United States,[46] Lopez v. United States,[47] and White v. United States,[48] all of which provoked heated dissent, the Court sustained the use of evidence obtained by participant monitoring, reasoning essentially that since the monitoring party is in any event privy to the information revealed, and free to make it public, his recording or transmittal of the conversation verbatim does not significantly increase the threat to the suspect's personal security.[49]

In the White case, where the issue received its most thorough airing, the plurality opinion regarded participant monitoring as constitutionally indistinguishable from the use of informers, whose testimony the Court in 1966 had ruled admissible. Of the two decisions involving informers, one concerned a sale of narcotics to an agent in the suspect's home. To the contention that since the agent had misrepresented himself, the invitation to enter was obtained by deceit, the Court asserted that where the home had been converted into an illicit place of business, to which all those who wished to purchase narcotics were welcome, that business was entitled to no greater protection than if it were conducted on the street.[50] The other and more difficult case concerned Jimmy Hoffa, who was convicted of jury tampering on testimony offered by an erstwhile friend. This man, released from prison when he offered his services to the government as an informer, proceeded to elicit incriminating statements from Hoffa in the latter's hotel suite. This episode was regarded by the Court as merely an example of misplaced confidence: Hoffa, in revealing his secrets, had assumed the risk that his companion might report to the police.[51] While the Court held the question open, it may be presumed that the same result would follow if the informer were not a friend of the suspect but deliberately wormed his way into his confidence to obtain information.

Given this background, the Court in the White case disposed of the issue easily. Since the suspect must in any event be on his guard whenever he chooses to confide in someone, neither his spontaneity of utterance nor his sense of security would be further diminished by the possibility that his companion is not only an informer but a "walking bug." Despite the impassioned dissent of Justice Harlan that participant monitoring constitutes a greater invasion of privacy than use of an unwired informer, the Court's position appears to be sound or at least consistent, especially when one considers that informers are notoriously unreliable, and it is often to a suspect's advantage not to have the informer's word taken at face value. What clearly requires reassessment is the original premise that the deliberate "planting" of an informer near a suspect for the purpose of reporting confidential conversations, does not require judicial supervision. It is the unregulated use of informers, far more than the possibility that they might be electronically equipped, that poses a real peril to a democratic society.[52]

Strenuous efforts over the years to repeal or amend Section 605 so as to allow some wiretapping by government agents (who were in any event widely disregarding the law, but could not, at the federal level and in the exclusionary states, use the evidence in court), failed in Congress less because of the strength of the opposition than because of the inability of advocates of such a bill to agree on the safeguards it should contain.

These efforts, spurred by a soaring crime rate and facilitated by some adroit compromises in Congress during a presidential election year, finally bore fruit with the enactment of the Omnibus Crime Control Act of 1968. Title III[53] of the act introduced the first comprehensive federal scheme for regulating mechanical eavesdropping. Some of its provisions are long overdue. Thus the act prohibits and makes subject to stringent penalties all private wiretapping and electronic eavesdropping. Evidence yielded by an illegal surveillance is inadmissible in federal and state courts. A civil cause of action is created which allows the victims of unlawful interception to collect liquidated and punitive damages and reasonable attorneys' fees. The sanctions apply to illegal law enforcement activity as well as private eavesdroppers.

However, Title III authorizes law enforcement eavesdropping for a wide range of offenses on standards of probable cause and particularity that are similar to those required for regular search warrants. The officer applying for an order is required to certify to the judge that traditional law enforcement methods have failed to solve the case, or explain why they are unlikely to succeed if used. Interception orders may run up to thirty days but surveillance must cease once the objective of the order has been achieved. Renewal is possible under the same conditions as govern issuance of the original order. The intercepted communications are placed in the custody of the court, and persons subjected to surveillance must subsequently be served with an inventory disclosing the dates on which interceptions took place. Several features of the act have aroused great controversy:

(1) The large number of crimes for whose prosecution interception is permitted. Federal officers may eavesdrop to gather evidence of such

serious offenses as murder, kidnapping and sabotage, as well as numerous offenses linked to organized crime, including gambling and dealing in dangerous drugs. State officers, however, may eavesdrop in connection with any "crime dangerous to life, limb, or property and punishable by imprisonment for more than one year. . . ."

(2) Many judges may issue interception orders. Such orders may be issued by all federal district and Court of Appeals judges and by state judges "of general criminal jurisdiction."

(3) Many law enforcement officials may authorize applications for orders. To be sure, at the federal level only one person, the Attorney General (or an Assistant Attorney General specially designated by him) may authorize an application; but at the state level the authorization may be given by the principal prosecuting attorney of the state or any of its political subdivisions. Thus the act makes it possible for literally hundreds of officials to authorize applications for orders, and hundreds of judges to issue them.

(4) The length of time over which interceptions are permitted. In the Berger case the Court regarded interceptions over two months as constitutionally impermissible; whether it would consider a one-month period less objectionable remains to be seen.

Under the reporting provisions of the act, prosecutors and judges must furnish to the Administrative Office of the United States Courts complete information on applications and orders for interceptions. Statistics compiled by that office show that during 1971 installation of eavesdropping devices was judicially authorized in a total of 816 cases, although in only 792 were they actually used; additionally, 228 renewals were approved. In only a handful of interceptions were microphones employed; the great majority (753) involved the tapping of telephone wires exclusively. Seventy percent (570) of the authorizations were for investigation of gambling offenses, with drug crimes accounting for the next highest number (126). Evidence obtained from the eavesdropping had resulted, as of December 31, 1971, in 2,818 arrests and 322 convictions. Three jurisdictions accounted for nearly ninety percent of all legal eavesdropping; the federal government received 285 authorizations, New York 254, and New Jersey 187. Perhaps the small number of authorizations for the rest of the country reflects, in part, the great expense involved: the average cost per interception was $4,599, and one ran as high as $67,860.[54]

The most disquieting feature of the act's operation thus far is one that may have profound implications for the entire law of search and seizure: the apparent readiness of judges to grant interception orders. It is perhaps indicative of the state of judicial scrutiny of warrant applications generally that between June 20, 1968, when the act went into operation, and December 31, 1971, all but two of the 1,889 applications for orders made to federal and state judges were granted. Even conceding that the reporting requirements of the act would induce prosecutors to exercise great care in applying for orders, the number of rejections still seems incredibly small.

One provision of the act states that this law does not prevent the President from taking necessary measures "to protect the Nation against actual or potential attack or other hostile acts of a foreign power, to obtain foreign intelligence information deemed essential to the security of the United States, or to protect national security information against foreign intelligence activities," nor restricts his authority to "protect the United States against the overthrow of the Government by force or other unlawful means, or against any other clear and present danger to the structure or existence of the Government."[55] Attorney General John N. Mitchell construed this language to mean that the President may authorize eavesdropping without prior judicial approval on persons suspected of domestic subversion. This controversial interpretation of the act was rejected by the Court in a case decided on June 19, 1972. The Court ruled that neither the statute nor the Fourth Amendment confers such authority on the President. The statute, in this provision, merely disclaims any intention "to limit or disturb such powers as the President may have under the Constitution. In short, Congress simply left presidential powers where it found them." However, the Court strongly intimated that it would be possible to grant judicial authorization for domestic security surveillance on a more flexible standard of probable cause, and with a less strict time limit, than are required by the act for surveillance of "ordinary crimes," in view of the "long range" nature of this type of surveillance and the difficulty of identifying the "exact targets." In fact, the opinion virtually invited Congress to amend the act in these particulars.[56]

VIII. ADMINISTRATIVE SEARCHES

Like mechanical eavesdropping, periodic inspection of dwellings by housing, health, and fire inspectors, as required by modern municipal codes, postdates the eighteenth-century milieu in which the Fourth Amendment was framed; however, administrative inspections differ from eavesdropping and conventional searches in that they look to the correction of actual and potential hazards to the public safety rather than to the securing of evidence. This factor was considered crucial when the issue of a warrant requirement for municipal inspections came before the Court in 1959.[57] Since the object of this type of search is not prosecution, it was regarded by the majority as merely touching upon the "periphery" of interests protected by the Fourth Amendment; the privacy of the householder must therefore give way to the paramount public interest in preserving a healthy urban environment. The decision was roundly criticized for making it possible for police to employ inspectors to ferret out evidence; for enabling inspections to be made for personal or political reasons; and, in general, for construing the Fourth Amendment in such a way as to shield suspects who misuse their privacy, but not to protect law-abiding citizens who value privacy for its own sake.

In 1967 the Court reversed itself and affirmed that the "basic purpose" of the Fourth Amendment "is to safeguard the privacy and security of individuals against arbitrary invasions by government officials,"[58] regardless of their object. Recognizing, however, that inspection schemes would be rendered unworkable if the quantum of proof needed for a warrant were similar to that required in a criminal case, the Court jettisoned the usual probable cause standard as inappropriate, and substituted instead a flexible test based upon such factors as the condition of the area to be inspected and the time elapsed since the last inspection, rather than specific knowledge of the condition of the dwelling to be entered. Whether the decision will significantly add to the householder's sense of security against unreasonable inspections is debatable. It has been cogently argued that, given the relative ease of obtaining a warrant, and an ex-parte proceeding in which the citizen cannot appear to explain his reasons for refusing inspection, the grant of a warrant will usually be virtually automatic. A procedure more appropriate to the end in view would give the householder notice of the impending warrant application so that he may appear in court to state his objections.[59]

More recently the Court has held, over sharp dissent, that a public assistance grant may be made conditional upon periodic visits to the home by a caseworker. A warrant to enter is not required since a caseworker is neither a person in "uniformed authority" nor permitted to "snoop," and because the public has a legitimate interest in seeing to it that the money it spends (in this instance, for support of a dependent child) is properly used.[60]

IX. THE EXCLUSIONARY RULE IN LAW

The most controversial feature of the Court's development of the Fourth Amendment is its handling of the problem of enforcement. Since a search takes place during the investigation stage of a case, the right to security against unreasonable search, unlike most other procedural safeguards, is not within the power of the trial court to enforce. Nor, because of the secrecy which surrounds the preparations for a search, is it usually possible to invoke the advance protection of an injunction,[61] as is commonly done when First Amendment freedoms are threatened. Yet in the absence of an effective means of enforcing its restrictions, the amendment stands in danger of becoming a dead letter, a mere admonition to good conduct on the part of the police. It was to prevent the Fourth Amendment from becoming a forgotten part of the Bill of Rights that in 1914, in Weeks v. United States,[62] the Court broke with common law precedent and ordered the exclusion from federal trials of evidence obtained through unconstitutional search, a rule which nearly 50 years later, in Mapp v. Ohio,[63] was extended to trials in the states. Under common law the manner in which evidence is acquired is immaterial; if the evidence is trustworthy it is admissible. This position is still maintained by the British courts and those of nearly all countries the world over, yet Mapp was not as dramatic a departure from American state practice as may appear: gradually, between 1914 and 1961, about one-half of the states had of their own volition adopted the exclusionary rule.

Comparisons with British judicial practice, which are frequently made by critics of the exclusionary rule, are unfair since the need for an exclusionary policy depends in large measure on the extent of police misconduct, which the policy is designed to discourage. Whatever the situation in Britain, in the years preceding the Mapp decision it had become abundantly clear to the Court that the Fourth Amendment was being commonly and often flagrantly violated, and was perhaps the provision of the Bill of Rights least respected by the police.

Those who have opposed the exclusionary rule (and they have included such eminent judges and scholars as Benjamin N. Cardozo and John H. Wigmore) take essentially the position that it attempts to do justice in a roundabout way, by turning a policeman's infraction of law into a criminal's ticket to freedom. In Cardozo's oft-quoted words, "[t]he criminal is to go free because the constable has blundered."[64] The more rational course would be to convict the criminal and punish the policeman; in this way, the interests of victims of illegal search against whom nothing is found, and who gain nothing from the exclusionary rule, would also be served. This contention, admirably logical as it appears, nevertheless overlooks the realities of the situation: policemen are practically never prosecuted for searching unlawfully, while administrative discipline has proven inadequate. As for remedies in tort (civil suit), these are defective for a variety of reasons: the amount recoverable in a trespass suit is often geared to the extent of injury to property, but a search usually causes little damage; also, even where punitive damages can be awarded, malice must be shown; again, juries have shown themselves more favorably disposed to a policeman who uncovers evidence of crime than to the obviously guilty person who sues him; finally, policemen are not men of means from whom large sums can be recovered, and this discourages aggrieved parties from suing them. Those against whom no incriminating evidence has been found are reluctant to file suit for a different reason: they do not want to draw public attention to the fact that they have been under police scrutiny. The kind of suit which might prove an effective deterrent to illegal search, and at a lesser social cost than exclusion—a quasi-judicial action, or one before a judge without a jury, against the state or city which employs the officer—does not currently exist in any American jurisdiction.

The Supreme Court's move to deter illegal search by state officers actually developed in two stages. The Mapp decision imposed the exclusionary rule, but it did not say that the Fourth Amendment's standard in its entirety had been carried over into Fourteenth Amendment due process. The exclusionary rule, it may be observed, does not dictate the content of search standards; it merely requires that whatever those standards are, whether stringent or lax, they must be adhered to if the fruits of the search are to be admissible.

In Wolf v. Colorado,[65] the 1949 decision which Mapp overruled, the Court took the position that only such protections as are at the "core" of the Fourth Amendment are guaranteed by due process against infringement by the states. (The core was never laid bare by the Court except insofar as the exclusionary rule was held *not* to be a core protection.) The Mapp decision clearly catapulted the exclusionary rule into a position at the core of the amendment; but did it also require the states to follow federal search standards, or did it merely hold that seizures made in violation of core protections (whatever they were) would henceforth be inadmissible? In 1963 the Court answered this question in Ker v. California[66] by imposing a single constitutional standard for federal and state searches alike.

Adoption of the Weeks rule for federal trials did not stir much controversy; the federal government at the time exercised a limited jurisdiction in criminal law so that the rule affected only a handful of offenders. Whatever controversy there was in the succeeding years focused on the increasing tendency of state courts to follow the federal example. In contrast, the Mapp decision—which inaugurated the Warren Court's "constitutional revolution" in the area of defendants' rights—unleashed a storm of criticism, but not until 1971 did any of the Justices make a serious effort to discard the rule. That year, however, it became clear that the future of the exclusionary rule was likely to become a major constitutional battleground. Chief Justice Burger, a long-time implacable foe of the rule, called for its abandonment in both federal and state cases.[67] Justice Blackmun apparently supported him, although more guardedly.[68] Justice Harlan, in his penultimate Fourth Amendment opinion[69] before retiring, stated that he wished to discard both Mapp and Ker, but would have retained the Weeks rule. Harlan, who like Justice Frankfurter had voted with fair consistency in favor of a liberal interpretation of Fourth Amendment protections but had dissented in Mapp because of the issue of federalism, thought that the single constitutional standard adopted in Ker had caused the Court to relax requirements for federal searches in order to grant some leeway to state law enforcement. Burger conceded, however, that until an effective tort remedy is legislated, the exclusionary rule should remain in effect so as to avoid giving police "the impression . . . that an open season on 'criminals' had been declared."[70] Here Burger was clearly appealing to the federal and state governments to legislate the kind of remedies which might allow the Court to free them from the grip of the exclusionary rule.[71]

The Chief Justice was also critical of the inflexibility of the rule, which applies to all official infractions without regard to the character of the violation. He believed the Court should offer "rationally graded responses" and not treat "vastly dissimilar cases as if they were the same."[72] While Burger did not elaborate on his position, it is indeed a serious question whether the rule, as it operates today (and even assuming that it carries a far greater deterrent power than it appears to), always serves to advance the cause of justice. The Court understandably does not want trial judges (of whom it is probably mistrustful, in any event) to get bogged down in the task of distinguishing between flagrant violations and errors in judgment. But does the rule serve to deter the police when, to cite an extreme example, evidence is excluded not through any fault of theirs but because the warrant under which the seizure was made was improperly issued through the carelessness or ignorance of the magistrate?

The Weeks opinion itself did not involve any specific constitutional provision, and in its subsequent opinions the Court oscillated between the Fourth and Fifth Amendments in an effort to settle on a constitutional basis for the exclusionary rule, sometimes (as in the pre-Weeks case of Boyd v. United States)[73] joining the two in a mystical union. The Fifth Amendment in this context has a certain advantage since, unlike the Fourth, it addresses itself to the enforcement problem by expressly forbidding a compelled incrimination, but it is novel to consider the use of an unlawful seizure from a passive victim as an incrimination. More recently, the Court has settled on the Fourth Amendment as the appropriate constitutional instrument. In other words, it is reasonable to construe the amendment to allow the imposition of an exclusionary rule if this is regarded as necessary to ensure compliance with its provisions.[74]

X. THE EXCLUSIONARY RULE IN ACTION

The essential purpose of the exclusionary rule is, of course, to deter unlawful search by making the quest unprofitable. If police were prohibited from using evidence so obtained, the Court believed, they would more frequently conform to the requirements of the Fourth Amendment in order to maintain acceptable conviction records. A decade after the Mapp decision it is still not possible to arrive at any sound judgment as to whether, or to what extent, this belief was in fact justified.

The sole important empirical study conducted prior to the Mapp decision in a State (Illinois) which had of its own volition adopted the exclusionary rule, concerned Chicago, and indicated only qualified success in deterring police from making unlawful searches. In 1950 the Chicago Municipal Court suppressed evidence in 19 percent of narcotics cases, 25 percent of weapons cases, and an incredible 81 percent of gambling cases.[75] These figures indicated also that the more serious the crime, the more likely the police were to heed the legal requirements so as not to imperil the chances for successful prosecution.

In the years since the Mapp decision a number of studies, embracing questionnaires,[76] field observation,[77] and statistical analyses,[78] have focused, directly or indirectly, on the effect of the exclusionary rule in reforming police search practices. At the risk of oversimplification, one may summarize the findings as follows: as a result of Mapp, police officials now place much greater emphasis on providing their men with instruction in the law, but there is something of a gap between police education and performance. To some extent police misconduct continues, since the norms found within the police organization, particularly the attitudes of superior officers and the emphasis placed on solving crime, are more important determinants of police behavior than judicial rules. Moreover, the reasoning underlying the exclusionary rule is undermined by the fact that prosecution of offenders is not always the object of police searches; a large number (perhaps the majority) of unlawful searches are carried out not with eventual prosecution in mind, but to keep suspected criminals under some sort of surveillance and constraint. This harassment centers around vice, gambling, narcotics abuse, and other crimes where evidence to sustain a successful prosecution is difficult to obtain. The police believe, perhaps correctly, that the public is interested more in crime rates than in conviction rates.

One of these studies analyzed the nature of police allegations concerning discovery of evidence in narcotics misdemeanor cases in New York City, and concluded that "police officers often fabricate testimony to avoid the effects of Mapp-based motions to suppress illegally seized evidence."[79] This conclusion was based on the striking fact that the cases in which police claimed to have found narcotics hidden on the suspect dropped from over 30 percent in 1960-1961 to 5 percent in 1966; conversely, the percentage of cases in which, following the Mapp decision, the police claimed to have found evidence that was clearly visible (that is, held in the suspect's hand, dropped or thrown down by him, or openly exposed in premises), rose dramatically. That some policemen have resorted to perjury in order to prevent the exclusion of evidence is, from the writer's knowledge, widely believed by trial judges, yet it has been suggested that in this particular instance the contrasting patterns in police statements may possibly be accounted for by a change in tactics: "a police officer without a warrant may rush a suspect, hoping to produce a panic in which the person will visibly discard the narcotics and give the officer cause to arrest him and a legitimate ground to use the evidence."[80]

The most recent study, by Professor Dallin H. Oaks,[81] is comprehensive, indeed magisterial, in its analytical discussion of the purpose of the rule, its survey of the other studies, and its detailed proposals for further research. Where it may be least satisfactory is precisely the area in which it is most original: an analysis, based on statistical material, of police performance in Chicago, Washington, D.C., and Cincinnati. Oaks believes that the expected improvement in police conduct as a result of the exclusionary rule has largely failed to materialize. Such an assessment finds much support in the literature. Whether Oaks' own data point in this direction is a different matter.

Oaks' findings may be summarized as follows:

(1) In Chicago in 1969 evidence was thrown out in 33 percent of narcotics cases, 24 percent of weapons cases, and 59 percent of gambling cases. (The suppression rate in Chicago thus remains about as high as it was in 1950).

(2) In sharp contrast, the District of Columbia's courts in 1965 excluded evidence in only 4 percent of narcotics felonies, 2 percent of gambling felonies, and 1 percent of weapons felonies.

(3) In Cincinnati, arrests and convictions in narcotics and weapons cases showed no significant variation between the five year period which preceded the Mapp decision and the six year period which followed it.

What are we to make of these data? In the first place, it is unclear why Oaks apparently expected a significant change in police behavior in Chicago. Whatever the factors which in 1950 were responsible for large-scale noncompliance with the law, they would surely not change automatically with the superimposition of the federal exclusionary rule on the preexisting state rule.[82]

The figures for the District of Columbia seem to provide impressive corroboration for the claimed effectiveness of the rule. Yet Oaks discounts the evidence as equivocal. The contrast between Chicago and the District, he says, is attributable to "differences in the receptivity of judges to claims of illegal search and seizure and differences in the structure of the system, as well as differences in police behavior."[83] This is a tantalizing statement, but the asserted differences in judicial receptivity and police behavior are not explained. The only difference that Oaks develops is that in Chicago there is no screening by prosecutors of police charges prior to the initial hearing; whereas in the District prosecutors carefully review all cases before presenting them to the court, dropping such charges as might be challenged successfully through a motion to suppress evidence. However, since the charges dropped by prosecutors (for whatever reason) are said to number about 10 percent of the total, the contrast between Chicago and the District is still impressive.

As for Cincinnati, one can draw the inference that the exclusionary rule has failed as a deterrent in that city only if one assumes that observance of legal requirements by the police should result in lower arrest and conviction rates. However, an illegal search does not necessarily signify that the police would have been unable to obtain a warrant. In studying the cases brought before the Supreme Court and state appellate courts, one is struck by the number of instances in which warrants could have been readily obtained if only the police had taken the trouble to apply for them. More important, assuming the Mapp rule had not been imposed, would arrest and conviction rates for narcotics and weapons cases have remained constant, or would they have increased, reflecting the sharp rise in the crime rate during the 1960s?[84] If the latter, it might be contended that the rule has indeed proved effective in reducing the number of unlawful searches in Cincinnati.

Interviewing of patrolmen and detectives—the men who actually carry out searches—may be more productive than other forms of investigation in assessing the impact of the exclusionary rule. This method has the additional advantage of being less expensive and time-consuming. One such project was conducted on a small scale in 1970, in which nineteen New York City police officers were interviewed[85] concerning their attitudes on the decision in the stop-and-frisk case of Sibron v. New York.[86] Only three of the officers regarded the search of Sibron as unreasonable. Twelve regarded it as reasonable, while the remaining four thought the search was unreasonable only because it had been delayed for too long. (Sibron was shadowed for eight hours before being searched.) Even more striking, ten of the officers thought it would be morally right for them to "doctor" their testimony in order to help convict the guilty.

The focal point of empirical studies has been the exclusionary rule as it has affected police practices. Not one published study has attempted to gauge the reaction of trial judges. This is a gap that deserves to be filled.

At one time it was implicitly assumed that when the Supreme Court issues a ruling, it is faithfully (if not cheerfully) implemented at lower judicial levels. Thus the study of constitutional law usually began and ended with analysis of Supreme Court opinions and consideration of their probable impact on government and society. In recent years, however, attention has belatedly been paid to the question of how some of these decisions are actually being enforced in the federal and state courts.

The writer has for some time been examining the extent of judicial compliance with Supreme Court search and seizure decisions. This requires, first of all, an exhaustive review of judicial opinions (and, where available, transcripts of suppression hearings) in the jurisdictions to be studied; secondly, extensive interviewing of judges, prosecuting and defense attorneys, and law enforcement officials; and finally, some courtroom observation of the way in which motions to suppress evidence are handled. Interviews are particularly important since most opinions of trial courts, even at the federal level, go unreported and, like transcripts of suppression hearings, are difficult to locate. Since a nationwide or even regional study is obviously beyond the capacity of any one individual, it is to be hoped that other scholars will pursue this matter further.

One major though not insuperable problem that confronts the investigator is the sophistication and complexity of Fourth Amendment law. This demands a more exhaustive knowledge of constitutional law than would be necessary for a comparable study of any other procedural protection. A study of the reaction of trial courts to issues raised by the Miranda warnings, for example, is simple by comparison to the evaluation of judicial handling of such matters as probable cause and stop-and-frisk.

While the subject of judicial compliance with Supreme Court decisions in any area of constitutional law deserves serious attention, judicial compliance as it affects Fourth Amendment cases is of critical importance. In most other fields of constitutional law resistance or defiance cannot easily be camouflaged, but in search and seizure cases the judge has a variety of methods at hand for resisting compliance with Supreme Court decisions without appearing to do so.[87] His determination of the constitutionality of the search may depend on the answers he gives to such questions as: was probable cause properly established? was the warrant properly issued? was it sufficiently specific? In the case of a warrantless search, was there knowing consent to the search? did a legitimate arrest precede the search and thereby give it legal color? Very often it is simply a matter of taking the word of the police as against that of the defendant, something that the judge is free to do. (Exclusion of evidence is a question of law rather than fact, and is therefore decided by the judge rather than the jury.) To be sure, an appellate court might reverse the trial judge, but most convictions are not appealed and, even when they are, the appellate court might itself be no more sympathetic to Supreme Court precedent than was the trial court. There is, the writer is persuaded, a close correlation between the way in which the police react to Supreme Court decisions and the way in which some judges will enforce those decisions, for the relationship between law enforcement officials and trial judges tends to be close.

Nevertheless, a note of caution is in order. What will at times appear to the investigator to be evidence of judicial resistance of the Court's mandate, may in reality no more than reflect the inability of some trial judges to absorb the body of constitutional principles which has been developed (and not always with consistency) with such amazing speed in the last decade. Judicial error is, of course, a two-edged sword; it will sometimes work in favor of defendants' rights (though with less frequency) as well as against them. The establishment of seminars and institutes, which was proposed by Professor Katz in 1966,[88] to keep judges abreast of developments in the law of search and seizure, is widely supported by trial judges. Unfortunately, whatever instruction trial judges receive is still largely self-instruction.

The safeguarding of the right of privacy and personal security deserves to be one of the overriding concerns of the American polity. This right lies at the heart of the Fourth Amendment, which is the foremost constitutional instrument for its protection. In the words of Justice Brandeis, the amendment "conferred, as against the government, the right to be let alone—the most comprehensive of rights and the right most valued by civilized man."[89] The Supreme Court has, in recent years, made a conscious and powerful effort to infuse this right with greater potency. Whether the Court's policy is being thwarted at lower judicial levels, is a subject which demands more sustained attention by lawyers and social scientists than it has so far received.

NOTES

1. 367 U.S. 643 (1961).
2. 388 U.S. 41 (1967).
3. 389 U.S. 347 (1967).
4. 395 U.S. 752 (1969).
5. United States v. Rabinowitz, 339 U.S. 56, 66 (1950).
6. Harris v. United States, 331 U.S. 145, 157 (1947) (dissenting opinion).
7. Interview, December 5, 1961.
8. See his opinions for the Court in Davis v. United States, 328 U.S. 582 (1946); and Zap v. United States, 328 U.S. 624 (1946).
9. Chambers v. Maroney, 399 U.S. 42 (1970), which is discussed below in section III.
10. 331 U.S. 145 (1947).
11. Marron v. United States, 275 U.S. 192 (1927), marks the actual beginning of the shift, but this decision was severely qualified shortly afterwards in Go-Bart Importing Co. v. United States, 282 U.S. 344 (1931), and United States v. Lefkowitz, 285 U.S. 452 (1932).
12. 334 U.S. 699 (1948).
13. 339 U.S. 56 (1950).
14. American Law Institute. (1970) Model Code of Pre-Arraignment Procedure (Tent. Draft No. 3, 1970). xix, xx.
15. 395 U.S. 752 (1969).
16. 387 U.S. 294 (1967).
17. Taylor, T. (1969) Two Studies in Constitutional Interpretation. p. 48. Columbus: Ohio State University Press.
18. 399 U.S. 42 (1970).
19. Coolidge v. New Hampshire, 403 U.S. 443 (1971). This restriction, however, applies only to objects lying beyond the limited area in which, consonant with the Chimel decision, an incidental search may be carried out; evidence found on the prisoner himself and in the area within his reach continues to be seizable even though its discovery was anticipated.
20. Id. at 477-478.
21. 392 U.S. 1 (1968).
22. 392 U.S. 40 (1968).
23. 392 U.S. at 16.
24. Id. at 30.
25. 392 U.S. at 39 (dissenting opinion).
26. Id. at 35, n.1.
27. Miranda v. Arizona, 384 U.S. 436 (1966).
28. In the Terry case the officer's apprehension of danger was based on personal observation. However, in a recent case the Court approved a frisk carried out on the basis of an informer's tip that the man in question was armed. While the informer was known to the officer, his reliability was not established, and he did not state the source of his information. Adams v. Williams: 40 U.S. L. W. 4724 (1972). In this case the Court also made explicit what in the Terry opinion was only implicit: that the police may stop a person acting suspiciously for investigation. "A brief stop of a suspicious individual, in order to determine his identity or to maintain the status quo momentarily while obtaining more information, may be most reasonable in light of the facts known to the officer at the time." Id.

29. 384 U.S. 436 (1966).

30. Frazier v. Cupp, 394 U.S. 757 (1969).

31. See Katz v. United States, 389 U.S. 347 (1967).

32. The suggestion is made in Cahey v. Mazurkiewicz, 431 F. 2d 839, 843 (3rd Cir. 1970).

33. Stoner v. California, 376 U.S. 483 (1964).

34. Coolidge v. New Hampshire, 403 U.S. 443 (1971).

35. Olmstead v. United States, 277 U.S. 438 (1928).

36. Justice Holmes' famous dissent in this case, in which he referred to wiretapping as "dirty business," was based not on constitutional considerations but on the illegality of wiretapping under the law of the state (Washington) where it took place.

37. Nardone v. United States, 302 U.S. 379 (1937).

38. Goldman v. United States, 316 U.S. 129 (1942).

39. Silverman v. United States, 365 U.S. 505 (1961).

40. 388 U.S. 41 (1967).

41. 389 U.S. 347 (1967).

42. Id. at 351.

43. Lanza v. United States, 370 U.S. 139 (1962).

44. Gouled v. United States, 255 U.S. 298 (1921).

45. 387 U.S. 294 (1967). Actually, the "mere evidence" rule was implicitly discarded in Schmerber v. California, 384 U.S. 757 (1966), where the Court ruled that a compulsory blood test to determine whether a person was intoxicated while driving may be made on probable cause, without the delay of securing a warrant, since the alcoholic level of the blood diminishes with the passage of time, thus eroding the evidence. Blood, even when saturated with alcohol, can scarcely be regarded as anything other than "mere evidence."

46. 343 U.S. 747 (1952).

47. 373 U.S. 427 (1963).

48. 401 U.S. 745 (1971).

49. Where the "bugging" takes place in the post-indictment stage of a case, the admission is excluded on the ground that it was elicited without advice of counsel. Massiah v. United States, 377 U.S. 201 (1964).

50. Lewis v. United States, 385 U.S. 206, 211 (1966).

51. Hoffa v. United States, 385 U.S. 293, 302 (1966).

52. See Lewin, N. (1971) "Privacy and the 'Third-Party' Bug." New Republic 164 (April 17, 1971): 12-17. However, so long as informers are regarded as indispensable instruments of law enforcement, a change in the Court's attitude is most unlikely. In a controversial 1967 decision, McCray v. Illinois, 386 U.S. 300, the Court held that an affidavit for a search warrant based upon information provided by an informer need not disclose his identity. By allowing his identity to be kept secret, the law protects an undercover agent from possible reprisals and preserves his usefulness; but it opens the door to serious and virtually undetectable abuses, and a difficult burden is placed on a defense counsel who may wish to challenge the reliability of an informer whose name he does not even know.

53. 18 U.S.C. #2510-2520.

54. Administrative Office of the United States Courts. (1972) Report on Applications for Orders Authorizing or Approving the Interception of Wire or Oral Communications. Washington, D.C. The act exempted consensual surveillance from its restrictions; data on this type of eavesdropping are therefore unavailable.

55. 18 U.S.C. #2511 (3).

56. United States v. United States District Court for the Eastern District of Michigan 40 U.S.L.W. 4761 (1972). The Court left open the question whether interception of the communications of foreign powers or their agents may be authorized by the President. (70-153).

57. Frank v. Maryland, 359 U.S. 360 (1959).

58. Camara v. Municipal Court, 387 U.S. 523, 528 (1967).

59. See LaFave, W. R. Administrative Searches and the Fourth Amendment. 1967 Supreme Court Review (Kurland, ed.) 1, 27-35.

60. Wyman v. James, 400 U.S. 309 (1971).

61. Where a specific and continuing pattern of violations was shown (the entry of Baltimore police into numerous homes to search for suspects, without probable cause to believe that the suspects were inside) the conduct was enjoined by the Fourth Circuit in Lankford v. Gelston, 364 F. 2d 197 (1966).

62. 232 U.S. 383 (1914).

63. 367 U.S. 643 (1961).

64. People v. Defore, 150 N.E. 585, 587 (N.Y. 1926).

65. 338 U.S. 25 (1949).

66. 374 U.S. 23 (1963).

67. Bivens v. Six Unknown Named Agents of Federal Bureau of Narcotics, 403 U.S. 388, 411 (1971) (dissenting opinion).

68. Id. at 430 (dissenting opinion).

69. Coolidge v. New Hampshire, 403 U.S. 443, 490 (1971) (concurring opinion).

70. 403 U.S. at 421.

71. In Bivens v. Six Unknown Named Agents of Federal Bureau of Narcotics, 403 U.S. 388 (1971), the Court recognized a federal cause of action for violations of the Fourth Amendment by federal officers, but did not reach the question whether the official position of the agents rendered them immune to liability.

72. Id. at 419.

73. 116 U.S. 616 (1886). This case, which involved a forced production of business records in a forfeiture proceeding, implicitly adopted the exclusionary rule, but this aspect of the decision was drastically limited in Adams v. New York, 192 U.S. 585 (1904).

74. Under the Fifth Amendment exclusion would be considered a vindication of the right, regardless of its deterrent effect.

75. Comment. (1952) "Search and Seizure in Illinois: Enforcement of the Constitutional Right of Privacy." Northwestern Law Review 47 (September-October): 493-507.

76. Nagel, S. S. (1965) "Testing the Effects of Excluding Illegally Seized Evidence." Wisconsin Law Review 1965 (Spring): 283-308; Katz, M. (1966) "The Supreme Court and the States: An Inquiry into Mapp v. Ohio in North Carolina. The Model, the Study, and the Implications." North Carolina Law Review 45 (December): 119-151.

77. Skolnick, J. H. (1966) Justice Without Trial. New York: John Wiley; Tiffany, L. P., McIntyre, D. M. Jr., and Rotenberg, D. L. (1967) Detection of Crime: Stopping and Questioning, Search and Seizure, Encouragement and Entrapment. Boston: Little, Brown. 95-205.

78. Comment. (1968) "Effect of Mapp v. Ohio on Police Search-and-Seizure Practices in Narcotics Cases." Columbia Journal of Law and Social Problems 4 (March): 87-104; Oaks, D. H. (1970) "Studying the Exclusionary Rule in Search and Seizure." University of Chicago Law Review 37 (Summer): 665-757.

79. Comment, "Effect of Mapp v. Ohio" 87.

80. Oaks 699, n. 90.

81. Cited at n. 78.

82. Professor Oaks may have had in mind the transformation of the Chicago Police during the 1960s from an inefficient, politically shackled force into one of the most thoroughly professional forces in the country (notwithstanding the unfortunate conduct of some officers during the 1968 Democratic National Convention).

83. Oaks 687-688.

84. The number of arrests in the nation on narcotics charges jumped from 29,613 in 1963 to 162,177 in 1968, and on weapons charges from 43,608 to 83,721. Federal Bureau of Investigation, Uniform Crime Reports (1963), 104; (1968), 111.

85. The interviewer was Joseph P. Davey, an attorney and at that time a graduate student of the writer.

86. See section V above.

87. Some judges express their antagonism boldly. In a recent report on the Boston trial courts, one judge is quoted as saying: "the day I throw out a warrant that uncovers 100 decks of heroin is the day they'll throw a net over my head." Another remarked to a defense counsel: "We don't follow those Supreme Court decisions here." Bing, B. and Rosenfeld, S. S. (1971) "The Quality of Justice: In the Lower Criminal Courts of Boston." Criminal Law Bulletin 7 (June): 393-443, at 438.

88. Katz, 139.

89. Olmstead v. United States, 277 U.S. 438, 478 (1928) (dissenting opinion).

CONFESSIONS AND SELF-INCRIMINATION

nor shall any person be . . . compelled in any criminal case to be a witness against himself

From the Fifth Amendment
to the U.S. Constitution

O. JOHN ROGGE received his J.S.D. in 1931 at Harvard Law School. He has served as counsel for the Securities and Exchange Commission, and assistant and special assistant for the U.S. Attorney General, at which office he was, between 1939 and 1941, in charge of the Criminal Division of the Department of Justice. His publications include *Our Vanishing Civil Liberties* (1949), *Why Men Confess* (1959), *The First and The Fifth* (1960), *The Official German Report* (1961), and *Obscenity Litigation in 10 American Jurisprudence Trials* (1965), as well as several long articles in various law reviews. He is at present in private practice.

Chapter 3

CONFESSIONS AND SELF-INCRIMINATION

O. JOHN ROGGE

I. OUR ACCUSATORIAL METHOD

The tendency of our courts to exclude confessions, except in the form of a guilty plea with a defendant's lawyer by his side, is one of the mainstays of our accusatorial method, a method that stands in sharp contrast to the inquisitional technique in use on the mainland of Europe and in Communist countries. The writer would carry our method to its logical, as well as wise, conclusion.

In the writer's view, any confession which a defendant repudiates in court should for that reason alone be inadmissible in evidence. Then we shall fulfill the spirit of our accusatorial method and also its implicit promise. Moreover, such a course will make for stronger, not weaker, law enforcement. The United States Supreme Court under Chief Justice Warren was approaching this position, but had not quite reached it in its extensions of the right to counsel and of the privilege against self-incrimination, or right of silence as the bench and bar are increasingly calling it,[1] and its exclusions of confessions in both state and federal cases.[2] Miranda v. Arizona gave further substance to the critical yet prophetic comment of Justice White in his dissenting opinion in Escobedo v. Illinois: "The decision is thus another major step in the direction of the goal which the Court seemingly has in mind—to bar from evidence all admissions obtained from an individual suspected of crime, whether involuntarily made or not."[3] Or, as he put it in his dissenting opinion in Miranda in which Justices Harlan and Stewart joined, the Court's result in that case "adds up to a judicial judgment that evidence from the accused should not be used against him in any way, whether compelled or not."[4] This is as it should be.

If a defendant wants to stand up with his lawyer beside him and plead guilty, well and good; that is one thing. A large majority of deviants do just this anyway. That is how prosecutors rack up such high percentages of convictions year after year. But if a defendant pleads not guilty, the prosecutor ought to be bound to prove his case from sources other than the defendant's own mouth, or the defendant goes free. Then we shall truly have an accusatorial system.

Prosecutors and those of like mind have assailed the Supreme Court's exclusionary rulings. Often they have quoted the statement of Justice Jackson, concurring in Watts v. Indiana,[5] that counsel for the suspect would mean "a real peril" to law enforcement. Justice Harlan in his dissenting opinion in Miranda, in which Justices Stewart and White joined, relied upon Justice Jackson's concurring opinion and expressed a similar fear: "[F]or if counsel arrives, there is rarely going to be a police station confession."[6] Justice Clark in his dissenting opinion in Miranda was even more gloomy as to the Court's extension of the right of silence to police interrogation: "Such a strict constitutional specific inserted at the nerve center of crime detection may well kill the patient."[7]

In the writer's opinion, those who insist upon empowering the police to question suspects in the absence of counsel, thus importing another bit of the inquisitional system, are mistaken when they assert that such a measure is essential to law enforcement. On the contrary, counsel for suspects will be a help rather than a hindrance in handling deviants. Indeed, such counsel will prove to be a boon to law enforcement, for they will find out from suspects what their stories are. True, if a suspect is guilty, counsel will then try to negotiate a solution with the prosecutor; but this usually happens after indictment or other comparable charge anyway. Therefore, let us put counsel for the suspect in as good a bargaining position as the prosecutor. Let us give the suspect the right to counsel during the interrogation stage. And let us exclude confessions, except in the form of a guilty plea with a defendant's lawyer by his side.

II. GUILTY PLEAS

Even with our accusatorial method, the large majority of deviants plead guilty because human beings, whether guilty or innocent of the offense charged, feel a

compulsion to confess to something. It has even been adumbrated that some individuals commit offenses in order to make confessions.

It may come as a surprise to many, but in the eighty-six United States District Courts having purely federal jurisdiction, the number of defendants in such cases during the seven-year period ended June 30, 1954 who pleaded either guilty or nolo contendere amounted to the surprising figure of 224,920 out of a total of 268,620. Of the remainder, 23,274 were dismissed, 6,988 were acquitted, and 13,438 were convicted. Reduced to percentages this means, if one excludes the defendants who were dismissed, the astounding figure of 91.67 percent for those who pleaded either guilty or nolo contendere. If one includes the defendants who were dismissed, the figure becomes 83.70 percent. These figures exclude those charged as juvenile delinquents but include immigration cases. The immigration cases were almost entirely confined to the five federal districts touching the Mexican border and the pleas of guilty of defendants in these cases amounted to almost 98 percent. If immigration cases are omitted, the figure becomes 87.67 percent if one excludes the defendants who were dismissed, and 77.16 percent if one includes them.[8]

Comparable figures for the fifteen years from June 30, 1954 follow:[9]

Table 1. Guilty Pleas

Fiscal Year Ended June 30	Total Defendants Terminated	Total Convicted	Convicted by Plea of Guilty or Nolo Contendere	Percent Convicted by Plea of Guilty or Nolo Contendere of Total Terminated	of Total Convicted
1955	38,900	33,855	31,148	79.9	92.0
1956	31,811	27,567	25,029	78.7	90.8
1957	29,725	26,254	23,867	80.3	90.9
1958	30,469	26,808	24,256	79.6	90.5
1959	30,729	27,033	24,793	80.7	91.7
1960	30,512	26,728	24,245	79.5	90.7
1961	31,226	28,625	24,830	79.5	86.7
1962	33,110	28,511	24,639	74.4	86.4
1963	24,845	29,803	25,924	74.4	86.9
1964	33,381	29,170	26,273	78.7	90.0
1965	33,718	28,754	25,923	76.9	90.1
1966	31,975	27,314	24,127	75.5	88.3
1967	31,535	26,344	23,131	73.3	87.8
1968	31,843	25,674	22,055	69.3	85.9
1969	32,796	26,803	23,138	70.5	86.3

Although the percentage of defendants in the federal court who pleaded guilty has fluctuated somewhat and has declined a little in recent years, the large majority still pleaded guilty.

The story in our state courts is not far different, although here one is handicapped by a lack of statistics. Some of the best state court statistics come from the Bureau of Criminal Statistics of the California Department of Justice, and the Administrative Office of the Courts of New Jersey. In California for the 13-year period from 1952 through 1965, of the total number of dispositions, less those certified to the juvenile courts, the percentage of those who pleaded guilty was rather consistently in the neighborhood of 65 percent.[10] In recent years, as in the case of the federal figures, the percentage of defendants who pleaded guilty declined a little but it still remained in the neighborhood of 60 percent. The percentages for the six years following 1964 are: 1965—62.9 percent; 1966—61.2 percent; 1967—59.8 percent; 1968—59.5 percent; 1969—63.0 percent; 1970—60.9 percent. According to the New Jersey statistics, the number of defendants who pleaded either guilty or non vult exceeded by more than two-and-a-half times the number who went to trial.[11]

In Santobello v. New York,[12] where the Court in an opinion by Chief Justice Burger described plea bargaining as "an essential component of the administration of justice,"[13] Justice Douglas, in two footnotes to his concurring opinion, cited these statistics:

> In 1964, guilty pleas accounted for 95.5% of all criminal convictions in trial courts of general jurisdiction in New York. In 1965, the figure for California was 74.0%. President's Commission on Law Enforcement and Administration of Justice, Task Force Report: The Courts 9 (1967).

> In 1964, guilty pleas accounted for 90.2% of all criminal convictions in United States district courts. *Ibid.* In fiscal 1970, of 28,178 convictions in the 89 United States district courts, 24,111 were by pleas of guilty or *nolo contendere*. Report of Director of Administrative Office of U.S. Courts, for Period July 1 through Dec. 31, 1970, Table D-4, p. A-26.[14]

A recently published report of the American Bar Foundation states that the proportion of defendants who elected to plead guilty rather than stand trial ranged from 33 percent to 93 percent in the various states, with a median figure of 66 percent.[15]

As Dean Edward L. Barrett, Jr., of the new law school of the University of California at David pointed out in his background material for the twenty-seventh American Assembly held in 1965 at Arden House on the Harriman (New York) campus of Columbia University, "the overwhelming majority (at least three-quarters over-all) of all persons brought to the courts will plead guilty and not involve courts, prosecutors, and defenders in the time and expense of contested cases."[16]

III. TREATMENT OF CONFESSIONS

In the small percentage of contested cases that we do have, the United States Supreme Court has been invalidating many confessions which defendants repudiated in court. It has done this in two lines of cases: one for the federal courts, and the other in state cases.

Three-quarters of a century ago, in Bram v. United States,[17] Justice, later Chief Justice, White in the Court's opinion tied the inadmissibility of a challenged confession in a case in the federal courts to an individual's right of silence under the Fifth Amendment:

> In criminal trials, in the courts of the United States, whenever a question arises whether a confession is incompetent because not voluntary, the issue is controlled by that portion of the Fifth Amendment, . . . commanding that no person "shall be compelled in any criminal case to be a witness against himself."[18]

The challenged material consisted of certain answers which a triple-murder suspect gave to an interrogator.

Professor Wigmore was harshly critical of Justice White's opinion. At one point he stated that Bram "reached the height of absurdity in misapplication of the law."[19] and at another, called the identification of the exclusion of coerced confessions and the Fifth Amendment's right of silence as "erroneous, both in history, principle, and practice."[20] One can suggest, on the contrary, that, just as the Fourth and Fifth Amendments support each other, so the exclusion of challenged confessions and the Fifth Amendment's right of silence are but two sides of the same coin.

More recently in federal trials we have what is known as the McNabb-Mallory rule. McNabb v. United States;[21] Mallory v. United States.[22] McNabb involved three members of a clan of Tennessee mountaineers by that name who were charged with the murder of an officer of the Federal Alcohol Tax Unit. Two of them were questioned for a number of hours over a period of two days. During this period all three gave confessions. The other case involved a 19-year-old youth named Mallory who was charged with rape in the District of Columbia. He was taken into custody between two and two-thirty o'clock in the afternoon, subjected to a polygraph (lie detector) test beginning a little after eight o'clock in the evening, and alleged to have confessed by nine-thirty. In both cases the defendants objected to their confessions. The Supreme Court held the confessions to be invalid because they were obtained as a result of persistent questioning plus a failure to take the prisoners before a United States Commissioner or other committing authority without unnecessary delay. In between the two decisions came the Federal Rules of Criminal Procedure, promulgated in 1946, which in rule 5(a) requires that an arrested person be taken before the nearest available committing authority "without unnecessary delay."

In Mallory the Court drew a distinction between time taken to verify a claim by an arrested person that he was innocent and time used to obtain a confession: "Circumstances may justify a brief delay between arrest and arraignment, as, for instance, where the story volunteered by the accused is susceptible of quick verification through third parties. But the delay must not be of a nature to give opportunity for the extraction of a confession."[23]

In state cases the Court threw out confessions which it found to be involuntary on the ground that they violated the due process clause of the Fourteenth Amendment. However, by involuntary the Court meant almost any confession which it regarded as unfairly obtained. As Chief Justice Warren explained in Blackburn v. Alabama:[24] "Thus a complex of values underlies the stricture against use by the state of confessions which, by way of a convenient shorthand, this Court terms involuntary, and the role played by each in any situation varies according to the particular circumstances of the case."[25]

The line of state cases in which the Court invalidated convictions based on confessions began with Brown v. Mississippi[26] in 1936. Then came Chambers v. Florida[27] where Justice Black wrote eloquently for a unanimous Court on the dangers of a secret inquisitional method:

> The determination to preserve an accused's right to procedural due process sprang in large part from the knowledge of the historical truth that the rights and liberties of people accused of crime could not be safely entrusted to secret inquisitorial processes. The testimony of centuries, in governments of varying kinds over populations of different races and beliefs, stood as proof that physical and mental torture and coercion had brought about the tragically unjust sacrifices of some who were the noblest and most useful of their generations. The rack, the thumbscrew, the wheel, solitary confinement, protracted questioning and cross questioning, and other ingenious forms of entrapment of the helpless or

unpopular had left their wake of mutilated bodies and shattered minds along the way to the cross, the guillotine, the stake and the hangman's noose.[28]

A high point in the exclusion of confessions came in June 1949, the last month that Justices Murphy and Rutledge sat, when the Court invalidated convictions in three different cases from three different states.[29] It was in one of these that Justice Frankfurter stated: "Ours is the accusatorial as opposed to the inquisitorial system."[30]

In the first part of the 1950s, during the time of the Vinson Court with Justices Murphy and Rutledge gone and in the midst of the cold war, there was somewhat of a retreat in the exclusion of confessions.[31] But under Chief Justice Warren the Court returned to its course. At each of many of its recent terms, just as it has set aside a number of convictions because defendants have been denied the effective assistance of counsel, so it has invalidated a number of convictions because they were based upon confessions. As Justice Frankfurter commented in another connection:

It would be comfortable if, by a comprehensive formula, we could decide when a confession is coerced so as to vitiate a state conviction. There is no such talismanic formula. Every Term we have to examine the particular circumstances of a particular case in order to apply generalities which no one disputes.[32]

Many of the recent rulings produced leading cases. Often there were leading cases in every year and in 1961, as in 1949, there were three: Fikes v. Alabama (1957),[33] Payne v. Arkansas (1958),[34] Spano v. New York (1959),[35] Blackburn v. Alabama (1960),[36] Rogers v. Richmond (1961),[37] Reck v. Pate (1961),[38] and Culombe v. Connecticut (1961).[39]

In Spano as well as Blackburn Chief Justice Warren wrote the opinion. In both cases the Court was unanimous for reversal, although in Spano there were concurring opinions, and in Blackburn Justice Clark concurred in the result. Spano confessed after eight hours of questioning, Blackburn after eight or nine hours. Also, in Spano a fledgling police officer who was one of Spano's buddies told him that if he did not confess the officer would be in trouble with his superiors. In the Court's opinion excluding Spano's confession, Chief Justice Warren explained:

The abhorrence of society to the use of involuntary confessions does not turn alone on their inherent untrustworthiness. It also turns on the deep-rooted feeling that the police must obey the law while enforcing the law; that in the end life and liberty can be as much endangered from illegal methods used to convict those thought to be criminals as from the actual criminals themselves.[40]

In Blackburn Chief Justice Warren, on behalf of himself and seven of his brethren, reasoned:

> Since Chambers v. State of Florida . . . this Court has recognized that coercion can be mental as well as physical, and that the blood of the accused is not the only hallmark of an unconstitutional inquisition. A number of cases have demonstrated, if demonstration were needed, that the efficiency of the rack and the thumbscrew can be matched, given the proper subject, by more sophisticated modes of "persuasion." A prolonged interrogation of an accused who is ignorant of his rights and who has been cut off from the moral support of friends and relatives is not infrequently an effective technique of terror. . . .

> [A]s important as it is that persons who have committed crimes be convicted, there are considerations which transcend the question of guilt or innocence. Thus, in cases involving involuntary confessions, this Court enforces the strongly felt attitude of our society that important human values are sacrificed where an agency of the government, in the course of securing a conviction, wrings a confession out of an accused against his will. This insistence upon putting the government to the task of proving guilt by means other than inquisition was engendered by historical abuses which are quite familiar.[41]

In 1961, in Reck v. Pate, the Court reached back a quarter-century to upset an Illinois conviction in 1963. In another leading case decided in that year, Rogers v. Richmond, a police chief in Connecticut had obtained a confession from a suspect after he pretended that he was about to have the suspect's wife brought in for questioning. The state courts accepted the confession, and in doing so were influenced by the consideration that the probable reliability of the confession was a circumstance of weight in determining its voluntariness. But the United States Supreme Court reversed, reasoning that the probable truth or falsity of a confession had nothing to do with its voluntariness or admissibility. If it was not voluntary in the broad sense in which the Court uses the word, it was not admissible. Justice Frankfurter, author of the Court's opinion, spoke unequivocally:

Our decisions under that Amendment [Fourteenth] have made clear that convictions following the admission into evidence of confessions which are involuntary, i.e., the product of coercion, either physical or psychological, cannot stand. This is so not because such confessions are unlikely to be true but because the methods used to extract them offend an underlying principle in the enforcement of our criminal law: that ours is an accusatorial and not an inquisitorial system—a system in which the State must establish guilt by evidence independently and freely secured and may not by coercion prove its charge against an accused out of his own mouth. [Footnotes omitted.] To be sure, confessions cruelly extorted may be and have been, to an unascertained extent, found to be untrustworthy. But the constitutional principle of excluding confessions that are not voluntary does not rest on this consideration. Indeed, in many of the cases in which the command of the Due Process Clause has compelled us to reverse state convictions involving the use of confessions obtained by impermissible methods, independent corroborating evidence left little doubt of the truth of what the defendant had confessed. Despite such verification, confessions were found to be the product of constitutionally impermissible methods in their inducement. Since a defendant has been subjected to pressures to which, under our accusatorial system, an accused should not be subjected, we were constrained to find that the procedures leading to his conviction had failed to afford him that due process of law which the Fourteenth Amendment guarantees.[42]

At the same term and in the same year as Gideon v. Wainwright,[43] where the Court extended the right to counsel to all defendants in all state criminal cases, the Court also reversed convictions based on confessions, again in three different cases from three different states: Fay v. Noia[44] (New York), Lynumn v. Illinois,[45] and Haynes v. Washington.[46] In Fay v. Noia the Court reversed such a conviction, even though the defendant Noia had allowed the time for a direct appeal in the state courts to lapse. Noia had two co-defendants, Bonino and Caminito, who were convicted with him. Both took direct appeals but lost in the state reviewing courts.[47] Ultimately, however, Caminito succeeded in having the Court of Appeals for the Second Circuit throw out his confession.[48] Judge Jerome N. Frank wrote for the court:

It has no significance that in this case we must assume there was no physical brutality. For psychological torture may be far more cruel, far more symptomatic of sadism. Many a man who can endure beatings will yield to fatigue. To keep a man awake beyond the point of exhaustion, while constantly pummelling him with questions, is to degrade him, to strip him of human dignity, to deprive him of the will to resist, to make him a pitiable creature mastered by the single desire—at all costs to be free of torment. Any member of this or any other court, to escape such anguish, would admit to almost any crime. Indeed, the infliction of such psychological punishment is more reprehensible than a physical attack: it leaves no discernible marks on the victim. Because it is thus concealed, it has, under the brutalitarian regimes, become the favorite weapon of the secret police, bent on procuring confessions as a means of convicting the innocent.[49]

Then Bonino got the New York Court of Appeals to reverse his conviction.[50] The Supreme Court, affirming the Second Circuit, freed Noia.

In Malloy v. Hogan,[51] Justice Brennan noted that the Court, in Haynes v. Washington,[52] had "held inadmissible even a confession secured by so mild a whip as the refusal, under certain circumstances, to allow a suspect to call his wife until he confessed."[53] After a reference to the "marked shift to the federal standard in state cases," Justice Brennan then made this significant comment: "The shift reflects recognition that the American system of criminal prosecution is accusatorial, not inquisitorial, and that the Fifth Amendment privilege is its essential mainstay."[54]

The next term marked another high in the protection of an individual's right of silence. There were no less than a half-dozen decisions enforcing it in one way or another. In the order of their rendition, they were: Doughty v. Maxwell (Feb. 24, 1964),[55] extending Gideon not only retrospectively but also to defendants who had pleaded guilty; Massiah v. United States (May 18, 1964),[56] reversing a federal conviction because of the introduction into evidence of the defendant's incriminatory statements made after indictment to federal agents in the absence of his counsel; Malloy v. Hogan (June 15, 1964),[57] making the Fifth Amendment's right of silence applicable to the states; Murphy v. Waterfront Comm'n of New York Harbor (June 15, 1964),[58] holding state-compelled testimony and its fruits inadmissible in a federal criminal prosecution; Jackson v. Denno (June 22, 1964),[59] reversing a state conviction based on a confession because the trial judge left the question of the confession's voluntariness to the jury without passing on this question independently first himself; and Escobedo v. Illinois (June 22, 1964),[60] excluding a suspect's confession given in the absence of his counsel.

Jackson v. Denno arose in New York. After its rendition, the New York Court of Appeals in People v. Huntley[61] announced that in cases involving contested confessions, whether the cases were concluded or not, there would be a hearing on voluntariness before the trial judge. As to future trials the court further stated: "The Judge must find voluntariness beyond a reasonable doubt before the confession can be submitted to the trial jury. The burden of proof as to voluntariness is on the People."[62] In concluded cases, such hearings became known as "Huntley hearings." Huntley himself had such a hearing but lost before the trial judge.[63]

IV. MIRANDA v. ARIZONA

The stage was now set for Miranda v. Arizona,[64] and Bram v. United States[65] finally came fully into its own. The Court, in extending the Fifth Amendment's right of silence to police questioning, commented through Chief Justice Warren that "this question, in fact, could have been taken as settled in federal courts almost 70 years ago . . . "[66] with Bram, and quoted from it.

With Miranda, those in custody must be advised of their right to remain silent and to counsel, either retained or appointed. If they are not so advised, any statements which they give during such detention will not be admissible in evidence. Chief Justice Warren in the Court's opinion twice detailed what Miranda requires. Near the beginning he wrote:

> Our holding will be spelled out with some specificity in the pages which follow but briefly stated it is this: the prosecution may not use statements, whether exculpatory or inculpatory, stemming from custodial interrogation of the defendant unless it demonstrates the use of procedural safeguards effective to secure the privilege against self-incrimination. By custodial interrogation, we mean questioning initiated by law enforcement officers after a person has been taken into custody or otherwise deprived of his freedom of action in any significant way. As for the procedural safeguards to be employed, unless other fully effective means are devised to inform accused persons of their right of silence and to assure a continuous opportunity to exercise it, the following measures are required. Prior to any questioning, the person must be warned that he has a right to remain silent, that any statement he does make may be used as evidence against him and that he has a right to the presence of an attorney, either retained or appointed. The defendant may waive effectuation of these rights, provided the waiver is made voluntarily, knowingly and intelligently. If, however, he indicates in any manner and at any stage of the process that he wishes to consult with an attorney before speaking there can be no questioning. Likewise, if the individual is alone and indicates in any manner that he does not wish to be interrogated, the police may not question him. The mere fact that he may have answered some questions or volunteered some statements on his own does not deprive him of the right to refrain from answering any further inquiries until he has consulted with an attorney and thereafter consents to be questioned.[67]

To make doubly sure, he went over the same ground again before taking up the facts of the four cases involved in that decision:

To summarize, we hold that when an individual is taken into custody or otherwise deprived of his freedom by the authorities and is subjected to questioning, the privilege against self-incrimination is jeopardized. Procedural safeguards must be employed to protect the privilege, and unless other fully effective means are adopted to notify the person of his right of silence and to assure that the exercise of the right will be scrupulously honored, the following measures are required. He must be warned prior to any questioning that he has the right to remain silent, that anything he says can be used against him in a court of law, that he has the right to the presence of an attorney, and that if he cannot afford an attorney one will be appointed for him prior to any questioning if he so desires. Opportunity to exercise these rights must be afforded to him throughout the interrogation. After such warnings have been given, and such opportunity afforded him, the individual may knowingly and intelligently waive these rights and agree to answer questions or make a statement. But unless and until such warnings and waiver are demonstrated by the prosecution at trial, no evidence obtained as a result of interrogation can be used against him.[68]

To many police officers and prosecutors, the Court's requirements in Escobedo and Miranda seem revolutionary. But to those familiar with our legal history, the Court's extensions in Escobedo of the right to counsel, and in Miranda of the right of silence to police questioning, seem as natural developments of our accusatorial method; developments which will not reach their full fruition until any confession which a defendant repudiates in court will for that reason alone be inadmissible in evidence.

At the same term as its Miranda ruling, the Court in Davis v. North Carolina[69] not only threw out a confession in a state case without the help of Miranda, but also by its reliance in reaching its results on the Fifth Amendment's right of silence (made applicable to the states by the due process clause of the Fourteenth Amendment), blended the two lines of cases for the federal and state courts on the exclusion of confessions. Davis was an escaped convict who was captured and interrogated about a rape-murder. Miranda was not applicable under Johnson v. New Jersey.[70] Nevertheless, Chief Justice Warren in the Court's opinion reasoned:

The standard of voluntariness which has evolved in state cases under the Due Process Clause of the Fourteenth Amendment is the same general standard which applied in federal prosecutions—a standard grounded in the policies of the privilege against self-incrimination. Malloy v. Hogan, 378 U.S. 1, 6-8 (1964).

The review of voluntariness in cases in which the trial was held prior to our decisions in Escobedo and Miranda is not limited in any manner by these decisions. On the contrary, the fact that a defendant was not advised of his right to remain silent or of his right respecting counsel at the outset of interrogation, as is now required by Miranda, is a significant factor in considering the voluntariness of statements later made. . . .[71]

Justice Clark, in a dissenting opinion in which Justice Harlan joined, complained about the Court's new emphasis in confession cases on an individual's Fifth Amendment right of silence:

> This case goes against the grain of our prior decisions. The Court first confesses that the rule adopted under the Fifth Amendment in Miranda v. Arizona, . . . i.e., that an accused must be effectively advised of his right to counsel before custodial interrogation, is not retroactive and therefore does not apply to this case. See Johnson v. New Jersey, ... However, it obtains the same result by reading the Due Process Clause as requiring that heavy weight must be given the failure of the State to afford counsel during interrogation as "a significant factor in considering the voluntariness of statements. . . .[72]

Even before this case and Miranda, it had been argued that the recent decisions of the Supreme Court in effect, if not in form, had applied the McNabb Mallory rule to the states.[73] Now there is no longer any doubt that the rules excluding confessions are the same for the state as for the federal courts.

Before Miranda, as one puts together the results of the various decisions of the United States Supreme Court voiding confessions, particularly the results in three cases—

Mallory v. United States[74] where the Court excluded a confession obtained after less than two hours of questioning;

Massiah v. United States[75] where the Court held inadmissible an incriminating statement made by an indicted defendant in the absence of his counsel; and

Escobedo v. Illinois[76] where the Court ruled out a suspect's confession given in the absence of his counsel and the decisions of the lower courts extending Escobedo (for instance, the Court of Appeals for the Third Circuit in United States ex rel. Russo v. New Jersey,[77] and the California Supreme Court in People v. Dorado[78]) to suspects who do not have or do not request counsel;

one could see that the courts were approaching the writer's position of excluding from evidence any confession which a defendant repudiates in court. Miranda took this process one step further. And this, the writer repeats, is as it should be.

Indeed, the District of Columbia Circuit in the application of the Mallory rule in a recent case, Alston v. United States,[79] reversed a conviction based on a confession obtained in only about five minutes of questioning. Chief Judge David L. Bazelon based his opinion on the ground that the arresting officers had not taken the defendant before a committing magistrate as quickly as possible. He relied heavily upon two other recent District of Columbia Circuit cases. In one, Greenwell v. United States,[80] the court excluded an oral confession made after arrest and while the police vehicle was parked for the purpose of obtaining the confession before proceeding to the committing authority. According to the police, the defendant confessed within a few minutes. In ruling against the confession, Circuit Judge J. Skelly Wright wrote for the court: "One purpose of the Mallory doctrine was to eliminate swearing contests between police and defendants as to what each said and did, by commanding that the defendant be promptly presented."[81] In the other, Spriggs v. United States,[82] the court excluded a confession which a police officer obtained during a form-filling process. Circuit Judge Charles Fahy in the court's opinion distinguished not only between the time taken to verify an arrested person's claim of innocence and time used to obtain a confession, but also between questions which the police ask to make sure they are not charging the wrong person and questions which they ask to elicit a confession. With reference to the case at hand, he wrote:

> The *McNabb-Mallory* exclusionary rule does not permit the use at trial of evidence of a repudiated confession obtained by secret interrogation during a form-filling process such as here occurred after arrest on probable cause and prior to arraignment. It is of little consequence that the officer says he advised Spriggs he need make no statement and if he did it would be used against him. Under the law Spriggs was entitled to be taken to a magistrate for public advice by the magistrate as to his rights, including his right to counsel with an opportunity to obtain counsel.[83]

Some other recent pre-Miranda confession cases deserve mention. The Tenth Circuit reversed the conviction for spying of George J. Gessner because it was based on a confession which the court held inadmissible in evidence.[84] Gessner was an Army nuclear weapons specialist who deserted, went to Mexico City, contacted the Soviet Embassy, and passed atomic secrets to the Russians. For this he got a life sentence. The court was "in complete accord with the government's contention that the military interviewers treated Gessner with admirable decency."[85] Also, the court agreed "with the government that the evidence does not indicate that Gessner was in any way physically abused. . . ."[86] Nevertheless, he was mentally sick and his confession was obtained from him by considerable questioning without the presence of counsel. Despite the fact that it might not be possible to try him again, the court reversed, saying at the close of its opinion:

> In remanding this case we are not unmindful that further prosecution under the Atomic Energy Act may not be possible although Gessner's betrayal of the United States is despicable, sorely testing the administration of justice as an individual case. Further, his statement to the trial court, when given the right of allocution at sentencing, is nauseating. This record reflects no travesty on justice. It does reflect complete fairness of prosecution and appeal upon the part of the government, careful and competent adjudication, and complete dedication of appointed defense counsel to a cause which to them, as to us, is distasteful but reflects the legal profession at its best.[87]

Subsequently, the government dropped the case because it lacked sufficient evident without Gessner's confession to try him again. Gessner, who has a high I.Q., on his part had referred to President Johnson as "the Mr. Pecksniff we have in the White House—a horse poverty warrior, full of promise but of no performance."[88]

The Second Circuit set aside the conviction of Samuel Tito Williams, who was convicted of the murder of 15-year-old Selma Graff in the course of a burglary of the Graff apartment, because the conviction was based on coerced confessions. The court realized: "As there was no evidence against Williams at the trial, other than the confessions which we now hold to have been inadmissible, a retrial may be unlikely."[89]

The New York Court of Appeals in People v. Waterman[90] as well as in other cases, a number of which were cited with approval by the Supreme Court in Massiah v. United States,[91] ruled inadmissible confessions or other statements of an indicted defendant obtained by the authorities in the absence of his counsel. In Waterman the court held:

> Any secret interrogation of the defendant, from and after the finding of the indictment, without the protection afforded by the presence of counsel, contravenes the basic dictates of fairness in the conduct of criminal causes and the fundamental rights of persons charged with crime.[92]

This holding was quoted by the Supreme Court in Massiah. People v. Meyer[93] extended Waterman to a pre-indictment but post-arraignment statement: "We thus conclude that any statement made by an accused after arraignment not in the presence of counsel as in Spano, DiBiasi and Waterman is inadmissible."[94]

In People v. Friedlander[95] the New York Court of Appeals threw out a confession made before arraignment, but after the defendant had consulted with a lawyer who told the officer in charge "to arrest and arraign"[96] the defendant. The court reasoned:

> The right to counsel is fundamental . . . and statements obtained after arraignment not in the presence of counsel are inadmissible . . . as are statements obtained where access has been denied . . . and this is so even when counsel cannot obtain access, due to physical circumstances. . . . So it is here.[97]

In People v. Donovan,[98] this court invalidated a confession taken by police from a suspect after counsel had been denied access to him; and in People v. Faila,[99] it reached the same result as to a confession in the prospect of being taken from a suspect when an attorney sent by the suspect's father asked to see the suspect.

The New York Appellate Division, First Department, in reversing a first-degree murder conviction in People v. Taylor,[100] held that where a suspect "has asked to see his family or his family have asked to see him, and such request is denied, any confession thereafter obtained by the police will be inadmissible against him upon his trial."[101] However, in this instance the Court of Appeals modified the order of the Appellate Division by requiring a Huntley-type hearing to determine the voluntariness of the confession,[102] which the First Department thereafter directed to be held.[103]

New York State Supreme Court Justice J. Irwin Shapiro dismissed indictments against three anti-Castro Cubans because the indictments were based on confessions taken from the defendants out of the presence of their lawyer, who was in the station house.[104] The three allegedly confessed to firing a bozooka shell from Queens County into the East River near the United Nations on December 11, 1964 in order to divert attention from a speech that Major Ernesto Che Guevara, a chief aide of Premier Fidel Castro, was making to the United Nations General Assembly.

Another recent confession case tried before Miranda involved six defendants and the confession of one of them.[105] Although all the names in the confession were blanked out, save that of the confessing party, the Second Circuit, Circuit Judge Leonard P. Moore dissenting, nevertheless reversed as to the five on the ground that the confession of the one might have rubbed off on them. Ironically enough, there was a good case against the defendants without the confession. As the court noted:

To be sure the evidence apart from Jones' confession was ample for convictions on all counts if the jurors believed Kuhle, as we have relatively little doubt it would have even without the impressive corroboration which the confession furnished.[106]

The trial, which lasted a month in the federal district court in Brooklyn, produced sensational accusations of murder threats, Cosa Nostra activity, and the attempted intimidation of the assistant United States attorney who tried the case. Judge Moore wrote in his dissent: "For all practical purposes, the decision must of necessity seriously affect all future multi-defendant trials. . . . For all practical purposes any confession in any multi-defendant trial becomes unusable or inadmissible."[107] But the difficulty to which Judge Moore addressed himself becomes nonexistent if prosecutors will just give up their reliance on confessions.

V. POST-MIRANDA CONFESSION CASES

Although Miranda was to be applied prospectively, the Warren Court continued to throw out confessions even in cases tried before Miranda where, on a consideration of the "totality of the circumstances,"[108] it regarded the confessions as involuntary.[109]

In addition, the Warren Court made further extensions of the right of silence and the right to counsel. In Mathis v. United States[110] the Court extended Miranda to statements and documents obtained from a prisoner by an Internal Revenue agent. The Court, speaking through Justice Black, held: "We reject the contention that tax investigations are immune from the *Miranda* requirements for warnings to be given a person in custody."[111]

In Orozco v. Texas[112] the Court extended Miranda to admissions which an individual made to police officers while he was in the process of being arrested in his bedroom at the boarding house where he lived. The Court, again in an opinion by Justice Black, held "that the use of these admissions obtained in the absence of the required warnings was a flat violation of the Self-Incrimination Clause of the Fifth Amendment as construed in *Miranda.*"[113]

However, and somewhat surprisingly, the Court held in Jenkins v. Delaware[114] that Miranda did not apply to persons whose re-trials commenced after the date of that decision if their original trials had begun before that. Lower courts had divided on the issue.[115]

A number of trial judges found Miranda congenial to their way of thinking and gave it a sympathetic application. For example, in People v. Allen,[116] New York State Supreme Court Justice Nathan R. Sobel ruled that a statement elicited from a rape suspect in his home by the arresting officers, without first warning him of his right to remain silent and to counsel as required by Miranda, was inadmissible in evidence. The complainant was the suspect's mother-in-law. She, her paramour, and police officers went to her son-in-law's home. The officers asked him if he had raped his mother-in-law. He replied that he had not, but that he had had intercourse with her consent. He was then placed under arrest. In ruling his statement inadmissible, Justice Sobel reasoned:

> "Compulsion" under the Fifth Amendment and its State counterpart does not have its precise dictionary meaning. It has no relationship to "coercion" and is applicable in many settings not related to any "critical stage." Compulsion is simply questioning in any setting (civil proceeding, administrative or departmental hearing, grand jury and all court proceedings) where a criminal fact may be elicited. . . .
>
> I read *Miranda* to hold that the mere "fact of custody" is inherently "compulsive" in its Fifth Amendment sense; that as soon as a person is deprived of "his freedom of action" adversary proceedings commence and the privilege protects him from questioning, routine or otherwise, which seeks to elicit a criminal or clue fact. . . .
>
> To summarize, what the Court has done is to move the commencement of "adversary proceedings" to the point of "custody"—backwards from "focus" in point of time. This the Court deemed essential when "compulsion" rather than "critical stage" became the new test. . . .
>
> Presumably when a police officer is merely investigating there will be no custody if the questioning takes place outside the police station. Since the burden of proof is on the People, the police officer's testimony of his subjective intention not to "arrest" should not suffice. An objective test is required—one which encompasses in scope primarily the prior existence of probable cause to arrest—but also the place, nature, the duration of the questioning and all other relevant circumstances. Whether the interrogation was in fact custodial should not turn on the actual or professed intent of the police officer but rather on all the objective evidence. . . .
>
> Since *Miranda,* police have presumably been alerted to the circumstances under which such warnings must be given. . . . The fourfold warning should be given before engaging in any "first" custody questioning at the scene, upon "arrest" and in the police car.[117]

However, the Appellate Division, Second Department, reversed.

In a publicized case, Edgar H. Smith, Jr.,[118] had been in the death house in Trenton State Prison for fourteen years—longer than any other condemned person had spent in Death Row in United States penal history—for the murder of 15-year-old Virginia Zielinski, a Ramsey High School cheer leader whose bludgeoned body was found in an isolated gravel pit in Mahwah, a rural community in Bergen County, New Jersey. The Federal Supreme Court refused to review the Third Circuit's affirmance of Circuit Judge John J. Gibbons' decision that Smith's confession, given in 1957, was the result of a combination of coercion circumstances which made that confession involuntary under federal constitutional standards.

While in the death house, Smith wrote a best selling book, *Brief Against Death.* His writing ability attracted the attention of William F. Buckley, Jr., the conservative author and commentator, who brought the case to national attention.

Similarly, Federal District Judge John R. Bartels in Brooklyn, in United States ex rel. v. Mancusi[119] in 1971 overturned the 1953 confessions and conviction, of a Long Island potato picker on the ground that under the totality of the circumstances his confessions were involuntary.

Whatever trial and reviewing courts may have thought about Miranda, they continued to throw out repudiated confessions under the Burger Court about as readily as they had come to throw them out under the Warren Court. A publicized case is that of Thomas A. Ruppert, who was alleged to have caused the conflagration that occurred on December 20, 1965 at the Jewish Community Center in Yonkers in which 12 persons perished.[120] The defendant told Dr. Zvi Almog (doctor of philosophy), the director of the Center, that everytime there was a fire he had been accused of it. Almog reported this to the police. In the course of time the defendant made a full confession to the police. Thereafter he repeated his confession to Almog. The trial court suppressed the confession to the police because the Miranda warnings had not been given, although the confession occurred before Miranda; the trial occurred after Miranda. However, the trial court permitted the confession to Almog and the defendant was convicted. The Appellate Division affirmed, but the court of appeals reversed and directed a new trial as well as a Huntley hearing on the confession to Almog. This time the trial court suppressed the confession to Almog and dismissed the indictment. The Appellate Division reversed. But the court of appeals in turn reversed the Appellate Division and held that the confession to Almog was tainted, because it was a rehash of the suppressed confession to the police, and ordered the reinstatement of the trial court's orders suppressing the confession to Almog and dismissing the indictment.

Thus it is that currently prosecutors would seem to be seeking Federal Supreme Court review a little more frequently than in the recent past. No less than a half-dozen illustrations from four different states are: Stidham v. Swenson,[121] where the Federal Eighth Circuit held that a Missouri trial judge's finding that a confession was not "involuntary as a matter of law" before submitting it to the jury did not meet the requirements of Jackson v. Denno;[122] United States ex rel. Smith v. Yeager,[123] where the Federal Third Circuit sustained Circuit Judge Gibbons' invalidation of the confession which New Jersey obtained against Edgar H. Smith, Jr., who became the friend of William F. Buckley, Jr.; People v. Ruppert,[124] where the New York Court of Appeals threw out the confession of Thomas A. Ruppert, the alleged incendiary, invalidated his murder conviction and ordered the reinstatement of the order of the trial court dismissing the indictment; United States ex rel. Rivera v. McKendrick,[125] where the Federal Second Circuit on the totality of the circumstances decided that New York Police officers who showed a robbery suspect's photograph to the victim and then conducted a one-on-one showup engaged in impermissible suggestive pretrial identification procedures; Commonwealth v. McCloskey,[126] where the Pennsylvania Supreme Court quashed an indictment on the ground that an investigating grand jury judge relied upon private counsel to advise witnesses of their Fifth and Sixth Amendment rights rather than advising them himself; and United States ex rel. Gockley v. Myers,[127] where the Federal Third Circuit ruled that a Pennsylvania's prisoner's arrest without probable cause on a bad check charge fatally tainted his murder confession, which was obtained during his counselless detention on the bad check charge. In all of these cases save the first, the Burger Court denied review.

VI. EFFECT OF EXCLUSIONARY RULINGS

Prosecutors and those of like mind in this country have especially complained about four of the United States Supreme Court's rulings: McNabb v. United States,[128] Mallory v. United States,[129] Escobedo v. Illinois,[130] and Miranda v. Arizona.[131] Each one in turn they have asserted would mean the end of law enforcement.

In July and August 1965 Deputy United States Attorney General Ramsay Clark and David C. Acheson, the United States Attorney for the District of Columbia, flouting the Mallory rule, issued administrative instructions to the District's Police Chief John B. Layton authorizing arresting officers there to question suspects for up to three hours before arraignment. The United States Senate passed a bill to the same effect.[132] Three Senators—Democratic Senator John J. McClellan of Arkansas, and the Republican Senators Roman L. Hruska of Nebraska and Hugh Scott of Pennsylvania—questioned the new appointee to the Supreme Court, Justice Abe Fortas, on the point. He hedged by going in opposite directions at the same time: "I believe that adequate opportunity by police to interrogate persons who are suspected or accused is absolutely essential to law enforcement. But such a person should be brought before a magistrate as soon as possible to determine probable cause."[133]

In Great Britain likewise there were those who denounced the exclusionary course. Lord Shawcross, who was attorney general for Great Britain from 1945 to 1951, would even borrow "from the *juge d'instruction* of continental systems." He contended: "It is notorious that under our existing procedures the police have, in general, no power to compel anyone—be he suspect or merely witness—to disclose anything or to answer any question. Why on earth not?"[134]

Statistics on the effect of exclusionary rulings on law enforcement are scarce, but they have been accumulating. Professor Yale Kamisar gathered some on two rulings· Mallory v. United States,[135] which came up from the District of Columbia; and People v. Cahan,[136] a search and seizure case in which the Supreme Court of California, in the words of Justice Stewart in the Court's opinion in Elkins v. United States, "resolutely turned its back on many years of precedent and adopted the exclusionary rule."[137] Professor Kamisar's findings, contrary to what prosecutors and those in accord with them contend, indicate that these exclusionary rulings resulted in somewhat more effective law enforcement rather than less.[138]

After Mallory, both Chief Robert Murray and Deputy Chief Executive Officer Howard Covell of the District of Columbia Police Department testified that the percentage of solutions of major crimes had increased through the years. Covell testified in 1959, and Murray the following year. Here is part of Covell's testimony:

> Mr. Santangelo: As a matter of fact, it appears to me that the percentage of solutions of the major crimes has increased down through the years?
>
> Chief Covell: I would say yes.
>
> Mr. Santangelo: For the last 3 years let us say, the homicides, rapes, and aggravated assaults, your percentage of solutions has increased, has it not?
>
> Chief Covell: I would say yes, but that also comes from, and I say this with modesty, from an increased efficiency of the Police Department and better coordination of law enforcement agencies throughout the entire metropolitan area. I think that the cooperation of all departments in this area reflects in each other's department to some extent. . . . During the fiscal year 1958 there was a total of 51 percent of all part 1 crimes [major offenses] solved as compared with 49.5 during 1957 [the Mallory year].

The rate of clearance in 1958 is second to the highest; that was 55.6 attained by the Department since the installation of the present system of reporting, which was made in 1948.[139]

The next year Chief Murray continued the account:

Mr. Santangelo: . . . Can you tell us what your experience in 1959 was with respect to the solution of crimes of criminal homicide and the other major crimes? . . .

Chief Murray: . . . The average is 52.5. . . .

Mr. Santangelo: Last year, in 1958, the percentage of solution of crimes was 51 percent, and in the year 1959 it was 52.5 percent. So your percentage of efficiency has increased to that extent. Is that a correct statement?

Chief Murray: Yes sir; plus the fact that we have had a few more men to help us clear it. . . .

Mr. Santangelo: Your percentage of solutions has increased in the cases of robbery.

Chief Murray: Yes, sir; we have, I think, a very good record in the clearance of robberies, 65 percent.

Mr. Santangelo: That rose from 61.3.

Chief Murray: Yes, sir. . . .

Mr. Santangelo: In aggravated assault, you also have gone up from 84.3 to 88 percent. In housebreaking, which is another difficult thing to solve, you have gone up from 50.5 to 54 percent. Is that correct?

Chief Murray: Yes, sir.[140]

In the third year after Mallory, the United States Attorney for the District of Columbia, Oliver Gasch, in a speech in Washington, D.C., to the Twelfth Annual Conference, National Civil Liberties Clearing House, made some statements about law enforcement which must seem incredible to many prosecutors:

In fact, *Mallory* questions, that is to say, confessions or admissions, are of controlling importance in probably less than 5% of our criminal prosecutions. At the present time, due largely to the conscientious cooperation of our Chief of Police and in accordance with the teaching of the decisions and our lectures on it, the police are making better cases from the evidentiary standpoint. Extensive investigation prior to arrest of suspects has resulted. The accumulation of other evidentiary material has become standard operating procedure.[141]

The Cahan statistics are equally arresting. In the 13-year period from 1952 through 1964, including three pre-Cahan years, the Cahan years, and six post-Cahan years, not only did the number of felony defendants (less juvenile) in

California superior courts almost double, but also the percentage of convictions stayed fairly steady, and even increased a little:[142]

Table 2. Cahan Statistics

	Number of Defendants	Number of Convictions	Percentage of Convictions
1952	17,006	14,238	83.7
1953	18,372	15,864	86.3
1954	19,882	17,359	87.3
1955	17,850	15,236	85.4
1956	19,648	16,875	85.9
1957	22,985	19,646	85.5
1958	26,054	22,564	86.6
1959	26,539	22,939	86.4
1960	28,751	24,816	86.3
1961	32,175	27,960	86.9
1962	31,228	27,084	86.7
1963	32,894	28,393	86.3
1964	32,569	27,830	85.4

Less than two years after Cahan, Attorney General, later Governor, Edmund G. Brown wrote:

The over-all effects of the *Cahan* decision, particularly in view of the rules now worked out by the Supreme Court, have been excellent. A much greater education is called for on the part of all peace officers of California. As a result, I am confident they will be much better police officers. I think there is more cooperation with the District Attorneys and this will make for better administration of criminal justice.[143]

In March 1972, most of the more than 70 Connecticut state and local policemen who studied Federal Supreme Court decisions in a criminal law course at the University of New Haven, came out with a wholehearted acceptance of the Warren Court's rulings affecting police work. A New Haven detective wrote on his examination at the end of the course: "Although I would probably be stoned at a police union meeting for saying so, I think that almost every controversial Supreme Court decision has aided in the professionalization of law enforcement."[144]

Dramatic support for the writer's thesis that confessions are not the key to law enforcement came from a study by New York State Supreme Court Justice Sobel. His study showed that of the first 1,000 indictments since the New York

Court of Appeals decided People v. Huntley[145] on January 7, 1965, fewer
than 10 percent involved confessions:

Based on the Huntley statistics, as fortified by the individual
experiences of the trial judges consulted, it is safe to estimate that
"confessions" constitute part of the evidence in *less* than 10 percent of all
indictments. This would include admissions and exculpatory statements.
An examination of the trial minutes of several judges indicates that
confession doctrine is charged in one out of twenty cases tried. . . .[146]

Justice Sobel further wrote:

Indeed little or no harm to successful law enforcement would result if
the courts were to outlaw all but "volunteered" confessions—i.e., outlaw
any confessions "elicited" by *interrogation*. . . .
The "historical" fact is that law enforcement has always depended
more on *judicial* confessions than on police station confessions. At the
appropriate time, with the aid of counsel, those who do not volunteer
confessions to the police will make a judicial confession to the court—i.e.,
plead guilty. This had been the "experience in *all* jurisdictions at *all* times
whether there has been a confession to the police or not; whether there is
much or little evidence and often when there is insufficient evidence. This
is a commonplace of 'adjudication. . . .' "[147]

According to press accounts Justice Sobel, in discussing his study before the
New Jersey Bar Association, derided the usual police contention that confessions
are the backbone of law enforcement as "carefully nurtured nonsense." In a
telephone interview he added: "Confessions do not affect the crime rate by
more than one-hundredth of one per cent, and they do not affect the clearance
of crime by more than one per cent."[148]

The next month the Chief of Detectives of the City of Detroit, Vincent W.
Piersante, in a letter to Professor Jerold Israel of the Michigan Law School,
disclosed that in the nine months from January 20, 1965 (the date his
department decided to notify suspects of their right to counsel and that of
silence) and October 31, 1965, confessions were obtained in 56.1 percent of the
homicide cases (as against 53.0 percent in 1961), and were essential in only 9.3
percent of the cases (as against 20.9 percent in 1961).[149]

District Attorney Evelle J. Younger of Los Angeles County conducted a
survey to test the effect of People v. Dorado[150] and Miranda upon the
prosecution of felony cases. He entitled his survey simply *Dorado-Miranda
Survey*. The Dorado part covered 1,297 cases and was for the week December
13-17, 1965. The Miranda part covered 2,780 cases and was for the three-week
period that ended July 15,1966. The survey demonstrated two things: that

confessions were relatively unimportant, and that suspects talked despite advice by the police that they had a right to remain silent and to counsel and, if they were indigent, to free legal counsel. At the complaint stage Dorado and Miranda caused difficulty in only one percent of the cases. At the trial stage confessions were unimportant in but 10 percent of cases in the Miranda part, and less than that in the Dorado part. Mr. Younger wrote:

> The results appear to justify the following conclusions: . . .
> 2. Confessions are essential to a successful prosecution in only a small percentage of criminal cases.
> 3. The percentage of cases in which confessions or admissions were made has not decreased, as might have been anticipated, because of the increased scope of the admonitions required by Miranda. . . .
> 5. If an individual wants to confess, a warning from a police officer, acting as required by recent decisions, is not likely to discourage him. Those who hope (or fear) these decisions will eliminate confessions as a law enforcement tool will be disappointed (or relieved).[151]

In a telephone interview, Mr. Younger admitted: "I'm amazed by our findings. Like most prosecutors I had assumed that confessions were of the utmost necessity in the majority of cases."[152] He further explained: "The most significant things about our findings are that suspects will talk regardless of the warnings and that furthermore it isn't so all-fired important whether they talk or not."[153]

A few other law enforcement officials have expressed comparable views. Two of these—Brendan T. Byrne, the prosecutor in Essex County, New Jersey, and Richard Sprague, chief trial lawyer in the Philadelphia district attorney's office—spoke of their experiences as a result of orders after Escobedo to the police in their jurisdictions to warn suspects of their rights and to provide them with lawyers in case of indigency where requested after the warning. Both stated that no confessions have been lost as a result of the warnings and the offer of counsel. Mr. Sprague, who had opposed the warning system, said: "I hate to admit it, but on the basis of our early reports we haven't lost a single confession, except to racket men and hardened criminals who never talk anyway."[154]

Sixth Circuit Judge George Edwards, who was Police Commissioner in Detroit during 1962 and 1963, told the Midwestern Conference of Attorneys General in December 1965, before Miranda, that he ran the Detroit Police Department under the same rules as those announced in recent decisions of the Supreme Court and that as a result, law enforcement in Detroit became more effective.

Judge Edwards and his assistants convinced most people that they were moving toward making law enforcement "more nearly equal in its application to all people, regardless of race or color."[155]

At the sixtieth annual meeting of the National Association of Attorneys General held in May 1966, after Escobedo but before Miranda, the clear consensus was that Escobedo had had little effect on the rate of confessions. Furthermore, confession rates remained stable even in those states where Escobedo had been extended to require the police to warn suspects of their rights. In addition, Jack P. F. Gremillion, Attorney General of Louisiana and president of the association, stated that even the presence of lawyers during interrogation had not "hurt the confession rate a bit." He further contended that ever since Escobedo, lawyers had been present in the back rooms of police stations: "If the suspects haven't got the money we appoint lawyers for them, and it hasn't made a bit of difference as far as confessions go."[156]

Brooklyn District Attorney Aaron E. Koota took the position in 1965 that a persons should have access to a lawyer "at the moment he comes into contact with the law."[157] But the next year, an election year, he told 52 graduating Housing Authority policemen that the Court's Miranda ruling "shackled" law enforcement agencies, making it possible for vicious criminals to escape punishment.[158]

A recent book, Neal A. Milner's *The Court and Local Law Enforcement: The Impact of Miranda,* [159] assesses the impact of Miranda on the police departments of Racine, Madison, Green Bay, and Kenosha, Wisconsin, during the first fourteen months after the decision. These four cities are the central cities of the four standard metropolitan statistical areas of Wisconsin outside of Milwaukee. The author summarizes the consequences of Miranda this way:

1. The decision was less likely to be opposed in the more professionalized department and more completely understood in the most professionalized department.

2. The decision did not basically change the decentralized and often unsystematic communications process used to inform police departments about innovation, although it did increase somewhat the activities of the prosecutors in Racine and Kenosha. The existing levels of participation and professionalization were generally unchanged; however, these levels seemed related to certain departments' attitudes, perceptions, and characteristics of the communications process. . . . The Madison department's adoption of new incentives for greater education was the most tangible evidence that *Miranda* may increase professionalization, but we must

remember that this change occurred in a department that was already relatively highly professionalized.

3. On the surface, the decision generally led to greater standardization and routinization of interrogation procedures. The more professionalized the department the more bureaucratized and formalized these procedures appeared to be.

4. Multiple clearances lessened as a result of the decision.[160]

As to the impact of Miranda on conviction rates, only the Madison and Racine police departments had information which allowed such considerations, and in both communities the conviction rate remained stable during late 1966 and early 1967. In Racine there were signs that Miranda gave defense counsel greater leverage in plea bargaining, for the percentage of defendants who were found guilty of an offense less serious than the one with which they were originally charged was three times greater for the first six months of 1967 than during the first half of 1966. However, in Madison the percentage of those who were held guilty on a lesser charge declined during the first six months of 1967, as against the first half of 1966.

If Miranda did result in greater plea bargaining, that in the writer's view is all to the good for a bargained plea also results in a resolution, at least for the time being, of the controversy between the defendant and the people.

There was evidence, not only in this volume but also in two other studies: Richard J. Medalie, Leonard Zeitz and Paul Alexander, *Custodial Police Interrogation in our Nation's Capital: The Attempt to Implement Miranda;*[161] and Cyril D. Robinson, *Police and Prosecutor Practices and Attitudes Relating to Interrogation as Revealed by Pre- and Post-Miranda Questionnaires: A Construct of Police Capacity to Comply;*[162] that efforts by police departments as well as by the FBI at encouraging acceptance of Miranda were severely limited. As Milner put it, referring to the FBI: "No real attempt was made to inform the police that the decision may be evidence of the need to re-evaluate the role of the police in a democratic society."[163] The FBI issued a study entitled "Police Interrogation—the Miranda Rule"[164] as well as a supplement.[165] The supplement concentrated upon a discussion of the means for avoiding situations where the Miranda warnings were required. A portion of the supplement made this clear:

> Particular caution is necessary if the interrogation of a criminal suspect *in a law enforcement office* is to be kept *noncustodial* so that the *Miranda* warning and waiver procedure need not be followed. The invitation to the office should be handled in such a way that it clearly *is* an invitation, not a

command, order, or arrest. A true invitation can be extended by mail, telephone or friend. The officer can personally contact the suspect and accompany him to the office if he is willing to go. . . . Once the invited suspect reaches the law enforcement office, the conditions of the interrogation should be kept as *noncustodial* as possible. Allow him all available courtesies, such as permission to use the telephone. If the facilities are suitable, conduct the interrogation in some semi-public place such as a desk in the corner of the police department lobby, or in a large room where other desks are occupied by police clerical personnel in the performance of their regular duties.[166]

Medalie, Zeitz and Alexander found that defendants as well as police officers made an insufficient use of Miranda. Their study showed that approximately 40 percent of the defendants in their study who were arrested in the post-Miranda period stated that they had given statements to the police and that an astonishingly small number of defendants—only 7 percent of the persons arrested for felonies and serious misdemeanors in the District of Columbia during fiscal 1967—requested counsel from the Precinct Representation Project. They ended their study with the hope "that a curbing of the more egregious police practices, an educational campaign by the bar to help sensitize the citizenry to their legal rights, and the use of the law students in the station house to help the legal manpower problem may help alleviate some of the difficulties in implementing *Miranda.*"[167]

Cyril D. Robinson suggested that the responsibility for implementing Miranda be shifted from the police to the city government, the prosecutor, and the legislature.[168]

If the FBI as well as the police showed a lack of enthusiasm for Miranda, this was to be expected. Human beings make radical changes at what seems to be a snail's pace.

As for the effect on the crime rate of the Court's exclusionary rulings, even the former United States attorney for the District of Columbia conceded: "Prosecution procedure has, at most, only the most remote causal connection with crime. Changes in court decisions and prosecution procedure would have about the same effect on the crime rate as an aspirin would have on a tumor of the brain."[169]

There are those who have suggested that the solution for misconduct of the police in the procurement of coerced confessions and in illegal searches and seizures simply is "to see to it that our police are selected and promoted on a merit basis, that they are properly trained and adequately compensated, and that they are permitted to remain substantially free from politically inspired interference."[170] The California Supreme Court answered that suggestion when it explained in Cahan why it decided to adopt the exclusionary rule:

We have been compelled to reach that conclusion because other remedies have completely failed to secure compliance with the constitutional provisions on the part of the police officers with the attendant result that the courts under the old rule have been constantly required to participate in, and in effect condone, the lawless activities of law enforcement officers. . . .

Experience has demonstrated, however, that neither administrative, criminal nor civil remedies are effective in suppressing lawless searches and seizures. The innocent suffer with the guilty, and we cannot close our eyes to the effect the rule we adopt will have on the rights of those not before the court.[171]

Unfortunately, before the dust had a chance to settle on the Miranda controversy, the Congress, looking to effects rather than causes, sought in the Omnibus Crime Control and Safe Streets Act of 1968,[172] which we shall next consider, to modify Miranda as well as Mallory v. United States[173] by adding a new section, 3301, to Title 18.

VII. OMNIBUS CRIME CONTROL AND SAFE STREETS ACT OF 1968

The new section 3501 which the Congress added to Title 18 by the Omnibus Crime Control and Safe Streets Act 1968 provides in paragraph (b) with reference to Miranda:

The trial judge in determining the issue of voluntariness shall take into consideration all the circumstances surrounding the giving of the confession, including (1) the time elapsing between arrest and arraignment of the defendant making the confession, if it was made after arrest and before arraignment, (2) whether such defendant knew the nature of the offense with which he was charged or of which he was suspected at the time of making the confession, (3) whether or not such defendant was advised or knew that he was not required to make any statement and that any such statement could be used against him, (4) whether or not such defendant had been advised prior to questioning of his right to the assistance of counsel; and (5) whether or not such defendant was without the assistance of counsel when questioned and when giving such confession.

The presence or absence of any of the above-mentioned factors to be taken into consideration by the judge need not be conclusive on the issue of voluntariness of the confession.

With reference to Mallory, section 3501(c) permits up to six hours and sometimes even longer before taking a person into custody before a committing authority. It provides:

. . . and if such confession was made or given by such person within six hours immediately following his arrest or other detention: *Provided,* that the time limitation contained in this subsection shall not apply in any case in which the delay in bringing such person before such magistrate or other officer beyond such six-hour period is found by the trial judge to be reasonable considering the means of transportation and the distance to be traveled to the nearest available such magistrate or other officer.[174]

The minority members of the Senate Judiciary Committee Joseph D. Tydings, Thomas J. Dodd, Philip A. Hart, Edward V. Long, Edward M. Kennedy, Quentin N. Burdick and Hiram L. Fong, felt that the provisions of section 3501(a) and (b) are "squarely in conflict" with Miranda and that these provisions "will almost certainly be held unconstitutional."[175] They further thought that section 3501(c) was "obviously intended to repeal" Mallory and "would leave the 'without unnecessary delay' provision of rule 5(a) of the Federal Rules of Criminal Procedure as a rule without a remedy."[176]

Once there is legislation such as section 3501, it is the job of the bar and bench to work it into the existing legal system. The results will not always be those which the drafters had in mind. So it may be with this section.

Two state reviewing courts in cases in which confessions were thrown out held that section 3501 did not apply to state courts. The Pennsylvania Supreme Court so held in Commonwealth v. Bennett,[177] as well as in Commonwealth v. Ware.[178] The court of appeals in Michigan so held in People v. Whisenant.[179] In Ware, the Federal Supreme Court at first granted certiorari,[180] but later changed its mind for the reason that the judgment below rested on an adequate state ground.[181]

In Commonwealth v. Bennett, the Pennsylvania Supreme Court had a second ground of decision. The Omnibus Crime Control and Safe Streets Act of 1968 was not to be applied retroactively. Federal District Judge Robert Van Pelt ruled similarly in United States v. Barber:[182] "This court is unwilling to say that what were constitutional rights until a few months ago can be relegated to a lesser position retrospectively, even by the Congress of the United States."

In United States v. Schipani,[183] involving "electronic surveillance," District Judge Jack B. Weinstein stated: "In short, the Omnibus Crime Control and Safe Streets Act of 1968 has not affected the common law rules applicable to this case."[184]

In Government of Virgin Islands v. Williams[185] District Judge Almeric L. Christian, in the course of granting a defense motion to suppress a confession, stated that section 3501 was not applicable to Virgin Islands prosecutions.

The ways of members of the bar are such that counsel for the defendants in United States v. White[186] contended that section 3501 expanded the Miranda protections. The Second Circuit was not persuaded.

The Ninth Circuit in United States v. Halbert[187] expressed the view that section 3501 was to ameliorate the effect of Mallory but only insofar as delay in taking an accused person before a committing magistrate was concerned. The Ninth Circuit was of the opinion that Mallory was still good law and not inconsistent with section 3501.

United States v. Robinson[188] involved confessions to a homicide by a patient at St. Elizabeths Hospital, Washington, D.C. The District of Columbia Circuit, on the totality of the circumstances, ruled all of the confessions to be involuntary and felt that the restrictions of section 3501 were not relevant. Senior Circuit Judge Charles Fahy wrote for the court:

> Under *Mallory* a confession made during a period of unnecessary delay in complying with the requirement that the defendant be taken before a magistrate is inadmissible at his trial. This judicial rule of evidence has been deemed essential to effectuation of procedural Rule 5 because of the importance of the Rule in the administration of the criminal law. Moreover, 18 U.S.C. §3501(c) does not nullify this judicial rule of evidence, but only restricts its application in circumstances which are not relevant to the case before us.[189]

Of course, there have been some applications of section 3501.[190] However, it is safe to say that up to this point this new section has caused scarcely more than a ripple on the broad stream of the law.

VIII. THE BURGER COURT

Even without the Omnibus Crime Control and Safe Streets Act of 1968, confessions would have been more easily admissible in evidence under the Burger Court than they were under the Warren Court. In Harris v. New York[191] the Court held that a statement by an arrested defendant which violated the guidelines in Miranda could nevertheless be used for impeachment purposes if the defendant took the stand. Justices Douglas, Brennan and Marshall dissented. Justice Brennan closed his dissent, in which Justices Douglas and Marshall joined, with this paragraph:

> The objective of deterring improper police conduct is only part of the larger objective of safeguarding the integrity of our adversary system. The "essential mainstay" of that system, *Miranda v. Arizona,* 384 U.S., at 460, is the privilege against self-incrimination, which for that reason has occupied a central place in our jurisprudence since before the Nation's birth. Moreover, "we may view the historical development of the privilege as one which groped for the proper scope of governmental power over the

citizen. . . . All these policies point to one overriding thought: the constitutional foundation underlying the privilege is the respect a government . . . must accord to the dignity and integrity of its citizens." *Ibid.* These values are plainly jeopardized if an exception against admission of tainted statements is made for those used for impeachment purposes. Moreover, it is monstrous that courts should aid or abet the law-breaking police officer. It is abiding truth that "[n]othing can destroy a government more quickly than its faulure to observe its own laws, or worse, its disregard of the charter of its own existence." *Mapp v. Ohio,* 367 U.S. 643, 659 (1961). Thus, even to the extent that *Miranda* was aimed at deterring police practices in disregard of the Constitution, I fear that today's holding will seriously undermine the achievements of that objective. The Court today tells the police that they may freely interrogate an accused incommunicado and without counsel and know that although any statement they obtain in violation of *Miranda* cannot be used on the State's direct case, it may be introduced if the defendant has the temerity to testify in his own defense. This goes far toward undoing much of the progress made in conforming police methods to the Constitution. I dissent.[192]

At the next term in Riddell v. Rhay,[193] the Court let stand a state court conviction which was obtained by the use on cross-examination of a statement elicited from the defendant in violation of Miranda. The defendant was convicted of an assault. In the course of an argument over the conduct of a neighbor's dog, a rifle which the defendant carried discharged, the bullet striking his neighbor in the foot. The only real issue at the trial was that of intent. The defendant, testifying on his own behalf, said he did not intend for the rifle to go off and did not have his finger on the trigger when it did fire. On cross-examination, however, the prosecution was permitted to confront him with a statement obtained from him in violation of Miranda in which he told the police, "I cocked the hammer and pulled the trigger. I thought the rifle was aimed towards the ground and only intended to scare Mr. Lewis [the neighbor]." Justice Douglas, in a dissent in which Justice Brennan concurred, wrote:

> A denial of certiorari in this case would illustrate the rewards that would flow to those police interrogators who, deliberately or otherwise, ignore the restrictions placed upon them by *Miranda*: restrictions necessary to safeguard the privilege against self-incrimination and to insure the reliability of statements elicited in the police-dominated atmosphere of an incommunicado custodial interrogation. . . .
>
> The lesson of *Miranda* is that the effective determination of guilt all too

often rests on the ruses and strategems employed in an incommunicado police interrogation, not on the evidence and testimony elicited in the impartial surroundings of a trial court. . . .

The exclusionary rule is a recognition that the vision of law enforcement authorities is often narrowed by their total immersion in the never-ending war against crime. If we permit the legitimate desire to win that war to undermine constitutional guarantees of liberty, our victory will indeed by fleeting. I would grant this petition.[194]

Harris does require that the trustworthiness of the statement used for impeachment purposes, in the words of Chief Justice Burger in the Court's opinion, "satisfies legal standards."[195] What application the Court will make of this requirement in order to water down Miranda more than the Omnibus Crime Control and Safe Streets Act of 1968 already has, remains to be seen.

The Warren Court held in Jackson v. Denno[196] that the trial judge had to find a confession to be voluntary before letting it go to the jury. This left the question of the standard of proof to be applied in determining voluntariness. Some courts required proof beyond a reasonable doubt; other courts sanctioned a standard of proof less strict than that beyond a reasonable doubt, including proof of voluntariness by a preponderance of the evidence.[197]

In Lego v. Twomey[198] an Illinois trial judge let a confession go to the jury after finding it voluntary by a preponderance of the evidence. The Illinois Supreme Court affirmed the judgment of conviction[199] and the federal courts let this conviction stand. In the Federal Supreme Court, Justice Brennan, in a dissenting opinion in which Justices Douglas and Marshall joined, concluded with these two paragraphs:

If we permit the prosecution to prove by a preponderance of the evidence that a confession was voluntary, then, to paraphrase Mr. Justice Harlan, we must be prepared to justify the view that it is no more serious in general to admit involuntary confessions than it is to exclude voluntary confessions. I am not prepared to justify that view. Compelled self-incrimination is so alien to the American sense of justice that I see no way that such a view could ever be justified. If we are to provide "concrete substance" for the command of the Fifth Amendment that no person shall be compelled to condemn himself we must insist, as we do at the trial of guilt or innocence, that the prosecution prove that the defendant's confession was voluntary beyond a reasonable doubt. In my judgment, to paraphrase Mr. Justice Harlan again, the command of the Fifth Amendment reflects the determination of our society that it is worse to permit involuntary self-condemnation than it is to deprive a jury of probative evidence. Just as we do not convict when there is a reasonable doubt of guilt, we should not permit the prosecution to introduce into evidence a defendant's confession when there is a reasonable doubt that it was the product of his free and rational choice.

I add only that the absolute bar against the admission of a defendant's compelled utterance at his criminal trial is fundamentally an expression of the American commitment to the moral worth of the individual. What we said in *Winship* bears repeating here. "[U]se of the reasonable-doubt standard is indispensable to command the respect and confidence of the community in applications of the criminal law. It is critical that the moral force of the criminal law not be diluted by a standard of proof that leaves people in doubt whether innocent men are being condemned." *Id.,* at 364. I believe that it is just as critical to our system of criminal justice that when a person's words are used against him, no reasonable doubt remains that he spoke of his own free will.[200]

What the Warren Court would have done in certain situations is often, probably usually, hard to say. But in Lego v. Twomey it is safe to suggest that the Warren Court would have held that the trial judge had to find the confession involuntary beyond a reasonable doubt before letting it go to the jury. The Burger Court ruled otherwise.

As one surveys the course of the Burger Court one is reminded, albeit remotely, of what a legal scholar, David Jardine, wrote about the rights of deviants after the Restoration of the Stuarts in the person of Charles II in 1660 with what they were under the Commonwealth with Oliver Cromwell, and before. He wrote:

> The law then for the first time became a protection to the subject against the power of the Crown; and so well considered and substantial were the improvements then introduced, that they continued after the Restoration, and through the tumultuous and sanguinary reign which succeeded it. Though the barriers were still insufficient entirely to stop the encroachments of bad princes, encouraged and promoted by unprincipled judges, the administration of the criminal law, even in the evil days of Charles II, was always better than it had been before the Commonwealth; for the tide of improvement, having once set in, steadily continued to flow, until at length the increase of knowledge, and the power and proper direction of public opinion, led to the final subjection of prerogative to law at the Revolution of 1688.[201]

The tide of new rights for defendants having set in, the change from the Warren Court to the Burger Court will not greatly impede it. The Burger Court will not invalidate as many confessions as did the Warren Court. Also, the Burger Court sustained the constitutionality of the provisions of the Organized Crime and Control Act of 1970 that protect a witness only against the use of his testimony and its fruits and not from prosecution for offenses which his testimony reveals;[202] whereas the Warren Court would have found such provisions to violate the Fifth Amendment privilege against self-incrimination. But in the area of the right to counsel, as well as in other due process areas, the Burger Court will surpass the Warren Court, just as future Courts will surpass the Burger Court.

IX. THE LITTLE BIG DIFFERENCE

One measure of a society's development is the extent to which there is an absence of stress on obtaining confessions from its deviants. To the extent that there is an absence of such stress, it is treating its deviants as adults rather than as children.

For our part, we do have contested criminal cases. By way of contrast, in the Soviet Union as well as in other countries where the Communists have come to power, there are practically no contested criminal cases. Practically all deviants confess. This little big difference should be our concern.

In our political cases, the Smith Act prosecutions of leaders of the American Communist Party, of the more than 130 individuals who were indicted and the 114 who were convicted, not one confessed during trial and only one pending appeal: Mrs. Barbara Hartle, a defendant in the Seattle prosecution who stood by her associates through the trial, then contacted the FBI, confessed, and withdrew her appeal.[203]

By way of contrast, in the Moscow purge trials of 1936-1938 all the defendants confessed; so did nearly all the defendants in subsequent cases.

Moreover, we should not try to do indirectly what we should not do directly. We should not stress compulsory testimony acts; or make use of such devices as the required records exception; or registration, licensing and reporting provisions for the purpose of obtaining confessions.

Our accusatorial method has helped us to develop a more independent and mature citizenry than Eastern countries have. With us an individual does not have to be submissive when the state points an accusing finger at him: he has a right to remain silent, along with a right to counsel; to a formal accusation; to bail in nearly all cases; to a public trial; to be confronted with his accusers; and to be proved guilty beyond a reasonable doubt. We should not let any of these rights atrophy, least of all the right of silence and the right to counsel. The compulsory confession of one's sins and the naming of one's associates may be standard operating procedure in authoritarian regimes, but it is unbecoming a free people.

An individual, as to any accusation which may tend to incriminate him, should have an absolute right to remain silent. Furthermore, any confession which has been obtained from an accused who has not been taken promptly upon arrest before a committing authority, and any confession which an accused repudiates in court, should not be admissible in evidence.

Lawyers, legal writers, and courts have differed considerably in their estimates of the right to remain silent and the inquisitional technique. Bentham, writing in 1824, in his *Rational of Judicial Evidence,* attacked the right to remain silent. He saw no reason why an accused should not be compelled under pain of contempt to speak. If one was innocent one had nothing to hide, and if one was guilty such a course was not unjust. Here was the way he answered some of the arguments he attributed to those who favored this right:

> 2. The old woman's reason. The essence of this reason is contained in the word *hard*: 'tis hard upon a man to be obliged to criminate himself. Hard it is upon a man, it must be confessed, to be obliged to do anything that he does not like. . . . What is no less hard upon him, is, that he should be punished: but did it ever yet occur to a man to propose a general abolition of all punishment, with this hardship for a reason for it? . . .
> 3. The fox-hunter's reason. This consists in introducing upon the carpet of legal procedure the idea of fairness, in the sense in which the word is used by sportsmen. . . .
> 4. Confounding interrogation with torture; with the application of physical suffering, till some act is done; in the present instance, till testimony is given to a particular effect required: On this occasion it is necessary to observe, that the act of putting a question to a person whose station is that of defendant in a cause, is no more an act of torture than the putting the same question to him would be, if, instead of being a defendant, he were an extraneous witness. . . .
> 5. Reference to unpopular institutions [Courts of Star Chamber and High Commission]: Whatever Titius did was wrong; but this is among the things that Titius did; therefore this is wrong; such is the logic from which this sophism is deduced.[204]

Wigmore answered Bentham with the suggestion that the inquisitional technique lent itself to bullying and the use of physical torture: "The real objection is that *any system of administration which permits the prosecution to trust habitually to compulsory self-disclosure as a source of proof must itself suffer morally thereby.* The inclination develops to rely mainly upon such evidence, and to be satisfied with an incomplete investigation of the other sources. The exercise of the power to extract answers begets a forgetfulness of the just limitations of that power. The simple and peaceful process of questioning breeds a readiness to resort to bullying and to physical force and torture. If there is a right to an answer, there soon seems to be a right to the expected answer, that is, to a confession of guilt. Thus the legitimate use grows into the unjust abuse; ultimately, the innocent are jeopardized by the encroachments of a bad system. Such seems to have been the course of experience in those legal systems where the privilege was not recognized."[205]

Sir James Stephen, an English lawyer and judge who drafted the Indian Code of Civil Procedure, in his *History of the Criminal Law of England* earlier made the same point as Wigmore: "During the discussion which took place on the Indian Code of Civil Procedure in 1872, some observations were made on the reasons which occasionally lead native police officers to apply torture to prisoners. An experienced civil officer observed, 'there is a great deal of laziness in it. It is far pleasanter to sit comfortably in the shade, rubbing red pepper into a poor devil's eyes than to go about in the sun digging up evidence.' "[206]

However, Wigmore disagreed with Bentham only up to a point: he agreed with him in his condemnation of the equation of the inquisitional process with torture. If physical force was not in fact used, Wigmore did not condemn confessions obtained as a result of the inquisitional technique. When a court wrote: "So the inquisition of torture is restored, only without the rack and thumbscrew";[207] Wigmore commented: "This attitude of maudlin sentimentality, repeating the misnomer of 'torture,' has not disappeared ever since Bentham's day. . . ."[208]

More recently Lord Shawcross, likewise in agreement with Bentham, argued:

> Take our English doctrine against self-incrimination. On what ethical grounds is it to be supported? Of course, these rules about the admissibility of statements by accused persons are very ancient. I know that is usually enough to justify anything in my country, however unrealistic. They arose in medieval times when illiterate prisoners often were subjected to torture in order to extort confessions. The statements thus obtained often were made in the hope of escaping further suffering, and so were not to be relied upon. But nowadays adequate safeguards usually exist to prevent the extortion of statements which are false, and the question which ought to attract the attention of ordinary citizens not too steeped in our ancient and sometimes outworn legal traditions is whether, in addition, we ought to take the elaborate precautions we do to discourage criminals—or, indeed, innocent but suspected citizens—from speaking the truth?[209]

If Lord Shawcross meant to say that the right of silence arose because of the unreliability of coerced confessions, he is wrong in his history. The right of silence finally established itself, it bears repeating, because the Puritans were unwilling to name their associates.

Lord Shawcross also does not comprehend the devastating use which the Communists have made of the inquisitional technique. In the light of our present knowledge, the world should have done not only with this technique but also with the confessions it produces.

An accused should have an absolute right to remain silent as to any incriminating situation involving him. The government could still require the keeping of records in appropriate situations. A taxpayer, for instance, could be required to keep records for the determination of the amount of his tax liability. Or again, a shopkeeper could be required to keep records to be used to determine ceiling prices. But the only result that should follow from a failure to keep such records, or a refusal to produce them if kept, in situations incriminating to the individual would be a pecuniary loss to him and, furthermore, such pecuniary loss should bear some relation to the object for which the government required the records to be kept. If a taxpayer failed to keep appropriate records, his gross income must be increased or claimed deductions might be disallowed. If a shopkeeper failed to keep appropriate records, his ceiling prices might be lowered. However, in neither case should the individual's right to remain silent, including his right to refuse to produce records as to any incriminating situation, be infringed. Shapiro v. United States,[210] which enunciated the required records doctrine, should be overruled the next time the Court has the question before it. However, the Burger Court is less likely than was the Warren Court to do this.

Chief Justice Weintraub of the New Jersey Supreme Court, who told New Jersey judges and prosecutors to ignore the Third Circuit's ruling in United States ex rel. Russo v. New Jersey,[211] nevertheless expressed the thought that the courts "are drifting toward the abolition of all confessions," and that intellectually he "could not resist such a course."[212] In time the majority of us will agree. Judges, in their exclusionary rulings and extensions of the right to counsel and that of silence, will prove to have been wiser than lawyers and legal writers and even wiser than they themselves have realized.

In September 1960, on the occasion of the visit to this country of lawyers from England, Scotland, and Australia for the 83rd annual meeting of the American Bar Association, the writer and his wife had as their guests a British solicitor and his wife, Mr. and Mrs. S. E. Mann. One evening just before dinner the writer made a comment about British self-restraint. Mr. Mann responded, "Then our greatest export is the rule of law." The writer replied, "yes."

That was all there was to this part of the conversation. Nothing more needed to be said. One can hope that the day will arrive when one can have a conversation with a Russian or a Chinese person in which so few words will cover so large an area of understanding.

NOTES

1. More than 75 years ago, District Judge Peter S. Grosscup in United States v. James, 60 Fed. 257, 265 (N.D. Ill. 1894) referred to the Fifth Amendment's privilege against self-incrimination both as the privilege of silence and the right of silence. Justice Douglas in his dissenting opinion in Ullmann v. United States, 350 U.S. 422, 445, 446, 449, 454 (1956), in which Justice Black concurred, did likewise. In Miranda v. Arizona, 384 U.S. 436, 444, 453, 460, 465, 466, 467, 468, 469, 470, 471, 473, 479, 495, 497 (1966), Chief Justice Warren writing for the Court, repeatedly referred to the privilege as the right of privilege of silence or the right to remain silent. This writer has usually referred to the privilege as the right of silence. See O. J. Rogge, *The First and the Fifth,* 138-203 (1960); O. J. Rogge, "Compelling the Testimony of Political Deviants," 55 Mich. L. Rev. 163 (1956); id. at 375, 388-404 (1957).

2. 384 U.S. 436 (1966), rev'g 98 Ariz. 18, 401 P.2d 721 (1965), Westover v. United States, 342 F.2d 684 (9th Cir. 1965), and Vignera v. New York, 15 N.Y. 2d 970, 207 N.E. 2d 527, 259 N.Y.S. 2d 857 (1965), and aff'g California v. Stewart, 62 Cal. 2d 571, 400 P.2d 97, 43 Cal. Rptr. 201 (1965).

3. 378 U.S. 478, 495 (1964).

4. 384 U.S. at 538.

5. 338 U.S. 49, 59 (1949).

6. 384 U.S. at 516 n.12.

7. Id. at 500.

8. See O. J. Rogge, *Why Men Confess,* 148 (1959).

9. See Annual Report of The Director of the Administrative Office of The United States Courts, Table D4 (1955-1969). For the years 1955-1961, juvenile delinquents are excluded. See also Federal Offenders in the United States District Court (Administrative Office of The United States Courts, 1963-1968).

10. California Bureau of Criminal Statistics, "Crime & Delinquency in California: Felony Defendants Disposed of in California Courts," 4 (1970); Id. at 36 (1968); Id. at 100 (1967); Id. at 83 (1966); California Bureau of Criminal Statistics, "Crime in California," 118 (1964); Id. at 51 (1959); Id. at 57 (1956); Id. at 17 (1952). This series of reports began in 1952.

11. See O. J. Rogge, *Why Men Confess,* 149 (1959).

12. 404 U.S. 257 (1971).

13. Id. at 260.

14. Id. at 264, n.1-2.

15. Silverstein, *Defense of the Poor in Criminal Cases In American State Courts* 92-93 (1956). The 66 percent figure includes 6 percent of the defendants who pleaded guilty to lesser offenses.

16. E. L. Barrett, "Criminal Justice: The Problem of Mass Production," in *The Courts, The Public, and The Law Explosion,* 107-108 (Harry W. Jones, ed., 1965).

17. 168 U.S. 532 (1897).

18. Id. at 542.

19. 3 Wigmore, Evidence §821 n. 2 (3d ed. 1940).

20. 8 Wigmore, Evidence §2266 (3d ed. 1940).

21. 318 U.S. 332 (1943).

22. 354 U.S. 449 (1957).

23. Id. at 455.

24. 361 U.S. 199 (1960).

25. Id. at 207.

26. 297 U.S. 278 (1936).

27. 309 U.S. 227 (1940).

28. Id. at 237-238.

29. Harris v. South Carolina, 338 U.S. 68 (1949); Turner v. Pennsylvania, 338 U.S. 62 (1949); Watts v. Indiana, 338 U.S. 49 (1949).

30. 338 U.S. at 54.

31. See, e.g., Stein v. New York, 346 U.S. 156 (1953) (Known as the "Reader's Digest case," because the murder there involved was committed in the course of a robbery of some Reader's Digest mail); Burns v. Wilson, 346 U.S. 137 (1953); DeVita v. New Jersey, and Grillo v. New Jersey, 345 U.S. 976 (1953), denying cert. to 11 N.J. 173, 93 A.2d 328 (1952).

32. Kingsley Int'l Pictures Corp. v. Bd. of Regents, 360 U.S. 684, 696 (1959) (concurring opinion).

33. 352 U.S. 191 (1957).

34. 356 U.S. 560 (1958).

35. 360 U.S. 315 (1959).

36. 361 U.S. 199 (1960).

37. 365 U.S. 534 (1961).

38. 367 U.S. 433 (1961).

39. 367 U.S. 568 (1961).

40. 360 U.S. at 320-321.

41. 361 U.S. at 206-207.

42. 365 U.S. at 540-541.

43. 372 U.S. 335 (1963).

44. 372 U.S. 391 (1963), aff'g 300 F.2d 345 (2d Cir. 1962).

45. 372 U.S. 528 (1963).

46. 373 U.S. 503 (1963).

47. People v. Bonino, 291 N.Y. 541, 50 N.E.2d 654 (1943), aff'g 265 App. Div. 960, 38 N.Y.S.2d 1019 (1942).

48. 222 F.2d 698 (2d Cir.), cert. denied, 350 U.S. 896 (1955).

49. Id. at 701.

50. People v. Bonino, 1 N.Y.2d 752, 135 N.E.2d 51, 152 N.Y.S.2d 298 (1956).

51. 378 U.S. 1 (1964).

52. 373 U.S. 503 (1963).

53. 378 U.S. at 7.

54. Id. at 7.

55. 376 U.S. 202 (1964).

56. 377 U.S. 201 (1964).

57. 378 U.S. 1 (1964).

58. Id. at 52.

59. 378 U.S. 368 (1964); accord, Boles v. Stevenson, 379 U.S. 43 (1964); McNerlin v. Denno, 378 U.S. 575 (1964); Owen v. Arizona, 378 U.S. 574 (1964); Catenzaro v. New York, 378 U.S. 573 (1964); Harris v. Texas, 378 U.S. 572 (1964); Pea v. United States, 378 U.S. 571 (1964); Del Hoyo v. New York, 378 U.S. 570 (1964); Muschette v. United States,

378 U.S. 569 (1964); Oister v. Pennsylvania, 378 U.S. 568 (1964); Lopez v. Texas, 378 U.S. 567 (1964); Lathan v. New York, 378 U.S. 566 (1964); Senk v. Pennsylvania, 378 U.S. 562 (1964); United States ex rel. Gomino v. Maroney, 231 F. Supp. 154 (W.D. Pa. 1964).

60. 378 U.S. 478 (1964).

61. 15 N.Y.2d 72, 204 N.E.2d 179, 255 N.Y.S.2d 838 (1965). At the time of Jackson v. Denno there were three different rules for determining the voluntariness of confessions: the New York rule, the orthodox rule, and the Massachusetts rule. Under the New York rule, if there was a factual conflict in the evidence as to the voluntariness of a confession over which reasonable men could differ, the judge left the question of voluntariness to the jury. This rule was followed in some 15 states, the District of Columbia, Puerto Rico, and six federal circuits. Under the orthodox rule, the judge heard all the evidence and ruled on voluntariness for the purpose of the admissibility of the confession; and the jury considered voluntariness as affecting the weight or credibility of the confession. This rule was followed in some 20 states and three federal circuits. Under the Massachusetts rule the judge heard all the evidence and ruled on voluntariness before allowing a confession into evidence; if he found the confession voluntary the jury was then instructed that it must also find the confession was voluntary before it could consider it. This rule was followed in 14 states and two federal circuits. The law in Nevada on the point apparently had not been settled. See 378 U.S. at 410-423.

In People v. Huntley, the New York Court of Appeals adopted the Massachusetts rule. The Wisconsin Supreme Court adopted the orthodox rule. State v. Burke, 133 N.W.2d 753 (Wis. 1965).

Jackson v. Denno was applied retrospectively in Rudolph v. Holman, 236 F. Supp. 62 (M.D. Ala. 1964). The petitioner in this case was also the petitioner in Rudolph v. Alabama, 375 U.S. 889 (1963).

62. 15 N.Y.2d at 78, 204 N.E.2d at 183, 255 N.Y.S.2d at 843-844.

63. People v. Huntley, 46 Misc. 2d 209, 259 N.Y.S.2d 369 (Sup. Ct. 1965).

64. 384 U.S. 436 (1966).

65. 168 U.S. 532 (1897).

66. 384 U.S. at 461.

67. Id. at 444-445.

68. Id. at 478-479.

69. 384 U.S. 737 (1966), rev'g 339 F.2d 770 (4th Cir. 1964), aff'g 221 F. Supp. 494 (E.D.N.C. 1963).

70. 384 U.S. 719 (1966).

71. 384 U.S. at 740.

72. Id. at 753-754.

73. Ritz, "Twenty-five Years of State Criminal Confession Cases in the U.S. Supreme Court," 19 Wash. & Lee L. Rev. 35 (1962); see Enker & Elsen, "Counsel for the Suspect: Massiah v. United States and Escobedo v. Illinois," 49 Minn. L. Rev. 47, 88 (1964). Broeder, in "Wong Sun v. United States: A Study in Faith and Hope," 42 Neb. L. Rev. 483, 564-594 (1964), argued that McNabb should be extended to the states.

74. 354 U.S. 449 (1957).

75. 377 U.S. 201 (1964).

76. 378 U.S. 478 (1964).

77. 351 F.2d 429 (3d Cir. 1965), judgment vacated sub nom. New Jersey v. Russo, 384 U.S. 889 (1966).

78. 394 P.2d 952, 40 Cal. Rptr. 264 (1964), 398 P.2d 361, 42 Cal. Rptr. 169, cert. denied, 381 U.S. 937 (1965).

79. 348 F.2d 72 (D.C. Cir. 1965).

80. 336 F.2d 962 (D.C. Cir. 1964). But cf. State v. Myers, 140 N.W.2d 891 (Iowa 1966).

81. 336 F.2d at 968.

82. 335 F.2d 283 (D.C. Cir. 1964).

83. Id. at 285. But in Pyles v. United States, 362 F.2d 959 (1st Cir.), cert. denied, 385 U.S. 994 (1966), the court held that a suspect's inculpating answer to a question asked by a policeman who had apprehended him fleeing a robbery scene, had disarmed him, and was holding him at gunpoint, was not as a matter of law inadmissible.

In State v. Randolph, 406 P.2d 791 (Ore. 1965), the court held that un unlicensed Oregon motorist's admission to an officer that he was driving the car which hit a parked car was admissible at his trial on a charge of driving without a license, even though the officer did not advise him of his Fifth and Sixth Amendment rights.

84. Gessner v. United States, 354 F.2d 726 (10th Cir. 1965).

85. Id. at 729.

86. Ibid.

87. 354 F.2d at 731.

88. New York Times, March 9, 1966, p. 6, col. 1.

89. United States ex rel. Williams v. Fay, 323 F.2d 65, 69 (2d Cir. 1963), cert. denied, 376 U.S. 915 (1964).

90. 9 N.Y.2d 561, 175 N.E.2d 445, 216 N.Y.S.2d 70 (1961).

91. 377 U.S. 201, 205 n.5 (1964).

92. 9 N.Y.2d at 565, 175 N.E.2d at 448, 216 N.Y.S.2d at 75.

93. 11 N.Y.2d 162, 182 N.E.2d 103, 227 N.Y.S.2d 427 (1962).

94. Id. at 165, 182 N.E.2d at 104, 227 N.Y.S.2d at 428.

95. 16 N.Y.2d 248, 212 N.E.2d 533, 265 N.Y.S.2d 97 (1965).

96. Id. at 250, 212 N.E.2d at 533, 265 N.Y.S.2d at 98.

97. Id. at 250, 212 N.E.2d at 534, 265 N.Y.S.2d at 98.

98. 13 N.Y.2d 148, 193 N.E.2d 628, 243 N.Y.S.2d 841 (1963).

99. 14 N.Y.2d 178, 199 N.E.2d 366, 250 N.Y.S.2d 267 (1964).

100. 22 App. Div. 2d 524, 256 N.Y.S.2d 944 (1965).

101. Id. at 526, 256 N.Y.S.2d at 946.

102. 16 N.Y.2d 1038, 213 N.E.2d 321, 265 N.Y.S.2d 913 (1965). But in In re Williams, 49 Misc. 2d 154, 267 N.Y.S.2d 91 (Family Ct. Ulster County 1966), the court held the principal case not applicable to a juvenile, and voided a confession taken without first notifying the parent or other person legally responsible as required by section 724 of the N.Y. Family Ct. Act.

103. 25 App. Div. 2d 516, 267 N.Y.S.2d 1 (1966).

104. People v. Novo, Sup. Ct., June 9, 1965. For further recent pre-Miranda cases where the courts voided confessions or other incriminating statements, see United States v. Middleton, 344 F.2d 78, 81-82 (2d Cir. 1965) (two-hour delay) ("Any period of delay becomes unreasonable if used, as here 'to carry out a process of inquiry that lends itself, even if not so designed, to eliciting damaging statements' to support the arrest and ultimately the defendant's guilt"); Jones v. United States, 342 F.2d 863 (D.C. Cir. 1964) (arrested on a warrant issued in another state, and not taken before the nearest available

commiting authority); (arresting officer testified that the defendant confessed within two or three minutes after the questioning began); Seals v. United States, 325 F.2d 1006 (D.C. Cir. 1963), cert. denied, 376 U.S. 964 (1964) (three-hour delay); United States ex rel. Kemp v. Pate, 240 F. Supp. 696, 707 (N.D. Ill. 1965). ("Once the accusatory process and the attempt to elicit incriminating statements has begun, the failure to warn the suspect of his absolute constitutional right to remain silent and the failure to give him an opportunity to consult with counsel is a violation of the Constitution.")

In Killough v. United States, 315 F.2d 241, 245 (D.C. Cir. 1962), the court held "that a reaffirming confession which, though it followed a hearing, was made soon after an earlier confession obtained during unlawful detention which preceded the hearing, was 'a result' of that illegality and must be excluded."

In Johnson v. United States, 344 F.2d 163, 166 (D.C. Cir. 1964), the court concluded that a defendant's inadmissible confession could not be used to cross-examine him if he took the stand at his trial and "merely offered his own version of the events charged in the indictment." But in United States v. Curry, 358 F.2d 904, 910 (2d Cir. 1966), the Second Circuit, with reference to a suppressed confession, said: ". . . if the defendant offers testimony contrary to the facts disclosed by evidence which has been suppressed, the government may in the interest of truth use this illegally obtained evidence to establish facts collateral to the ultimate issue of guilt."

Also, in Fredericksen v. United States, 266 F.2d 463, 464 (D.C. Cir. 1959), the court held that "a spontaneous and voluntary exclamation" of an accused person in a police lineup was admissible over a Mallory objection. Thereafter a practice seemed to develop in the District of Columbia of offering in evidence apologies by accused persons to complaining witnesses. See, e.g., Veney v. United States, 344 F.2d 542, 543 (D.C. Cir. 1965); Copeland v. United States, 343 F.2d 287 (D.C. Cir. 1964). This led Circuit Judge J. Skelly Wright in his concurring opinion in Veney to comment:

> For some time now I have been curious and concerned about evidence offered by the Government, appearing again and again in criminal case records, showing that the defendant, at the lineup or other confrontation with the complaining witness, had, while in the presence and custody of the police, "spontaneously and voluntarily" applogized for his misdeed.
>
> [I] t appears to me that the time is ripe for some soul searching in the prosecutor's office before it offers any more "spontaneous" apologies in evidence.

In United States ex rel. Martin v. Fay, 352 F.2d 418 (2d Cir. 1965), where the defendant claimed that he pleaded guilty because of a coerced confession obtained from him in the absence of counsel, the Second Circuit held, in the words of another of its recent decisions: "A voluntary guilty plea entered on advice of counsel is a waiver of all non-jurisdictional defects in any prior stage of the proceedings. . . ." Id. at 419.

But in United States ex rel. Kuhn v. Russell, 252 F. Supp. 70 (M.D. Pa. 1966), the court gave habeas corpus relief because the state court trial judge at the time of sentence under a guilty plea considered the defendant's pretrial statement taken while he was without the benefit of counsel.

The Delaware Supreme Court adopted "the federal McNabb-Mallory rule within the framework of the facts of the case before us," where a delay of 36 hours in bringing the defendant before a committing magistrate was in violation of a Delaware statute. Vorhauer v. State, 212 A.2d 886 (Del. 1965). The Michigan Supreme Court took a similar step in People v. Hamilton, 359 Mich. 410, 102 N.W.2d 738 (1960).

In Evalt v. United States, 359 F.2d 534 (9th Cir. 1966), the court, partly because of Estes v. Texas, 381 U.S. 532 (1965), held that newspaper reporters who, with the sheriff's permission, interviewed a federal criminal defendant and obtained his confession, could not be used as witnesses against him.

105. United States v. Bozza, 365 F.2d 206 (2d Cir. 1966).

106. 365 F.2d at 218.

107. Id. at 228.

108. Clewis v. Texas, 386 U.S. 707, 708 (1967), quoting from Fikes v. Alabama, 352 U.S. 191, 197 (1957).

109. Clewis v. Texas, 386 U.S. 707 (1967); Beecher v. Alabama, 389 U.S. 35 (1967); Sims v. Georgia, 389 U.S. 404 (1967); Greenwald v. Wisconsin, 390 U.S. 519 (1968); Darwin v. Connecticut, 391 U.S. 346 (1968).

110. 391 U.S. 1 (1968).

111. Id. at 4.

112. 394 U.S. 324 (1969).

113. Id. at 326.

114. 395 U.S. 213 (1969).

115. For a collection of the cases, see id. at 215 n.3.

116. 50 Misc. 2d 897, 272 N.Y.S.2d 249 (Sup. Ct. Kings County 1966), rev'd, 28 A.D.2d 724, 281 N.Y.S.2d 602 (2d Dep't 1967).

117. 50 Misc. 2d at 903-905, 272 N.Y.S.2d at 255-257.

118. United States ex rel. Smith v. Yeager, 451 F.2d 164 (3d Cir.), cert. denied, 404 U.S. 859 (1971).

119. 326 F. Supp. 1366 (E.D.N.Y. 1971).

120. People v. Ruppert, 29 N.Y.2d 519, 323 N.Y.S.2d 985, 272 N.E.2d 493 (1971), 26 N.Y.2d 437, 311 N.Y.S.2d 481, 259 N.E. 2d 906 (1970), cert. denied, 92 S.Ct. 281 (1971).

121. 443 F.2d 1327 (8th Cir. 1971), cert. granted, 40 U.S.L.W. 3351 (U.S. Jan. 24, 1972).

122. 378 U.S. 368 (1964).

123. 451 F.2d 164 (4d Cir.), cert denied, 404 U.S. 859 (1971). Thereafter, Smith's counsel successfully entered into plea bargaining with the prosecutor, Smith pleaded guilty and went free on probation. See New York Times, Dec. 7, 1971, at p. 1, cols. 3-4.

124. 29 N.Y.2d 519, 313 N.Y.S.2d 985, 272 N.E.2d 493 (1971), 26 N.Y.2d 437, 311 N.Y.S.2d 481, 259 N.E.2d 906 (1970), cert. denied, 92 S.Ct. 281 (1971).

125. 448 F.2d 30 (2d Cir. 1971); cert. denied, 40 U.S.L.W. 3316 (U.S. Jan. 10, 1972).

126. 443 Pa. 177, 227 A.2d 764, cert. denied, 40 U.S.L.W. 3286 (U.S. Dec. 20, 1971).

127. 450 F.2d 232 (3d Cir. 1971), cert. denied, 40 U.S.L.W. 3352 (U.S. Jan. 24, 1972).

128. 318 U.S. 332 (1943).

129. 354 U.S. 449 (1957).

130. 378 U.S. 478 (1964).

131. 384 U.S. 436 (1966).

132. New York Times, Sept. 1, 1965, p. 29, col. 1.

133. New York Times, Aug. 6, 1965, p. 1, cols. 2-3, p. 11, col. 1.

134. Lord Shawcross, "Police and Public in Great Britain," 51 A.B.A.J. 225, 228 (1965), reprinted under the title "Crime Does Pay Because We Do Not Back Up the Police." New York Times, June 13, 1965 (Magazine): pp. 44, 49.

135. 354 U.S. 449 (1957).

136. 44 Cal. 2d 434, 282 P.2d 905 (1955).

137. 364 U.S. 206, 220 (1960).

138. Kamisar, "Public Safety v. Individual Liberties: Some 'Facts' and 'Theories,' " 53 J. Crim. L., C & P.S. 171, 188-192 (1962).

139. "Hearings Before a Subcommittee of the House Committee on Appropriations, District of Columbia Appropriations," 1960, 86th Cong., 1st Sess. at 440-441 (1959); see Kamisar, supra note 457, at 191.

140. "Hearings Before a Subcommittee of the House Committee on Appropriations, District of Columbia Appropriations," 1961, 86th Cong., 2d Sess. at 619-620 (1960); see Kamisar, supra note 457, at 191-192.

141. Unpublished address by Oliver Gasch, Twelfth Annual Conference, National Civil Liberties Clearing House, "Law Enforcement in the District of Columbia and Civil Rights," March 25, 1960, at 3, on file in Minnesota Law School Library.

142. California Bureau of Criminal Statistics, "Crime in California," 118 (1964); Id. at 51 (1959); Id. at 57 (1956); Id. at 17 (1952). This series of reports began in 1952.

143. Letter from Edmund G. Brown, Attorney General of the State of California, Dec. 7, 1956, on file with the Stanford Law Review, and quoted in Note, 9 Stan. L. Rev. 515, 538 (1957), and in Elkins v. United States, 364 U.S. 206, 220-221 n.15 (1960).

144. Quoted in J. Kandell, "Connecticut Police Back Warren Court After Law Study," New York Times, March 28, 1972, p. 45, cols. 1-5.

145. 15 N.Y.2d 72, 204 N.E.2d 179, 255 N.Y.S.2d 838 (1965).

146. Sobel, "The Exclusionary Rules in the Law of Confessions: A Legal Perspective–A Practical Perspective," 154 N.Y.L.J. 1, 4 (Nov. 22, 1965).

147. Id. at 5.

148. See New York Times, Nov. 20, 1965, p. 1, cols. 5, 6; Nov. 22, 1965, p. 39, col. 1.

149. Letter from Vincent W. Piersante to Jerold Israel, Dec. 17, 1965, on file in the Michigan Law School Library, and summarized in Kamisar, "Has the Court Left the Attorney General Behind? –The Bazelon-Katzenbach Letters on Poverty, Equality and the Administration of Criminal Justice," 54 Ky. L.J. 464, 479-480 n.37 (1966).

150. 62 Cal. 2d 338, 398 P.2d 361, 42 Cal. Rptr. 169 (1965), cert. denied, 381 U.S. 937 (1965).

151. Younger, Dorado-Miranda Survey (Aug. 4, 1966), on file in the Office of the District Attorney of Los Angeles County.

152. Zion, "Report Questions Confession Role," New York Times, Aug. 19, 1966, p. 20, col. 3.

153. Zion, "So They Don't Talk," New York Times, Aug. 21, 1966, p. 13, col. 1.

154. New York Times, Nov. 20, 1965, pp. 1, 70, col. 6.

155. New York Times, Dec. 7, 1965, p. 33, cols. 5, 6.

156. Zion, "Prosecutors Say Confession Rule Has Not Harmed Enforcement." New York Times, May 18, 1966, p. 27, col. 1.

157. New York Times, Nov. 22, 1965, p. 39, col. 1.

158. New York Times, Aug. 13, 1966, p. 1, col. 1; Sept. 5, p. 17, col. 1.

159. Sage Publications, 1971.

160. Id. at 226-227.

161. 66 Mich. L. Rev. 1347 (1968).

162. (1968) Duke L. J. 425.

163. Milner, *The Court and Local Law Enforcement,* 65-66, Sage Publications, 1971.

164. Washington: FBI National Academy (May, 1967).

165. July, 1967.

166. Id. at 9-10, quoted in Milner, *The Court and Local Law Enforcement,* 66, Sage Publications, 1971.

167. R. J. Medalie, L. Zeitz & P. Alexander, "Custodial Police Interrogation in Our Nation's Capital: The Attempt to Implement Miranda," 66 Mich. L. Rev. 1347, 1400 (1968).

168. C. D. Robinson, "Police and Prosecutor Practices and Attitudes Relating to Interrogation as Revealed by Pre- and Post-Miranda Questionnaires: A Construct of Police Capacity to Comply," (1968) Duke L. J. 425.

169. Quoted by Chief Justice Warren in the Court's opinion in Miranda v. Arizona, 384 U.S. 436, 441 n.3 (1966), from Herman, "The Supreme Court and Restriction on Police Investigation," 25 Ohio St. L. J. 449, 500 n.270 (1964).

170. Inbau & Reid, *Criminal Interrogation and Confessions,* 208 (1962).

171. People v. Cahan, 44 Cal. 2d 434, 445, 447, 282 P.2d 905, 911-912, 913 (1955), quoted with approval in Elkins v. United States, 364 U.S. 206, 220 (1960).

172. 82 Stat. 197 (codified in scattered sections of 18 and 47 U.S.C.).

173. 354 U.S. 449 (1957).

174. A 1967 act for the District of Columbia permitted detention and questioning for a period of three hours. 81 Stat. 735, D.C. Code §4-140a (Supp. 1970-1971).

175. 2 U.S. Code Cong. & Ad. News 2211 (1968).

176. Id. at 2216.

177. 439 Pa. 34, 264 A.2d 706 (1970).

178. 438 Pa. 517, 265 A.2d 790 (1970).

179. 19 Mich. App. 182, 172 N.W.2d 524 (1969), rehearing, 21 Mich. App. 518, 175 N.W.2d 560 (1970), aff'd, 384 Mich. 693, 187 N.W.2d 229 (1971).

180. Pennsylvania v. Ware, 92 S. Ct. 1254 (1972).

181. 40 U.S.L. W. 3512 (U.S. April 24, 1972).

182. 291 F. Supp. 38, 41 (D. Neb. 1968); accord, Sheer v. United States, 414 F.2d 122, 125 (5th Cir.), cert. denied, 396 U.S. 946 (1969). In Reinke v. United States, 405 F.2d 228 (9th Cir. 1968), the government in its brief in the Ninth Circuit conceded that section 3501 should have prospective application only.

183. 289 F. Supp. 43 (E.D.N.Y. 1968). For subsequent proceedings, see 293 F. Supp. 156 (E.D.N.Y. 1968), aff'd, 414 F.2d 1262 (2d Cir. 1969).

184. 289 F. Supp. at 60.

185. 306 F. Supp. 1104 (D. Virgin Islands 1969).

186. 417 F.2d 89 (2d Cir. 1969), cert. denied, 397 U.S. 912 (1970); accord, Grooms v. United States, 429 F.2d 839 (8th Cir. 1970).

187. 436 F.2d 1226 (9th Cir. 1970).

188. 439 F.2d 553 (D.C. Cir. 1970).

189. Id. at 563-564.

190. United States v. Stevens, 445 F.2d 304 (6th Cir. 1971); United States v. Smith, 418 F.2d 1294 (5th Cir. 1969).

191. 401 U.S. 222 (1971), aff'g 25 N.Y.2d 175, 303 N.Y.S.2d 71, 250 N.E.2d 349 (1969); accord, United States v. Cranston, 453 F.2d 123 (2d Cir. 1971); cf. People v. Taylor, 27 N.Y.2d 327, 318 N.Y.S.2d 1, 266 N.E.2d 630 (1971), where the New York Court of Appeals held that defendants in a robbery prosecution had waived their Miranda

rights without the presence of counsel and despite the fact that counsel had been assigned to them at their arraignment on an unrelated robbery charge. See Dershowitz & Ely, "Harris v. New York," 80 Yale L. J. 1198 (1971).

Until the Federal Supreme Court's decision in Harris, the weight of authority was to the contrary. Many of the cases are collected in 401 U.S. at 231 n.4 (Brennan, J.) (dissenting opinion), and 25 N.Y.2d at 178 n.1, 303 N.Y.S.2d at 74 n.1 (Fuld, C. J.) (concurring opinion).

192. 401 U.S. at 231-232.

193. 404 U.S. 974 (1971).

194. Id. at 974, 976, 977-978.

195. 401 U.S. at 224.

196. 378 U.S. 368 (1964).

197. The cases are controled in Lego v. Twomey, 404 U.S. 477, 479 n.1 (1972).

198. 404 U.S. 477 (1972). In Stidham v. Swenson, 443 F.2d 1327 (8th Cir. 1971), cert. granted, 404 U.S. 1058 (1972), the Eighth Circuit held that a trial court's finding that a confession was not "involuntary as a matter of law" before submitting it to the jury did not meet the requirements of Jackson v. Denno, 378 U.S. 368 (1964). Cf. Erving v. Sigler, 453 F.2d 843 (8th Cir. 1972).

199. People v. Lego, 32 Ill. 2d 76, 203 N.E.2d 875 (1965).

200. 404 U.S. at 494-495.

201. D. Jardine, *A Reading on The Use of Torture in The Common Law of England* 70 (1837).

202. Kastigar v. United States, 40 U.S.L.W. 4550 (U.S. May 22, 1972), aff'g 440 F.2d 954 (9th Cir. 1971); accord, Zicarelli v. New Jersey State Comm'n of Investigation, 40 U.S.L.W. 4560 (U.S. May 22, 1972), aff'g 55 N.J. 249, 261 A.2d 129 (1970); Sarno v. Illinois Crime Investigating Comm'n, 40 U.S.L.W., 4563 (U.S. May 22, 1972), writ of cert. to 45 Ill. 2d 473, 259 N.E.2d 267 (1970), dismissed as improvidently granted.

203. Ironically enough, she went to prison while her co-defendants had their convictions reversed on appeal with a direction to enter a judgment in their favor. Huff v. United States, 251 F.2d 342 (9th Cir. 1958).

204. 7 Works 452-455 (Bowring ed. 1843).

205. 8 Wigmore Evidence §2251, p. 309 (3d ed. 1940).

206. Vol. 1 at 441 (1883).

207. People v. Arrighini, 122 Cal. 121, 126, 54 Pac. 591, 593 (1898).

208. 8 Wigmore, Evidence §2251 n.5 (3d ed. 1940).

209. Shawcross, "Police and Public in Great Britain," 51 A.B.A.J. 225, 227 (1965), reprinted under the title "Crime Does Pay Because We Do Not Back Up the Police," New York Times Magazine, June 16, 1965, pp. 44, 49.

210. 335 U.S. 1 (1948).

211. 351 F.2d 429 (3d Cir. 1965), judgment vacated sub nom. New Jersey v. Russo, 384 U.S. 889 (1966).

212. See New York Times, Dec. 11, 1965, p. 1, col. 1; p. 42, cols. 2, 3. New York State Supreme Court Justice Samuel H. Hofstadter and Shirley R. Levitan proposed "enactments by statute, when possible, and by constitutional amendments, when necessary," which would provide, with reference to police questioning in the station house:

As soon as the inquiry ceases to be general in nature, and a mere search for information, and the police focus their attention in suspicion of a particular person—to the extent that they wish to constrain him to further interrogation—they must take him before a judicial officer. There in a court house—not a police station—his questioning may be continued *by the police in the presence of the magistrate.*

Hofstadter & Levitan," Let the Constable Blunder: A Remedial Proposal," 20 Record of N.Y.C.B.A., 629, 630 (1965). The danger with this proposal is that our magistrate will become like the French *juge d'instruction.*

PART III.

FROM FIRST COURT APPEARANCE

TO TRIAL

Chapter 4

JUSTICE IN THE ACCUSATION

In all criminal prosecutions, the accused shall enjoy the right to . . . be informed of the nature and cause of the accusation

From the Sixth Amendment
to the U.S. Constitution

DELMAR KARLEN received his B.A. at the University of Wisconsin in 1934 and his LL.B. at Columbia University in 1937. After several years' law practice and military service as U.S. Army Judge Advocate, he joined the law faculty of the University of Wisconsin. He has also taught at New York University and University of Chicago. Dr. Karlen has been active on many American Bar Association task forces and also law consultant to several foreign governments. He is the author of *Appellate Courts in the United States and England* (1963), *Law in Action* (1964), *The Citizen in Court* (1964), *Anglo-American Criminal Justice* (1967), *Judicial Administration: The American Experience* (1970), and has contributed to *Encyclopedia Britannica, Encyclopedia Americana, Encyclopedia of the Social Sciences,* and other important publications. At present he is Director and Vice President of the Institute of Judicial Administration.

J. LAWRENCE SCHULTZ received a B.A. cum laude from Yale University in 1967, majoring in an honors program, History, the Arts, and Letters. He was articles editor of the Harvard Law Review before receiving his J.D. cum laude from Harvard in 1970. He then clerked for Judge Irving R. Kaufman of the Second Circuit Court of Appeals. In the summer of 1970 Schultz was director of projects studying the U.S. Forest Service and the Bureau of Reclamation for Ralph Nader's Center for the Study of Responsive Law. He is Research Director of the Juvenile Justice Standards Project at New York University Law School, where he teaches.

Chapter 4

JUSTICE IN THE ACCUSATION

DELMAR KARLEN and
J. LAWRENCE SCHULTZ

I declare the trial opened. Yours is the first word. For it must justly be the pursuer who speaks first and opens the case, and makes plain what the action is.

Athene to the Furies, from Aeschylus,
The Eumenides, 11, 582-584

I. THE PROBLEM OF PROSECUTORIAL DISCRETION

The decision to bring a criminal prosecution is in a sense more critical than the decision to convict. Not only is every conviction preceded by a prosecution, but prosecution alone, even if it ends in acquittal, can bring severe economic, psychological, social, and physical hardship. To be accused of crime, "may disrupt the defendant's employment, drain his financial resources, curtail his associations, subject him to public obloquy, and create anxiety in him, his family, and his friends" (United States v. Marion, 1971).

Clear notice to the defendant, guaranteed by the Sixth Amendment, is the beginning of justice in a criminal accusation—but only the beginning. Its importance lies primarily in two of its functions: to permit the accused to prepare his defense, and to allow a determination of the fairness of the accusation in advance of trial.

It is to this latter question, the justice of the accusation, that the present chapter is addressed. Who holds the power to accuse of crime, and how is that power controlled to protect the accused against abusive prosecutions?

Prosecutors can err to the unfair detriment of the defendant in three directions: by bringing an accusation based on insufficient evidence that the accused committed the crime alleged; by singling out one among many similar offenders for prosecution because of some factor beyond the authority of the prosecutor to consider; or by applying the criminal law inappropriately, for reasons of policy inconsistent with some ideal norm. Following a brief overview of common patterns of accusation, the present and potential effectiveness of available controls for protecting against these three kinds of abuses will be assessed.

A. Serious, Minor, and Juvenile Offenses

The process by which an accusation is made varies from state to state, even from court to court. In all jurisdictions, however, minor offenses are handled differently than more serious crimes. The principal difference is that more governmental screening before trial is required in the case of major prosecutions.

Still, both kinds of process can be described in broad terms and discussed together, since each entails the same kinds of problems in controlling the prosecutor's discretion. Parenthetically, it must be noted that the same cannot be said of the special procedures that state and local governments ordinarily use for dealing with most juvenile offenders. These procedures must for the most part remain beyond the scope of this chapter. Briefly, it is useful to observe that officials empowered to proceed against juvenile offenders probably exercise greater discretion than do prosecutors who enforce criminal laws against adults. This is primarily so because statutory definitions of juvenile offenses are broader than most criminal codes. Also, juvenile trial proceedings have not traditionally been hedged by the same safeguards as adult criminal trials (although the direction is now toward increasing these protections). These two key characteristics expand discretionary power over juveniles regardless of whether, as is sometimes true, statutes concerned with juvenile offenders also explicitly grant discretion not to proceed formally against a juvenile offender. As will be seen, trial procedures and the nature of criminal statutes are decisive to limiting prosecutorial discretion.

B. The Prosecutor

In the adult criminal justice system, the key figure for screening in most jurisdictions is an official known as the "district attorney," although in some states he is called "commonwealth attorney," "state's attorney," "county attorney," "county prosecutor," "solicitor," or "prosecuting attorney," and so far as a federal prosecution is concerned, the "United States Attorney." Hereafter, he will be called simply, "prosecutor." Around him revolve various institutions and procedures, which will be described after he and his role have been delineated (see generally, President's Commission, 1967: 73-76).

The district attorney is a local official, normally serving a single county and usually popularly elected for a term of two or four years. In a rural area, he may serve only part-time, being allowed to practice law in civil cases on the side, but in a metropolitan area of any size he is likely to be a full-time official, and have several lawyer assistants, possibly also a staff of detectives, investigators and accountants. The district attorney's office in Manhattan (one of New York City's five boroughs) has a staff of about 260 persons all of whom are full-time employees appointed on a nonpolitical basis by the head of the office, who himself has been elected and reelected for more than 20 years on nomination of all parties. This is the exception rather than the rule, however, for in most communities the district attorney is an underpaid creature of politics, often seeking and going on to higher office, hampered by an inadequate staff.

As a rule, responsibility for criminal prosecution is decentralized, fragmented, and uncoordinated above the local level. In only three states, Rhode Island, Delaware, and Alaska, is there no local district attorney, all criminal prosecutions being supervised by the state attorney general's office. While the other states also have attorneys general, they ordinarily have little to do with criminal prosecutions. Their main work is to represent the state in civil litigation. Occasionally they prosecute the violation of a taxing or regulatory statute of statewide ramification, and occasionally they step into a situation where local law enforcement has broken down because of corruption or incompetence, appointing a special prosecutor to take over some or all of the cases that would normally be handled by the district attorney. Generally speaking, however, the prosecution of serious state crimes is in the hands of local district attorneys, who are largely autonomous.

Federal prosecutions are also highly localized and also subject to political influence. The federal judicial system is divided into 93 districts, each having its own trial court and its own United States Attorney, a local lawyer appointed by the President, confirmed by the Senate, and directly responsible to the United

States Department of Justice. His job is to represent the federal government in both civil and criminal litigation. He handles in federal court all prosecutions of federal crimes committed within his district. These are relatively few in number because the federal government, being one of limited powers enumerated in the Constitution, has no jurisdiction to define crimes for the nation as a whole. Ordinary crimes are a matter of state law, prosecuted in state courts, normally by local district attorneys.

C. Minor Offenses

In some jurisdictions, the prosecutor confines his activity to the trial courts of superior jurisdiction and has nothing to do with minor offenses. They are considered the concern of the police and the minor courts.

1. Minor Traffic Vilations

For example, in most states a class of offenses viewed as relatively trivial, and therefore unlikely to engage a prosecutor's attention, is comprised of routine violations of traffic laws. Typically, an accused motorist is apprehended, or his car is identified as illegally parked or licensed, and the police officer writes out the familiar ticket. This not only commands the accused to appear in a specified court at a specified time, but also informs him of the charge against him. If and when he appears in court, the charge will be read aloud to him or summarized orally. He may plead "guilty," in which case sentence will be imposed forthwith, or "not guilty," in which case a trial will be held to determine his guilt or innocence. The trial may take place immediately or be postponed to a later hour or day to suit the convenience of the judge, the accused and the police officer.

Indeed, the offense may be considered so trivial that the motorist is not required to appear in court at all. He may be allowed to "plead guilty" on a form printed on the ticket, and if he so pleads (or "pleads guilty" by failing to respond to the ticket—a practice of questionable validity), he may send a fine, fixed according to a rigid schedule, to the court by mail, or pay it in person at a "violations bureau"—a clerical office often located at a police station but functionally an adjunct of the traffic court. In these cases, only if the accused wishes to dispute the charge against him or ask a lower than ordinary fine, must he appear in court for a judicial hearing.

2. Variations on the Theme: Other Minor Offenses

Minor nontraffic offenses generally are not processed as automatically as traffic tickets, and defendants normally do not avoid a trip to the courthouse (see Miller and Remington, 1962: 113-120; Miller, 1970). Common to all kinds of processing for minor violations, however, is the traffic-ticket pattern of a final judgment following close upon arrest, with little intermediate screening and processing. Typically, minor offenders may be tried immediately at their first appearance before a judicial officer, called a "magistrate," "commissioner," or "justice of the peace," on the basis of a "complaint" drafted by police or a prosecutor. Prosecutions may also be initiated by a "warrant" for arrest or of a "summons" for the appearance of the defendant in court, which are also issued by a judicial officer on request of the police, a prosecutor, or even a private citizen victimized by a criminal offense.

Because lack of involvement by prosecutors and immediate final trial on the basis of the initial charging or arresting document are the hallmarks of processing accusations of minor offenses, the discretion in deciding which of these prosecutions shall go forward is exercised primarily by police. Discretion is sometimes exercised on an individualized ad hoc basis, as where a police officer sends a middle-class, respectably dressed drunk home in a taxi but arrests a skid row derelict indulging in the same conduct and charges him with public drunkenness. Sometimes it is exercised on an institutionalized, policy basis, as where laws against such offenses as public intoxication or peddling without a license are either systematically ignored or systematically enforced. Police officers also exercise discretion in the kind of accusations they make against persons whom they arrest. For the same conduct, a motorist might be charged with reckless driving or merely speeding.

In addition to police discretion, citizen discretion is important. Most crimes are not observed by police, and the vast majority of crimes are never reported. When a crime is reported—usually by the victim—it is probably on the basis of a highly individualized judgment. A wife who has been assaulted by her husband may or may not complain, and if she does, may later withdraw the charge. A merchant who has been given a bad check may or may not go to a magistrate to swear out a warrant, depending mostly upon whether he has been able to secure private satisfaction. If he reports the offense and later receives payment, he will probably attempt to drop the charge. In all probability, he will be allowed to do so, because in minor cases, the wishes of the victim are given almost controlling weight.

D. Serious Crimes: The Prosecutor's Role

1. Initiating Prosecutions

With respect to felonies and serious misdemeanors, however, the prosecutor's role is paramount—far more important than is popularly recognized. In television, movies, and novels, the prosecutor is almost always seen in a courtroom (no doubt a reflection of the perhaps artificial drama of the criminal trial system itself). But that is not where all of his work, or the most important part of it is done. The other function he performs is to decide what persons are to be prosecuted and for what crimes. He exercises with respect to serious crimes the same kind of discretion that is exercised with respect to minor crimes by police officers.[1] The prosecutor also possesses veto power over the discretionary decisions made by police officers and private citizens to bring accusations with respect to certain kinds of crimes. If the prosecutor considers it unwise to allocate his limited time and resources to the prosecution of gambling or prostitution cases, they will not be prosecuted, regardless of how the police and complaining citizens may feel. They have no power to activate the judicial machinery; only the prosecutor has that power. His decisions affect not only the particular cases that come to his attention, but also the general thrust of police activity. If the prosecutor refuses to prosecute a certain type of crime, there is little point in the police continuing to make arrests for it.

Most criminal codes are so broad and replete with obsolete and unworkable prohibitions that their literal, full enforcement would be impossible.[2] There are not enough police to arrest, attorneys to prosecute, judges to try or jails to hold all the people who violate the criminal law, or even those relatively few whose crimes are known to law enforcement authorities. If there were, society would not tolerate total enforcement, for in most states that would mean not only the end to church bingo games but the cessation of many forms of sex which Dr. Kinsey and others consider perfectly normal.

In view of the limited resources available, priorities in law enforcement must be assigned and choices made. The prosecutor must and does exercise judgment as to what prosecutions shall be brought. How he exercises it depends not only on his personal views, but also on his relationships with other law enforcement authorities and on public attitudes. This explains why such crimes as prostitution, gambling, drug abuse, pornography, and homosexuality are prosecuted in some communities, but not in others. The incidence of such crimes may be as great in one city as another, but the crime statistics of prosecutions and convictions emanating from the two cities may diverge very markedly. They may even vary widely from time to time in a single community as the laws against such crimes are alternately ignored and enforced, sometimes depending on the proximity of forthcoming elections.

2. Dropping Charges

The power of a prosecutor before trial is not exhausted with his decision to file an information or present a case to the grand jury. Even after the filing of an indictment or information, he maintains control. One thing he can do is enter a nolle prosequi, stopping the prosecution. In some states, the consent of the trial court is required, but this is hardly ever withheld. Judges recognize that the screening of cases by the police and magistrates is often perfunctory and they are inclined to place greater trust in the judgment of the prosecutor.

Another important power of the prosecutor is to engage in what is commonly called "plea bargaining." The idea is that the accused agrees to plead guilty to a lesser offense than that originally charged in return for the prosecutor dropping the greater charge with its heavier possible penalty and sometimes also promising to recommend to the court a lenient sentence. Judges usually respect such bargains, although they need not do so. Plea bargaining is no longer a secret, under-the-table operation, but a well recognized, widespread and openly acknowledged procedure. It is defended on the ground that it eliminates the expense, delay and uncertainty of contested jury trials, and on the ground that it mitigates the effect of Draconian laws mandating punishments beyond anything that is sensible in terms of community protection or the rehabilitation of offenders. Most plea bargaining, however, is not based on such humanitarian considerations, but upon crowded calendars in the courts and the necessity of disposing of a vast volume of cases without trial. It is a procedure that is subject to grave abuse and that often leads to the unequal treatment of offenders (Harvard Law Review, 1970a: 404).

Finally, a prosecutor has power to confer immunity from prosecution on some persons who are guilty of criminal conduct. These are people who claim their constitutional privilege against self-incrimination[3] but whose testimony is necessary to convict other persons. Under some statutes, a witness may be compelled to answer incriminating questions as a matter of course in the investigation of specific types of crime, but he is immune from prosecution in consequence of his answers. Under other statutes, the prosecutor is given discretion to offer immunity to a recalcitrant witness, although sometimes he is required to secure the approval of the trial judge or of members of the grand jury. He is normally careful in exercising this power, because, in view of the very early stage in questioning that the privilege can be claimed, he cannot be sure of the extent of the "immunity bath" he is conferring. If immunity is granted by a state authority, it protects a witness not only from a state prosecution, but also from a federal prosecution; and vice versa.

3. Controlling the Prosecutor's Discretion

Lest there be any misunderstanding of what has been said, it should be noted that the exercise of discretion by a prosecutor is often more deserving of commendation than blame. If "crime in the street," meaning the commission of crimes of violence such as murder, robbery, forcible rape and mugging, is the problem most urgently needing attention, as many responsible persons believe, it may well be irresponsible for a prosecutor to divert the limited resources of law enforcement under his control to the prosecution of "victimless crimes" such as prostitution, abortion, homosexuality, drunkenness, drug abuse and pornography. There is plenty of room for argument as to what crimes are truly "victimless" and as to which of these and other crimes, if any, should be ignored, but there can be little doubt that a prosecutor has difficult but necessary policy choices to make—choices fraught with grave social consequences. "It is the duty of the prosecuting attorney to solve the problem of public order using the criminal code as an instrument rather than as a set of commands" (Arnold, 1932).

Inevitable as prosecutorial discretion may be, however, such power over public policy and private lives invites misuse. As indicated earlier in this chapter, prosecutors can wrongly prosecute someone in three ways. First, they may charge someone on the strength of too little evidence to believe that the person in fact committed the crime. Second, although the evidence to charge a selected defendant may be sufficient, the decision to charge itself may be made on the basis of factors other than those a prosecutor may legitimately consider. In particular, a prosecutor may overlook many persons who violate a law or ordinance, and select only a few violators to accomplish some end other than the enforcement of the law that was violated.

The more subtle, more difficult to define, but no less important misuse of the prosecutor's power involves his choice of law enforcement policies. Should limited resources be devoted to removing all illegal drug users from the streets, or should large-scale sellers be the target? Should drunks be prosecuted or referred to a medical detoxification unit? Should complex prosecutions be initiated against industrial polluters? While these questions do not involve "rights of the defendant" in so acute a form as an arbitrary or baseless decision to prosecute, society as a whole, including defendants, has a strong interest in the appropriate use of the criminal law—at least in having important policies about the uses of the criminal laws determined openly, in a manner permitting rational public review and choice.[4]

In the following sections, various means for controlling these abuses are discussed. To anticipate, there are several devices—primarily grand juries, preliminary hearings, and, to a lesser extent, discovery before trial—commonly used in the pre-trial stages of major criminal prosecutions that are designed in some degree specially to guard against prosecutorial abuse, especially against arbitrary or groundless prosecutions. That these devices are in many ways unsatisfactory should not promote a conclusion that the decision to accuse is virtually "lawless" and uncontrolled (see Packer, 1968: 290-291). Other controls over a prosecutor's discretion exist: the right to a public trial and conviction by proof beyond a reasonable doubt, the constitutional prohibition of overly broad or vague statutes, such less important judicial doctrines as "desuetude" or "entrapment," political constraints, certain "administrative law" devices, and the growth of means other than prosecution for handling some problems traditionally defined as crime. These latter controls, potentially if not well in many ways at present, seem to offer better opportunities than the formal review procedures for reducing abuse and making policy judgments responsive to rational public preferences.

II. REVIEW OF SUFFICIENCY OF EVIDENCE TO PROCEED WITH PROSECUTION

A. The Grand Jury

Prosecution for a serious crime is instituted by one of three different forms of accusation: indictment, information or presentment (see generally Karlen, 1967: 149-153). An indictment is returned by a grand jury on the basis of evidence presented to it by the prosecutor. An information is filed by the prosecutor on his own initiative. A presentment is made by a grand jury on its own initiative. The drafting of indictments and presentments as well as informations is practically always done in the prosecutor's office, for, as will be shown later, the prosecutor is considered an essential part of the grand jury's machinery.

The grand jury is an accusing body, not one which determines guilt or innocence. It was inherited from England, where it was abolished in 1933. In all American states it survived a tide of abolition sentiment that crested during the 1930s (see Younger, 1955), but only in slightly more than half of them is it used as a regular and indispensable step in the prosecution of felonies or (in a few states) serious misdemeanors. In the remaining states, the prosecutor has the option of proceeding on his own initiative by information in lieu of grand jury indictment. While he may use the grand jury to buttress his own judgment in questionable or sensitive cases or to compel the pre-trial production of testimony needed by him for a successful prosecution, he seldom does so. For example, in California, where the prosecution has the option of bypassing the grand jury, informations are used in about 90 percent of all felony cases. (Stanford Law Review, 1956: 644).

The Federal Constitution does not require indictment or presentment by grand jury in any state prosecution (Hurtado v. California, 1884) but requires it in federal prosecutions for any "capital or otherwise infamous" crime, a phrase which has been interpreted to require grand jury action to initiate any prosecution that might result in imprisonment more than for one year (Federal Rules of Criminal Procedure, Rule 7[a]). Since the states are free to dispense with grand juries or to limit their use, it is not surprising that great variations exist from state to state. In South Carolina, indictment is required by the state constitution for any crime where the punishment may exceed a fine of $100 or imprisonment for 30 days (South Carolina Constitution, Article I, Section 17). In Florida, it is required only in capital cases (Florida Constitution, Article I, Section 15[a]). Between these extremes are other varieties of state constitutional rules, the most common being a provision that grand jury indictment is required in all felony cases. This of course allows the district attorney to proceed by information in all misdemeanor cases. In a few states grand jury indictment is required by statute rather than constitutional provision (Orfield, 1947: 142-144). In the federal courts and in those of a number of states, the accused, with the consent of the district attorney, may waive his rights to indictment. If he does, the case may be prosecuted by information.

The grand jury is composed of laymen, usually 12 to 23 in number (as was formerly the case in England) although in some states there may be as few as five members. They are normally chosen by lot from tax or voting rolls to serve for relatively short periods of time and then melt back into the communities from which they came. In rural areas, grand juries sit briefly and infrequently; in metropolitan areas, several grand juries may be in session simultaneously and their members may serve for a month or more.

Grand jury sessions are secret and private. Witnesses, having been supoenaed by the prosecutor, are sworn and heard one by one, and excused as soon as they finish testifying. Ordinarily the accused is not present, although he may be invited to appear as a witness and tell his story if he wishes, or even be compelled to appear (see United States v. Winter, 1965). If he does appear, courts have held that he has no right to have his attorney present with him before the jury, although he may have a right to have an attorney nearby for consultation (see Duke Law Journal, 1967), and to be warned of his right against self-incrimination (Birzon and Girard, 1966).

The prosecutor or his deputy is always present however, for it is his job to present evidence and examine witnesses in support of the indictment he has drafted. If the grand jurors agree that a particular person should be tried for a particular crime, it is marked a "true bill," but if they decide against prosecution, it is marked "no bill" or "ignored." The indictment, if voted, is all that is made known for most states prohibit inquiry into the conduct of grand jury proceedings and bar access to a transcript of the proceedings. Secrecy may not be lifted even if the defendant wishes to prove that the prosecutor acted improperly in securing the indictment (Calkins, 1965), although the trend is otherwise. Some states now automatically disclose grand jury transcripts in every case (see Sherry, 1962). Generally defendants may have access to their own grand jury statements (Columbia Law Journal, 1968: 311), and they may have access to the statements of witnesses the government relies upon at trial, either in all instances for cross-examination, or upon the showing of a "particularized need" (Dennis v. United States, 1966; Pittsburgh Plate Glass v. United States, 1959; United States v. Youngblood, 1967).

Because the prosecutor so largely controls its proceedings, the grand jury is often regarded as little more than his puppet. It can investigate crime and make accusations on its own initiative proceeding by presentment rather than indictment, but it seldom does. Most, if not all, of its attention is focused on cases presented by the prosecutor. He has virtually unlimited discretion not to present a potential case, for no one is likely to know about it or be in a position to challenge his estimate that the evidence is insufficient to proceed. Even when a grand jury appears to act independently, refusing to indict in a case presented to it, its action may be the result of a hint or suggestion from the prosecutor himself. Grand jurors seldom have the time or resources to familiarize themselves with all the facts in the cases before them. This is particularly true where the volume of prosecutions is great and the cases routine. The prosecutor may introduce any evidence to help his case, even if it would not be admissible under the rules of evidence applicable in a criminal trial, or even if the evidence was illegally obtained by police and could therefore be suppressed prior to the trial (Lawn v. United States, 1956; West v. United States, 1966; United States v. Cox, 1965).

This is not to imply that courts exercise no control over the activities of grand juries. The usual formula is that grand juries may only seek by appropriate means information relevant to an investigation properly authorized for a legitimate law enforcement purpose (Oklahoma Press Publ. Co. v. Walling, 1946). They may be forbidden to issue a "report" censuring some action unless they also bring in an indictment, although such reports are often permitted (Harvard Law Review, 1961: 590). Some courts require that prosecutors prove the necessity of resorting to a grand jury's powers to compel the production of evidence or the elicitation of testimony (in re Dionisio, 1971). Indictments may be suppressed if they are based on insufficient or entirely on incompetent evidence (People v. Howell, 1958) or if prosecutors rely on hearsay evidence when direct evidence is available (in this way prosecutors protect their direct evidence introduced at trial against impeachment by contradictory direct testimony recorded in grand jury minutes) (United States v. Arcuri, 1969).

Nevertheless, while theoretically the grand jury is a screening device to examine and reject baseless accusations without exposing the accused to unfavorable publicity, in fact it may be less important as a shield for the innocent than as a tool for the prosecutor. It enables him to secure sworn testimony in secret from cooperative witnesses. Without it, he would have no power to compel testimony in advance of trial—a serious handicap, especially when dealing with professional criminals working in organized gangs or white collar criminals acting under expert legal advice.

The grand jury is a declining institution. As noted earlier, it has already been abolished in England and is consistently used only in about half the American states. The trend away from proceeding by indictment in favor of proceeding by information will probably continue, because the added costs and delays entailed by use of the grand jury seem hardly counterbalanced by any real protection afforded the accused.

B. Judicial Review

1. Warrant Requirements and Arraignment

Often the first court review of the evidence supporting a prosecution occurs when the commissioner, magistrate, or justice of the peace issues a warrant authorizing the arrest of a suspect (Miller and Remington, 1962: 113-120). Even though a warrant may not be legally necessary to bring a prosecution when a suspect is validly arrested, law enforcement authorities may still rely on it as giving an imprimatur of judicial concurrence in the charging decision (Miller, 1970: ch. 3). Following arrest, the accused is brought before a judicial officer for "arraignment," at which normally bail (if any) is set and the accused is formally charged, informed of his rights, perhaps asked to plead guilty or not guilty, and asked in serious cases if he desires a preliminary hearing. Theoretically, the arraignment also presents a second opportunity for judicial review of the adequacy of the evidence on which the charge is based. In practice, there is no effective control of the decision to prosecute through either the warrant or arraignment devices. Judges often sign applications for warrants without reading them, or after only a perfunctory examination.[6] At the arraignment, the accused has no opportunity to protest the charge.

2. Preliminary Hearing

A potentially better protection for the rights of the accused than grand jury indictment is the preliminary hearing. This is a procedure designed to take place shortly after arrest, usually before the filing of a formal accusation. Its purpose is to have a magistrate decide whether there is enough evidence to justify holding the accused for trial. If a preliminary hearing is held, the prosecution presents its evidence and the accused has a right to make a statement himself and to call witnesses in his behalf. He is warned that anything he says may be used against him at a subsequent trial and that he is under no obligation to call witnesses or testify himself. At the conclusion of all the evidence, the magistrate decides whether there is sufficient evidence to hold the accused. If an indictment or information has already been filed, the accused is "bound over" for trial. If no formal accusation has been filed, the accused is "bound over" for action by the grand jury or the prosecutor.

In the United States (unlike England, where "committal proceedings," as they are called, have supplanted grand jury action) the preliminary hearing has not achieved its full potential for screening out unfounded charges and preventing them from going to trial. There are several reasons.

First, the preliminary hearing is not mandatory (see Goldsby v. United States, 1895; United States v. Funk, 1969; Sciortino v. Zampano, 1968). In states where the grand jury is used, its indictment is considered a sufficient basis for requiring trial. In some states where the grand jury is not used, the prosecutor's information is given the same effect as an indictment. This means that the defendant may be brought to trial without any preliminary hearing having been held.

Second, the accused may and often does waive the right to a preliminary hearing when he is entitled to one.[7] This may be because he intends to plead guilty anyway, or has already pleaded guilty at arraignment; because, unrepresented by counsel, he is ignorant of the nature of a preliminary hearing; or because he and his lawyer, assuming he has one, consciously conclude that there is little to be gained from a hearing at which the prosecution is not required to produce all of its evidence, but only enough to make out a prima facie case. A high waiver rate also may merely indicate that prosecutions are effectively screened prior to the initiation of prosecutions. (In some states the prosecution must also consent to waive a preliminary hearing, but consent is normally given, especially in view of the fact that the district attorney does not need the preliminary hearing to compel answers from cooperative witnesses. He can use the grand jury for that purpose.)

Third, preliminary hearings when held tend to be perfunctory and dominated by the prosecutor.[8] They are often conducted by rural justices of the peace untrained in the law, or by lawyer-magistrates who lack sufficient competence, knowledge, skill or interest to do the kind of screening that ought to be done. They are often held in courtrooms that are noisy and crowded, with defendants, lawyers, police officers and bail bondsmen milling around in great confusion—an atmosphere not conducive to rational inquiry. The defendant, from inability or design, unless the prosecutor's case is weak, usually conducts a minimal cross-examination of government witnesses and presents none of his own. Both defense counsel and the prosecutor consider it tactically unwise in most cases to disclose their evidence at this early stage.

Fourth and finally, dismissal of a charge at a preliminary hearing is not necessarily conclusive. Since the hearing is not a trial, the charge can be reinstated without twice putting the accused in jeopardy. This practice is barred by statute in some states, but permitted in others (see Graham and Letivin, 1969: 110-116; University of Pennsylvania Law Review, 1958: 602-603).

Despite these defects, the preliminary hearing is probably the most promising available method of securing effective review of the adequacy of the prosecutor's case prior to trial. Even as presently constituted in most states, the defendant has far more opportunity to challenge the prosecutor at an adversary proceeding before a judge than does the grand jury. At a preliminary hearing, in contrast to a grand jury proceeding, the defendant can confront government witnesses, compel the production of evidence on his own behalf, and secure a full transcript of the hearing. He may also be represented by counsel and have the advantage of rules of evidence applicable in full criminal trials. Depending on such factors as the degree of prior screening, the rules of evidence applied, the availability of counsel, and the quality of the hearing official, more than 40 percent of preliminary hearings may result in dismissal, or the figure may be as low as 1 or 2 percent[9] (Hall et al., 1969: 850-851).

Liberalizing pretrial discovery rules, guaranteeing effective assistance of counsel, and raising the status of the hearing officers would remove the major present impediments to effective preliminary hearings. In view of their potential, and the importance of protecting the accused against prosecutions unsupported by sufficient evidence,[10] there are strong arguments for courts reconsidering the traditional view that the "due process" clauses of the Fifth and Fourteenth Amendments do not require a preliminary hearing or some reasonable alternative screening procedure. Control of baseless accusations alone justifies fashioning a powerful preliminary hearing, even though it is not designed to protect against either arbitrary prosecutions—those involving defendants unfairly selected from among a large number of similar offenders—or unwise uses of the criminal law.

3. Review by motion to suppress; challenging the sufficiency of an indictment or information

When evidence is seized by law enforcement authorities without a search warrant, but incident to an arrest, the defendant may indirectly secure judicial review of the adequacy of the evidence available to the arresting authorities by moving to suppress the seized evidence, thus preventing its use at trial (see Mapp v. Ohio, 1961). The practical effect of a successful motion may be to make a prosecution impossible (and the exclusionary rule, as it is usually called, has for this reason come under increasing criticism recently; see Wingo, 1971), essentially on the ground that the law enforcement process was wrongly initiated, even if sufficient evidence to prosecute was developed as a result of the arrest. Since there is no general right to "suppress" an entire prosecution on the ground that the defendant was illegally arrested or "seized" under the Fourth Amendment, the availability of this remedy turns on the fortuitous circumstance whether a warrantless search accompanied the arrest.

In every case, the defendant can move to quash an indictment or information on the ground that it is defective in form, or that the acts alleged as criminal in fact do not constitute a crime. Also, in some states the accused can make a motion to quash an indictment because of the insufficiency of evidence before the grand jury. Again, all these procedures are designed to stop the unfounded prosecution—not those where a defendant is singled out unfairly or because of unsound policies.

D. Disclosure of Prosecutor's Case

1. Notice

The guarantee that the accused "be informed of the nature and cause of the accusation," originally applicable to federal prosecutions, is now considered a fundamental element of "due process of law" protected against state infringement as well (Smith v. O'Grady, 1941; Snyder v. Massachusetts, 1934). It is not sufficient for an indictment or information merely to echo the language of a criminal statute. It must specify the facts upon which a violation of the statute is alleged with sufficient particularity to permit the defendant to prepare a refutation of the allegations, to permit courts to decide whether the facts alleged constitute a criminal violation, and to allow a future determination whether any subsequent prosecution would unconstitutionally put the accused in "jeopardy" twice for the same conduct (Russell v. United States, 1962; Stirone v. United States, 1960; United States v. Cavalcante, 1971; Gaither v. United States, 1969). The notice requirement, however, does not require the government to reveal the evidence upon which it will try to prove its charges. It is only a minimal guarantee of fundamental fairness, although an essential one (see Scott, 1957).

2. Discovery

Disclosure of the evidence relied on by the prosecution is generally thought of primarily as a way to permit the defendant to prepare for trial, taking some of the gamesmanship out of determining guilt or innocence. But requiring disclosure forces prosecutors to reveal their cases, so it also can strengthen the hand of the defense in attempting to induce the prosecutor to drop a case or negotiate a guilty plea to a lesser charge. Discovery may also "expos[e] any latent procedure or constitutional issues . . . prior to trial" (American Bar Association Project, 1970: Standard 1.1[a] [iv]) including fatal defects in the prosecutor's intended evidence, and thus reduce the danger that a prosecution unlikely to result in conviction will proceed to trial.

The inadequacies of grand jury action, preliminary hearings and motions to suppress evidence in disclosing the basis of charges against the accused have already been noted. While discovery in criminal cases is in a rudimentary stage of development in the United States, it exists on a larger scale than is generally recognized—although on a peacemeal basis. What is lacking is a comprehensive set of rules explicitly recognizing the accused's right to pre-trial discovery, defining its extent and providing a simple, workable procedure for disclosure.

Informal disclosure of some or a great deal of the prosecution's evidence is sometimes made to defense counsel. This, however, depends upon a relationship of confidence between the prosecutor and the defense lawyer, and is a matter of grace, not right. A variety of formal rules which at least tangentially affect the accused's right to learn what is in the prosecution's files may be summarized as follows (see Karlen, 1967: 159-167):

(1) It is a violation of due process for a prosecutor at the trial to knowingly suppress evidence favorable to the accused.
(2) In many, although not all, states, the names of witnesses for the grand jury are required to be endorsed on the indictment. This, however, does not reveal the substance of their testimony. Furthermore, prosecution witnesses not so named are allowed to testify.

(3) In the federal courts and some states, the pre-trial statement of a witness who testifies for the prosecution must be made available to the accused for purposes of cross-examination.
(4) A few states have provided by statute that the accused is entitled to inspect his own statement or confession in the hands of the prosecution.
(5) In some states motions by the defense to inspect scientific, laboratory reports have been successful.
(6) In the federal courts and a few states, the defense before trial is entitled to obtain documents and tangible objects which were obtained from or belong to him or which were obtained from others by seizure or process. [11]

This hodge-podge of miscellaneous, uncoordinated rules, varying from state to state, item by item, is obviously unsatisfactory. What is needed is a comprehensive and articulate regulation of discovery. There is a growing recognition that such a reform is needed. It may soon be provided by an amendment to the federal rules of criminal procedure, and if so, it will probably be widely copied in the states.

Model standards recently approved by the American Bar Association Project on Minimum Standards for Criminal Justice (1970: 46) provide an excellent basis for movement toward nation-wide liberal discovery rules. These proposals would permit freer discovery than presently available in any jurisdiction in the United States, state or federal. Probably the most useful proposal among them for revealing weak prosecutions is the recommendation that the prosecutor be required to disclose all of the witnesses he intends to call at trial, "together with their relevant written or recorded statements." (American Bar Association Project, 1970: Standard 2.1 [a] [1]).

III. PROTECTIONS AGAINST ARBITRARY OR DISCRIMINATORY PROSECUTIONS

So far we have primarily considered means for stalling prosecutions based on inadequate evidence of guilt. Deficient as these devices may be in some respects, they are collectively, and in combination with other devices and doctrines which will be discussed in parts IV and V of this chapter, fairly efficient in weeding out most weak cases. The most important reason for this relative success is that the evil to be averted, prosecuting people who are innocent of wrongdoing, is clear and incontroversial. Also, the principal upon which the evil may be avoided is simple in concept, if not always in application: find out what the prosecutor's case is, and permit a judge, jury, or the defendant himself to assess it. The second danger of abuse—singling out a wrongdoer on some illegitimate basis—is more controversial, in the sense that reasonable men and women will disagree as to when prosecutions should be barred or law enforcement otherwise hampered to avoid it. It is also more difficult to prove, even in cases of clear overreaching.

A. Proof of Prosecutor's Abuse of Discretion

Courts will not dismiss a charge merely because the defendant shows that he was singled out for accusation when many similarly situated are not subject to similar accusations. He is not entitled to a dismissal of a charge of gambling or intoxication or speeding because other gamblers or speeders or drunks are not charged. His only possible recourse is to prove that he is the victim of conscious persecution rather than prosecution. To succeed in such a direct attack, he must show that the prosecutor intentionally discriminated against him, for example because of his race (see Oyler v. Boles, 1962; Two Guys from Harrison-Allentown v. McGinley, 1961; Yick Wo v. Hopkins, 1886; Massachusetts v. Hornig, 1963; People v. Gray, 1967). The fact that police and prosecutors together control most of the key evidence about law enforcement patterns that might reveal a design to discriminate, and the high burden of proof that defendants must meet to prove deliberate bias, renders this remedy effective only against blatant discrimination, and only then when the defendant has the initiative and resources to make a case. This kind of attack is usually rejected out of hand (Miller, 1970: 171, 336).

A simple expedient that would greatly lessen the burden on a defendant to prove discrimination where it exists, without inhibiting legitimate law enforcement policies, would be to require that police and prosecutors maintain complete public records and file regular reports concerning arrests, prosecutions, and dispositions. This practice would also help reduce unjustified inconsistencies in law enforcement patterns and deliberate or inadvertant adherence to unwise policies that do not rise to the level of bias (discussed in part "V" below).

B. Discriminatory Grand Jury Selection

The accused may be able to defeat a prosecution tainted with bias without showing actual discrimination directed against him, if he can prove that a grand jury which indicted him was selected in some impermissible way. Even though states may choose not to use grand juries, courts do not tolerate discrimination in the operation of whatever system the state opts for (see Beck v. Washington, 1962; Costello v. United States, 1956; Bartlett, 1967; Yale Law Journal, 1965).

The strongest showing of this kind available to the defendant is proof that he was indicted by a grand jury specially selected in some unusual way because of some irrelevant characteristic of the defendant himself, such as his race (Collins v. Walker, 1964).

A more difficult defense, one that courts do not always recognize, is presented by a showing of discrimination in the selection of all grand juries in a jurisdiction over a period of time, including the one that indicted the defendant. The state's rejoinder may be that it treated the defendant no differently than anyone else and thus that the defendant lacks "standing" to raise the issue. Courts may permit the defendant to bypass this objection by asserting as his own the rights of the wrongly excluded potential grand jurors (in latinate jargon, the "jus tertii"), primarily on the ground that only the defendant is sufficiently motivated to redress the discrimination.

Some courts may limit this defense to members of the "same class" as those wrongly excluded from the grand jury, although there is no evidence to justify the apparent assumption behind this rule that class members (blacks, for example) tend to be more lenient in judging other members of the same class. Since there is also little justification for use of "benign quotas" in grand jury selection, ensuring somy pre-set mixture of races, the better rule is to forbid selections based on race in every case.

At present, the utility of showing racial or other bias in grand jury selection is limited not only by the "one class" rule and standing problems, but, as in attempts to show actual discrimination by the prosecutor, by the difficulty of proof, especially when most of the relevant evidence is controlled by the government. Some courts properly take into account the government's possession of the decisive records by permitting indirect proof of discriminatory selection through random sampling of grand jury compositions during the period that the defendant was indicted (Colson v. Smith, 1971).

C. Desuetude

Occasionally a defendant can defeat a prosecution by securing a declaration that the criminal law sought to be enforced against him had remained so long dormant and unused that it could no longer be revived except by legislative reenactment (see United States v. Elliott, 1967; Berry, 1966; Fuller, 1968; Bickel, 1957). Although nominally directed at the validity of the statute, the doctrine of "desuetude" (which we inherited from Scotland rather than England) is probably best understood, and most reliably applied, as an indirect method of proving discriminatory enforcement. Although courts may rely upon the rationale that legislatures at some point "intend" to repeal dormant laws, normally statutes are struck down as desuetudinous only when an illegitimate and discriminatory purpose is the only reasonable motive for their sudden resuscitation (even though no such motive can be proved). Thus, courts will not normally declare statutes unenforceable merely because they have not been used for a long while.

This is probably a sound practice—a law against grazing too many animals on a city commons may be perfectly valid although long unenforced due to a dearth of urban sheeps and cows. To apply the doctrine other than to permit inferential proof of a prosecutor's discrimination would leave courts without apparent standards for second-guessing legislative intent. The safer course in such cases is probably not repeal, but simply reinterpretation of an old law in light of modern circumstances. Since the appropriate remedy in the case of a discriminatory prosecution is to quash the prosecution, not repeal the law, the doctrine of desuetude might be dispensed with altogether. The enforcement of a dormant law might then become an element in the proof of discriminatory intent— perhaps shifting the burden to the prosecutor to show a legitimate reason for the prosecution.

D. Entrapment

"Desuetude" is only of secondary importance in protecting against arbitrary prosecutions, is rarely invoked by defendants, and is practically desuetudinous itself judged by the paucity of decisions that apply it. The same cannot be said of the difficult concept of "entrapment," a doctrine which serves a unique role. Increasingly advanced by litigants, the "entrapment" defense continues to trail after it a state of confusion which the Supreme Court has twice attempted, futilely, to dispel (Sherman v. United States, 1958; Sorrells v. United States, 1932).

As usually formulated, entrapment is a "defense" involving two elements of proof, permitting an accused to relieve himself of liability for committing a criminal act. First, a court or trial jury must find that the government "induced" or "encouraged" the defendant to commit the crime. The defendant has the burden of proving this threshhold element, although the extent of his burden is unclear. If "inducement" is shown, then the government may defeat the defense by proving that the defendant was "predisposed" to commit the crime even if the government had not induced him to do it. "Predisposition" may normally be shown by proof that the defendant had committed similar crimes in the past, had been predisposed to do so, or had "readily acquiesced" in the government's inducement—had jumped at the bait (Sherman v. United States, 1958; Sorrells v. United States, 1932). A minority view, twice rejected by a majority of the

Supreme Court over strong dissents, would ignore the subjective "predisposition" element altogether, and ask only whether the government's inducement was likely to snare otherwise "innocent" people into committing crimes.[12]

The difficulty with entrapment lies in the necessity to balance legitimate law enforcement needs against at least two different kinds of possible abuse. "Inducement" of crime is generally recognized as an acceptable, because necessary, police technique in investigating crimes with no immediate victims. These generally fall into two classes. First, the only victim of so-called "victimless crimes"—such as obscenity, prostitution and other sex crimes, gambling, or drug and alcohol abuse—is the general public, or the "public morality." Similarly, the victim of a second class of crimes—such as bribery of public officials or politically motivated crimes directed against the government— is the general public, rather than any individual.

The only feasible way for police to prove the commission of either of these kinds of crime is often for a government agent to pose as a participant in the crime, since otherwise no witness to the crime would be motivated to report it. Participation, however, often requires that the government agent actively encourage or solicit the criminal act (by, for example, offering a bribe or offering to buy narcotics). Whenever the government agent does anything actively to promote the commission of a crime, the problem of entrapment arises.

It is commonly recognized that the entrapment defense is designed to protect two different kinds of values threatened by police promotion of crime. First, "innocent" people should not be seduced by the government to commit crimes. "The function of law enforcement is the prevention of crime and the apprehension of criminals. Manifestly, that function does not include the manufacturing of crime" (Sherman v. United States, 1958). Second, courts should not tolerate outrageous law enforcement practices, even if the defendant is "really guilty."

It may be that by attempting to protect both of these interests simultaneously, the doctrine of entrapment performs only the second function well, protecting against the most blatant abuses of law enforcement power while slighting the function of protecting the "innocent" against arbitrary prosecution (see Yale Law Journal, 1969; Rotenberg, 1963; Harvard Law Review, 1960; Donnelly, 1951).

Specifically, the two-step "inducement" and "predisposition" formula is awkwardly designed to serve its stated purpose, to separate the guilty from the innocent. Thus, one purpose of the entrapment defense is to prohibit convicting people for committing crimes "manufactured" by the government. But all crimes "induced" by a government agent are "manufactured" by the government. If the government had not induced such crimes, they would never have been committed. It does not matter that the defendant was "predisposed" to commit a crime, or that he "readily acquiesced" in it—still, the precise crime for which he is prosecuted would not have occurred without the government's inducement. Thus, in every case where inducement is proved, yet the entrapment defense is defeated by proof of "predisposition," the defendant is convicted for committing a crime "manufactured by the government"—a practice which, as the Supreme Court has recognized, serves no proper function of law enforcement authorities.

The implication of the above analysis is not, however, that no persons induced by the government to commit crimes should be prosecuted and convicted. Such a rule would unjustifiably interfere with what is clearly a proper law enforcement function—to detect crime and convict people who commit it, without government inducement. Rather, the implication may be that entrapment should not be seen as a "defense" insofar as it is designed to separate the "guilty" from the "innocent." It might better be viewed as part of the government's normal burden of proving the guilt of the accused.

The crime induced by the government is not a legitimate subject of prosecution, but crimes that would have been committed without the government's intervention are legitimate law enforcement targets—provided that the government can prove that the same crime would have been committed beyond a reasonable doubt even if the government had not induced a particular act. Thus, the entrapment "defense" might be more clearly formulated if it required that the government prove in every case beyond a reasonable doubt that its "inducement" of the crime was irrelevant—that the crime would have been committed anyway but with a different co-participant.

An important function of this formulation would be to prevent the government from prosecuting people it only suspects of one kind of crime (e.g., giving bribes) by encouraging them to commit another kind of crime (e.g., to take a bribe offered by a government undercover agent). More generally, the test would limit the police's and prosecutor's present discretion to induce suspicious or undesirable persons to commit a crime that that person would otherwise not have committed, but to support the prosecution by proof of "predisposition." Such proof amounts to conviction for having a "criminal character," and the practice of inducement in such cases amounts to the administration of a character test. But the prosecutor's legitimate function is to prosecute criminal activity, not people who are criminally inclined. The reformulation would thus simply require that the criminal activity, not the bad character, of the defendant be established in cases involving government inducement, just as it presently must be proved in every other kind of criminal case.

IV. PERVASIVE LEGAL CONTROL OF PROSECUTOR'S DISCRETION

Limiting the discussion of the prosecutor's discretion to specific devices designed in part specially to control it may leave the impression that the prosecutor has more leeway than he has in practice. In fact, the most fundamental and effective control of prosecutorial discretion, essential to all the other mechanisms but potent even without them, is the elementary requirement that eventually the prosecutor prove beyond a reasonable doubt, to the satisfaction of a jury in serious cases if the defendant so demands, that the accused violated a legitimate criminal law.

A. Proof at Trial

Prosecutors, whose reelections tend to be guaranteed, are generally more concerned with establishing a reputation among lawyers, judges, and law enforcement officers as sound judges of good prosecutions than with pleasing any particular constituency. Partly this is a matter of professional pride, and partly a pragmatic concern with establishing credibility among judges before whom the prosecutor must regularly appear (Skolnick, 1967: 57-58). A recent study found that in deciding whether to charge, prosecutors as a rule applied the "beyond a reasonable doubt" standard of proof they would have to meet at trial, rather than the more lenient "probable cause" standard required by law (Miller, 1970: 22-23).

But the prospect of an eventual jury trial affects more than the prosecutor's standard of proof. He will also consider such factors bearing on the prospects of conviction as the popularity of the criminal statute violated and the likely reception his key witnesses will have before a jury. Most prosecutors will avoid prosecuting a crime like statutory rape, for example, except under aggravated circumstances, because the jury may consider the "victim" as guilty as the defendant.

Ignoring the role of the potential trial, and especially jury trial, in controlling a prosecutor's discretion (including his policy decisions) not only unjustifiably magnifies his power. It also discounts the danger of permitting inefficient administration of criminal justice to increase the prosecutor's power artificially, by reducing the importance of the trial. By aggravating the harm that the mere pendency of a criminal charge can do, delays in criminal courts increase pressure on defendants to forego their right to a trial and to plead guilty to charges they might defeat if given an early chance.[13] It is no tribute to the plea bargaining system that the criminal process would collapse almost everywhere without it.

B. The Substantive Law

None of the controls discussed thus far would have any effect if the criminal law itself gave the prosecutor unlimited discretion. A law that forbade everything would in effect delegate to the prosecutor complete discretion to decide what was illegal and what permissible. Criminal laws are not only codes of conduct, but also delegations of authority to the officials who enforce them, including prosecutors. The breadth of the delegation of power increases to the extent that the law proscribes more acts than the legislature intends, the public expects, or resources permit to be prosecuted. Thus, laws that are vague as well as broad permit particularly broad discretion, and therefore risk the most serious abuses. To illustrate, probably murder statutes are virtually never abused, while statutes defining so-called victimless crimes (referred to earlier), which together account for about half of all arrests in the country each year (President's Commission, 1967: 5-8) are easily abused.

Statutes that delegate too much discretion to prosecutors and other officials administering the criminal law, or which are too vague for an average person to apply as a guide to his conduct, violate the due process guarantees of the Fifth and Fourteenth Amendments (see Palmer v. City of Euclid, 1971; Lanzetta v. New Jersey, 1939). Through the "vagueness doctrine," courts thus require legislatures to retain a minimal degree of control over the definition of crimes, and therefore over the conduct of prosecutors. The potential reach of the vagueness doctrine for this purpose is uncertain, however, since early cases stressed the alternative requirement reflected in the doctrine, that criminal statutes provide reasonable notice of the acts prohibited (see Connally v. General Construction Co., 1926: 391). Only recently has the function of limiting courts' and law enforcement officials' discretion become prominent (Coates v. Cincinnati, 1971; cf. United States v. Marion, 1971).

A second important constitutional limitation on the power of the legislature to delegate discretion to the prosecutor is enforced through the "overbreadth" principle, which prohibits even specific criminal laws to infringe too greatly on the freedom of speech and press protected by the First Amendment (Harvard Law Review, 1970b). The overbreadth doctrine serves a narrower function than the prohibition against vagueness, but it does so in a vital area. Even without the overbreadth rule, any conviction for activities protected by the First Amendment could be overturned on appeal. But reversing individual convictions would not redress the evil of permitting statutes to remain in force that allowed prosecutions of protected speech. Because the very threat of criminal prosecution can seriously inhibit the exercise of First Amendment rights, statutes permitting such prosecutions may be struck down even if a large part of the activity they prohibit is not protected by the Constitution. Indeed, if a defendant can show a special danger of "irreparable injury" to his right to free expression from a prosecution, he may secure a federal court injunction barring the prosecution, rather than having to wait (as he normally would) to raise the defense at trial or after conviction (Younger v. Harris, 1971; Dombrowski v. Pfister, 1965).

V. STRUCTURING PROSECUTORS' POLICY DECISIONS

The controls discussed so far are reasonably adequate to forestall most baseless prosecutions, but provide no more than minimal protection against arbitrary or discriminatory prosecutions, and (with the exception of the jury trial) are almost totally ineffective to ensure consistent application of sound law enforcement policies. This is true largely because legal controls enforceable primarily through the inflexibile remedy of dismissing prosecutions are insufficiently sensitive to protect against any but clear abuses. To take law enforcement policies out of the hands of individual prosecutors and to ensure their even-handed enforcement requires more subtle controls.

It has been found that most prosecutors consider such nebulous factors as the possible harm prosecution may cause to the criminal law system and to the defendant in determining whether to bring a charge, or whether to charge less than the most serious crime supported by the evidence. In making their calculations, they weigh such diverse matters as the defendant's past criminal record, the seriousness of the offense, whether prosecution is necessary to achieve the purpose behind the law violated (for example, the usual remedy for passing a bad check is to force the wrongdoer to make it good, under threat of prosecution if payment is not forthcoming), and whether the relationship between the perpetrator and victim makes prosecution inappropriate (domestic disputes involving technical crimes will rarely lead to prosecution) (Subin, 1966: ch. 3; Miller, 1970: chs. 10-13). The complexity of these decisions guarantees that effective policy will vary arbitrarily over time and among different individual prosecutors—and will reflect no one's ideas about the proper uses of the criminal law other than the prosecutor's—in the absence of appropriate controls.[14]

A. Political Constraints

Public opinion, reinforced by the sanction of defeat at the polls, is the ultimate control over a prosecutor's conduct. But unless he blunders badly, reelection is usually guaranteed. The electorate may oust a corrupt, indolent, or incompetent prosecutor, but its attention will rarely be captured by the minimally adequate prosecutor, whatever his policies. Conceivably, also, a prosecutor who grossly abused his discretion by vindictive action against an individual or by consistently ignoring crimes committed by particular ethnic, religious, political, or economic groups could be removed from office directly through impeachment by the legislature, or indirectly as a result of his disbarment or conviction for "bad faith" administration of his office. Or he might be replaced by a special prosecutor, who in some states can be appointed by the attorney general and in others by the courts. Such drastic remedies, however, are rarely invoked (Miller, 1970: ch. 20; University of Pennsylvania Law Review, 1955).

B. Administrative Law Techniques

A more promising approach is to make prosecutors' policies self-consistent and visible enough to attract outside scrutiny by interested persons through a range of techniques that have long been used for these purposes in administrative settings other than the prosecutor's office.[15] Thus, some supervising authority, or the prosecutor's office itself, might be required to promulgate written policies. Prosecutors might be required to state in writing their reasons for their decisions. The decisions themselves might be subject to routine review by higher administrative authority. The actual decisions of the prosecutor might be regularly reviewed by an outside body—such as a citizens' panel or an arm of the legislature—to test their consistency with written policy. Individual defendants who believed the decisions in their cases to be inconsistent with stated policy might have recourse to an outside administrative official, such as an ombudsman, or to the court. These procedures have worked well, by and large, to rationalize and make accessible to public influence the actions of other administrative agencies, and there seem no valid reasons why they should not be applied to prosecutors as well.

C. Diversion (see generally, NIMH, 1971)

Regardless of formal protections against abuse, the sensitivity with which society responds to its problems is strictly limited by the variety of responses available to it. If the only answer to drunkenness in a community is the local lock-up, drunks will be jailed if they are not ignored (and they will not be ignored if they present a problem of any magnitude). If there are no facilities for treating mental illnesses, many people who should receive treatment will eventually be prosecuted when their mental problems lead to crimes. Political controls and administrative control techniques cannot supply alternative ways of answering social ills. Developing such alternative answers may be the most important and constructive approach to making the best use of the criminal law and diluting the prosecutor's control over how it will be used.

Alternatives to criminal prosecution may be either voluntary or involuntary. The traditional examples of coercive alternatives include civil commitment for treating of mental illness, narcotics addiction, and alcoholism (Miller, 1970: ch. 14-15). Compulsory commitment procedures, however, raise the same kinds of dangers of abuse, may lead to similar conditions of incarceration if "treatment" is not available in practice, and may include fewer protections than criminal prosecutions (see Hickey and Rubin, 1971; Kaplan, 1969; Georgetown Law Journal, 1969).

For these reasons, a hopeful development in recent years has been the growth in many cities of pilot projects that offer the defendant, with the consent of the prosecutor, an alternative to prosecution that he can accept or reject. Would-be defendants may avoid a conviction by agreeing to enter an alcohol treatment program, for example, or by successfully completing a brief trial period designed to help them establish more stable lives through counseling, training, and employment. Such pre-trial intervention programs were successful enough in Washington and New York City that they have passed from the experimental stage to become a routine diversion route from the criminal courts of those cities, and other such programs are beginning to operate throughout the country.[17]

Diversion projects do not suffer from the negative quality of some of the other controls discussed in this chapter. They do not limit the prosecutor's options, but expand them. As outside constraints, however, they transfer power from the prosecutor and diffuse it through other agencies and individuals. Although they are no substitute for legal protections against the arbitrary exercise of power, they lessen the potential for abuse by making the criminal law less important, and permit a more graded, reasoned response to social problems than the often destructive weapon of the criminal law.

NOTES

1. In other jurisdictions, the prosecutor wields even more power. His activities are not confined to the superior courts but extend as well to the minor courts. He controls the prosecution not only of serious crimes, but also of most minor offenses, usually excluding only traffic infractions of a routine nature and violations of municipal ordinances.

2. The relation between the substantive criminal law and the prosecutor's discretion is discussed in part III.B of this chapter.

3. The privilege against self-incrimination is guaranteed against federal infringement by the United States Constitution, Amendment V, and against state infringement by the "due process" guarantee, Amendment XIV (see Murphy v. Waterfront Commission, 1963).

4. As noted at the beginning of this chapter, since we are concerned here with protecting the accused's interests, we will not consider ways to control a prosecutor's decision *not* to charge a potential defendant with a crime. It can fairly be said, however, that prosecutors presently enjoy virtual immunity from review of these decisions (see United States v. Cox, 1965), at least prior to the filing of an indictment and information (see University of Pennsylvania Law Review, 1955). The policy-regulating mechanisms— political constraints, administrative law devices, and alternatives to the criminal law— discussed in part "V" of this chapter are probably most realistically suited to bringing a degree of control to these negative decisions (see Yale Law Journal, 1955, recommending criminal prosecutions directed by private complaining victims, with court approval).

5. That obvious and serious dangers inherent in permitting grand juries to condemn without indicting illustrates that the public trial is the surest protection against prosecutorial caprice.

6. This was the finding of the American Bar Foundation study of prosecution procedures in Michigan, Kansas, and Wisconsin (Miller, 1970: 54).

7. Preliminary hearings were waived by 66-90 percent of the defendants to whom they were offered in a sample analyzed in the American Bar Foundation study (Miller, 1970: 110).

8. This was the overall finding of the Bar Foundation study (Miller, 1970: ch. 4).

9. HALL, L. Y. KAMISAR, W. LAFAVE; J. ISRAEL, (1969: 850-851). The American Bar Foundation study found that the dismissal rate following preliminary examination in all three states studied ran below 10 percent (Miller, 1970: 83-84). Furthermore, if defendants who waived preliminary examinations were included in the sample, the study found that "[a] n average dismissal rate of 2 percent of all persons entitled to preliminaries is probably a substantially accurate reflection of current practice."

10. Normally it is said that "probable cause" to believe the defendant committed the crime charged must be found at a preliminary hearing to avoid a dismissal. It is unclear whether this is the same or a different standard in theory or practice than that applied to justify (1) arrest; (2) grand jury indictment or presentment; and (3) refusal of the court to dismiss a case against a defendant during or following a jury trial.

11. Rules governing disclosure of grand jury proceedings are discussed in part II.A. of this chapter.

12. See Kadis v. United States (1967). Kadis has not spurred a general exodus from the traditional approach, as, for example, United States v. Greenberg, (1971) illustrates.

13. United States v. Ewell (1966: 120): An important function of the right to a speedy trial guaranteed by the Sixth Amendment is to "limit the possibilities that long delay will

impair the ability of an accused to defend himself." Of course, delays also pressure the prosecutor to compromise.

14. California Law Review (1969: 526, 529), reporting wide variations of opinion among different prosecutors in a single office concerning the proper disposition of the same case.

15. A leading advocate of this approach is Kenneth Culp Davis (1969: 188-190, 224-225). See also, California Law Review (1969).

16. An exhaustive list of possible objections is analyzed, and each convincingly refuted by Abrams (1971).

17. See, e.g., National Committee for Children and Youth, "Project Crossroads: A Final Report to the Manpower Administration, U.S. Department of Labor" (1971; L. Leiberg, Director). The Manpower Administration is presently supporting similar pre-trial intervention projects in ten cities.

CASES

Beck v. Washington, 369 U.S. 541 (1962).

Coates v. Cincinnati, 402 U.S. 611 (1971).

Collins v. Walker, 329 F.2d 100 (5th Cir. 1964), cert. denied, 379 U.S. 901 (1964).

Colson v. Smith, 438 F.2d 1075 (5th Cir. 1971).

Connally v. General Constr. Co., 269 U.S. 385 (1926).

Costello v. United States, 350 U.S. 359 (1956).

Dennis v. United States, 384 U.S. 855 (1966).

Dombrowski v. Pfister, 380 U.S. 479 (1965).

Gaither v. United States, 413 F.2d 1061 (D.C. Cir. 1969).

Goldsby v. United States, 160 U.S. 70 (1895).

Hurtado v. California, 110 U.S. 516 (1884).

In Re Dionisio, 442 F.2d 276 (7th Cir. 1971).

Kadis v. United States, 373 F.2d 370 (1st Cir. 1967).

Lanzetta v. New Jersey, 306 U.S. 451 (1939).

Lawn v. United States, 350 U.S. 359 (1956).

Mapp v. Ohio, 367 U.S. 643 (1961).

Moss v. Hornig, 314 F.2d 89 (2d Cir. 1963).

Murphy v. Waterfront Comm'n, 378 U.S. 52 (1963).

Oklahoma Press Publ. Co. v. Walling, 327 U.S. 186 (1946).

Oyler v. Boles, 368 U.S. 448 (1962).

Palmer v. City of Euclid, 402 U.S. 544 (1971).

People v. Gray, 254 Cal.App.2d 256, 63 Cal.Rptr. 211 (1967).

People v. Howell, 3 N.Y.2d 672 (1958).

Pittsburgh Plate Glass Co. v. United States, 360 U.S. 395 (1959).

Russell v. United States, 369 U.S. 749 (1962).

Sciortino v. Zampano, 385 F.2d 132 (2d Cir. 1967), cert. denied, 390 U.S. 906 (1968).

Sherman v. United States, 356 U.S. 369 (1958).

Smith v. O'Grady, 312 U.S. 329 (1941).

Snyder v. Massachusetts, 291 U.S. 97 (1934).

Sorrells v. United States, 287 U.S. 435 (1932).
Stirone v. United States, 361 U.S. 212 (1960).
Two Guys From Harrison—Allentown, Inc. v. McGinley, 366 U.S. 582 (1961).
United States v. Arcuri, 282 F.Supp. 347 (E.D.N.Y.), aff'd., 405 F.2d 691 (2d Cir. 1968),
    cert.denied, 395 U.S. 913 (1969).
United States v. Cox, 342 F.2d 167 (5th Cir.), (en banc), cert. denied, 381 U.S. 935 (1965).
United States v. Decavalcante, 440 F.2d 1264 (3d Cir. 1971).
United States v. Elliott, 266 F.Supp. 318 (S.D.N.Y. 1967).
United States v. Ewell, 383 U.S. 116 (1966).
United States v. Funk, 412 F.2d 452 (8th Cir. 1969).
United States v. Greenberg, 444 F.2d 369 (2d Cir. 1971).
United States v. Marion, 40 U.S.L.W. 4092 (Dec. 20, 1971).
United States v. Winter, 348 F.2d 204 (2d Cir.), cert.denied, 382 U.S. 955 (1965).
United States v. Youngblood, 379 F.2d 365 (2d Cir. 1967).
West v. United States, 359 F.2d 50 (8th Cir.), cert.denied, 385 U.S. 867 (1966).
Yick Wo v. Hopkins, 118 U.S. 356 (1886).
Younger v. Harris, 401 U.S. 37 (1971).

CONSTITUTIONAL PROVISIONS

Florida Constitution, Article I, Section 15(a).
South Carolina Constitution, Article I, Section 17.
United States Constitution, Amendments V, VI, XIV.

REFERENCES

ABRAMS (1971) "Internal policy: guiding the exercise of prosecutorial discretion."
    University of California Law Rev. 19: 1.
American Bar Association Project on Minimum Standards for Criminal Justice, "Standards
    Relating to Discovery and Procedure Before Trial (Approved Draft, 1970)." Chicago:
    American Bar Association.
AESCHYLUS, The Eumenides (R. Lattimore, trans., 1953). Chicago: University of Chicago
    Press.
ARNOLD (1932) "Law enforcement: an attempt at social dissection." Yale Law J. 42: 17.
BARTLETT (1967) "Defendant's right to an unbiased federal grand jury." Boston
    University Law Rev. 47: 551.
BERRY (1966) "Spirits of the past—coping with old laws." University of Florida Law Rev.
    17: 24.
BICKEL, A. (1962) The Least Dangerous Branch. Indianapolis: Bobbs-Merrill.
BIRZON and GERARD (1966) "The prospective defendant rules and the privilege against
    self-incrimination in New York." Buffalo Law Rev. 15: 595.
California Law Review (1969) [Comment] "Prosecutorial discretion in the initiation of
    criminal complaints." 42: 519.
CALKINS (1965) "Grand jury secrecy." Michigan Law Rev. 63: 455.

Columbia Law Journal (1968) [Note] "Discovery by a criminal defendant of his own grand jury testimony." 68: 311.

DAVIS, K. (1969) *Discretionary Justice*. Baton Rouge: Louisiana State Press.

DONNELLY (1951) "Judicial control of informants, spies, stool pigeons, and agents provocateurs." Yale Law J. 60: 1091.

FULLER, L. (1968) *Anatomy of the Law*. New York: Mentor.

Georgetown Law Journal (1969) [Symposium] "The right to treatment." 57: 673.

GRAHAM and LEWIN (1969) The Preliminary Hearing in Los Angeles.

HALL, L., Y. KAMISAR, W. LAFAVE, J. ISRAEL (1969) *Modern Criminal Procedure*. St. Paul: West.

Harvard Law Review (1970a) [Note] "The unconstitutionality of plea bargaining." 83: 404.

---(1970b) [Note] "The First Amendment overbreadth doctrine." 83: 844.

---(1961) [Comment] "The California grand jury—the grand jury as an investigatory body." 74: 590.

---(1960) [Note] "Entrapment." 73: 1333.

HICKEY, W. and S. RUBIN (1971) *Civil Commitment of Special Categories of Offenders*. Washington: Government Printing Office.

KAPLAN (1969) "Civil commitment: as you like it." Boston University Law Rev. 49: 14.

KARLEN, D. (1967) *Anglo-American Criminal Justice*. New York: Oxford University Press.

LEIBERG, L. (1971) National Committee for Children and Youth, Project Crossroads: A Final Report to the Manpower Administration, United States Department of Labor.

MILLER, F. (1970) Prosecution: The Decision to Charge a Suspect With a Crime. Boston: Little, Brown.

MILLER and REMINGTON (1962) "Procedures before trial." Annals 339: 113.

United States National Institutes of Mental Health (1971) *Diversion from the Criminal Justice System*. Washington: Government Printing Office.

ORFIELD, L. (1947) *Criminal Procedure From Arrest to Appeal*. New York: New York University Press.

PACKER, H. (1968) *The Limits of the Criminal Sanction*. Stanford: Stanford University Press.

President's Commission on Law Enforcement and Administration of Justice (1967) *Task Force Report: The Courts*. Washington: Government Printing Office.

ROTENBERG (1963) "The police detection practice of encouragement." Virginia Law Rev. 49: 871.

SCOTT (1957) "Fairness in accusation of crime," Minnesota Law Rev. 41: 509.

SHERRY (1962), "Grand jury minutes: the unreasonable rule of secrecy." Virginia Law Rev. 48: 668.

SKOLNICK (1967) "Social control in the adversary system," J. of Conflict Resolution 11: 52.

Stanford Law Review (1956) [Comment] "Some aspects of the California grand jury system." 8: 631.

SUBIN, H. (1966) *Criminal Justice in a Metropolitan Court*. Washington: Government Printing Office.

University of Pennsylvania Law Review (1958) [Note] "Preliminary hearings on indictable offenses in Philadelphia." 106: 602.

---(1955) [Note] "Prosecutor's discretion." 103: 1057.

WINGO (1971) "Growing disillusionment with the exclusionary rule." Southwestern Law J.
    25: 573.
Yale Law Journal (1969) [Note] "Applying estoppel principles in criminal cases." 78:
    1046.
———(1965) [Note] "The defendant's challenge to a racial criterion in jury selection: a
    study in standing due process, and equal protection." 74: 919.
———(1955) [Comment] "Private prosecution: a remedy for district attorneys' unwarranted
    inaction." 65: 209.
YOUNGER (1955) "The grand jury under attack III." J. of Criminal Law, Criminology and
    Police Science 46: 214.

Chapter 5

THE RIGHT TO COUNSEL

In all criminal prosecutions, the accused shall enjoy the right to . . . have the assistance of counsel for his defense

From the Sixth Amendment
to the U.S. Constitution

WILLIAM M. BEANEY received his A.B. at Harvard, 1940, his LL.B. at University of Michigan, 1947, and his Ph.D. at University of Michigan in 1951. He has taught at Princeton University at which, from 1964-1969, he was Cromwell Professor of Law. At present he is Professor of Law, University of Denver. Dr. Beaney is author of *The Right to Counsel in American Courts* (1955) and co-author (with A. T. Mason) of *American Constitutional Law* (4th ed. 1968) and *The Supreme Court in a Free Society* (rev. ed. 1968), as well as numerous articles and reviews.

THE RIGHT TO COUNSEL

WILLIAM M. BEANEY

INTRODUCTION

In an adversary system, the right of all persons faced with loss of liberty to have the assistance of counsel seems obvious. Yet, as shown below, the right to counsel, especially for indigents, is of relatively recent origin, its expansion to various stages of the criminal justice system has been slow and erratic and the actual effectiveness of the right in practice difficult to measure. While a substantial increase in the enjoyment of the right to counsel has taken place in the past quarter-century, the potentiality for greater improvement in the actual furnishing and functioning of counsel is obvious. The material which follows attempts to show first, the development of the concept of the right to counsel; second, the various proceedings to which it has been extended;[1] third, the problem of waiver and guilty pleas; fourth, methods of providing counsel for indigents; fifth, the effectiveness of the counsel received by indigents. In addition to relying on written sources, many of them embodying empirical

AUTHOR'S NOTE: I wish to acknowledge assistance in the preparation of this paper by two advanced students at the College of Law, University of Denver. Barbara Lynn Hosford aided in the collection of materials and preparation of footnotes. David K. Rees was a highly valued aide in research and drafting labors.

studies, the writer has relied on his own observations and interviews resulting from a still unpublished study of the judges of the Denver District Court.

The right to counsel is indeed curious, reflecting a mixture of idealism and practical considerations so characteristic of our system of justice. Lofty judicial assertions of the extensive rights of an accused are juxtaposed with all-too-easy acceptances of waiver which minimize or thwart an accused's right in practice. Counsel may be made available but not given adequate investigative assistance. Post-conviction practices vary greatly. One warning is called for: while this essay is not intended to serve as a digest of the multitude of cases or a complete bibliography of the voluminous writings dealing with the right to counsel, it does document the ungenerous, technical manner in which American courts have tended in the past to deal with right to counsel claims, as well as displaying the diversity with which courts in different jurisdictions even now regard the nature and scope of the right.

THE RIGHT TO COUNSEL—BACKGROUND AND DEVELOPMENT

Historically, the right to counsel has meant no more than the right to retained counsel, a protection not legally recognized fully in English felony cases until 1836.[2] The American practice, however, as reflected in early state constitutional provisions and the sixth amendment of the United States Constitution, clearly allowed the retention of counsel. A number of states showed even greater concern for indigents by enacting statutes providing for appointment in capital cases, or in all felonies.[3] The seeming generosity of even the most sweeping of these acts was limited, however, by the casualness with which many judges advised defendants, and a facile judicial doctrine of ready acceptance of waiver of the right, especially in connection with pleas of guilty.

The landmark decisions tell us something about judicial attitudes but only hint at actual practices. In the classic case of Powell v. Alabama,[4] nine black youths, accused of raping two white women, were convicted and sentenced to death in a farcical proceeding in which only the most superficial assistance of counsel was provided. A Tennessee attorney appeared at the arraignment on the first day of trial and asked if he could appear with local appointed counsel. The judge agreed to this, saying that he had appointed all the members of the local bar for the arraignment and had assumed they would continue if the defendants did not retain counsel. An inconclusive colloquy between judge and local bar representatives ended with one of the local attorneys agreeing to help the visitor from Tennessee. Despite this aid, however, the defendants were convicted. In reversing, the Supreme Court stressed that the special characteristics of the defendants, including their youth, illiteracy, ignorance, as well as community hostility, indicated the need for effective appointment of counsel. Justice Sutherland emphasized the vital role of counsel: "Even the intelligent and educated layman has small and sometimes no skill in the science of law. . . . He requires the guiding hand of counsel at every step in the proceedings against him."[5] Just ten years later, however, in Betts v. Brady[6] the Supreme Court refused to hold that every felony defendant needed counsel. By a 6-3 vote the Court, speaking through Justice Roberts, applied the "fair trial rule" which required "fundamental fairness" in state criminal trials,[7] and found that based on the totality of facts Betts had been afforded a "fair trial." Professor Kamisar in a devastating analysis of the Betts trial record[8] shows how unrealistic was the Court's cavalier assessment of the simplicity of the case and the unlikelihood that counsel could have rendered useful assistance to the defendant.

While adhering to the post-hoc "fair trial" rule in reviewing state cases, the Court during this period gave an expansive interpretation to the sixth amendment right to the assistance of counsel in federal proceedings. Using, or more realistically, misusing historical data, the Court, in the 1938 case of Johnson v. Zerbst,[9] discovered at this rather late date that the Constitution required an offer of free counsel to indigents in all federal felony cases. Furthermore, in cases where the defendant waived his right, the Court insisted that trial judges determine whether the waiver was intelligent, and reflect that finding in the case record. Still, the burden of proof remained on those convicted without counsel to show in a habeas corpus proceeding that their original waiver of counsel was constitutionally tainted.[10]

It should be noted that before 1964 no method was provided for paying federal appointed counsel for their services, nor were they given expert and investigative assistance, nor was there any systematic way of appointing counsel for federal defendants. Some judges were quite casual about it, appointing young attorneys or any attorney within the court with the expectation that they would plead their clients guilty. Other judges in important and difficult cases had no compunction about asking prominent attorneys to serve defendants without compensation. Hence, because of the varying judicial practices, and the lack of incentive for appointed attorneys, the quality of the counsel defendants received even in federal cases was, in many instances, highly suspect.

Thus well into the 1950s we had a dual system with respect to the right to counsel; federal courts granting the right unless intelligently waived on the record—the states, guided by the United States Supreme Court, engaged in a process of assessing on a case-by-case basis whether counsel was needed by indigent defendants because of the nature of the case or characteristics of the defendants. There were, however, several trends in the Supreme Court's review of state cases that portended change. First, in all capital cases, it became increasingly apparent that counsel had to be provided.[11] Second, in lesser felonies, the Court became more generous in discovering circumstances that justified appointment.[12] Third, waivers were looked upon with increasingly greater suspicion.

The 1960s marked the great change. In Mapp v. Ohio[13] the Supreme Court indicated that it would no longer allow the states to operate under a less stringent standard of due process than the federal government. Two years later, the Supreme Court ended this dichotomy in right to counsel cases, and in Gideon v. Wainright[14] overruled Betts, thus burying the "fair trial" doctrine, and establishing the rule that unless an intelligent waiver was obtained, free counsel must be provided all indigents accused of a serious crime.

MISDEMEANORS

It was not until 1972 that the Gideon rule was applied to misdemeanor cases. Argersinger v. Hamlin[15] handed down on June 12, 1972 held that whenever an accused was in danger of being deprived of his liberty he must, absent a knowing and intelligent waiver, receive appointed counsel. Thus the Court viewed the right to the assistance of counsel as more extensive than the right to trial by jury, which, in Baldwin v. New York,[16] the Court had limited to cases where imprisonment of six months or more was imposeable.

An opinion, concurring only in the result, written by Justice Powell (Justice Rehnquist concurring) argued for a Betts-type rule in which a judge would decide whether, based on the nature of the offense, the characteristics of the defendant, and the likelihood of a prison sentence, counsel should be appointed in a specific petty case. The justices feared the chaos that would result and also viewed the decision as opening the door to a constitutionally based need for counsel in proceedings where important privileges could be lost (automobile license) or where property rights were adversely affected.

In spite of the fears of Justices Powell and Renquist, and to a lesser degree Chief Justice Burger, the Argersinger decision seems justified as a solution to a problem that had been widely recognized.

The President's Commission in 1967 reported that: "In many lower courts defense counsel 'do not regularly appear, and counsel is either not provided to a defendant who has no funds; or, if counsel is appointed, he is not compensated.' "[17] Rather, it has been pointed out that the normal pattern in most states is for a defendant accused of a misdemeanor, or petty offense to appear pro se, usually either pleading, or being found, guilty.[18]

Even when the plea of guilty is undoubtedly wise, the availability of counsel on a defendant's behalf to speak about sentencing is clearly a matter of considerable significance. Lower court judges take, or seem to take, greater interest in proceedings with counsel present, especially when one or more interesting legal issues are raised. Additionally, few defendants are aware that prosecutors will often reduce charges or sentences in return for a guilty plea.

That counsel can accomplish a great deal for many defendants is apparent from this writer's observation of the situation in Denver, Colorado, where second- and third-year law students under Supreme Court authorization frequently appear for indigent misdemeanants in lower courts and enjoy considerable success in having cases dismissed or charges reduced by plea bargaining. These students are particularly helpful in cases involving youthful, ignorant, or minority group defendants.

Recognizing the role counsel can play in misdemeanor cases, the Judicial Research Foundation conference agreed that "lower courts are obligated to provide counsel for indigent defendants charged with any misdemeanor where conviction could involve deprivation of liberty," but they confessed that "many lower court judges are ignoring this requirement in misdemeanor cases," due to judicial obstinacy or lack of means for providing or compensating appointed counsel.[19]

In spite of the "obligation" to provide counsel in misdemeanor cases referred to above, it is clear that, except for a handful of states, the legal obligation has been unfulfilled in the past. A national survey reported in 1968 that California and to a somewhat lesser degree, Illinois, Massachusetts, Minnesota, and New Hampshire were the only "full counsel" jurisdictions.[20] Colorado should now be added to this list.[21] But in general the national picture has been one of trial, pleas of guilty, or findings of guilt, without the assistance of counsel in the bulk of misdemeanor cases. Even in states which give the judge discretionary power to appoint, the burden of a heavy docket and a lack of an efficient method of supplying counsel have made appointment an exception rather than the rule in most jurisdictions. Argersinger, whether it is applied prospectively or retrospectively, promises to produce vast change in the treatment of alleged misdemeanants.

COUNSEL AND THE STAGES OF A FELONY PROCEEDING

Initial Appearance

Normally, the first official proceeding to which a defendant is exposed after being booked (see Chapter 3) is the initial appearance before a magistrate. As the police must bring the accused before a magistrate without unreasonable delay, there is seldom time for an indigent to be provided counsel.[22] In a few instances, an efficient, well-staffed public defender office may conduct a daily jail census, enabling it to provide counsel even at the initial appearance. However, this practice is extremely rare.[23]

At the initial appearance, an indigent and any other defendant without counsel will be advised of his right to retain counsel, and that counsel will be appointed for him if he is indigent. If the suspect can provide bail, this is usually taken by the court as a sign that the defendant is not destitute, and the offer to appoint is withdrawn. In any event, the decision that defendant cannot afford counsel does not commonly signify that counsel will be appointed immediately. Depending on the jurisdiction, assignment may not be made until the preliminary hearing (if held) or arraignment. Even if appointment is made within a reasonable time of the initial appearance, several days may elapse before appointed counsel actually interviews the defendant for the first time.

The importance of this time lag between arrest and appearance of counsel should not be minimized. If, as all statistics show, the state and the defendant are engaged in most cases in a bargaining situation, the ready access of the state to the defendant before he has the assistance of counsel frequently means that statements have been made (in spite of warnings), witnesses for defendant have disappeared and police tests of various kinds have been conducted. As Silverstein concluded: ". . . In general, an unrepresented defendant is more likely to plead guilty than one who has counsel, even though this is not true in some counties."[24]

Grand Jury and Preliminary Hearing

We can quickly dismiss a discussion of the right to counsel at grand jury proceedings, because counsel is not permitted to be present in the jury room and substantial handicaps are placed on his attempt to defend his client or advise witnesses, some of whom may be under investigation themselves. Whatever the historical basis for viewing this unique proceeding as an important protection for the accused, the modern grand jury, controlled and manipulated by the prosecutor hardly merits a place in any rational concept of an adversary proceeding.[25] Even on such a vital matter as invoking the privilege against self-incrimination, the ludicrous situation arises of a layman forced to decide whether it is necessary to ask to be allowed to consult counsel, waiting impatiently outside the jury room to determine whether he should respond to questions. The refusal of the law to allow counsel at grand jury proceedings is especially ironic in view of the Supreme Court's recent view of the preliminary hearing.

In most jurisdictions, the preliminary hearing rather than the grand jury is used to determine whether probable cause exists sufficient to hold the defendant for trial. In Coleman v. Alabama[26] where the Supreme Court held that where a preliminary hearing is utilized, indigent defendants must be offered legal representation, the Court pointed out that there were four functions a defense attorney could perform for his client which rendered this stage of the proceedings "critical." First, a lawyer by skillfully examining witnesses might be able to create holes in the prosecution's case sufficient to persuade the magistrate that no probable cause exists, and the defendant should be released. Second, statements can be drawn from prosecution witnesses which can later become valuable for impeachment. Third, counsel can use the preliminary hearing as a discovery tool. Fourth, the preliminary hearing may be influential in a judge's decision to reduce bail or grant an early psychiatric examination.[27]

The Coleman case was not without its drawbacks, however. After ruling that the defendant had a right to counsel, the Court remanded the case to determine whether the error had been "harmless."[28] Justice White, concurring,[29] thought the net result of the decision would be fewer preliminary hearings in jurisdictions where the prosecutor might avoid a preliminary by simply proceeding expeditiously to the grand jury. Among the dissents, that of Chief Justice Burger was most prophetic of a new "strict construction" approach to the rights of criminal defendants. It had taken the Court "nearly two centuries," he pointed out, to " 'discover' a constitutional mandate for a preliminary hearing." He concluded that "here there is not even the excuse that conditions have changed; the preliminary hearing is an ancient institution."[30] The Chief Justice also underlined the anomaly of requiring counsel at the preliminary hearing while denying the assistance of counsel at the equally critical grand jury inquiry.

Arraignment

As yet, the Supreme Court has not declared that defendants have an absolute right to counsel at arraignment. In Hamilton v. Alabama[31] the Court held that in capital offenses arraignment was a "critical stage" and, consequently, counsel should be appointed. In White v. Maryland,[32] the Court extended the

Hamilton principle to a case arising from a Maryland procedure in which the client had pled guilty at the preliminary hearing where he appeared pro se. Later, after obtaining counsel, White changed his plea and the prosecutor introduced his original plea as evidence at trial. As White had been uncounseled when he first pled, and could not have known all the legal options available, the Supreme Court held that his prior plea could not be used against him. Again, however, this case involved a petitioner who had been sentenced to death.

Though no case explicitly gives the indigent defendant the right to counsel at arraignment in non-capital cases, the logic of other right to counsel cases implies that such a right exists. It is now firmly established that the indigent defendant has a right to counsel at every critical stage of the proceeding in non-capital as well as capital cases.[33] It is also clear that a defendant may lose fundamental rights through his actions at an arraignment. First, he may plead guilty to a charge to which there is a valid defense. Second, he may plead nolo contendere, or not guilty by reason of insanity, pleas with which most laymen are unfamiliar. Third, in some cases, it may be of critical importance to begin plea bargaining at an early stage of the proceeding. Thus it is clear that the arraignment is a "critical stage" of the criminal process, and counsel should be made available to all indigents before a plea is accepted.

Trial

Gideon v. Wainright[34] made clear that the right to assistance of counsel applies at the very least to the trial itself. Long before Gideon, courts had generally expected counsel to be reasonably well prepared in advance of trial; although some appointments were made shortly before trial, counsel should be in reasonably good physical and mental health, sober, and attentive to the proceedings. Yet, courts have emphasized again and again that errors of commission or omission, or tactics which misfire, are not sufficient to show that defendant was deprived of his right to effective assistance of counsel.[35] Some courts have insisted that appointed counsel should be required to perform at a higher level than retained counsel, presumably on the ground that selection of counsel by the state makes the state more responsible than one retained. The logic of this is not overwhelming, since the state grants the license to practice, and many defendants who fail to qualify as indigents have little realistic chance of counsel.

Appeal

The right to counsel in appellate proceedings in federal courts is based on 28 U.S.C.§1915 (1970). According to this section, any court of the United States may appoint counsel for an indigent defendant who may then take an appeal in forma pauperis. In this manner all normal court costs are waived. The statute also requires, however, that "An appeal may not be taken in forma pauperis if the trial court certifies in writing that it is not taken in good faith."[36] Consequently, much of the earlier litigation in this area was concerned with the trial court's discretion in finding that the appeal was not being taken in good faith. In the 1957 case of Johnson v. United States,[37] the Court held that the finding of the trial court was not final, and could be reversed on appeal. The Court also stated that under the rule in Johnson v. Zerbst,[38] the Court of Appeals must afford counsel to an indigent who wishes to challenge the certification ruling.

A year later, the Court in Ellis v. United States, citing Johnson, pointed out that "In the absence of some evident improper motive, the applicant's good faith is established by the presentation of any issue that is not plainly frivolous."[39] The Court affirmed the indigent's right to have appointed counsel to help him and said that such counsel must be an advocate for the defendant rather than an amicis curie screening agent of frivolous appeals for the Court.

The Court recognized that there will be instances in which appointed counsel may wish to withdraw. "If the court is satisfied that counsel has diligently investigated the possible grounds for appeal, and agrees with counsel's evaluation of the case, then leave to withdraw may be allowed and leave to appeal may be denied."[40]

In Coppedge v. United States[41] the Court, speaking through Chief Justice Warren, again affirmed the indigent's right to appointed counsel in cases where there has been no showing of bad faith. Warren, however, rejected a subjective standard of good faith (i.e., one discretionary with the trial judge), and opted for an objective standard of determining good faith. Warren concluded that "We consider a defendant's good faith in this type of case demonstrated when he seeks appellate review of any issue not frivolous."[42]

In Coppedge, Warren attempted to lay down workable standards which the lower courts could apply in determining whether an appeal was being made in good faith. In so doing, he weakened the requirements laid down by Congress which gave great discretion to the trial judge and severely restricted that discretion.

The reason for the Chief Justice's concern is reflected in Jones v. United States in which the Court of Appeals in a per curiam decision pointed out that ". . . grounds appearing 'frivolous' to one judge may constitute reversible error in the eyes of another."[43] To support this statement the Court had some impressive statistics. The Court pointed out:

From September 1, 1957—February 28, 1959, we decided 24 appeals in which we granted leave to appeal in forma pauperis although the District Court had previously denied leave on the ground that the appeal lacked merit. *We reversed the conviction in 11 of the 24 cases.* In 6 of the other cases the convictions were affirmed by split decisions. Thus in 17 of the 24 cases at least one judge of this court thought the conviction should be reversed. In all 17 of the cases, the Government had opposed the petition for leave to appeal in forma pauperis.

A free society should be ready to assume the burden of infinitely more than 24 appeals to avert 11 miscarriages of justice. Concern for our docket should not attenuate the right of every indigent to point out, with the aid of counsel what may prove to be errors. If time of the bench and bar is spent in a review of cases lacking merit, it is the price we must pay for a system of justice that shields the poor man from "invidious discrimination"[44] [quoting Griffin v. Illinois]

In short, the Warren Court had evidence, nor merely visceral feelings, that the poor were being treated unfairly in the appellate procedure. In the federal counsel cases, Johnson, Ellis, and Coppedge, the Supreme Court took steps to try and remove the inequalities of the appellate system. The federal system is a safe place to start. Hardly anyone questions the right of the Supreme Court to set standards of procedure in federal courts. These decisions, however, were precursers of the Supreme Court's applying these same federal standards to the states.

Griffin v. Illinois[45] was an early indication that the Warren court meant to set the standards for the states in appellate procedures. In this case the Court held that the equal protection clause of the fourteenth amendment gave indigents the right to a transcript from which they could prepare an appeal. Perhaps as important as the decision itself, was the flavor of the language in which it was couched. Justice Black states: "There is no meaningful distinction between a rule which would deny the poor the right to defend themselves in a trial court and one which effectively denies the poor an adequate appellate review according to all who have money enough to pay the costs in advance—[At] all stages of the proceedings the Due Process and Equal Protection Clauses protect persons like petitioners from invidious discrimination."[46] It was a natural next step to hold in Douglas v. California that in first appeals "granted as a matter of right to rich and poor alike . . . from a criminal conviction"[47] it is reversible error for the state to refuse to appoint counsel to an indigent defendant.

The Douglas protection does not apply to instances in which the defendant wishes to take a non-discretionary appeal. The logic of this position is not apparent. Why should it be easier for a rich man to appeal to the Supreme Court than a poor one? If anything, the argument would seem to be stronger for appointing counsel in cases of discretionary appeals. A prisoner who can fill out the proper forms in a non-discretionary appeal can at least assure himself of his day in court. In discretionary appeals, however, merely getting into the court may be half the battle. An indigent defendant will usually have little expertise in presenting legal issues in such a way as to arouse the interest of a Supreme Court Justice who must necessarily give each discretionary appeal less than his full attention.

In Douglas, the defendants were accused of 13 felonies including robbery, assault with a deadly weapon, and assault with intent to commit murder. There is no indication, therefore, that the Douglas doctrine would apply to a misdemeanor case. People v. Sanders[48] specifically holds that there is not a right to appointed counsel in appeals of misdemeanor cases.

A final question raised by the Douglas case concerns the possible obligations of a court-appointed attorney who feels that the grounds for appeal are in fact frivolous. In Anders v. California,[49] the Court rejected California's procedure by which a judge might accept a letter from the attorney that he felt there were no valid grounds for appeal. Instead, the Court laid down the additional requirement that the attorney file a brief containing any possible arguments for the defendant,[50] although as the dissenters argued, such a brief was unlikely to change the result.

Once an Anders-type brief has been filed, there is no obligation on the part of the court to appoint a second counsel if it feels there would be no point in doing so.[51]

Post-Conviction Right to Counsel—Sentencing, Parole, Probation

In the 1947 case of Townsend v. Burke, the Supreme Court, speaking through Justice Jackson, ruled that the absence of appointed counsel at sentencing, "when aggravated by circumstances showing that is resulted in the person actually being taken advantage of, or prejudiced, does make out a case of violation of due process."[52]

The leading case construing the right to counsel at the sentencing stage is Mempa v. Rhay,[53] which has caused no little confusion in the lower courts. Mempa was convicted of joy riding and placed on probation. Under Washington procedure[54] his sentence was deferred. Subsequently, he was involved in a burglary and his probation was revoked. At this time he was sentenced to a ten-year term in the penitentiary with a recommendation that he be paroled after one year. Mempa, however, was not afforded an attorney at the probation revocation-sentencing procedure. On appeal, the Supreme Court reversed, in a decision whose scope has yet to be finally determined. The narrowest interpretation is that Mempa only assures a right to counsel at sentencing. That this is the narrowest construction was made clear in McConnell v. Rhay.[55] In this case, which applied Mempa retroactively, the Court, in a per curiam decision, stated:

> This Court's decisions on a criminal defendant's right to counsel at trial, *Gideon v. Wainwright*, 372 U.S. 335 (1963); at certain arraignments, *Hamilton v. Alabama*, 368 U.S. 52 (1961); and on appeal, *Douglas v. California*, 372 U.S. 353 (1963), have been applied retroactively. The right to counsel at *sentencing* is no different.[56] [emphasis added]

In this sense, Mempa can be seen as one more step in a progression. Under the old Betts v. Brady rule, there was no right to counsel at trial unless special circumstances were alleged. Townsend was decided when Betts was still good law. Hence it is not surprising that it should have been couched in language stressing "aggravated circumstances," a rationale merely consistent with the Betts approach. When the Court in 1963 abandoned the Betts "fair trial" rationale, the reasoning behind Townsend became suspect. Mempa applies absolutely the right to counsel provided in Gideon to indigents at the time of sentencing.[57]

The source of confusion in this case comes from Justice Marshall's statement that: "All we decide here is that a lawyer must be afforded at this proceeding whether it be labeled a revocation or probation or deferred sentencing."[58]

The perplexing question about Mempa is to what procedures other than that of Washington does it apply? Does it stand merely for the proposition that one is entitled to counsel at sentencing? At probation revocation? Or does it cover all post-conviction hearings?[59] Justice Marshall's statement based on whether the proceeding is labeled deferred sentence or probation revocation, seemingly implies that Mempa applies to probation revocation hearings as well.

Surprisingly, however, many lower courts have construed Mempa to apply only to sentencing.[60] Proponents of this position rely on the fact that Justice Marshall pointed out how valuable it would be to have counsel at sentencing. Secondly, they point out that the facts of Mempa differ from a normal probation revocation proceeding in which sentence has already been imposed. Third, they point out that probation is not a matter of right; hence there is no right to counsel either based on the sixth amendment, or on the due process clause of the fourteenth.

On the other hand, there is a series of cases holding that there is a right to counsel at probation revocation.[61] Perhaps the best reasoned of these cases is the Hewett case in which Judge Winter[62] stated:

As we read *Mempa* we are persuaded, unlike the majority of the decisions which deny the right to counsel, that it cannot be limited to its narrow factual context. The principle which undergirds that decision is broad indeed, "appointment of counsel for an indigent is required at *every stage* of a criminal proceeding where substantial rights of a criminal accused may be affected." [emphasis supplied] 389 U.S. at 134, 88 S.Ct. at 257. While the right to counsel applies to "criminal proceedings," we have little doubt that the revocation of probation is a stage of criminal proceedings. Even if a new sentence is not imposed, it is the event which makes operative the loss of liberty.[63]

It should be pointed out that probation revocation is not an administrative matter. The hearings are before a judge; not an administrative body, and the judge must make a factual decision as to whether or not the terms of probation have in fact been violated. In some cases, the hearing may go into the question of whether or not a second crime has been committed. In short, we are not dealing here with a purely formal hearing in which the attorney's presence will make only an occasional difference. Rather, we are dealing with a proceeding in which the attorney's training and ability to marshall facts and cross-examine witnesses may be of crucial importance. If American courts are to avoid "invidious discrimination"[64] Mempa should be construed to apply to all probation revocation proceedings, not merely those in which sentence has been deferred.

Similar to the question of Mempa's application to probation revocation hearings is its application to parole hearings. As with probation revocation, there is abundant authority which indicates that there is no right to counsel at a parole revocation hearing on the basis of either the sixth amendment, due process,[65] or equal protection.[66]

The key to this line of cases is the case of Escoe v. Zerbst.[67] In holding that under federal law a person had a right to a hearing before his probation was revoked, the Court held that there was no constitutional protection which applied to probation revocation hearings. Cardozo stated: "Probation or suspension of sentence comes as an act of grace to one convicted of a crime, and may be coupled with such conditions in respect of direction as Congress may impose."[68] The logic of this dictum has been applied to parole revocation hearings and has been a chief weapon in the arsenal of those opposing a right to counsel at parole revocation hearings. A case affirming this point of view is Hyser v. Reed.[69] This case takes particular significance as it was written by Judge, now Chief Justice, Burger. In it he held that the sixth amendment applies only to criminal prosecutions; that parole revocation is not a criminal prosecution; and that, consequently, there is no sixth amendment right to counsel.

The 1964 case of Jones v. River,[70] illustrates another argument used by those who feel there is no right to counsel at a parole revocation proceeding. This argument reflects a reverence for administrative expertise. In rejecting a due process argument that there is a right to counsel at parole revocation proceedings the Court held:

> ... When a person accused of crime has been tried, defended, and if he wishes, has exhausted his rights of appeal, the period of contentious litigation is over. The problem then becomes one of an attempt at rehabilitation and the progress of that attempt should be measured, not by legal rules, but by the considered judgment of those who make it their professional business. So long as that judgment is fairly and honestly exercised, a judgment which is subject to judicial review, we think there is no place for *required* counsel representation in the matter of parole revocation.[71]

There are, however, cases which have held that there is a right to counsel in parole revocations. In Earnest v. Willingham, the Court stated that:

> the [Parole] Board is required to provide substantially the same type of hearing for one violator as another, so long as the Board allows retained counsel at revocation hearings it must provide such for those financially unable to hire one.[72]

While this case is certainly support for those who would urge a broad interpretation of Mempa, it does not base its decision on Mempa. Rather, the Court is concerned with a Griffin-like invidious discrimination. The problem with such a holding is that it permits regulations[73] such as one in effect at Leavenworth penitentiary in which no counsel, either hired or appointed, were permitted at parole eligibility hearings, a regulation which was upheld in Schwartzberg v. United States Board of Parole.[74]

Other cases, however, have interpreted Mempa to hold that there is a right to counsel in parole revocation hearings.[75] In Commonwealth v. Tinson, the Court stated:

> The Commonwealth argues that this case is different from [Mempa] because [Mempa] involved "sentencing" while here sentencing has already taken place. This distinction is completely untenable. We are helped not at all in determining constitutional rights by attaching artificial labels to describe the proceeding before us. Our reply to the commonwealth's argument here is the same as our reply in *Johnson*,[76] to the argument

that the actual sentencing was merely a formality: "an opportunity was present for action by counsel designed to foster his client's interest . . . [appellant] therefore had a right to counsel at that time."[77]

Thus, the area of post-conviction right to counsel is one which has seen a widening since Townsend v. Burke. In Townsend, the Court, operating in the era of Betts doctrine, was unwilling to hold that an absolute right to counsel existed at sentencing. Rather, it stated that when aggravated circumstances existed, lack of counsel might be grounds for a reversal on the grounds that due process had been violated. With the adoption of Gideon, the Townsend doctrine was bound to go. Mempa v. Rhay holds that there is an absolute right to counsel at sentencing, thus completing the process.

A question remains, and courts have split over whether Mempa applies to parole revocation and probation revocation proceedings. As these proceedings seriously affect people's liberties, and counsel can be of assistance, Mempa should be read to include the right to counsel at parole and probation revocations as well as at the sentencing stage.

COLLATERAL ATTACK PROCEEDINGS

In 1963 the Supreme Court, through the cases of Fay v. Noia,[78] Townsend v. Sain,[79] and Sanders v. United States,[80] significantly widened the scope of the federal court's power to grant writs of habeas corpus. In Townsend Chief Justice Warren listed six instances in which the federal court must grant an evidentiary hearing to a habeas corpus applicant.[81] Thus, with Townsend, the Court made it clear that under certain circumstances habeas corpus petitioners shall have evidentiary hearings as a matter of right.[82] The question then becomes what the petitioners' rights are at that hearing, in particular: Does the expanded doctrine of Townsend imply a right to counsel at habeas corpus proceedings?

An analysis of this question must start with the fact that the courts have consistently held that habeas corpus proceedings are civil in nature and, therefore, that the sixth amendment right to counsel is within the discretion of the trial judge.

The United States Supreme Court has not spoken directly on this point. Those who support a rule that the appointment of counsel should be left to the discretion of the trial court point to Sanders v. United States, where the Court stated:

[W]e think it clear that the sentencing court has discretion to ascertain whether the claim is substantial before granting a full evidentiary hearing.

In this connection, the sentencing court might find it useful to appoint counsel to represent the applicant. cf. *Coppedge v. United States,* 369 U.S. 438, 446.[83]

In some jurisdictions, however, there has been a move away from this interpretation. In particular, there has been concern that while the sixth amendment does not apply to collateral attack proceedings, the due process clause of the fourteenth amendment may. But no court has gone so far as to say that in all collateral attack proceedings it is a denial of due process to fail to appoint petitioner counsel when he seeks it.

A few courts, feeling that some petitioners should have counsel, have recognized that there is no right to counsel at a collateral attack proceeding and that appointment of counsel is within the sound discretion of the judge, but have held that in certain instances his failure to appoint counsel will constitute an abuse of discretion.[84] The leading case in this area is Roach v. Bennett.[85] In this case the Court went back to Townsend and pointed out that:

> We must recognize that under Townsend v. Sain, 372 U.S. 293, 83 S.Ct. 745, 9 L.Ed.2d 770 (1963) (see also Tit. 28 U.S.C. §2254), a state prisoner is entitled to a hearing *in federal court* where "the fact-finding procedure employed by the state court was not adequate to afford a full and fair hearing" and "the material facts were not adequately developed at the state-court hearing."

> Implicit in these standards for an "adequate" and "fair" hearing, we recognize that under certain circumstances, it is not only a better practice to assign counsel, but it can be a necessary demand for compliance with due process requirements. Cf. Hampton v. State of Oklahoma, 368 F.2d 9 (10 Cir. 1966); Anderson v. Heinze, 258 F.2d 479 (9 Cir. 1958); United States ex rel. Wissenfeld v. Wilkins, 281 F.2d 707, 716 (2 Cir. 1960). Certainly, anything less than a meaningful presentation of the petitioner's claims is the equivalent of no hearing at all.[86]

Perhaps at this point a useful comparison can be drawn between the right to counsel in appellate proceedures and the same right in collateral attack proceedings. In appellate proceedings at first there was very limited right to counsel. This right was expanded in Coppedge v. United States[87] to include all non-frivolous appeals in federal cases. Finally the right was made absolute, regardless of frivolousness, to non-discretionary appeals both state and federal in Douglas v. California.[88] The right to counsel in collateral attack has followed a similar pattern, but has not been able to take the final step from the Coppedge to the Douglas level. Rather, Roach seems quite analogous to Coppedge. Roach only provides a right to counsel in collateral attack proceedings once the evidentiary standard established in Townsend and Sanders has been met. Hence, as in Coppedge, the right to counsel remains conditional.

A similar right may arise through an equal protection argument. In Griffin v. Illinois[89] the Court held that it was necessary to provide a free transcript to indigents wishing to appeal in order to avoid "invidious discrimination." Similarly, in People v. Shipman, Chief Justice Traynor, citing Griffin, held that:

> When, however, an indigent petitioner has stated facts sufficient to satisfy the court that a hearing is required, his claim can no longer be treated as frivolous and he is entitled to have counsel appointed to represent him. If relief is denied after the hearing, he is entitled to counsel, on appeal subject to the limitations set forth in the Nash case, supra, 61 A.C. 338, 39 Cal. Rptr. 205, 393 P.2d 405, for the issues involved may be as substantial as those that may be raised on appeal from a judgment of conviction.[90]

In this case Traynor specifically rejected the Douglas rationale and adopted a test of frivolousness—exactly the test which was applied in appellate proceedings under Coppedge.

The reluctance of the courts to declare an absolute right to counsel to petitioners in collateral attack proceedings is understandable. Of the thousands of collateral attacks which prisoners make each year, only a tiny fraction are more than frivolous.[91] As the Supreme Court held in Sanders, there is no right to a full evidentiary hearing in every petition of habeas corpus. Where, however, an evidentiary hearing is held, and the training and expertise of a lawyer might be of aid, the due process requirement of the fourteenth amendment should be broad enough to afford every person a right to counsel.

To say that an indigent can have a fair hearing without counsel is to ignore the lessons of Gideon and Douglas. If we are to have a system in which rich and poor are treated equally before the law, a lawyer must be afforded the indigent client in situations in which a legal calculation would be of value. This includes all hearings in which matters of fact or law must be decided upon by the court.

COUNSEL IN JUVENILE AND OTHER COMMITMENT PROCEEDINGS

In Re Gault[92] provided that in the adjudicatory phase of any juvenile proceeding which might result in commitment, the alleged offender has, among others, the right to be advised of his right to retain counsel, and, if unable to afford counsel, to have counsel appointed unless waived. As the opinion of the Court indicated, many of the states already had provisions by statute or rule for retained counsel's appearance, or notice of the right to assigned counsel, but the pattern of practice was spotty.

In the light of the professed objectives of juvenile proceedings, with paternalistic stress on rehabilitation, it appears that, the majority of youthful offenders lacked the assistance of counsel (before Gault) either because there was no legal requirement, the juvenile's or his parents' ifnorance of his right, the judge's lack of sympathy with legal provision of counsel causing inadequate advice, or an excessively ready waiver of the right by juvenile or parent.

Even after the decision in Gault it seems clear that juvenile courts still function for the most part without counsel for the alleged offender.[93] Quite different reasons explain this, but two seem pervasive. In the first place, juvenile proceedings, like many other decision points in the crime-correctional system, have not been viewed customarily as adversary in nature. Although the analogy may at first glance seem strained, juvenile proceedings resemble civil commitments (or even criminal commitments) for mentally ill persons.[94] The emphasis, in theory at least, is on treatment and early restoration to the community. These benevolent purposes have obscured and weakened the obvious need for safeguards for the affected person. Hence, embarrassed parents, especially those who have difficulty with their children, readily accept the juvenile judge as both judge and counselor, particularly if the cost of retaining counsel seems substantial. In criminal and civil commitment proceedings the medical profession, supported by nervous relatives and other interested parties (commonly the police and prosecutor in criminal commitments) are masters of the situation, with counsel either absent, as in most civil proceedings, or ill-equipped by training or experience to participate effectively as in the majority of criminal commitments.[95]

WAIVER AND NEGOTIATED PLEAS

In any proceeding in which the defendant has a right to counsel he may waive counsel if he choses to do so. In some cases the judge will refuse to accept the waiver, but such cases are exceptional. Before a court can accept a waiver, however, it must:

(1) Advise the defendant that he has the right to retain counsel and that time will be allowed for him to do so if need be, and if he is indigent counsel will be appointed for him at no cost if he so choses.

(2) Ascertain that the defendant knowingly, intelligently and unambiguously waives his right.

(3) Make a record that each of the above precautions has been taken.[96]

The history of the development of these safeguards has paralleled the development of the right to counsel. As early as Johnson v. Zerbst[97] Justice Black made the sensible suggestion that the facts and circumstances of a waiver should be placed in the record. Yet in numerous federal decisions following Zerbst waivers were upheld on the basis of dubious records.

Under the "fair trial" rule of the Betts period almost any evidence in the record that counsel had been waived was deemed sufficient to sustain a conviction. Thus it was held that failure to request counsel, a record of previous convictions, an expressed desire of the accused to represent himself, and written waivers were all sufficient evidences of waiver.

Only a clear showing of request and denial, typically in a capital case, or a waiver by an obviously incompetent defendant in non-capital cases were held to be denials of the right. Even in those few cases where a reversal was obtained, there was frequently an element of unfairness in the trial in addition to the failure of the court to secure a proper waiver.

The extent of this problem is reflected in Silverstein's classic study *Defense of the Poor,*[98] using 1962 (pre-Gideon) data. In 62 of 152 counties, Silverstein found 11 percent or more of defendants were without counsel.[99] Of these counties, waiver rates of 30 and 40 percent were not uncommon and one county in Georgia had a waiver rate of 85 percent.

There is also evidence that the method of assigning counsel to represent indigents will affect the waiver rate. Thus Silverstein found that only 4 out of 30 counties (13 percent) which utilized a public defender system had waiver rates of over 10 percent,[100] as contrasted to 58 out of 122 counties (48 percent) using an assigned counsel system.[101] Similarly Oaks, in his extensive study of the operation of federal district courts under the Criminal Justice Act of 1965, found that in the year following the Act's adoption waiver rates dropped from 20 to 17 percent.[102]

Oaks also underlined the importance of the habits of the particular court in assessing the waiver. Thus while 43 percent of the defendants in northern Mississippi were unrepresented, only 7 percent in southern New York were without counsel[103]

Quite obviously, relatively few defendants waive counsel and attempt to defend themselves. Most people who waive counsel have decided to plead guilty. The real problem of waiver, therefore, is normally bound up with the plea bargaining process. This fact takes on added significance, since, in our system of justice, a guilty plea is the rule, a plea of not guilty the exception.[104] Despite this fact, many guilty pleas are still taken without counsel.

This problem is extremely severe when one considers that plea bargaining is probably the area of criminal law least familiar to the layman. For instance, it has been my experience that many laymen are astounded to learn that the law will permit a defendant to plead guilty to a crime he did not in fact commit.

The need for an experienced negotiator in plea bargaining is also great. An attorney, knowledgeable about the possible defenses in a particular case, and who knows what normal standards of plea bargaining are, is in a much better position than his client to obtain the best possible disposition.[105] The point is that counsel can and does make a difference in even the simplest cases. Consequently, any standards of waiver should be extremely strict, and waiver should be accepted by judges only if a client insists that he does not want to see a lawyer.

METHODS OF AFFORDING REPRESENTATION

With the greatly expanded right to counsel came an administrative problem: How do you insure that indigent defendants actually receive counsel?[106] There are basically four schemes which are employed: (1) the assigned counsel system, (2) the voluntary defender system, (3) the public defender system, and (4) the mixed private-public system.[107]

Of the four systems now in use, the most prevalent in the United States has been assigned counsel. Under this system, the judge selects from among the members of the local bar an attorney to represent the indigent defendant. The appointments may be made either randomly or systematically. Under the random system, the judge selects an attorney, frequently one who is sitting in the back of the court room, and appoints him to represent the indigent. The problem with this method of appointment is that lawyers who hang around court rooms are frequently not the most qualified members of the bar. Other jurisdictions have a systematic system, in which all members of the local bar are appointed in regular order. A chief problem with this, however, is that a lawyer who does little besides estate planning and property work may suddenly be called to defend a client in a criminal trial. With virtually no experience in criminal work, and perhaps no trial experience at all, there is a serious question as to whether such attorneys can provide effective representation. Nor would a system relying solely on the appointment of criminal lawyers be an improvement. While this system would insure that the appointed lawyers are competent in the field of law, it would, in many communities, place such a heavy burden on such a small proportion of the bar as to be totally impracticable.

Assigned counsel systems also suffer from a severe lack of resources. In many jurisdictions assigned counsel are not compensated, and in the rest compensation is so small as to make the appointment financially disadvantageous to the assigned counsel. Additionally, there are practically never sufficient funds available for investigative and other costs necessary for the defense attorney to do an effective job of representation.[108] With such a disadvantageous position, there is a strong pressure on assigned counsel to dispose of his case quickly, or to go to trial with less than adequate preparation.

The assigned counsel system is not without its advantages. Of these perhaps the most important is that an assigned counsel, at least in theory, is free of political influences, and thus retains the independent relationship which traditionally exists between lawyer and client. Additionally, the assigned counsel system keeps many members of the bar in touch with the criminal courts as well as providing many young lawyers with valuable experience.

The second method of providing representation for indigents is by means of a voluntary defender system. Under this system an office is created which is funded by private sources. The courts may then refer all indigent defendants to this defender office. Indigent defendants are thus able to receive experienced, capable counsel, and, if the organization is sufficiently financed, may have adequate investigatory resources as well. Because of its independent nature, a voluntary system is free from political interference and can provide an effective defense for its client. The major drawback to such a system is that it is very difficult to maintain an office of the size required in a large urban area to properly represent all indigent defendants.

Increasingly, the most common type of representation available to the urban indigent defendant is the public defender. Public defender offices may be organized by city or state and are funded and controlled by the government. They have the advantage of being able to provide counsel experienced in criminal defense practice in all serious cases and many less serious ones.

There are, however, two major disadvantages to the public defender system. First, in most cities, providing adequate defense to indigents does not have a high political priority. Particularly in an era when popular opinion is against "coddling criminals," there is little incentive for the legislature or city counsel to appropriate large sums of money for a public defender office. Consequently, many public defender offices are woefully understaffed in terms not only of lawyers, but in investigative and clerical resources as well. This puts great pressure on each public defender to get his cases out of the way quickly. At times it takes a certain fortitude to keep the interests of each client in mind, rather than simply negotiating a plea in every case.

Even in cases which are taken to trial, the instances in which the public defender must ask the bailiff who the defendant is, and then quickly take him out to the hall to confer are all too numerous.

Additionally, public defender offices are bureaucracies. Consequently, there may be great internal pressure on the defenders to keep from alienating anybody by making an overzealous defense. Finally, because the public defender is hired by the state, there is a suspicion among many people, including defendants, that he is in league with the District Attorney and the judge, and is not an independent lawyer with only the interests of his client at stake.[109]

In spite of shortcomings, the better organized defender or defender-plus systems seem more effective in providing counsel. The federal system, at one time among the least effective, has now created a method through the Criminal Justice Act (as amended) that seems to ensure that if there is a waiver, it will be made after a clear offer of counsel. Three states, Alaska, New Jersey, and Colorado, have statewide, state-funded public defender systems. When a defender is available in every trial court, as is now the case in Colorado, the tendency is for the judge to ask counsel to speak with the defendant before accepting a waiver. In a few of the better organized county defender offices, a jail census is maintained on a daily basis by the public defender so that counsel can begin the defense or bargaining process on essentially the same basis as the accused.

It would be a distortion of reality to claim that a defender system solves all problems. If it is used on a state-wide basis it may increase state costs simply because the more casual assigned counsel system missed so many defendants. In Colorado for fiscal 1971 the cost of operating the statewide defender system was approximately $1.15 million compared with the other costs of all trial courts of approximately $10.34 million. Certainly, the cost of providing counsel for all defendants, even those who may decide subsequently to waive their right to counsel, seems minimal in light of the promise of greater fairness.

The fourth and least pervasive method of providing representation is the so-called mixed private-public system. Under this system an office is set up under the voluntary system, but public funds are appropriated to finance it. This system is, therefore, more independent than a public defender system, since the state has no bureaucratic control over the hiring and firing of personnel. Additionally the office has the advantages of the voluntary system, but has an additional source of funding.

CONCLUSION

The progression of the right to counsel, at least as far as "black letter law" is concerned, has been steady. Starting with the English right to retain counsel, the law in the United States arrived at a plateau in the 1930s, ensuring the indigent the right to counsel in capital cases where special need could be shown to provide the defendant with a fair trial. In the 1960s, the Warren court continued this progression by ensuring all indigents accused of serious crimes the right to be defended by counsel at virtually every stage of the criminal proceedings. And in Argersinger, a "strict constructionist" court has further expanded the scope of the right, so that indigent misdemeanor defendents are now protected. It remains to be seen whether Argersinger signals an end or the first step in a new progression.

The right to counsel in practice, however, has not kept pace with the broad sweep of the Court's decisions. Too often counsel is appointed too late to adequately protect his client. Similarly appointed counsel is frequently overburdened and underpaid. Seldom does he have adequate investigatory resources to prepare his case. Some of these problems are institutional—it is difficult to provide thorough, non-bureaucratic counsel to all indigents who need it. Nevertheless, the entire cost of the American Criminal Justice system is only $5 billion per year,[110] not a small sum to be sure, but hardly more than we spend on the federal space program alone.

If the practice of providing counsel to indigent defendants is to keep pace with the progress which has been made in legal doctrine, our society will have to spend considerably more than it has in the past. Only in this way can it come close to fulfilling its promise that no American shall be deprived of his freedom without the assistance of effective counsel.

NOTES

1. The material on the role of counsel at the interrogation-investigation state is covered in Chapter 3.

2. W. Beaney, *The Right to Counsel in American Courts* (1955). The book describes the historic development of the right to counsel and documents the great variations which existed in the United States prior to 1955. See also D. Fellman, *The Defendant's Rights* (1958); Fellman, "The Constitutional Right to Counsel in Federal Courts," 30 Neb. L. Rev. 559 (1951); Fellman, "The Federal Right to Counsel in State Courts," 31 Neb. L. Rev. 15 (1951); Fellman, "The Right to Counsel under State Law," Wis. L. Rev. 281 (1955).

3. See W. Beaney, supra note 2, at 238-239.

4. 287 U.S. 45 (1932).

5. Id. at 69.

6. 316 U.S. 455 (1942).

7. For a discussion of the "fair trial rule" see W. Beaney, supra note 2, Chapter 5.

8. Kamisar, "The Right to Counsel and the Fourteenth Amendment: A Dialogue on 'The Most Pervasive Right' of an Accused," 30 U. Chi. L. Rev. 1 (1962).

9. 304 U.S. 458 (1938).

10. See, e.g., Von Moltke v. Gillies, 332 U.S. 708 (1948); Annot., Right to Counsel, 93 L. Ed. 2d 137 (1950).

11. Hamilton v. Alabama, 368 U.S. 52 (1961).

12. See W. Beaney, supra note 2, at 230; Annot., Right to Counsel, 9 L. Ed 2d 1260, 1264 (1963).

13. 367 U.S. 643 (1961).

14. 373 U.S. 335 (1963).

15. Argersinger v. Hamlin, 407 U.S. 25 (1972).

16. 399 U.S. 66 (1970).

17. The President's Commission on Law Enforcement and Administration of Justice, *The Challenge of Crime in a Free Society,* 128-129 (1967). See *Law Enforcement in the Metropolis* (D. McIntyre, Jr. ed. 1967).

18. For a discussion of the plight of indigent defendants in misdemeanor cases see H. James, *Crisis in the Courts* (1968).

19. Judicial Research Foundation, *Struggle for Equal Justice,* 32 (1969).

20. Junker, "The Misdemeanant's Right to Counsel in American State Courts," 43 Wash. L. Rev. 719 (1968).

21. Colo. R. Crim. P. 44.

22. The applicable federal rule is Fed. R. Crim. P. 5(b). Similar requirements are found in the states' rules or statutes.

23. In some Colorado counties the public defender's office, with the assistance of law students, is able to provide counsel at the initial appearance.

24. L. Silverstein, 1 *Defense of the Poor in Criminal Cases in American State Courts,* 93 (1965).

25. See Steele, Jr., "Right to Counsel at the Grand Jury Stage of Criminal Proceedings," 36 Mo. L. Rev. 192 (1971). This is an excellent analysis attacking the present manner of using the grand jury as a device for reaching foregone conclusions without regard for the defendant's rights.

26. 399 U.S. 1 (1970).

27. Id. at 9. See Jennings v. Superior Court, 166 Cal. 2d 867, 428 P.2d 304, 59 Cal Rptr. 440 (1967). The case demonstrated how valuable counsel's services may be at the preliminary hearing stage.

28. Chapman v. California, 380 U.S. 18 (1967).

29. 399 U.S. 1, 17 (1970).

30. Id. at 22.

31. 368 U.S. 52 (1961).

32. 373 U.S. 59 (1963) (per curiam).

33. Coleman v. Alabama, 399 U.S. 1 (1970); United States v. Wade, 388 U.S. 218 (1967).

34. 372 U.S. 335 (1963).

35. Cf. Note, "The Right to Counsel and the Neophyte Attorney," 24 Rutgers L. Rev. 378 (1970).

36. 28 U.S.C. §1915 (1970).

37. 352 U.S. 565 (1957).

38. 304 U.S. 458 (1938).

39. 356 U.S. 674 (1958).

40. Id. at 675.

41. 369 U.S. 438 (1961).

42. Id. at 445.

43. 266 F.2d 924, 926 n.5 (D.C. Cir. 1959).

44. Id. at 926.

45. 351 U.S. 12 (1955).

46. Id. at 18.

47. 372 U.S. 353, 356 (1963).

48. 40 Ill. 2d 458, 240 N.E.2d 627 (1968).

49. 386 U.S. 738 (1967).

50. For an interesting case on the ramifications of Anders see In Re Smith, 90 Cal. Rptr. 1, 3 Cal. App. 3d 92, 474 P.2d 969 (1970).

51. See In Re Nash, 61 Cal. 2d 491, 393 P.2d 405 (1964); Fredericks v. Reinche, 152 Conn. 501, 208 A.2d 756 (1965); McLaughlin v. State, 32 Wis. 2d 124, 145 N.W.2d 153 (1960).

52. 334 U.S. 736, 739 (1947).

53. 389 U.S. 128 (1967).

54. Wash. Rev. Code Ann. §§9.95.200, 9.95.210 (1961).

55. 393 U.S. 2 (1968).

56. Id. at 3.

57. A court's error in appointing counsel must, however, be prejudicial. In Collins v. Commonwealth, 433 S.W.2d 63 (Ky. 1968) the court held that where the jury fixed the penalty at the statutory minimum there was no error.

58. Mempa v. Rhay, 389 U.S. 128, 137 (1967).

59. For discussion of the problems facing a prisoner in post-conviction hearings see Jacob and Sharma, "Justice After Trial: Prisoner's Need for Legal Services in the Criminal-Correctional Process," 18 Kan. L. Rev. 495 (1950).

60. See United States ex rel Bishop v. Brurly, 288 F. Supp. 401 (E.D. Pa. 1968); Holden v. United States, 285 F. Supp. 380 (E.D. Tex. 1968); Sammons v. United States, 285 F. Supp. 100 (S.D. Tex. 1968); United States v. Hartsell, 277 F. Supp. 993 (E.D. Tenn. 1967); Petition of Dubois, 84 Nev. 562, 445 P.2d 354 (1968); State ex rel Riffle v. Thorne, 153 W. Va. 76, 168 S.E.2d 810 (1969).

61. See Hewett v. North Carolina, 415 F. 2d 1316 (4th Cir. 1969); Ashworth v. United States, 391 F.2d 245(6th Cir. 1968); State v. Seymour, 98 N.J. Super. 526, 237 A.2d 900 (N.J. App. Div. 1968) (applying New Jersey laws); Perry v. Williard 247 Or. 145, 427 P.2d 1020 (1967).

62. For followers of Supreme Court politics it should be noted that Clement Haynsworth wrote a concurring opinion in which he subscribed to the views expressed by Judge Winter.

63. Hewett v. North Carolina, 415 F.2d 1316, 1322 (4th Cir. 1969).

64. Griffin v. Illinois, 351 U.S. 12, 18 (1956).

65. See Menechino v. Oswald, 430 F.2d 403 (2nd Cir. 1970); Earnest v. Willingham, 406 F.2d 681 (10th Cir. 1969); Rose v. Haskins, 388 F.2d 269 (6th Cir. 1968); Williams v. Patterson, 389 F.2d 374 (10th Cir. 1968); Schwartzberg v. United States Bd. of Parole, 399 F.2d 277 (10th Cir. 1968); Jones v. Rivers, 338 F.2d 862 (4th Cir. 1968); Dunn v. California, 401 F.2d 346 (9th Cir. 1968); Hyser v. Reed, 318 F.2d 225 (D.C. Cir. 1963); Fleming v. Tate, 156 F.2d 848 (D.C. Cir. 1946); Johnson v. Stucker, 203 Kan. 253, 453 P.2d 35 (1969) cert. denied, 396 U.S. 904 (1969); Robinson v. Cox, 77 N.M. 55, 419 P.2d 253 (1966); Broguglio v. New York State, 24 N.Y. 21, 298 N.Y.S.2d 704 (1969); State ex rel. London v. Pardon and Parole Comm., 2 Ohio St. 2d 224, 208 N.E.2d 137 (1965); Beal v. Turner, 22 Utah 2d 418, 454 P.2d 524 (1969).

66. See Martinez v. Patterson, 429 F.2d 844 (10th Cir. 1970).

67. 295 U.S. 490 (1935).

68. Id. at 492-493.

69. 318 F.2d 225 (D.C. Cir. 1963).

70. 338 F.2d 862 (4th Cir. 1964).

71. Id. at 874. See Rose v. Haskins, 388 F.2d 91 (6th Cir. 1968). Neither of the Jones or Rose decisions, however, was based in any way on the Mempa decision. In Broguglio v. New York State Bd. of Parole, 24 N.Y. 21, 298 N.Y.S.2d 704 (1969) the court distinguished Mempa citing McConnell v. Rhay, 393 U.S. 2 (1968), and holding Mempa to be strictly a sentencing case with no implications for either probation or parole revocation hearings.

72. 406 F.2d 681, 684 (10th Cir. 1969).

73. 28 C.F.R. §2.16 (Supp. 1971).

74. 399 F.2d 277 (10th Cir. 1968).

75. People ex rel. Combs v. La Vallee, 29 A.D.2d 128, 286 N.Y.S.2d 600 (1968).

76. Commonwealth v. Johnson, 428 Pa. 210, 230 A.2d 805 (1968). (In which the court held there was a right to counsel at the time of sentencing.)

77. 433 Pa. 328, 249 A.2d 549, 551-552 (1969). See Menechino v. Warden, 27 N.Y.2d 376, 318 N.Y.S.2d 449 (1971).

78. 372 U.S. 391 (1963).

79. 372 U.S. 293 (1963).

80. 373 U.S. 1 (1963).

81. "If (1) the merits of the factual dispute were not resolved in the state hearing; (2) the state factual determination is not fairly supported by the record as a whole; (3) the fact finding procedure employed by the state court was not adequate to afford a full and fair hearing; (4) there is a substantial allegation of newly discovered evidence; (5) the material facts were not adequately developed at the state-court hearing or (6) for any reason it appears that the state trier of fact did not afford the habeas applicant a full and fair fact hearing." 372 U.S. 293, 313 (1963).

82. See Hampton v. Oklahoma, 368 F.2d 9 (10th Cir. 1966); Dillon v. United States, 307 F.2d 445 (9th Cir. 1962); Larson v. Bennett, 160 N.W.2d 303 (Iowa 1968), cert denied, 393 U.S. 1036 (Iowa 1969); Brewer v. Bennett, 161 N.W.2d 749 (Iowa 1968).

83. 373 U.S. 1, 21 (1963).

84. See United States ex rel. Wissenfeld v. Wilkins, 281 F.2d 707 (2nd Cir. 1960).

85. 392 F.2d 743 (8th Cir. 1968). Some state courts have been willing to apply the due process approach while others have not. A note to Roach v. Bennett, supra at 748 n.3 states:

> Some courts have presented different approaches. E.g. in Alaska in a post conviction proceeding appointment of counsel is provided if the petition presents an issue requiring a hearing. Nichols v. State, 425 P.2d 247 (Alaska 1967). The rule is similar in Idaho. Austin v. State, 91 Idaho 404, 422 P.2d 71 (1966), but cf. Wilbanks v. State, 91 Idaho 608, 428 P.2d 527 (1967). In New York, an indigent is entitled to counsel upon request. People ex rel Jenks v. McMann, 27 A.D.2d 580, 275 N.Y.S.2d 399 (N.Y. App. 1966). Only a "possible basis" need be suggested. People ex rel. Williams v. La Vallee, 19 N.Y.2d 238, 225 N.E.2d 735 (1967). In Maryland appointment is required by court rule. Taylor v. Director, Patuxent Institution, 1 Md. App. 23, 266 A.2d 358 (1967). In Missouri it is discretionary, but preferred in all instances. Stave v. Garner, 412 S.W.2d 155 (Mo. Sup. Ct. 1967). In Kansas, only if substantial questions of law or triable issues of fact are presented. Carter v. State, 199 Kan. 290, 428 P.2d 758 (1967). See also Harper v. State, 201 So.2d 65 (Fla. 1967). It is reversible error in Pennsylvania to fail to make an appointment. Commonwealth v. Hoffman, 426 Pa. 226, 232 A.2d 623 (1967). See also Commonwealth v. Mitchell, 427 Pa. 395, 235 A.2d 148 (1967) where it is pointed out that the Pennsylvania rule makes appointment mandatory.

86. Id. at 748.
87. 369 U.S. 438 (1962).
88. 372 U.S. 353 (1963).
89. 351 U.S. 12 (1955).
90. 62 Cal. 2d 226, 230, 397 P.2d 993, 997, 42 Cal Rptr. 1, 5 (1965).
91. Brown v. Allen, 344 U.S. 443, 536-537 (1952). (Justice Jackson's concurring opinion.)
92. 387 U.S. 1 (1967).
93. Lefstein, Stapleton & Teitelbaum, "In Search of Juvenile Justice: Gault and Its Implementation," Law & Soc. Rev. 491 (1969).
94. See Heryford v. Parker, 396 F.2d 393 (1968) noted in 43 N.Y.U.L. Rev. 1004 (1968).
95. See *The Mentally Disabled and the Law* (F. Lindman & D. McIntyre eds. 1961); A. Matthews, Jr., *Mental Disability and the Criminal Law* (1970); R. Rock, *Hospitalization and Discharge of the Mentally Ill,* 157 (1968); Cohen, "The Function of the Attorney and the Commitment of the Mentally Ill," 44 Tex. L. Rev. 424 (1966); Kutner, "The Illusion of Due Process in Commitment Proceedings," 57 Nw. U. L. Rev. 383 (1962).
96. Miranda v. Arizona, 384 U.S. 436 (1966).
97. 304 U.S. 458 (1938).
98. L. Silverstein, 1 *Defense of the Poor in Criminal Cases in American State Courts,* (1965).
99. Id. at 91.
100. Id. at 98.
101. Id. at 91.

102. Subcommittee on Constitutional Rights of Senate Committee on the Judiciary, 90th Cong., 2d Sess., *The Criminal Justice Act in the Federal District Courts* 85 (Comm. Print 1969).

103. Ibid.

104. See L. Silverstein, supra note 98, at 90.

105. See D. Newman, *Conviction: The Determination of Guilt or Innocence Without Trial* (1966).

106. In addition to providing counsel for the indigent is the problem of securing counsel for the unpopular defendant. For a discussion of this problem see *Southern Justice*, 127 (L. Friedman, ed. 1964); Alexander, "The Right to Counsel for the Politically Unpopular," 22 L. in Transition 19 (1962); Note, "The Unpopular Criminal Defendant: His Right, Lawyer's Duty, Ways of Ensuring Both," 54 Ky. L. J. 584 (1964).

107. For case studies in particular states evaluating the methods of appointing counsel see Oaks & Lehman, *A Criminal Justice System and the Indigent: A Study of Chicago and Cook County* (1968); Benjamin & Pedeliski, "The Minnesota Public Defender System and Criminal Law Process," 4 L. & Soc'y Rev. 279 (1969); Bing & Rosenfeld, "The Quality of Justice: In the Lower Criminal Courts of Metropolitan Boston," 7 Crim. L. Bull. 393 (1971); Norris & Hammond, "The Right to Counsel, A Study of the Defense of Indigent Persons Accused of Crime in Michigan," 42 U. Det. L. J. 397 (1965); Palmer, "Indigent Defender Systems in New York: A Preliminary Report," 40 N.Y.S.B.J. 7 (1968); Note, "The Right to Effective Counsel and New York City Legal Aid," 1 N.Y.U. Rev. L. & Soc. Change 1 (1971).

For discussion on recurrent problems of implementing counsel appointment see *The Scales of Justice*, 91 (A. Blumberg, ed. 1970); A. Blumberg, *Criminal Justice* (1967); A Frebach, *The Rationing of Justice* (1964); *The Courts, The Public and the Law Explosion* (H. Jones, ed. 1965); Special Comm. of the New York City Bar Assoc. & the Nat'l Legal Aid & Defender Assoc., *Equal Justice for the Accused* (1959).

108. See generally Note, "The Indigent's Right to an Adequate Defense: Expert and Investigational Assistance in Criminal Proceedings," 55 Cornell L. Rev. 632 (1970); Comment, "Assistance in Addition to Counsel for Indigent Defendants: The Need for, the Lack of, the Right to," 16 Vill. L. Rev. 323 (1970).

109. See G. Smith, *A Statistical Analysis of Public Defender Activities* (1970); Casper, "Did You Have a Lawyer When You Went to Court? No, I Had a Public Defender," 1 Yale Rev. L & Soc. Action 4 (1971).

110. Ladinsky, "Lawyer Manpower in the Criminal Justice System," 61 Current History 9, 49 (1971).

Chapter 6

THE RIGHT TO BAIL REVISITED: A DECADE OF PROMISE WITHOUT FULFILLMENT

Excessive bail shall not be required

From the Eighth Amendment
to the U.S. Constitution

PATRICIA M. WALD graduated from Connecticut College for Women, 1948, and Yale Law School, 1951. She has served on the President's Commission on Crime in the District of Columbia and the President's Commission on Law Enforcement and Administration of Criminal Justice, as well as consulting work for the Office of Criminal Justice, Department of Justice, and for the National Advisory Committee on Civil Disorders and the National Commission on the Causes and Prevention of Violence. She has also been active in community, bail, and drug abuse law. She is author of *Bail in the United States* (1964), *Law and Poverty* (1965), and several law review pieces.

Chapter 6

THE RIGHT TO BAIL REVISITED: A DECADE OF PROMISE WITHOUT FULFILLMENT

PATRICIA M. WALD

I. THE RIGHT TO BAIL

A. The Purpose of Bail

Bail is the security that is required of someone accused of a crime to ensure that he will return for trial. It originated in medieval England as a way to relieve sheriffs of the cost and trouble of keeping people in the local gaols until visiting justices arrived on the scene to try them. Prisoners were released to personal friends or acquaintances who would vouch for their return, and present themselves as hostages if the accused fled (Freed and Wald, 1964; "Bail, An Ancient Practice Reexamined," 70 Yale L.J. 966, 1961). This kind of personal commitment still prevails in many countries. But in nineteenth-century America, the personal friend was replaced by the professional bail bondsman. In an urban, industrial and increasingly transient country, men did not always live out their lives in one place, and urban dwellers hesitated to become their brother's legal keeper. The commercial bondsman, for a price paid by the accused, would guarantee his appearance in court on pain of forfeiture of a sum on money set by the court. Bondsmen had no obligation to take clients they did not want or who could not pay their fees.

The basic purpose of bail, from society's point of view, has always been and still is to ensure the accused's reappearance for trial. But pretrial release serves other purposes as well, purposes recognized over the last decade as often dispositive of the fairness of the entire criminal proceeding. Pretrial release allows a man accused of crime to keep the fabric of his life intact, to maintain employment and family ties in the event he is acquitted or given a suspended sentence or probation. It spares his family the hardship and indignity of welfare and enforced separation. It permits the accused to take an active part in planning his defense with his counsel, locating witnesses, proving his capability of staying free in the community without getting into trouble.[1] In the past decade, studies have shown that those on pretrial release plead guilty less often, are convicted less often, go to prison less often following conviction than those detained before trial. This is true even when the study controls for factors such as employment at the time of arrest, retained or assigned counsel, family ties, past record and present charge. The factor of pretrial release alone shows up as a vitally controlling factor in the outcome of the trial and sentencing (Rankin, 1964;[2] Bellamy study, 1972).

The right to pretrial release also protects the integrity of our criminal justice system. The United States Supreme Court said:

> Unless this right to bail before trial is preserved, the presumption of innocence, secured only after centuries of struggle, would lose its meaning [Stack v. Boyle, 342 U.S. 4 (1951)].

B. When Bail Is Available and How It Is Set

Since colonial times, the majority of American citizens have enjoyed an absolute statutory or constitutional right to bail in noncapital crimes (Foote, 1965). On the other hand, if the charge is a capital one (or if they have already been convicted and are awaiting sentence or appeal) they have traditionally enjoyed only a discretionary right to bail. The Eighth Amendment of the United States Constitution grants a right to all United States citizens against "excessive bail," but it is silent on any explicit grant of an absolute right to bail. The Judiciary Act of 1789, however, did explicitly grant a right to bail in all noncapital cases before trial in the federal courts, a right, later embodied in Rule 46 of the Federal Rules of Criminal Procedure, which continued unchallenged until 1970 when the District of Columbia Court Reorganization and Criminal Procedure Act enacted preventive detention for certain felonies in the District of Columbia. Thus, the Supreme Court announced:

> From the passage of the Judiciary Act of 1789 . . . to the present Federal Rules of Criminal Procedure Rule 46(a)(1), federal law has unequivocally

provided that a person arrested for a non-capital offense shall be admitted to bail [Stack v. Boyle, 1951].

The vast majority of state constitutions (37) grant an absolute right to bail in noncapital cases; all but one (Illinois) have a constitutional prohibition against "excessive bail." Only a half-dozen states (i.e., Arizona, Maryland, New York, Texas, Virginia) do not grant an absolute right to bail in noncapital cases by either constitution or statute. Maine allows bail to be withheld for any crimes which at any time may have been capital. Rhode Island allows discretionary bail for crimes punishable by life imprisonment. Maryland excepts murder, burglary, rape and arson from the guarantee of bail; in New York, bail is in the judge's discretion for all felonies. Texas excepts an accused felon who has already been convicted of two prior felonies. Maryland and Arizona permit denial of bail for a crime committed while on pretrial release from another criminal charge. The District of Columbia allows pretrial preventive detention up to sixty days for a wide range of felonies. Juveniles are usually released or detained before trial at the discretion of the juvenile court, and, except in a few states, money bail is not ordinarily set for them.

But the constitutional or statutory right to have bail set has, however, never meant in practice an absolute right to freedom before trial. Until the past decade, judges almost always insisted on money bail or a surety bond from a bail bondsman before allowing an accused to go free pending trial. If the defendant could not afford the cash or the bondsman's price for standing surety, the defendant spent days or months—sometimes years—in jail until his trial. Although courts have always possessed inherent power to release accuseds without money deposit or surety bonds, until quite recently few judges used it. In 1966, a nationwide study of 11,000 felony defendants in 190 sample counties showed a median percentage of only 47 percent released before trial in large and medium sized counties and 39 percent in the smaller counties. In some counties, as few as 7 percent of all felony accuseds were released before trial (Silverstein, 1966).

Generally, state and federal laws and decisions provide that the amount or terms of bail shall be set by taking into account the nature of the offense charged, the weight of evidence against the accused, his finances, employment, record, moral character, family ties, past criminal record, and prior flights from custody. These factors are in theory to be considered only as indicators of his likelihood to show up for trial, not as indications of whether he will be a danger to the community meanwhile.

The range of conditions a judge may impose upon a pretrial defendant's release include:

Placing the person in the custody of a designated person or organization agreeing to supervise him during the release period

Restricting his right to travel, to associate with certain people or his place of abode

Requiring that he deposit cash or other security with the clerk of court (to be returned on performance of conditions of release)

Prohibiting possession of any dangerous weapon, indulgence in intoxicating liquors or drugs, or engaging in particular activities

Requiring that he report regularly to an officer of court or other designated supervisor

Any other condition necessary to assure appearance, including return to custody after certain hours (daytime or weekday work release)

Arizona law requires imposition of a condition of "good behavior" on felony defendants as well. [3]

In theory, every defendant should have the terms of his pretrial release set at an individualized hearing with counsel present (ABA Standards, 1968). But in practice, crowded court dockets often mean that bail is set pro forma based upon the charge and without regard to the individual characteristics of the defendant indicating reliability or nonreliability. In many jurisdictions, accuseds go free if they can pay the amounts listed in a bond schedule at the police precinct without ever going to court; otherwise, they must wait days or weeks for an individual arraignment. This kind of bond schedule as a substitute for prompt bail setting recently was declared unconstitutional by a federal court as a denial of due process and equal protection of the laws (Ackies v. Purdy, 322 F.Supp. 38 S.D. Fla. 1970).

Conditions originally set for release can generally be amended upon petition of either the prosecutor, the defense, or the court. Denial of a defendant's motion to reduce bail or change conditions to permit release is appealable (Stack v. Boyle, 1951; Moore, 1970). Pretrial release may also be revoked for failure to abide by the conditions set by the court, sometimes for new arrests or convictions, or for obstructing justice or threatening witnesses (ABA Standards, 1968) (Fernandez v. United States, 81 S.Ct. 642 (1961) (U.S. v. Gilbert, 425 F.2d 490, C.A. D.C. 1969).

II. BAIL REFORM

A. The Promise of Bail Reform

The decade of the 1960s saw the emergence of a significant bail reform effort in the United States. The effort drew upon the empirical studies of Caleb Foote and earlier critics of the money bail system which showed that:

Vast numbers of defendants spent months, even years, in jails before trial because they could not raise bail money;

The amount of bail set was generally based solely on the nature of the charge with little individual attention given to factors in the individual defendant's life that related to the likelihood he would flee;

The defendants who stayed in jail before trial for want of bail pled guilt or were convicted after trial more often and received prison sentences more often than those on bail and in virtually all cases lost their jobs and self-respect. Their families were often broken up and deprived of economic support;

The conditions in pretrial detention jails were usually worse than in the reformatories housing convicted prisoners;

Commercial bail bondsmen charged fees of 10 percent or more of the bond set by the court for doing virtually nothing;

Only a very small number of defendants (a few percent) actually fled to avoid trial (Freed and Wald, 1964).

Aroused by the insidious discrimination in the existing money bail system, reform efforts took two main routes; (1) investigative projects aimed at persuading judges to release more defendants on their own recognizance, and (2) legislation to require pretrial release when defendants met certain criteria. The Vera Foundation, sponsored by a civic-minded industrialist, Louis Schweitzer, mounted the Manhattan Bail Project in 1961, which sent law student investigators into the detention pens of New York City's teeming criminal courts to check out the residences, families, jobs, past records and other indicia of stability of defendants awaiting bail setting, and to make recommendations to the judges for the release without money bail of those with solid roots in the community. In the first year, the judges to whom the Vera investigators submitted their recommendations for release without money bail, based upon a point system for rating the accused's community ties, agreed to ROR (release on their own recognizance or promise to appear) prisoners in 59 percent of the cases. [4] That batting average later soared to a much higher percent. The project operated three years under Vera's auspices and released 3,500 defendants; the return rate of ROR'd defendants was 98.4 percent; there was no significant rate of rearrest while on release, and the released group fared far more successfully in acquittals, suspended sentences and probation than detained accuseds. At the end of the three years in 1964, Vera turned over the operation of the release project to the New York City Probation Department.

In the early sixties, too, Senator Sam Ervin of North Carolina of the Senate Subcommittee on Constitutional Rights of the Judiciary Committee began looking toward a legislative solution to the injustice of bail practices (Ervin, 1967). An Attorney General's Committee on Poverty and the Administration of Federal Criminal Justice, appointed by Attorney General Robert Kennedy, reported in 1963 on the appalling rates of pretrial detention due to indigency in 4 federal districts. (In one district 78 percent of the defendants could not raise $500 bail.) The study resulted in an Order to U.S. Attorneys to recommend release without money bail in federal courts whenever no substantial likelihood of flight existed. Bar Associations joined the ranks of bail reform with significant studies from the District of Columbia Junior Bar Section in 1963, and later in 1968 from the American Bar Association Project on Minimum Standards For Criminal Justice. In 1964, the Vera Foundation and the United States Department of Justice called together hundreds of key personnel in the state and federal criminal justice systems to urge them to undertake bail reform in their own communities (Proceedings of National Conference on Bail and Criminal Justice, 1964).

The President's Commission on Law Enforcement and the Administration of Criminal Justice in 1967 seconded the plea that bail projects be started to investigate defendants and recommend release without money bail whenever possible. It also suggested that legislation create a presumption in favor of such release (the Challenge of Crime in a Free Society, 1967). In the mid-sixties over 100 bail projects patterned after the Vera model were begun throughout the nation (Bail and Summons: 1965). In addition, several communities copied New York City's summons program which permitted the police themselves to release misdemeanants at the precinct if they had sufficient community ties. In 1970, New York City police released 27,000 arrestees at the stationhouse, thereby saving an estimated eight to ten hours of police time per case and a total of $2 million.

Legislative efforts at reform culminated on the federal level with the passage of the Bail Reform Act of 1966[5] (18 U.S. Code 3146). Applicable only to the federal courts and the District of Columbia, it (a) created a presumption in favor of release on recognizance without money before trial; (b) authorized a scale of "conditions of release" which the judge might impose during the pretrial period beginning with release on personal recognizance and an unsecured appearance bond and proceeding through third party custody, limitation of travel, residence or association, cash deposit of 10 percent of the amount of a bond into the court, returnable upon appearance, a surety bond, release into the community by day with return to custody at night, and finally any "other condition" thought appropriate to ensure that the defendant reappeared at trial. The judge was to make his decision on the proper conditions of release taking into account all "available information" about the nature and circumstances of the offense charged, the weight of the evidence, family ties, employment, financial resources, length of residence in the community, character and mental condition, record of convictions and appearances in prior cases. Regular rules of evidence did not apply to bail hearings.

Imposition of release conditions that resulted in the arrestee's incarceration or daytime release could be reviewed first by the judge who laid them down, anytime after 24 hours, then by the court with jurisdiction to try the case and finally by an appellate court. If the conditions were not changed to permit release, the judge had to state the reasons why in writing. The teeth of the Act were to lie in the severe criminal penalties for failure to appear at trial: $5,000 fine and/or five years in prison in a felony case; $1,000 and/or one year prison in misdemeanor cases. Defendants charged with capital crimes or already convicted and awaiting sentence or appeal could be detained only if the judge found that they posed a danger of flight or danger to the community. Defendants detained before trial were to be given full credit for any time in custody on any prison sentence subsequently rendered. It was hoped and optimistically expected in 1966 that states would quickly follow suit with little Bail Reform Acts.

In 1968, the American Bar Association's Minimum Standards Project published Pretrial Release Standards recommended for state and local criminal courts. They articulated a general policy in favor of release before trial, recommended the release of more defendants on their own promise to return and initiation of methods to provide the judicial officer with the facts he needed to set appropriate release conditions. They also endorsed the setting of nonmonetary conditions calculated to prevent commission of crime on bail as well as to deter flight. Reliance on money bail was to "be reduced to minimal proportions" and bondsmen to be abolished altogether and replaced where necessary by a returnable 10 percent cash deposit. Police-issued citations and judicially issued summons were to be encouraged, whenever possible, to avoid the necessity for custody after formal arrest. Arrested persons were to be taken before a judicial officer without unnecessary delay, and counsel appointed to represent the defendant at the bail hearing. Misdemeanants were automatically to be released on their own recognizance unless the prosecutor specifically opposed release. The factors to be considered in the judicial hearing on release followed the Bail Reform Act closely except that conditions could be imposed for the purpose of preventing renewed criminal activity as well as flight. Such conditions could include prohibitions from approaching particular persons, going to certain places, purchasing weapons or taking alcohol or drugs. Money bail could not, however, be used to prevent recidivism, and it was never to be set according to a preconceived bond schedule determined solely by the nature of the charge. Willful violation of release conditions could result in revocation of release, as could a finding of probable cause by a court or grand jury that the defendant had committed a new serious offense while on bail. Frequent reports were to be made to the court about the status of any defendant who failed to secure release within a two week period. [6] Detained defendants were to be tried within a definite time period or released from custody. Significantly, a provision for preventive detention was drafted but ultimately rejected by the ABA Committee.

B. The Counter Movement

The federal Bail Reform Act came under attack almost immediately, principally by law enforcement officials and trial judges in the District of Columbia who complained that it required the release of dangerous defendants accused of street crimes. Elsewhere, the Act was and continues to be generally conceded as a workable and worthwhile improvement on former bail practices. In 1969, the United States Court of Appeals for the District declared:

> The life of the Bail Reform Act has been marked by woefully inadequate awareness of its requirements by the lay public, resulting in often savage and invariably unfair criticism of judges for simply abiding by their sworn oaths to administer the laws of the United States [Leathers v. United States, 412 F.2d 169 (C.A. D.C. 1969)].

This same appellate court had unswervingly insisted that the spirit and the letter of the new law be carried out and that trial judges could not continue to set high money bail in order to prevent future crime. It had also required judges to explore fully the alternatives to money bail before allowing detention of any accused for failure to make a money bond (United States v. Allen, 386 F.2d 634 (1967) (J. Bazelon opinion); Leathers v. United States, 412 F.2d 169 (1969); United States v. Harrison, 405 F.2d 355 (1968); Banks v. United States, 414 F.2d 1150 (1969) cf. Vauss v. United States, 365 F.2d 956 (1966)).

Despite such herculean efforts, the Bail Reform Act failed to prevent a substantial percentage of defendants from continuing to be detained before trial. In the District of Columbia, 1968-1969 studies showed between 35 percent and 40 percent of defendants still being detained (Judicial Council Committee, 1969; National Bureau of Standards, 1970). In 1971, over 1,000 men were being held in a pretrial detention status in the D.C. Jail, a greater number than before bail reform efforts began. [7] Throughout the country, the number of man-days in detention for federal offenses has increased from 1.2 million in 1965 to 1.4 million in 1969; a 1.7 million figure is projected for 1971. The cost to federal taxpayers for pretrial detention has risen 58 percent from 4.5 million in 1965 to a projected 9.5 million in 1971 (testimony of Daniel J. Freed, based on U.S. Bureau of Prisons data, Hearings of Senate Subcommittee on Constitutional Rights on S. 895, 1971).

In the large cities, even those with bail projects,[8] a sizable pretrial detention population persists as well. In New York City, the birthplace of bail reform, a recent investigation by a City Council Subcommittee showed that 7,000 men and women were in city jails awaiting trial. The 1970 riots in the overcrowded Tombs brought home to the public their despair, degradation and bitterness, and the recent City Council Report shows little improvement since then (New York City Council Report, 1971). Ten years after the Manhattan Bail Project began, the New York City Council Subcommittee reports:

> Our present bail system constitutes a *de facto* system of preventive detention of the poor; the process by which a person is detained bears less relationship to considerations of justice or correction than to economic status. The bail hearing typically consumes about one or two minutes. A release on recognizance report if present at all under the limited existing program will mention family ties, local residence, employment, and criminal record. But if the prosecutor recommends a bail amount, it will probably be based solely on the charge and the past record. Defense counsel will just have met his client and will very likely do little more than acquiesce or ask for a lower amount. Evidence will rarely be taken on whether the defendant can afford the proposed amount. . . . As a result, over 40 percent of all defendants in New York City are remanded by the courts to detention, not because they are likely to commit a crime or jump bail, but because they lack sufficient resources either to post bond or to justify the risk of the bail bondsman.[9]

In California in 1967, there were 9,000 detainees in jail on one sample day; Philadelphia had an average daily population of over 1,600 detainees in 1968; one 1970 estimate places the total detained population in the country at 100,000 (Constitutional Limits on the Conditions of Pretrial Detention, 79 Yale L.J. 941-2 (1970)). Even the concept of bail reform has probably not permeated into most smaller counties and towns. On the other hand, a few dedicated people in a few smaller cities, not plagued by the tidal wave of urban crime, have accomplished a great deal. The Des Moines Pre-Trial Release Project releases 800 accuseds out of 1,600 a year on their own recognizance; another 400 post bail, and people in the community are working diligently to obtain release for the maximum number possible of the remaining 400 (Des Moines Model Corrections Project, 1971). Since 1964, they have released 3,800 accused, with a 2.4 percent nonappearance rate, and a savings of $222,500 annually in detention costs.

The question of why bail reform efforts have had so little impact in the big cities is an obvious one, and the answers are not hard to find.

Bail reform efforts have been literally starved to death: too few bail investigators, too few community resources to help those on release with job, housing, family and health problems. Judges can make rational decisions on the reliability of defendants only if they are provided with verified facts, usually by an independent investigator. Defendants who might be worthwhile risks, if some supervision and supportive help were given them in the community, are now denied release because judges do not think they can make it on their own.

A 1968-1969 study of the operation of the Bail Reform Act in the District of Columbia provides clues as to why more defendants are not released. The study found not enough information provided by defendants about their community roots was being verified by the Bail Agency investigators; either follow-up attempts at contacting families, employers, etc., were not being made when first efforts failed or were not being made at the right times or in the right ways (i.e., personal visits versus telephone calls); there were frequent snafus on obtaining police records or presentence reports needed to make reliable recommendations. As a result, the bail reports submitted to judges were often skimpy and the judges were hesitant to base a release decision on them. Inadequate use was being made of the judges' authority to use conditions of release such as third party custody and curfews, primarily because of a lack of community resources to provide the supervision intended by such devices. Federal Rule 46(h) requiring bi-weekly reports to the court on the status of all defendants had been ineffective for want of personnel to prepare and analyze the reports (Judicial Council Committee, 1968-1969).

There has also been an appalling amount of inaction on the part of many defendants' court-appointed attorneys in vindicating their bail rights. Of the nearly 1,000 defendants in the D.C. Jail in late 1970, 90 percent had court-appointed lawyers but one-third had never had any further contact with them after the initial appointment (American Friends Service Committee, 1970). An earlier survey showed only a small number of the attorneys had filed bail review motions to try to get their defendants released (Appendix D, Judicial Council Committee, 1968).

A large number of those currently accused of crime are already graduates of the criminal justice system, and have emerged unrehabilitated. Usually, the recidivist got into trouble to begin with because he was unemployed or underemployed, uneducated, came from a disrupted family or presently lives in one, is addicted to drugs or alcohol. On release, either before or after trial, he may indeed be a poor risk if no further help is given him in meeting conditions set by the court.

Two separate demonstration projects in New York City and Des Moines have, however, shown that a fair number of defendants not originally released on their own recognizance can secure release if they are reinterviewed and new pleas made to the court on their behalf. The New York Bail Reevaluation Project, run by Vera in 1966-1967, interviewed over 3,800 defendants who either had never been previously interviewed or had been passed over for recommendation for ROR. About 30 percent of this group were ultimately released through the project's renewed activity to get them ROR or to have their bail reduced and to find community resources to help them. The bail jump rate of this group was about 5 percent, and the estimated savings for fourteen months to the community in reduced detention costs were $400,000. Monitored telephones were also installed in jail to provide more access by the detainee to a bondsman or relatives. One in four of those with access to telephones were ultimately released, twice as many as in the control group who had no such access.

The Des Moines Model Corrections Project is another stunning example of how release rates can be increased with community commitment. The project set out to release at least 100 of the 400 annual detainees, and succeeded. Everyone released to the project showed up for trial and only 5 were arrested on new charges. The releasees had all been previously passed over for ROR for lack of community ties. The project required them as conditions of release to report daily to a counselor; to take courses in remedial reading, job training, drug abuse or alcoholism control, child care, budget planning. Some needed psychiatric counselling; the largest number needed help in locating and keeping jobs. There was no doubt the project dealt with a problem population without significant roots: 30 percent had drug and drinking problems; 53 percent had prior convictions. Yet almost all showed they could, with help, stay out of trouble during the pretrial period and return for trial. Those enrolled in the project, moreover, had a much lower rate of prison sentences (29 percent) after conviction than those in a control group (73 percent). The project staff consisted of half professionals and half community people. [10]

Failure of bail reform to make a greater impact on the detention problem in urban cities may also be attributable to the concentration of narcotics addicts in such centers. Judges are quite vocal in articulating their reluctance to release addicts whom they feel will almost inevitably revert to thefts, robberies, or prostitution to obtain the money to satisfy their habit. In 1968, 45 percent of the admissions to the D.C. Jail were found to be users of drugs, predominantly heroin. The scarcity and limited capacity of community-based narcotics treatment programs in most cities and, until the advent of methadone, the relatively poor success rates of such programs has meant that an addict-defendant is virtually doomed to detention. In Washington, a community narcotics program, in operation since 1969, supervises and treats some addict defendants during the pretrial period, but the need in most cities far outstrips the resources. The recent survey of New York City detention facilities by the City Council Subcommittee found that a majority of the inmate population were drug users, yet very limited treatment programs, primarily methadone detoxification, existed to help them.

Finally, the dilemma of bail reform in the sixties raises fundamental questions about whether any part of the criminal justice system can be significantly improved until all of it is. The sheer numbers of accuseds that have steadily mounted in this decade too often have meant interminable delays until trial; which, in turn, can mean greater chances for flight or the commission of new crimes. One New York study (Vera Study on Bail Jumping, 1968) showed that a released defendant had to make several court appearances before his case came to trial. [11] The overall jump rate in the study among ROR'd defendants had gone up to 9.4 percent as compared to the 1.6 percent rate in the original Vera project. The overall jump rate for all releasees—both ROR's and money bail—was 13.9 percent. In Washington, many of the defendants listed as "no shows" actually came to the courthouse but got lost in the wrong courtroom or got discouraged by too many "dry runs" and left before their case was finally called. Bench warrants for "no shows" were seldom served promptly; revocation proceedings were rare for failure to observe conditions; and even convictions for failure to appear usually brought only sentences concurrent with those imposed for the main offense. [12]

In retrospect, bail reform efforts in the sixties have probably had their greatest impact in releasing good risk defendants who might otherwise have had to pay a bondsman or go to jail. They did not, however, do very much to solve the problem of the defendant who needs supportive help in the community to succeed on release. Nor have they reduced the staggering costs society and the individual still pay for detaining persons not yet convicted of any crime. Finally, the abhorrent conditions under which presumptively innocent men are detained, have, on the whole, gotten worse, not better, due to overcrowding, physical deterioration of facilities, and a steadfast refusal to allocate adequate funds to this part of our criminal justice system.

III. THE FOCUS SHIFTS TO PREVENTIVE DETENTION

A. The Preventive Detention Law

Thus far, a major factor in the bail equation has been omitted. That is the fear of judges that accuseds will commit new and "dangerous" crimes while on release. (Judges' rating of what crimes are "dangerous" vary widely and may include prostitution, drug use and petty theft.) This fear of repetition of crimes has probably been the major factor in the nonrelease of accuseds. At the time the Bail Reform Act was passed in 1966, legalized preventive detention was considered but rejected in favor of giving the new law a chance. What few figures existed at that time on the rate of crime on bail showed a relatively low recidivist rate (Ervin, 1967). Once enacted, however, the Bail Reform Act was attacked, primarily in the District of Columbia where street crimes came within its orbit, for requiring the release of dangerous criminals onto the streets, despite the fact that our federal jurisprudence had never allowed bail to be set for any reason except to deter flight. In 1969, the administration proposed a Preventive Detention law for all federal courts which was, however, ultimately enacted for crimes committed in the District of Columbia alone. It allows pretrial detention of persons (1) accused of "dangerous crimes," defined to include robbery, burglary and housebreaking, arson, rape, sale or distribution of illegal drugs, or (2) accused of "crimes of violence," defined to include murder, rape, carnal knowledge, mayhem, kidnapping, robbery, burglary, manslaughter, extortion, blackmail, assault, or attempt to conspiracy to commit any of the foregoing. To be eligible for detention, those accused of so-called violent crimes must also have been convicted of another "crime of violence" within the past ten years, or be on bail, probation, or pretrial release from such a crime, or be diagnosed as an addict. Also detainable is one accused of any offense who subsequently threatens, intimidates or injures any prospective witness or juror for the purpose of obstructing justice.

A detention proceeding can be initiated by motion of the prosecutor, either at the initial appearance before the judge or later when the man was already on release. Unless the prosecutor moves for a continuance (maximum 3 days) or the defense counsel so moves (maximum 5 days), the hearing will be held immediately. The accused may be detained pending the hearing. A suspected addict may be detained 3 days for examination of his condition.

At the hearing itself, before detaining the accused, the judge, on the basis of the same factors prescribed for determining release under the Bail Reform Act, plus "past conduct," must determine that no condition or combination of release conditions can assure the safety of the community or any other person. He is also to determine that, except in the case of one accused of obstructing justice, there is a "substantial probability" that the accused committed the crime charged.

The law provides for a right to counsel for the accused at the detention hearing and an opportunity to present information by proffer or live witnesses. (Whether there is a right to subpoena witnesses is unclear.) It does not require that the government's evidence be live testimony nor that the accused have the right to confront any witnesses against him. Information presented to the judge at the hearing need not conform to the rules pertaining to admissibility "in a court of law."

If the defendant testifies at the hearing, his testimony may not be used against him "on the issue of guilt" but it may be used for impeachment at his trial and is admissible in proceedings for failure to appear, or to impose additional penalties for crimes committed during release and in proceedings for violations of release conditions.

A detained defendant is to be housed "to the extent practicable" in facilities separate from convicted persons, afforded "reasonable opportunity for private consultation with counsel" and, "for good cause shown," allowed time out of jail to help prepare his defense in the custody of the United States marshal or other appropriate person. He shall be given priority for trial to the extent "consistent with sound administration of justice," and at the end of 60 days the detention order is to terminate if he is not brought to trial, and release terms are to be set under the regular provisions of the law.[13]

The constitutionality of the preventive detention law is yet to be determined by the courts. The issues raised in one judicial attack, subsequently dismissed on technical grounds, Dash v. Mitchell, – F. Supp. – (D.C. D.C. 1972), include the following:

(1) Does the Eighth Amendment grant an absolute right to bail in noncapital cases? The Supreme Court has never ruled on this question. Carlson v. Landon, 342 U.S. 524 (1952) is interpreted by proponents of preventive detention to answer this question "No," but that was a close 1952 decision dealing with the detention of aliens pending deportation, not with citizens accused of crime. Stack v. Boyle, 342 U.S. 1, decided in the same term, contained a ringing endorsement of the importance of pretrial release to the presumption of innocence. Even if the Eighth Amendment does not grant an absolute right to bail in noncapital cases, does it mean that the legislature may set any limits

it wishes on that right, or only such limits as are reasonably necessary to prevent an intolerable or "excessive" risk of flight and/or criminal behavior?

(2) If it should be decided that the Eighth Amendment itself does not guarantee bail, is there a constitutionally guaranteed presumption of innocence which adheres to a defendant before trial so that he may not be put in jail solely to prevent new crimes, when the evidence of his dangerousness is based, at least in part, on the conclusion—arrived at without trial—that he is "substantially" guilty of the crime charged?

(3) Alternately, is the fact that there has been a right to bail in virtually every jurisdiction since 1789 made it so integral a part of "due process" that it cannot now be abandoned? An analogous line of reasoning was followed by the Supreme Court in In Re Winship 397 U.S. 358 (1970) when it found that the "beyond a reasonable doubt" standard of guilt necessary for conviction—nowhere mentioned in the Constitution—was nonetheless a part of due process.

(4) Must the legislative base of any preventive detention law show an ascertainable relationship between the types of crimes or the characteristics of offenders eligible for detention and those crimes or defendants that have been proven to have a significantly higher rate of recidivism during the pretrial period? A few statistical studies have attempted to show how many released defendants, potentially detainable under this law, are actually rearrested during the pretrial period. These studies have shown an actual rate of rearrests no greater than 1 out of 4 in any detainable category of crime or defendants studied (National Bureau of Standards, 1970) (Harvard Civil Rights, 1971).[14]

(5) Finally, there is the question whether preventive detention can be used when less restrictive alternatives have not been adequately tried first. The paucity of resources devoted to pretrial supervision and speedy trial of all offenders suspected of dangerousness belie any effort to curb pretrial crime by less drastic measures. Bail surveys have shown that roughly half of pretrial crime is committed after 60 days; hence, trial in 60 days should reduce the present rate of crime on bail by at least 50 percent, and perhaps more, since the sure knowledge of impending trial might deter some of the crime committed within the 60 day period as well.

(6) It was also asserted in the court challenge that the D.C. preventive detention law violates the Sixth Amendment because it denies a

defendant the right to confront or cross-examine witnesses at the detention hearing. Evidence of past crimes and misbehavior as well as evidence of the present crime can be introduced merely by proffer. Persons threatened with injuries, such as loss of government employment, suspension of welfare benefits or confinement as a juvenile delinquent or sexual psychopath have been allowed to confront their accusers as part of a due process hearing (Willner v. Committee on Character and Fitness, 373 U.S. 96 (1963); Greene v. McElroy, 360 U.S. 474 (1959); Peters v. Hobby, 349 U.S. 331 (1955); Jenkins v. McKeithen, 395 U.S. 411 (1969); Goldberg v. Kelley, 397 U.S. 254 (1969); In re Gault, 387 U.S. 1 (1969); Specht v. Patterson, 386 U.S. 610).[15]

The government's reply to these attacks on preventive detention takes the following lines (Mitchell, 1969; Hruska, 1969). There is no Eighth Amendment right to absolute bail. The mere fact that such an absolute right is not specifically granted in the Judiciary Act of 1789 speaks for itself. There is a long tradition of pretrial detention in England and Europe, and in fact judges have since 1789 used high bail as a way to keep dangerous offenders confined before trial. Capital crimes have always been detainable and many of the crimes for which detention is now sought were in fact capital crimes in 1789. Carlson v. Landon held that the Eighth Amendment does not require bail in all noncapital crimes. Pretrial defendants can already be jailed not only for want of bail but if the court finds it necessary to protect witnesses. Forty-nine states have excessive bail clauses in their Constitutions and 37 of these also have an absolute right to bail, thereby showing that they are not coextensive. Several lower court decisions have held that there is no constitutional right to bail before trial (U.S. ex. rel. Covington v. Coparo, 297 F.Supp. 203 (S.D. N.Y. 1969); Wansley v. Wilkerson, 263 F.Supp. 54 (W.D. Va. 1967)).

Furthermore, the presumption of innocence, according to the government, is only a rule of evidence at trial. Otherwise it would apply equally to those charged with capital crimes, or those who are now detained because of intimidation of witnesses, or lack of money bail. Similarly due process is not violated because not only capital defendants but defendants suspected of mental illness or obstructing justice may be detained before trial, as may those whom the judge feels will flee.

As to the uncertainty of predictions, the government points out that the same uncertainties are present in sentencing decisions, and before trial as well, insofar as predictions must be made at bail hearings on the possible flight of defendants. Predictions of future dangerous behavior are also involved in civil commitments for sexual psychopaths and the mentally ill. [16]

B. Preventive Detention in Practice

In the first ten months of operation in the District of Columbia, the preventive detention law (P.D.) has had no discernible impact on the crime rate. It has been invoked only with respect to 20 defendants out of 6,000 felony defendants entering the system during that period, and only 9 defendants have actually been subjected to P.D. hearings; 8 of the 9 hearings resulted in a detention order. In the other cases the motions for P.D. were withdrawn prior to hearing. Five of the ten detention orders were reversed on review or reconsideration, and one had to be dismissed when the grand jury refused to indict on the underlying offense. [17] The dearth of detention proceedings appears to be a result of the dubious status of the law's constitutionality and of the government's experience that, at least in the District of Columbia where a vigorous and aggressive Public Defender service exists, a P.D. hearing will be fought tooth and nail and is apt to entail a full-day's hearing and appeals. Prosecutors have also admitted off the record that they prefer the high money bail route which still exists for most dangerous offenders. This is in marked contrast to earlier assertions before the Act's passage by its proponents that P.D. was designed to make the bail system "honest" and prevent the hypocrisy of high bail to detain defendants thought to be dangerous (Kleindienst, 1970). If the 10 months of experience with P.D. in the District of Columbia have proved anything, it is that P.D. is merely an additional encrustation upon the continuing practice of keeping undesirables in jail through the setting of high bail. A substantial number of allegedly "dangerous" defendants are also being detained under the relatively obscure section of the new law which allows an accused already on parole or probation to be held for 5 days while the probation or parole authorities decide whether to revoke his release. The parole and probation authorities have almost invariably decided to take their wards back into custody when notified of their rearrest [18] (Vera-Georgetown Study on Preventive Detention, 1972).

Despite its infrequent invocation, several problems with the P.D. law have surfaced. One is the problem of what constitutes dangerousness and substantial probability of guilt. The government in the P.D. hearings so far has relied heavily on past arrests and indictments (sometimes even dismissed indictments or dropped charges) as proof of past dangerousness and merely "proffered" evidence about such alleged crimes through ex parte statements of witnesses or even oral accounts by the prosecutor without actually putting any live witnesses on the stand who could be cross examined by the defendant's counsel. Confessions, whether admissible at trial or not, are also used in such hearings. Sometimes mere suspicions or community complaints about a defendant have been aired about similar crimes occurring in the same neighborhoods for which the defendant has not even been formally charged. Juvenile records are frequently used. As to proof of the present charge, usually the arresting officer's testimony adduced at the preliminary hearing is relied on to establish "substantial probability" of guilt. On at least one occasion, no witnesses at all were offered and "substantial probability" of guilt was shown by the prosecutor's statement only.

Defense counsel in such proceedings must decide whether to request a closed hearing in order to save clients pretrial publicity. If they do so, they run the risk of perpetuating a disturbing practice of secret hearings where abuses can more easily occur and escape exposure to public view. The evils of secret hearings were sought to be avoided by the Sixth Amendment's right to a public trial. The Public Defender has generally chosen closed hearings, but recognizes that it is a Hobsen's choice. Some of the other hearings have been open. Press coverage was fairly intense for the first several open P.D. hearings but totally missing for several later hearings.

Obtaining review of preventive detention has been a frustrating process. Many of the detentions were for so short a period that review was impossible. In the cases where some type of judicial review was sought, either the defendant secured release before the review hearing or had the detention order lifted at review.

In the one attempt to obtain fullscale review of a detention order in an appellate court, the detention order was set aside and the defendant ordered to be held under the 5 day detention for parole revocation instead. In other cases, private counsel did not seek review at all. A class action brought by one of the defendants first preventively detained and later held for parole revocation along with the Public Defender Agency and other civic groups was dismissed by a three-judge federal court for lack of standing.[19] After 10 months, no appellate court has yet passed on the merits of the law.

A survey was made of what actually happened to a random sample of 200 persons out of 2,591 felony defendants processed in the first five months of the law. It showed that 33 percent of the 200, or 67, were prima facie eligible for detention under the statutory criteria of dangerous crimes or crimes of violence accompanied by the requisite past record or present probation, parole or bail status. But less than 2 percent of the total number of those technically eligible for detention were actually moved against under the law in this period.

Just over half of the sample had money bond set, which most could not meet; and just under half were released on nonfinancial conditions, usually after a Bail Agency recommendation. Twenty-two percent of the eligibles were already on probation or parole (Vera-Georgetown Study, 1972).

In November 1971 it was reported that the United States Attorney's office in the District of Columbia would attempt to deal with serious criminal repeaters through speeded up indictments (within one day of arrest), up-to-date "rap sheets" of past criminal records to present to the judge and immediate notification to the court of bail violations. Armed with indictments and accurate past records prosecutors would seek high bond in order to detain accuseds they thought dangerous (nothing was said in the report of how quickly the defendants would be brought to trial: Washington Evening Star, November 3, 1971). In light of the clear statutory command in the new law that money bail is not to be used as a release condition for the purpose of deterring crime, this new policy, if accurately reported, is of dubious legality. It does, however, strip the old high bail system of all pretense, and strongly suggests that preventive detention—whatever its legality or morality—has proved to be an impractical solution to the problem of crime on bail.

IV. THE SHAPE OF THINGS TO COME

The last decade has witnessed a tug of war between an idealistic bail reform movement which sought to free the maximum number of accuseds before trial and the backlash of a rising crime rate which sought to minimize the likelihood of an accused committing a new crime in the pretrial period. We have ended up with the worst of both worlds—continued use of high bail to clandestinely sentence those suspected of dangerousness to jail and the beginnings of a movement toward preventive detention to detain them outright. In this tug of war, we have lost sight of some of the original objectives of the bail reform movement entirely. It is time for a reassessment.

(1) Now, as ten years ago, it is still true that the vast majority of defendants who spend their pretrial time in jail are released outright after their trial or conviction. Out of 88,000 detainees in New York City in 1970, 64,000 were freed before or after trial; only 8 percent of detainees in Philadelphia in 1967 were ultimately sentenced to prison; 10-15 percent in Washington (Conditions of Pretrial Detention, 1970). Yet there is no question that the conditions of pretrial detention are typically far worse than prison: more security oriented, less programmed, no job training or education; more restricted access to visitors; less recreation and medical or psychiatric care; more overcrowding. The new wave of

corrections reform has so far bypassed pretrial detainees, despite the fact that bitterness and cynicism begins at the detention door and so must any genuine rehabilitation efforts. In some insane way we have reversed the entire process: we have more accuseds suffering worse deprivation in advance of trial than afterwards. The only way to right this wrong is for those in charge to recognize that fact, and begin to devote the proper share of the total criminal justice pie to pretrial programs. Before the passage of the Preventive Detention law, Deputy Attorney General Kleindienst promised:

> Ironically, the Bail Reform Act is responsible for the detention of hundreds of defendants who might be released under new procedures. This Administration is prepared to move vigorously to free these defendants, under some reasonable conditions, if they do not pose a threat to the community. But no movement in this direction is possible until the law comes to grips with the dangerous defendant.

The law is now in effect and it is time to collect on the promise of vigorous movement to free the rest of the defendants in jail for want of bail.

(2) One obvious need is for more comprehensive pretrial service agencies along the lines of the Des Moines Model Corrections Project and the Manhattan Court Employment Projects.

A Senate Bill sponsored by Sam Ervin (S. 895) would create pilot pretrial service projects in 5 federal districts; such an agency has also been recommended in the City Council Subcommittee Report for New York City to collect information from pretrial defendants, make release recommendations, supervise the conditions of release, report back to the court on violations, coordinate the efforts of private community groups to help; prepare the periodic reports to the Court on persons left in detention over a minimal period. To be really effective such agencies would have to provide job placement components, halfway houses, access to medical and psychiatric help, drug and alcoholic treatment programs. That is a tall order, and an expensive one, but the experience of the Des Moines project as well as pilot diversion programs in New York City (Manhattan Court Employment Project) and Washington, D.C. (Project Crossroads) suggest that such programs can work if enough resources are devoted to them. In the Manhattan project, one-half of all participants in a three-year period have had their cases dismissed after being helped to find employment; follow-up studies show they have had a markedly lower recidivism rate than the control group not accorded such services. Similar programs are being funded by the Department of Labor in 7 other cities. A few cities are beginning pretrial diversion programs for addict-defendants which condition their freedom on entrance into drug treatment programs (ABA Special Committee on Crime Prevention, 1972). Their early results look promising. A rational comparison of jail upkeep costs should easily convince communities that they can afford such projects.

For those defendants who society decides must be institutionalized before trial, equal protection requires that they not be treated worse than convicted felons. They deserve small institutions with decent medical, recreational, educational opportunities. It seems that few communities so far provide such basic decencies willingly, so it is probable that legal attacks will have to be made upon present intolerable detention conditions under the Equal Protection clause of the Fourteenth Amendment. Pretrial prisoners detained for want of bail money or even for lack of community ties must not be treated more severely than defendants convicted of crimes, nor should they be restricted any more than necessary to ensure their presence at trial or even to prevent them from committing new crimes. Maximum security prisons are not the least drastic alternative to accomplish either end (Constitutional Limitations on the Conditions of Pretrail Detention, 1970). The vast majority of pretrial detainees do not need censorship, restricted visitation and telephone rights, locked cells to insure that they will not flee. There is no excuse except convenience and tradition for treating them like convicted offenders and correctional authorities should be and in some cases are finally being called to task in court for such treatment (Wayne County Jail Inmates v. Wayne County Board of Commissioners, Mich. Circuit Court, 1971; Palmigrano v. Travisero, 317 F. Supp. 776 (D.C. R. I. 1970); Hamilton v. Love, 328 F. Supp. 1182 (E.D. Ark. 1971); Holt v. Sarver, 309 F. Supp. 362 (E.D. Ark. 1970). Detained defendants should secure by legislation or judicial declaration enforceable rights to adequate medical and psychiatric care, decent and uncrowded living conditions and maximum contact with their families and counsel; work release programs to maintain their jobs; these rights should be enforceable by release if they are violated. Similarly, the conditions of women detainees in many places, because of their relatively smaller numbers and briefer stays in detention, are more restrictive than for male prisoners. Such inequalities—indeed, even the separation of men and women prisoners in segregated institutions—need to be challenged under equal protection guarantees.

(3) The second and equally obvious point of entry into our present detention impasse is to set finite, definite legislative limits on the time anyone can be kept under restraints prior to trial.

Society can now put a man behind bars under the pretext of having set conditions of release and forget about him. It might be more willing to devote the resources to bring its high risk defendants to trial quickly if it knew they would automatically be released in the community after a certain period of time if not brought to trial. The National Crime Commission (Challenge of Crime in a Free Society, 1967: 154-157) and the ABA Standards Relating To Speedy Trial (1968) as well as S. 895 have endorsed specific limits on how long a man must wait for a trial. Time limits have already been enacted in several states such as California, New York and Florida, and in some federal courts (usually 3-6 months from arrest or indictment to trial). The Judicial Conference of the United States has formally asked the Supreme Court to amend the Federal Rules of Criminal Procedure to require all United States courts to set up "speedy trial" timetables (New York Times, November 1, 1971). Such limits are meeting heavy resistance from backed-up courts and prosecutors, but the resources now spent in detaining defendants should and can be transferred to bringing them to trial promptly, and pressures to delay in implementing the time-honored right to a speedy trial should be resisted. It stands to reason that any kind of pretrial supervision works best within finite time limits. Defendants are less likely to commit an offense if they face a date certain for trial on the old charge; they are more motivated to adhere to release conditions and make a genuine effort at rehabilitation when they know the day of reckoning is at hand. The resources of any supervising agency are more efficiently dispensed over many defendants for brief periods.

(4) The issue of the constitutionality of preventive detention should and will undoubtedly be settled by the courts within the next year or so. Even if the concept is upheld, the need will still remain for close monitoring of any such system to insure that hearings are fair and decisions based on reliable factual evidence and specific criteria. In this respect, the D.C. law is not a model of either clarity or fairness. A detention law should state specifically what it aims to prevent, i.e., crimes of violence to the person, and accord a defendant the right to confront evidence against him, etc. It should also be confined to persons accused of a limited number of crimes considered truly dangerous by community standards, and those with habitual patterns of committing such crimes in the past. Preventive detention should be a last resort, and not. allowable until other forms of release have been tried and proven unsatisfactory in controlling the defendant. It goes without saying that the results of research so far in predicting recidivism among pretrial defendants are most disappointing; much more refined research is needed to show if such predictions can be made or if they are impossible and society should face the truth that it is jailing people on hunches.

(5) A serious study also remains to be made of what kind of release conditions work in deterring flight and misconduct. The original bail reform

projects proved their hypothesis that defendants with community ties would not flee; they did not prove the opposite—that, if released, defendants without such roots would flee. [20] Many conditions now imposed routinely on releasees may be unnecessary, expensive to enforce, and provoke resentments. More empirical research is needed to show what techniques of supervision work best on what kind of defendants facing trial.

(6) Finally, the legality of setting money bail for poor defendants, no matter what the purpose, should be finally ruled upon by the Supreme Court. Heretofore the issue has been decided (in favor of money bail) only in a few isolated lower courts. The Supreme Court, on the other hand, has already ruled that states cannot deny free transcripts to indigent appellants (Griffin v. Illinois, 351 U.S. 12 (1956)) or free counsel to felony defendants (Gideon v. Wainwright, 372 U.S. 335 (1963)). These decisions would seem to indicate that money bail is suspect when it results in denial of freedom to poor defendants. The Court's latest rulings in Williams v. Illinois, 399 U.S. 235 (1970) and Tate v. Short, 401 U.S. 395 (1971) provide even closer analogies. They say that a person may not be incarcerated after conviction in lieu of a fine. It seems hard to distinguish between pretrial money bail and posttrial fine as the price of freedom. [21]

The Supreme Court's most serious excursion into the area of bail for criminal defendants involved the alleged excessiveness of bail set for Smith Act defendants in 1951 (Stack v. Boyle). [22] The court there emphasized that the function of bail was to insure appearance and that the amount of bail could not therefore be based solely on the charge, or on the past flights of other defendants accused of the same offense, but must be related to the individual's own case.

Nevertheless, the Court has in the past consistently turned down opportunities to decide the question of whether money bail violates equal protection of the laws (People ex rel. Gonzalez v. Warden, 21 N.Y. 2d 18, cert. den. 390 U.S. 973 (1968)). But see J. Douglas in Bandy v. United States, 81 S.Ct. 19708 (1960). ("Can an indigent be denied freedom, where a wealthy man would not, because he does not happen to have enough property to pledge for his freedom?") A lower federal court has refused to rule that New York State's money bail system is unconstitutional because money bail "is so thoroughly a part of our traditional procedures in criminal cases that nothing short of legislation can appropriately reform it" (U.S. ex rel. Shakur v. Commissioner of Corrections, 303 F. Supp. 309 (S.D. N.Y. 1969)). But after nearly 200 years the issue deserves consideration from the highest court. A recent class action brought on behalf of New York City detainees by the Legal Aid Society challenging the constitutionality of money bail for poor defendants, lack of due process in bail hearings, failure to pursue nonfinancial alternatives before imposing money bail or to verify information about the defendants in all cases suggests that decision may finally be imminent (Bellamy v. Justices, 1972).

Pretrial detention due to lack of bail remains the point of greatest impact in the criminal justice system where poverty punishes a man. Jails are still full of men and women who cannot make $500 bonds. If money bail were ruled out or its use severely restricted, society might be forced to concentrate on making nonfinancial release conditions work, and to bring defendants to trial promptly.

There is conceded risk involved in forcing such a decision, however. The outlawing of the money bail façade might result in a rash of ill-considered preventive detention laws to fill the vacuum. The experience with the juvenile detention system, where money bail does not predominate but unnecessarily high rates of detention do, does not provide a happy precedent;[23] neither does a close look at European experience, where those accused of minor offenses probably go free more often than in this country but those accused of major offenses are almost never released. For all of its faults, money bail still provides an automatic out for some accuseds who can raise it and who might otherwise be subjected to the vagaries of official predictions about their future conduct. Still, on balance, the widespread overuse of money bail to detain indiscriminately deserves to come to an end. To design a rational replacement may not be easy—in theory or in practice. Adequate resources for community supervision and prompt trials will be all that is required in most cases; in some cases, where a defendant has shown that he cannot be trusted, he may have to spend the pretrial period in halfway houses, or a special residence for those awaiting trial; in a few cases, money deposits may be a true deterrent to flight or misconduct. Those already on release, probation, or parole for prior offenses may face at least temporary revocation of their freedom. But one thing is certain: the bail system, as it now exists, is morally and practically bankrupt, and tinkering will no longer suffice.

NOTES

1. In some jurisdictions, a detained defendant may be compelled to appear in a lineup for a new offense while a released defendant may not. Rigney v. Hendrick, 355 F.2d 710, cert.den. 384 U.S. 975 (3rd Cir. 1966); cf. Butler v. Crumlish, 229 F. Supp. 565 (E.D. Pa. 1964). Unconvicted detainees may also be denied absentee ballots to vote. McDonald v. Board of Election Commissioners, 394 U.S. 802 (1969) See generally, "Constitutional Limitations on the Conditions of Pretrial Detention," 79 Yale L.J. 941, 946 (1970).

2. See generally, Ares, Rankin, Sturz, "The Manhattan Bail Project," 38 N.Y.U.L.Rev. 67 (1963) (59 percent of released had charge dropped or were acquitted compared to 23 percent of nonreleased control group; 21 percent of released group went to prison compared with 96 percent of nonreleased group.) Foote, "Compelling Appearance in Court: Administration of Bail in Philadelphia," 102 U.Pa.L.Rev.1031 (1954) Note, "A Study of the Administration of Bail in New York City," 103 U.Pa.L.Rev. 693 (1958) (detained defendants 2.5 times as likely to get prison sentences as released ones; released group got 4 times as many suspended sentences; 18 percent of the detained group acquitted compared with 48 percent of the released group).

See also McCarthy and Wahl, "The District of Columbia Bail Project, An Illustration of Experimentation and a Brief for Change," 53 Geo.L.J. 675 (1965); Foote, "The Coming Constitutional Crisis in Bail," 113 U.Pa.L.Rev. 959, 1125 (1965); Freed and Wald, *Bail in the United States* (1964), A Report to the Naional Conference on Bail and Criminal Justice; Silverstein, "Bail in the State Courts," 50 Minnesota L.Rev. 621 (1966); Goldfarb, *Ransom: A Critique of the American Bail System* (1966); Foote, "Studies on Bail," U.of Pa.Inst. of Legal Research (1966); Sachs, "Indigent Court Costs and Bail: Charge Them to Equal Protection," 27 Maryland L.Rev. 154 (1967); Note, "Bail Reform in the State and Federal Systems," 20 Vanderbilt L.Rev. 948 (1967); Smith, "Bail or Jail: Toward an Alternative," 21 Florida L.Rev. 59 (1968).

A 1972 study of several hundred New York City detainees prepared for a legal challenge on the constitutionality of money bail reaffirms the earlier studies. "A first offender who is detained in lieu of bail is more than three times as likely to be convicted and almost twice as likely to get a prison sentence as a recidivist with more than ten prior arrests who is released." Plaintiff's Memorandum in Bellamy v. Justices (App. Div., N.Y. Sup. Ct., First Dept.) p. 3.

3. Conditions of release have included affirmative action on the part of the defendant as well, i.e., attendance at alcoholism or narcotics treatment programs (Vauss v. United States, 365 F.2d 956, C.A. D.C. 1966); giving a handwriting sample in forgery cases (U.S. v. Orito, 424 F.2d 276, C.A. 9, 1970). Conditions such as periodic urinalyses, provision of handwriting samples, raise problems of self-incrimination. A court may also refuse to accept money alone, if it does not think that this will insure the defendant's appearance (U.S. v. Nebbia, 357 F.2d 303, C.A. 2, 1966).

4. The project initially excluded those charged with or having a prior record of narcotic offenses, homicide, rape, sodomy, sexual offenses involving children, or assault on a police officer. As the project progressed, some of the original exclusions were lifted.

5. See Hearings Before Subcommittee No. 5 of the House Committee of the Judiciary, 89th Cong., 2d Sess. (1966); Hearings on Federal Bail Reform of the Subcommittee on Constitutional Rights and the Subcommittee on Improvements in Judicial Machinery of the Senate Committee of the Judiciary, 89th Cong., 1st Sess. (1965); Summary Report of Hearings and Investigation of the Subcommittee on Constitutional Rights and Subcommittee on Improvements in Judicial Machinery of the Senate Committee of Judiciary, 88th Cong., 2d Sess. (1965); House Report No. 1541 and Senate Report No. 750; 111 Cong.Rec. 24520 (1965); 112 Cong.Rec. 12488.

6. A similar requirement had been provided for federal detainees in 1966 in revised Rule 46(f) of the Federal Rules of Criminal Procedure.

7. Obviously, a comparison of the gross number of detainees in jail at particular times has limitations as an indicator of the percentage of all arrestees being detained after

bailsetting. Those figures alone do not tell how many were arrested to begin with or how long most have been in jail. In the case of the District, for instance, pretrial periods have decreased somewhat since 1966 and arrests have increased.

8. A 1972 survey by the Office of Economic Opportunity showed no pretrial release projects in 23 states; and only 13 states with more than one project. California had the greatest number (10) and New York and Texas had 5 each.

9. A Vera Institute spokesman estimates 60 percent to 70 percent of those arrested and taken into custody in New York City receive a bail interview. A 1969 Vera study showed, however, that 56 percent of those interviewed but not released were detained because of lack of verification of their community ties. Schaeffer "The Problem of Overcrowding in Detention Institutions." But compare New York City Council Subcommittee Report to the effect that: "The possibility of qualifying for release on recognizance, a promising program initiated by VERA, but half-heartedly maintained by the Department of Probation, is remote at best."

10. A project was recently begun in Alleghany County, Pennsylvania, which utilizes community persons to maintain contact with the accused and refer him to needed services. Commercial bondsmen have been outlawed in the county. Pretrail Justice Federation Newsletter, March 1972.

11. The New York study showed, however, that the most jumping occurred early after release and just before disposition.

12. Another continuing problem is the lack of confidentiality of bail investigation interviews in some cities. The new D.C. Court Reorganization Act allows the bail report to be used for impeachment at trial in perjury or preventive detention proceedings. 23 D.C. Code 1303(d). In other jurisdictions, i.e., Montgomery County, Maryland, the bail interview is tape recorded for future use. This can discourage the flow of information from accused to bail interviewer, and thus cut down on the likelihood of a release recommendation.

13. Other portions of the law allow on accused's "dangerousness" to be taken into consideration in setting pretrial release conditions, except that money bail shall not be set to deter crime. A legislative presumption is created against release in the case of a convicted offender; the judge must find "by clear and convincing evidence that he is not likely to flee or pose a danger to any other person or the property of others." If already sentenced, the judge must find in addition that the appeal is "likely to result in a reversal." Finally, the law permits any accused already on parole or probation to be detained 5 days while the probation or parole authorities are notified to see if they wish to retake him into custody preliminary to revocation proceedings. New and stiffer penalties for crimes committed while on bail were enacted and made compulsorily consecutive to sentences imposed for the main crime. Failure to appear after notice was to be prima facie evidence of willful default, whether or not warnings of the applicable penalties were actually given to the defendant at the time of release. Actual notice need not have been received if "reasonable efforts" were made and the defendant by his own actions frustrated its receipt. Proceedings were established for revocation of release for violation of release conditions.

14. The Bureau of Standards study showed a rearrest rate of 17 percent for all felony defendants in the survey; only 5 percent of the rearrests being for serious felonies. No correlation was found between the type of crime charged and the severity of the crime for which the defendant was arrested on bail. There was a higher arrest rate for those charged with "dangerous" offenses (23 percent) but the accused of "crimes of violence" and all other felonies had the same rate of rearrests (17 percent). No single characteristic stated in

the law (employment, residence, past record, etc.) was found to be a reliable indicator of rearrest while on bail. The Harvard study attempted to use a "hunch" system for predicting recidivism (only 30 percent accurate) and then a complicated computer multivariant analysis combining all the factors listed in the law (only 40 percent maximum accuracy).

There have also been a few police and U.S. Attorneys' surveys showing a higher rate of rearrests on bail. These in turn have been criticized for poor methodology and inaccuracy. For a full account of such surveys, see Report of the Judicial Council Committee to Study the Operation of the Bail Reform Act in the District of Columbia (1968 and 1969); 1970 Preventive Detention, Hearings Before Subcommittee on Constitutional Rights, Senate Committee on Judiciary. The Report of the President's Commission on Crime in the District of Columbia (1967) also had a study of pretrial crime among accused felons on bail, showing a rate of 7.5 percent reindictment while on bail. Most of these surveys have counted all rearrests within the pretrial period, not just those within the first 60 days. Most do not take account of those arrests not ultimately culminating in convictions. None of the studies has produced any reliable predictive criteria for picking out those who will commit new crimes on bail.

15. Although regular bail hearings do not include such a right, to a full due process hearing with the right to confront accusers, the purpose of the detention hearing is arguably different. The bail hearing is to set conditions of release; the detention hearing decides if 60 days of incarceration is warranted.

16. Other grounds on which the law is being attacked include the failure to require a reasonable doubt standard in the proceeding and the vagueness of the standard "danger to the community or any person." Interference with the right to secure the effective assistance of counsel and impeding the right of a defendant to take the stand at the detention hearing by making his testimony usable against him for impeachment are other infirmities cited in the law. It has also been argued that detaining an addict violates Robinson v. California, 370 U.S. 660 (1962), since it punishes the status of addiction alone. The preventive detention proceedings also were attacked as being a denial of the equal protection of the laws to District citizens because they are applicable to federal offenses only in the District of Columbia. Thus, one accused of the same United States Code offense in Maryland or Virginia could not be detained whereas the D.C. defendant could. This ground of attack has recently been upheld by the U.S. Court of Appeals as it applies to the post conviction bail changes in the same Act. It was ruled that the older and more liberal bail standards of the Bail Reform Act would continue to apply to U.S. Code offenders in the District of Columbia. U.S. v. Thompson, 452 F.2d 1333 (C.A.D.C. 1971), cert. den. 405 U.S. 998.

17. The box score on P.D. defendants showed most were accused of crimes such as rape, armed robbery, narcotics sales. Twelve were already on pretrial release from other crimes, and seven had prior convictions. At the end of the 10 month survey period, 15 had been ultimately convicted of at least one of the pending charges; three were acquitted of or had the P.D. charge dropped; two still had their cases pending.

18. This experience tends to confirm the argument of opponents of P.D. that viable alternatives already exist to protect the community from most so-called dangerous offenders. The 5-day hold for probationers and parolees, of course, is not without its injustices too—parole and probation authorities now almost automatically terminate release and initiate revocation proceedings on new charges before any actual trial is had, and, if the man is ultimately found to be innocent of the new charge, he will still have spent needless time in jail. An independent study of P.D. in the District has estimated that 22 percent of

defendants eligible for detention are on parole or probation. The United States Attorney for the District has stated that in the past six months of 1971, 250 motions were made for 5 day detention "holds" on probationers and parolees. (Vera-Georgetown Study, 1972.)

19. Dash v. Mitchell—F. Supp.—(D.C. D.C. 1972) affm'd—U.S.—(1972). One of the three trial court judges dissented from the dismissal on the grounds that review should be granted as to the accused who had been first preventively detained, then held for parole violation, stating that "the nature of the case cries out for prompt judicial review."

20. For instance, the Women's House of Detention in Washington, D.C. (and probably elsewhere) has a large percentage of inmates awaiting trial who are prostitutes and addicts. Most cannot meet the permanent residence-legitimate employment criteria which figure so prominently in bail project point systems. Yet few contend that most such women either are likely to flee or that they present a danger of violence. The regular bail project criteria obviously need to be altered if pretrial release is not to be denied to such women, on a class basis.

Such women deserve to be released through a more flexible set of bail criteria, at least on an experimental basis, until some experience can be gleaned as to their nonflight and nondangerous propensities. That experience can then be used to alter the criteria for release on a more permanent basis.

21. In 1971, the Supreme Court, 402 U.S. 1006, remanded two cases to the Second and Eighth Circuit Court of Appeals with directions to consider the eligibility for credit against federal sentences of time served by defendants held in state jails in lieu of money bail. The Solicitor General of the United States had recommended to the Court that denial of such credit would amount to a denial of equal protection based on poverty. Memorandum of the United States filed in Supreme Court in Nelson v. United States and Gaines v. United States, (Nos. 6662 and 6704, 1971). See Gaines v. United States, 449 F.2d 143 (2d Cir. 1971) holding that "a man should not be kept imprisoned solely because of his lack of wealth."

22. In the 1971-1972 term, the court decided that it was constitutional for an Illinois bail law to charge a small administrative cost against a 10 percent cash deposit by the defendant as a guarantee of his appearance, even though he subsequently appeared. Schlib v. Kuebel, 404 U.S. 357.

23. Space has not permitted any discussion of two other critical detention problems against which we have made little or no headway in recent years. The first is how to handle bail setting in mass arrest situations during riots and civil disturbances. See, e.g., Report of the National Advisory Commission on Civil Disorders (1968) Ch. 13: Legal Services During the 1971 Mayday Demonstrations (D.C. Public Defender Service, 1971). The second area is the criteria for and administration of juvenile pretrial detention, where money bail is not involved, but where needlessly high rates of detention prevail nonetheless (N.C.C.D., Standard Guides for the Detention of Children and Youth, 1961; Aubry, "The Nature, Scope and Significance of Pre-Trial Detention of Juveniles in California," 1 Black L.J. 160 (1971). Juvenile overdetention can be traced principally to the wide discretion allowed judges in detaining juveniles for both criminal and noncriminal behavior under existing laws and to the lack of nonsecurity community resources for helping children in trouble.

REFERENCES

American Bar Association Special Committee on Crime Prevention and Control (1972) *New Perspectives on Urban Crime.*

American Bar Association (1968) *Standards Relating to Pretrial Release.*

American Friends Service Committee, Washington Pretrial Justice Program (1970) *Report on the Pretrial Justice Survey.*

Ares, C., A. Rankin, and H. Sturz (1963) "The Manhattan Bail Project." 38 N.Y.U.L. Rev. 67.

"Bail, An Ancient Practice Reexamined." (1961) 70 Yale L.J. 966.

Bail and Summons: 1965 (1966) Proceedings, Institute on the Operation of Pretrial Release Projects.

Bellamy v. Justices, Plaintiffs Memorandum (N.Y. Sup.Ct. 1972)

"Constitutional Limitations on the Conditions of Pretrial Detention" (1970) 79 Yale L.J. 941.

"Costs of Preventive Detention" (1970) 79 Yale L.J. 926.

Ervin, S. (1967) "The Legislative Role in Bail Reform." 35 Geo.Wash. L.Rev. 429.

Freed, D. and P. Wald (1964) *Bail in the United States.*

Foote, C. (1965) "The Coming Constitutional Crisis in Bail." 113 U.Pa.L.Rev. 959, 1125.

Hruska, R. (1969) "Preventive Detention: The Constitution and the Congress." 3 Creighton L.Rev. 36.

Kleindienst, R. (1970) "The case for pretrial detention." Address to American Trial Lawyers' Association, January 30.

Mitchell, M., Jr. (1969) "Bail reform and the constitutionality of pretrial detention." 56 Va.L.Rev. 1223.

Moore's Federal Practice (1970) Vol. 8A.

National Bureau of Standards (1970) *Compilation and Use of Criminal Court Data in Relation to Pretrial Release of Defendants.*

"Preventive Detention: An Empirical Analysis" (1971) 6 Harvard Civil Rights, Civil Liberties L.Rev. 289.

Prison Reform (1971) Proposed Legislation and Recommendations of the Subcommittee on Penal and Judicial Reform of the Committee on Public Safety of the Council of the City of New York.

Rankin, A. (1964) "The effect of pretrial detention." 39 N.Y.U.L.Rev. 641.

Rauh, C. and E. Silbert (1970) "Criminal law and procedure: District of Columbia court reform and criminal procedure act of 1970." 20 Am.U.L.Rev. 252.

Report of the Judicial Council Committee to Study the Operation of the Bail Reform Act in the District of Columbia (1968-1969).

Silverstein, M. (1966) "Bail in the state courts—a field study and report." 50 Minn.L.Rev. 621.

Vera Institute of Justice and Georgetown Institute of Criminal Procedure (1971) *Study of Preventive Detention in the District of Columbia: The First Ten Months.*

PART IV.

THE TRIAL STAGE

Chapter 7

THE JURY SYSTEM

In all criminal prosecutions, the accused shall enjoy the right to . . . an impartial jury.

From the Sixth Amendment
to the U.S. Constitution

RITA JAMES SIMON received her B.A. at University of Wisconsin and Cornell University, 1952, 1954, and her Ph.D. at University of Chicago, 1957. She has taught at University of Chicago, Columbia University, Yale University, and University of Illinois, where she is professor and former head of the Sociology Department, and also as a visiting professor, Hebrew University, Jerusalem. She has participated on the National Council on Legal Clinics' project on Professional Responsibility Among Law Students, the President's Commission on the Causes and Prevention of Violence, and in wide law and sociology editorial and writing activities. Her books are *The Jury and the Plea of Insanity* (1967), *As We Saw the Thirties* (1967), *Readings in the Sociology of Law* (1968), and *Public Opinion in the Formulation of Public Policy* (in preparation).

PRENTICE H. MARSHALL has been a law professor at the University of Illinois since 1967. Before that, he was a partner in the law firm of Mayer, Jenner, and Block in Chicago. He received his law degree from the University of Illinois. He has been the chairman of the Illinois Supreme Court Commission on Jury Instruction in Criminal Cases since 1961, the reporter for the Illinois Judicial Conference since 1967, and the project director for the American Bar Foundation Study of Appellate Courts since 1970.

Chapter 7

THE JURY SYSTEM

RITA JAMES SIMON and
PRENTICE MARSHALL

This chapter has two major themes. The first focuses on the extent and conditions under which constitutional provisions and statutes guarantee the right to trial by jury. In so doing it also considers recent Supreme Court decisions that have reinterpreted and redefined that right and the forms in which it may be acknowledged. The second theme is an evaluation of the efficacy of the system. It reviews some of the major empirical studies of jury behavior conducted by lawyers and social scientists in the last two decades.

I. THE RIGHT TO TRIAL BY JURY

While trial by jury in a criminal case may be "fundamental to the American scheme of justice"[1] and "ubiquitously guaranteed"[2] by the federal and state constitutions, it is erroneous to conclude that all persons accused of crime enjoy a right to trial by jury. The federal government may and many states do deny a jury trial to one accused of so-called petty crimes.[3] The youth who is prosecuted as a juvenile is frequently denied a jury trial.[4] Furthermore, within the past two years the Supreme Court has approved six member juries[5] and nonunanimous guilty verdicts[6] to the end that one must be somewhat apprehensive about the future of the institution which was created as a "barrier ... between the liberties of the people and the prerogatives of the Crown."[7] Nevertheless, there is a constitutional commitment to a defendant charged with a serious offense who prefers the "common-sense judgment of [laymen] to the more tutored but perhaps less sympathetic reaction of a judge": he shall have it.[8] This chapter is addressed to the exercise of that "right."

Like many of our legal institutions, the origins of trial by jury in criminal cases is obscure. Historians now reject[9] the assertion once made[10] that Magna Carta spoke of and sought to preserve trial by jury when it referred to a judgment of one's peers. That peer group function was more akin to our contemporary grand jury accusation. In the thirteenth century the trial of the ultimate issue was left to the devices of battle, ordeal or oath. But irrespective of the mysticism of its birth, by 1689 the jury in criminal cases, with its power to reject the Crown's accusation, had evolved to such a point that its preservation was one of the major purposes of the English Declaration and Bill of Rights.

The political leaders of the American colonial-revolutionary period recognized the jury as a check on governmental oppression. They also knew that this purpose could be frustrated by the government granting the accused his trial in a place far removed from the locale of his alleged transgression: by deporting him to England to stand trial for a crime allegedly committed in the colonies. Thus, the First Congress of the American colonies included "trial by jury" among its inventory of "essential rights and liberties."[11] The Declaration of Independence denounced the Crown's puppet judges and the denial "in many cases, of the benefit of trial by jury."[12] The United States Constitution twice explicitly guarantees the right insofar as federal prosecutions are concerned[13] and, in light of recent Supreme Court decisions, does so again in respect to state prosecutions by way of the due process clause of the Fourteenth Amendment.[14]

Today an accused is entitled to a trial by jury in following situations. If the prosecution is brought in a federal court and involves an offense for which the punishment may exceed six months, imprisonment and the defendant is prosecuted as an adult, the defendant is entitled to a trial by a jury of twelve whose verdict (either guilty or not guilty) must be unanimous.[15] On the other hand, if the maximum punishment does not exceed six months, imprisonment[16] or the accused is under eighteen and consents to be prosecuted as a juvenile[17] a jury can be denied.

The size of the federal jury, while prescribed by the Federal Rules of Criminal Procedure[18] is not constitutionally required.[19] A state jury of six persons sitting in a serious offense case has been approved by the Supreme Court in language which clearly indicates constitutional approval of a federal jury of less than twelve. "To be sure, the number should probably be large enough to promote group deliberation, free from outside attempts at intimidation, and to provide a fair possibility for obtaining a representative cross-section of the community. But we find little reason to think that these goals are in any meaningful sense less likely to be achieved when the jury numbers six, than when it numbers 12—particularly if the requirement of unanimity is retained."[20]

On the other hand, the requirement of unanimity of verdict in federal prosecutions is constitutionally protected according to a 5-4 majority of the Court.[21] Furthermore, it is presently required by the Federal Rules of Criminal Procedure [22] and an additional member of the Court has stated that he would look with disfavor on a departure from that standard.[23]

State prosecutions present a somewhat different picture. As a matter of fact every state assures the defendant some form of trial by jury in serious prosecutions[24] and the Supreme Court has held that this is constitutionally required by the due process clause of the Fourteenth Amendment if the potential punishment exceeds six months' imprisonment.[25] However, the Court has also held that the due process clause does not require either 12-person juries (juries of six have been approved)[26] or unanimous verdicts (9-3 verdicts have been approved).[27] Furthermore, in state proceedings the juvenile can be denied a jury trial without his consent if the state chooses to do so.[28]

So it is that we say that it is erroneous to conclude that all persons accused of crime enjoy a right to trial by jury. Many do but many do not and, of those who do, there are significant potential variations in the form in which they do enjoy it.

Assuming a situation in which the accused is entitled to a jury is there a correlative right to waive it? There is a division on the question whether the right to a jury trial is solely that of the defendant so that he has the unfettered right to waive it or whether the state also has an interest in trial by jury so as to allow waiver only with the consent of the prosecution or the court or both. The Federal Rules of Criminal Procedure condition waiver on the consent of the prosecution and the approval of the court.[29] The Rule has been sustained against an attack asserting that the right belongs solely to the defendant.[30] However, in reaching that conclusion the Supreme Court suggested that a defendant-only approach would pass constitutional muster and there is respectable state authority to the effect that the right does belong solely to the defendant and his waiver cannot be conditioned on prosecutor approval and cannot be denied by the court.[31]

If a defendant is entitled to a jury trial and waives it his waiver must be knowing and intelligent.[32] Because the decision to waive is a critical one affecting a potential constitutional right the defendant should be represented by counsel in order that his waiver be effective.[33] The elements of knowing and intelligent waiver have not been adequately articulated. Thus, there is no authority to the effect that the defendant must know all of the ingredients of a jury trial at the time of his waiver.[34] The courts have suggested that the defendant be apprised by the court of his right to a jury and the basic consequence that in the event he embraces that right it will be the jury and not the court who will determine his guilt.[35]

The primary purpose of the jury is to provide the accused with a safeguard against governmental oppression: the corrupt or overzealous prosecutor; the compliant, biased, or eccentric judge. It is an interposition between the accused and his accuser of the common-sense judgment of a group of fairminded laymen, representative of a cross-section of the district in which the defendant allegedly committed the offense with which he stands accused. Therefore, procedures must be established which will produce this representative cross-section of the community.

The final act of production is summoning or compelling to participate as jurors. Experience has taught that reliance on volunteers will seldom supply sufficient jurors to transact the business of the court and will never produce a true cross-section of the community. Ironic as it may be, in order to preserve this most cherished institution of a free people, compulsory participation is necessary.

The mechanics of compulsory participation are not difficult to fashion. Starting with the identifiable population of the district a representative sampling should be drawn who will be summoned for jury service. Over the years many devices have been used: volunteers, taxpayer-property owners, voter lists, telephone directories, city directories. It was doubtful that these techniques produced a true cross-section of the community. Today, under the impetus of the Jury Selection and Service Act of 1968, those charged with the responsibility of identifying and summoning prospective jurors have turned with increasing frequency to voter registration lists. One thing is clear: whatever the method of initial selection it may not result in the systematic exclusion of any socioeconomic group in the district.[36]

To save time and money it is not uncommon for the jury officials to make a periodic (e.g., annual) random selection from the total identifiable populace of the district and then, by term of court, make a further random selection of those who will be summoned to court for service during the particular term. Otherwise, all of the population would have to be placed in the random selection device for each term of court. In certain metropolitan areas, where prospective jurors are summoned every two weeks all year, the total population of the county could not reasonably be included in the random process every time prospective jurors were needed.

It is common for those initially drawn from the population to be contacted, normally by mail, and asked to complete a simple questionnaire to ascertain if they are eligible for service, entitled to be excused as a matter of right, or are confronted with immediate personal situations which would result in the imposition of a peculiar hardship upon them should they be required to serve. Again, however, this prescreening cannot be designed so as to exclude particular socioeconomic groups from the list of potential jurors. [37]

Irrespective of the preliminary mechanics employed, it is the uniform practice throughout the country for a group from the district to be summoned to the particular court for jury service during a particular period of time. Persons in receipt of this summons must respond under pain of contempt. Those who are summoned are in sufficient number to meet the anticipated needs of the court for the particular term. They are commonly referred to as the jury panel or venire. From them will be selected the jurors who will hear the cases set for trial during that term.

It is at this point in the proceeding that a defendant who believes that the selection procedures have been employed in either a constitutionally or statutorily improper manner voices his objection by way of a motion to quash or discharge the panel or venire. He asserts that because the process of initial selection was biased, he will not be able to obtain from the venire a trial jury which comports with the objective of a jury: a fair cross-section of the community.

Here another facet of fairmindedness occasionally arises. Has the entire population and hence the initial venire or panel been so exposed to information about the case or its participants as to render it impossible for a trial jury to be selected which can fairly and openmindedly sit in judgment of the accused? Implicit in this problem is another premise of the jury trial (indeed, the bench trial as well): the determination of guilt or acquittal should be made upon the basis of facts or evidence which are presented to the jury (or judge) in open court, in the presence of the accused and in accordance with constantly evolving rules of evidence. The defendant is entitled to a jury which has not prejudged the case. The problem here, which has been labeled with the catchy phrase "free press-fair trial" is that fact dissemination by an independent press is imperative to the preservation of a free society while, at the same time, an individual accused by the state is entitled to an orderly hearing at which his guilt or acquittal can be determined within the confines of principles which are calculated to safeguard him from the opinions of the masses as well as the oppression of the state. When the collective mind of the populace has been saturated by facts adverse to the accused we recognize the impossibility of the jury casting those facts aside and we permit therapeutic steps at this stage of the trial in the form of a challenge to the panel or venire on the basis of pretrial publicity, a continuance until the publicity and its effect subside or a transfer of the trial to a place where the publicity has not been so intense or the populace from which the jury will be drawn does not have the same degree of reason to identify with the publicity.[38]

Once the suggested challenges have been disposed of, we move into the process of selecting the trial jury which will hear the individual case. Here, from a mechanical standpoint, the jury officer (most commonly the judge or the clerk of the court) draws names at random from the previously randomly selected panel or venire. These persons are questioned by the judge and frequently by the prosecutor and counsel for the defendant in what is referred to as the voir dire examination and selection of the jury. Techniques vary from state to state and from locale to locale even within the federal court system. But, in essence, each juror discloses information about his or her background, familiarity with the case, friendship or acquaintance with persons involved in the case as defendant, lawyer or witnesses, attitudes toward certain facts which may be disclosed in the case or legal principles which may be involved, and a myriad of other factors which, in the almost uncontrolled discretion of the judge, will reflect upon the individual juror's ability and willingness to sit as a fair and impartial juror in the case.

If facts or circumstances develop during this interrogation which show that a juror cannot fairly judge the case, the juror may be challenged for cause by either the prosecution or defendant. The presiding judge rules on the challenges and if sustained that juror steps aside and another takes his place. Failure to sustain a defendant's challenge for cause is reviewable on appeal from a conviction. In practice few challenges for cause are made and even fewer are sustained. There is no limit to the number of jurors who can be challenged for cause.

Challenges for cause cannot be employed to produce a nonrepresentative jury. Thus, the Supreme Court has held it to be constitutionally impermissible in a capital case to excuse for cause all prospective jurors who voiced "conscientious or moral scruples" against the death penalty.[39] Automatic exclusion of such a broad segment of the populace cannot be tolerated consistent with the notion that the jury should be representative of a cross-section of the community.

In addition to challenges for cause, the so-called peremptory challenge enjoys nationwide acceptance. Here the defendant and prosecutor are granted a number of challenges fixed by statute or rule according to the gravity of the offense. These challenges may be exercised as their name indicates: without reason. Constitutionally based arguments that only the defendant should be granted peremptory challenges have been rejected.[40] So, too, has been the assertion that the defendant was denied equal protection and due process because the prosecutor used all his peremptories to exclude members of the defendant's race from the trial jury.[41] However, in regard to the latter complaint, the Court observed that a regular and systematic use of peremptories for the purpose of excluding a given socioeconomic group from jury participation would run afoul of the equal protection clause of the Fourteenth Amendment.[42]

Once the jury is selected and sworn to hear the case it becomes the judge of the weight of the evidence and the credibility to be given to the testimony of the witnesses. In some jurisdictions the presiding judge may comment on these matters but he may not compel the jury to accept his views.[43] Of course, if the evidence is so deficient that it cannot, as a matter of law, support a verdict of guilty beyond a reasonable doubt, the presiding judge should enter a judgment of acquittal without the jury's assent. But he may never direct a verdict of guilty.

Furthermore, as an ingredient of due process of law, the jurors must be admonished that they must not vote guilty unless they are convinced of the guilt of the defendant beyond a reasonable doubt.[44] In some jurisdictions, however, they are also instructed to pay heed to the views of their fellow jurors in arriving at their own conclusion.[45]

If the jury acquits the defendant that is the end of the matter. A verdict of not guilty cannot be challenged by the court or the prosecutor upon the ground that it is contrary to the evidence.[46] Thus, in fact the jury possesses a power of nullification which, from time to time, has been exercised in prosecutions which the jurors, as representatives of the community, regarded as particularly odious or unfair. Indeed, nullification is inherent in the Supreme Court's observation that the jury is "necessary to protect against . . . judges too responsive to the voice of higher authority."[47]

So much for procedural and statutory matters; we shift now to a consideration of the efficacy and worthwhileness of the system by reviewing empirical studies of jury behavior.

II. REVIEW OF EMPIRICAL STUDIES

A. General

Much of the recent empirical work on the jury system was done in the 1950s at the Law School of the University of Chicago under the financial auspices of the Ford Foundation.[48] The major focus of that effort was to find out how and why the jury functioned as it did. How it reached its decisions, what factors and which types of jurors most influenced those decisions, how responsive the jury was to the rules of law and evidence, to the testimony of experts and to the discipline of the court; and how the jurors felt about their service. One group of researchers concentrated on systematically comparing the verdicts reached by juries as opposed to those judges reported they would have reached if they were trying the same case. This procedure was used in some 3,576 criminal cases and some 4,000 civil actions. In total, over 550 judges representing all parts of the country participated in the survey.[49] Another team of researchers focused on the jury as a problem-solving group and examined the internal dynamics and decision-making processes of the jury; as well as selective external factors such as the influence of the jurors' statuses in the larger society on their verdicts and on the power or influence different types of jurors exerted on the group. In addition, there were others who interviewed jurors after they were released from jury duty and found out how they reacted to their experience. For example, did their service enhance or detract from their view of the jury as an institution, and did they consider the experience a valuable civic activity. Another researcher asked jurors to recreate from memory everything that happened in the jury room during their deliberation. By having each of the twelve participants provide his own version of the deliberating process, the researcher was able to fit each of the individual pieces of the puzzle together into one overall pattern that described how the jury reached the verdict it reported.

B. Comparison of Judge and Jury Verdicts[50]

The most significant, and for those critical of the jury, perhaps the most unanticipated result of the study was the degree of similarity between judges' and juries' verdicts. In criminal cases, the judges reported agreement with the jury's verdict 80 percent of the time; both agreed to acquit in 13 percent of the cases and to convict in 67 percent of the cases. In the 20 percent of the cases in which they disagreed, the jury was likely to acquit six times as often as the judge. Graphically, the results are shown below in Table 1.

Table 1. Judge and Jury Agreement and Disagreement on Guilty in Criminal Cases[51]

	Jury Found		
Judge Would Have Found	For Defendant	Against Defendant	Total Judge
For Defendant	13	2	15
Against Defendant	18	67	85
Total Jury	31	69	100

In civil actions the level of agreement was practically as high, 79 percent, but the pattern of disagreement was evenly balanced.

Table 2. Judge and Jury Agreement on Liability in Personal Injury Cases

	Jury Found		
Judge Would Have Found	For Plaintiff	For Defendant	Total Judge
For Plaintiff	44	10	54
For Defendant	11	35	46
	55	45	100

As Kalven has noted: The judge disagrees with the jury because he is more pro-plaintiff about as often as the jury disagrees with him because it is more pro-plaintiff. Whereas the greater leniency of the jury toward the criminal defendant is congruent with popular expectations, the equality of pro-plaintiff response between judge and jury in civil cases is in sharp contrast to popular expectations.[52]

A question often raised by those who are critical of the jury system is whether members of the jury are capable of, and in fact do they understand and follow the questions of law and facts that may be involved in any given trial. Kalven and Zeisel brought to bear the following data on that issue. At the end of every trial each of the judges participating in the study was asked to evaluate the case on the basis of how difficult or how easy he thought the issues involved were; and on whether he thought the weight of the evidence made it a "clear" or a "close" case. They then distributed the cases in which the judges and juries disagreed across the four categories shown below.

Cases Categorized by the Presiding Judge as:

| Judge and Jury | Clear | | Close | |
Disagree*	Easy	Difficult	Easy	Difficult
Percent	9	8	41	39
Frequency	(618)	(57)	(406)	(110)

*The authors offer no explanation for why the percentages do not add to 100.

These results dramatically refute the belief that the jury does not understand its task. The data show that there is no greater likelihood of judge-jury disagreement in difficult cases than in easy cases (9 v. 8 or 41 v. 39 percents) the higher rates of disagreement occurred in cases that the judges declared "close" (41 and 39 percents) as compared to those they believed clearly favored one side (9 and 8 percents). Certainly if the jury disagreed with the judge out of ignorance or incompetence it would be most likely to do so in the difficult cases. The fact that no such pattern exists, plus the fact that the judges and juries agree in 80 percent of all the criminal cases, are major considerations in the Kalven-Zeisel unequivocal conclusion that the jury understands its job and performs it competently.

C. Experimental Juries [53]

The basic thrust of the experimental procedure was to use real jurors who had been selected for jury duty in the typical manner and have them listen to recorded trials that had been adapted from cases previously tried in the courts, deliberate, and render a verdict. The juries' deliberations were also recorded. The distinctive characteristic of the experimental approach is that the same trial could then be played before many different juries. In total, more than 2,000 jurors participated in five of these trials; three were civil actions and two were criminal cases. Both of the latter involved a defense of insanity. [54] This part of the project focused primarily on the events inside the jury room: the topics that were discussed, by whom, at what length, and with what effect.

Although the two research teams examined the jury from different vantage points, the investigators who used an experimental approach reached much the same overall conclusions as did those whose findings were based primarily on the survey of judges. They are that the jury understands its task, wants to and does perform it competently, and believes that the experience was worthwhile. For example, in assessing jury deliberations reported in *The Defense of Insanity,* Simon observed:

the jurors spend most of their time reviewing the court record. By the time they have finished deliberating they have usually considered every bit of testimony, expert as well as lay, and every point offered in evidence. . . . The most consistent theme that emerged from listening to the deliberations is the seriousness with which the jurors do their job and the extent to which they are concerned that the verdict they reach be consistent with the spirit of the law and with the facts of the case.[55]

In criticizing the jury, Jerome Frank has written:

Prejudice has been called the 13th juror. . . . Mr. Prejudice and Miss Sympathy are the names of witnesses whose testimony is never recorded, but must, nevertheless be reckoned with in trials by jury.[56]

Empirical findings have these two characters barely visible and hardly audible. For example, in discussing an incest case that involved consideration of behavior that most people consider heinous and immoral, the jurors said that they were seeking a verdict that would best prepare the defendant, his family, and the community for the day when the defendant would eventually return to society. The jurors spent most of their deliberating time trying to piece together information about the defendant's life, his job, his friends, his ties to the community, etc., at the time he was having sex relations with his two daughters, in order to better understand why he did what he did. They then tried to connect the information they had about the defendant's early childhood with his illicit sexual activities. They discussed the various dispositions available to the defendant and tried to find a verdict that matched their own beliefs against the legal expectations about how persons of the category of this particular defendant should be treated.

Expert testimony, a topic about which critics of the jury system have based a significant portion of their case for the jury's incompetency and "wrong headedness," again finds the jury failing to "live down" to expectations. Members of a jury seem to recognize that their responsibility for interpreting the facts and making a decision differs from that of witnesses who are asked to provide opinions based on expert knowledge. In the cases studied, the juries did not always follow the advice implicit or explicit in the expert's testimony. For example, in a trial involving a defense of insanity to a charge of housebreaking (the case based on the famous Monte Durham trial heard originally in the District of Columbia) when the defendant was described by two psychiatrists as having a psychopathic personality with psychosis and when the defendant's testimony was jumbled and nonresponsive, and when his life history showed prior commitments to mental hospitals, 56 percent of the juries found the defendant not guilty by reason of insanity—a verdict consistent with the psychiatrists' testimonies. But in the incest trial, only 13 percent of the juries found the defendant not guilty by reason of insanity, even though testimony provided by two psychiatrists implicitly recommended that the defendant should be so found.[57]

In the housebreaking case, a defendant who was patently insane (as determined by his behavior in other contexts, his testimony, and his prior commitments to mental hospitals) but who had committed a seemingly rational crime (stealing for profit) in an intelligent manner (breaking into an empty house in the middle of the night) was found not guilty by reason of insanity by a majority of the juries.

In the incest case, a defendant who had never been committed to a mental institution, who held a responsible job as a lieutenant in the municipal fire department and whose condition was described by two psychiatrists as psychoneurotic, i.e., not psychotic, but who repeatedly committed acts that were unnatural and perverse, was found sane and responsible by almost all the juries.

Are the verdicts in the incest case evidence of the jury's failure or inability to understand expert testimony and therefore indicative of the jury's general incompetence? We do not think so. In listening to the jurors consider the expert testimony, it was not only clear that they understood the technical vocabulary as well as the essence of the testimony, but that they took upon themselves the difficult task of distinguishing how their role in the proceedings differed from or complemented that of the psychiatrists. During the deliberations the jurors discussed over and over again, "Who should have the final say about what happens to the defendant, a jury of laymen or a group of medical experts?" Most of the time the jury resolved its dilemma by spelling out for itself the separate tasks that the law expected each to perform. In essence, the jury concluded that the expert's testimony emphasized only one aspect of the problem, the clinical part, and that his testimony contributed little to the major dilemma that confronted the jury, that of placing the clinical or purely medical facts about the defendant into a moral-legal context. The jurors reminded each other that the court instructed them that the presence of a mental illness or aberration should not by itself excuse the defendant; that it was the jury's task to decide whether the particular manifestation of mental illness which the defendant exhibited met the norm of nonresponsibility specified by the rule of the law. Thus, the jury could consider the expert's testimony, understand it, choose to reject much of it, and still demonstrate intelligence about the substantive issues involved in the trial as well as the logic of the law they were instructed to apply.

When the Durham rule[58] was first adopted in the District of Columbia in

1954, one of the major criticisms leveled against it was that it would become a convenient vehicle whereby persons who had committed serious crimes could escape punishment for their behavior. The critics were especially apprehensive because they recognized that in many instances responsibility for applying and interpreting the rule would rest with the jury; and juries had acquired a notorious reputation for not understanding and properly applying legal rules. The basis for that reputation was not established by a systematic evaluation of the jury's performance but rather has been asserted by those who either have disagreed with a jury's decision in a particular case or who have sufficient prestige in the legal profession to make such assertions without adequate documentation. The experimental juries offer some data on the jury's ability to apply and interpret legal rules. A comparison of the verdicts reported by 22 juries who deliberated under the M'Naghten rule, as opposed to 26 juries who deliberated under Durham for the same trial, showed that instructions made some difference. None of the juries that deliberated under M'Naghten compared to five of the juries that deliberated under Durham, found the defendant not guilty by reason of insanity. The difference, or the pro-defendant bias as a result of using Durham as opposed to M'Naghten, is 19 percent (0 out of 22 = 0 percent, 5 out of 26 = 19 percent). It is not zero. But neither is it, as many critics of the Durham rule have feared, 100 or even 50 percent.

Jurors were also asked which rule they would recommend that the courts use in the future, M'Naghten or Durham.[59] Not unexpectedly the results showed a strong relationship between prior exposure and recommendation. For example, of those who deliberated under M'Naghten, 37 percent favored M'Naghten, 26 percent favored Durham, and 37 percent said it made no difference. Of those who deliberated under Durham, 45 percent favored Durham, 28 percent M'Naghten and 27 percent said it made no difference. But when these same jurors were asked to choose the rule of law that they would request the judge to read to the jury if they were the defendant's attorney and wanted to obtain a verdict of not guilty by reason of insanity, the results looked like this:

As Defense Attorney Jurors Recommend	Percent
M'Naghten Rule	19 (112)*
Durham Rule	49 (293)
No Difference	32 (184)

*The numbers in parentheses represent the number of jurors questioned.

These responses clearly demonstrate that the jurors understood the implications that the two rules have for the defendant. More than twice as many jurors recommended Durham as opposed to M'Naghten. Thus, when asked to step out of their role as jurors and into one in which they must identify with the defendant in the most partisan manner, the jurors recognize the pro-defendant advantages of Durham over M'Naghten that members of the bench and bar perceive. But in their role as jurors they did not allow those advantages to influence their verdicts as much as their critics feared.

D. Participation and Influence on the Jury

There is probably no other area of jury behavior that trial lawyers believe more important or about which they believe they have more expertise than that of predicting the kinds of people who are likely to have the most to say and the greatest influence in the jury room. Trial lawyers are interested in the socioeconomic and sociopsychological characteristics of prospective jurors as a practical matter. They believe that selecting a jury with the right combination of social characteristics can mean the difference between winning and losing a case. Researchers have asked two general questions about this issue. Are some jurors more influential than others in determining the group's decision; and, if they are, which types of jurors are most likely to have the greatest influence?

Analysis of more than one hundred civil jury deliberations showed that there were significant differences in jurors' performance by the educational, occupational, ethnic and racial, and sexual characteristics of the jurors. Those differences were manifest both in the amount and the quality of the juror's participation.[60] For example, one study showed that men talked more than women and said different kinds of things. Men were more likely to emphasize task-related topics while women were more likely to say things that reduced tension in the jury and served to unify the group. Men were more likely to initiate topics, women were more likely to react to comments or questions raised by men. Other studies showed that jurors who enjoyed higher socioeconomic status, i.e., held more prestigious jobs, had more education, were more likely to be elected foreman and to participate more actively in the discussions. Negroes and others who belong to minority ethnic groups were more likely to be sympathetic to the plaintiff and to favor higher awards for damages.

When these same characteristics were compared for criminal juries, the differences produced by socioeconomic status carried over; but the sex-role differences did not. In criminal juries, women talked as much as men and about much the same issues. The figures shown below in Table 3 compare relative participation in civil and criminal cases among jurors in different occupations.[61]

Table 3. Participation by Occupation in Civil and Criminal Juries

Juror's Occupation	Civil Juries (48)*	Criminal Juries (68)
Proprietors and Professionals	8.9	9.1
Clerical Workers	7.0	7.7
Skilled Laborers	6.3	7.6
Laborers	5.9	6.1

*The number in parentheses represents the number of juries involved.

The figures in Table 3 show that in both civil and criminal juries, jurors who occupy more prestigious occupations talk more than those who have less prestigious occupations. The tendency for jurors who belong to minority ethnic and racial groups to be more sympathetic to the defendant (just as they were more sympathetic to the plaintiff in the civil cases) also carried over to the criminal cases. The data on criminal juries were based on cases that involved a defense of insanity. It is reasonable to assume, however, that the jurors' behavior would generalize to other criminal proceedings and especially to those involving acts of violence or sexual crimes.

E. The Importance of the Deliberation

How often does it happen that jurors enter the jury room divided in their beliefs about the defendant's guilt in contrast to the frequency with which there is a consensus, even before the jurors begin to deliberate? Which pattern is more prevalent: one in which most people have formed an opinion before they enter the jury room and their opinions remain unchanged by what is said during the deliberations, or one in which most people are undecided before they begin to deliberate and the subsequent discussion determines their final decision?

One technique that was used to answer this question among experimental juries was to compare the jurors' individual verdicts as reported on questionnaires immediately after the trial but before the deliberations began, against the group's decision, and then to compare both verdicts against individual verdicts reported on a questionnaire following the group discussion. The results indicated that among 55 percent of the jurors there was no conflict between the opinions they held before they entered the jury room and the subsequent group decision. In other words, more than half the jurors formed an opinion before the deliberations began; and that opinion did not change as a result of the group discussion. An additional 16 percent were in juries that were unable to reach a consensus. They reported themselves as hung juries. The full pattern is described below in Table 3, 4 and 5. Note that of the 16 percent in hung juries, 12 had formed

Table 4. Relationship Between Individual and Group Decisions

Pre-deliberation Individual Verdicts	Verdict Reported by the Jury	Post-deliberation Individual Verdicts	Percent Jurors
NGI*	NGI	NGI	5
Guilty	Guilty	Guilty	50
NGI	Hung	NGI	3
NGI	Hung	Guilty	3
Guilty	Hung	Guilty	9
Guilty	Hung	NGI	1

*NGI = not guilty by reason of insanity.

opinions before the deliberation began and were not sufficiently moved by what was said in the discussion to change their opinions. Thus, a total of 67 percent of the jurors (55 percent of those in groups that reached consensus before the deliberations began plus an additional 12 percent in the hung juries) would have reached the same decision if there had never been a deliberation; in other words, if the court had polled the jurors individually right after the trial.

For the remaining 29 percent of the jurors, the pattern is as shown in Table 5. Among two-thirds of those jurors, or 19 percent of the total, the group discussion was significant. It changed their previously held individual verdicts

Table 5. Relationship Between Individual and Group Decisions

Pre-deliberation Individual Verdicts	Verdict Reported by the Jury	Post-deliberation Individual Verdicts	Percent Jurors
NGI	Guilty	Guilty	15
Guilty	NGI	NGI	4
NGI	Guilty	NGI	5
Guilty	NGI	Guilty	2
NGI	NGI	Guilty	2
Guilty	Guilty	NGI	1

and made them consistent with the majority. These jurors apparently did have a true change of belief, and were not responding to group pressure, because when they were given the opportunity to state privately what their verdicts were, they reported the same opinions as that reached by the group. Of the remaining 10 percent, two-thirds went along with the majority, but probably because they wanted to avoid a hung jury. Afterward in private, they reiterated an opinion that was still opposed to the group's verdict. The others shifted their verdicts in such a manner as to question whether they understood what was happening; but remember they constitute 3 percent of the total. Thus, for the 816 jurors described in Tables 4 and 5[62] the results show that in one out of three-and-a-half jury deliberations the group verdicts differ from those which the jurors would have reported if they were polled individually immediately following the trial.

Unlike the situation portrayed so dramatically in the movie, "Twelve Angry Men," it is extremely rare for one juror to hang the jury. In almost every instance in which there was a hung jury among the experimental civil and criminal juries, the size of the coalitions were 6-6, 7-5 or 8-4. In groups that reached consensus, in only about one in ten times did a minority coalition succeed in convincing a majority of the jurors to accept its point of view. Among those 10 percent, the size of the minority was five. There were no instances in which one juror or even two held out against the other ten or eleven and then succeeded in persuading them to their position.

The data, based on the experimental juries, match closely comparable information collected by Zeisel and Broeder in interviews with some 2,500 jurors who sat on real cases in Chicago and Brooklyn. They were asked to describe the distribution of votes on the first ballot in the jury room. For each jury, the first ballot votes were then compared against the jury's verdict. Table 6 shows the relationship between first ballots, which were taken before there was any substantive discussion about the case, and group verdicts.[62]

In referring to the data in Table 6, Kalven and Zeisel comment:

Table 6. First Ballot Votes by Jury Verdicts

Final Verdict	Guilty Votes on First Ballot (in percent)				
	0	1-5	6	7-11	12
Not guilty	100	91	50	5	—
Hung	—	7	—	9	—
Guilty	—	2	50	86	100
Total	100	100	100	100	100
Number of Cases	26	41	10	105	43

in the instances where there is an initial majority either for conviction or for acquittal, the jury in roughly nine out of ten cases decides in the direction of the initial majority. Only with extreme infrequency does the minority succeed in persuading the majority to change its mind during the deliberation. But this is only to say that *with very few exceptions the first ballot decides the outcome of the verdict.* And if this is true, then *the real decision is often made before the deliberation begins.* [64]

Consider the first ballot votes as comparable to the pre-deliberation verdicts, and note that the two sets of data (those from the experimental juries and those based on interviews with jurors who served on real cases) make the same point. Much of the time the deliberation does not decide the case. In other words, if the jurors were polled individually immediately following the trial and the majority opinion adopted as the group's decision, that verdict would match the verdict the jury eventually reports as its unanimous decision about 80 percent of the time.

There are those who claim, however, that it is in just that small proportion of cases in which the minority view does prevail that a man's life or entire future is likely to be at stake. They claim that cases in which the minority is successful are not randomly distributed but are indeed the most important cases because a principle or a life is on trial. Kalven and Zeisel comment:

> Perhaps [the deliberation] does not so much decide the case as bring about the consensus, the outcome of which has been made highly likely by the distribution of first ballot votes. The deliberation process might well be likened to what the developer does for an exposed film: it brings out the picture, but the outcome is pre-determined.

F. Jurors' and Judges' Evaluation of the Jury System

Some critics argue for the demise of the jury mainly on grounds that the participants find it an onerous and unrewarding task. Surveys that have been made of citizens who have served on the jury and of trial court judges, indicate the contrary. About twenty-five years ago some 1,500 jurors were surveyed in Utah concerning their reactions to having been called for jury duty.[66] The jurors were almost unanimous in their response that they found their service an interesting and worthwhile experience. They were strongly opposed to the idea of abolishing the jury system. Interviews with 1,500 jurors in New York City conducted about a dozen years ago revealed that among jurors who actually sat on a case and suffered no economic hardship, over 80 percent indicated that they would like to serve again.[67] In another survey of a medium-sized community in the Midwest, 94 percent of those who had ever served on a jury said they would like to do so again. Among a cross-section of residents of that same community, 90 percent said that if they were ever involved in a criminal case, they would prefer to have a jury over a bench trial.

The results of a national poll of some 1,060 trial judges in which the judges were asked to choose among three positions on the jury are reported in Tables 7 and 8.[68] Note that a large majority of the trial judges who, quoting Kalven "are daily observers of the jury system in action," find the jury's performance thoroughly satisfactory in both civil and criminal cases.[69] Thus the data that are available leave little basis for doubt that the jury is perceived as a positive and valuable institution by the public as well as the bench.

Table 7. Trial Judges' Opinions of the Jury System—Criminal Cases

Opinions of the Jury	Number	Percent
(1) Thoroughly Satisfactory	791	77
(2) Satisfactory if Certain Changes	210	20
(3) Unsatisfactory	29	3
Total	1,030	100

Table 8. Trial Judges' Opinions of the Jury System—Civil Cases

Opinions of the Jury	Number	Percent
(1) Thoroughly Satisfactory	661	64
(2) Satisfactory if Certain Changes	280	27
(3) Unsatisfactory	97	9
Total	1,038	100

G. Concluding Remarks

In the beginning of this chapter we noted that, in the last year or so, the Supreme Court has handed down decisions that make one somewhat apprehensive about the future of the jury.[70] In concluding this appraisal of the jury, we cannot avoid commenting on the irony of the timing of the Court's decisions. In the last two decades lawyers and social scientists have joined together in large-scale efforts to evaluate the jury system in more objective and scientific terms than had been done at any previous time. The results of parts of their study have only recently been published and there is still more to come. By and large what has been reported indicates that the jury system works well, that the participants perform their task with intelligence and interest, and that the juries' verdicts are consistent with those that experts, i.e., judges, claim they would have reached. These conclusions must be surprising to some distinguished members of the bench and bar who, even in the absence of systematic first-hand information, have been critical of the jury for a long time and have advocated limiting its use to certain types of cases or even abolishing it. That the court should act now, and that it should act in such a way as to diminish the role of the jury, when for the first time there is a systematic body of data available for evaluating the jury's performance, and when the data reported thus far provide such a positive image of the jury, is indeed ironic.[71]

NOTES

1. Duncan v. Louisiana, 391 U.S. 145, 149 (1968).

2. A. Amsterdam, B. Segal, M. Miller, *Trial Manual for the Defense of Criminal Cases,* §315 (ALI-ABA 1967).

3. See Rule 3(c)(1), Fed. R. Pro. Trial of Minor Offenses before U.S. Magistrates, 18 U.S.C.A.; Appendix to opinion of Harlan, J., Williams v. Florida, 399 U.S. 78, 138 (1970).

4. See 18 U.S.C. 5033.

5. Williams v. Florida, 399 U.S. 78, 86 (1970).

6. Johnson v. Louisiana, 40 LW 4524 (1972); Apodaca v. Oregon, 40 LW 4528 (1972).

7. 4 W. Blackstone, *Commentaries,* 349 (Cooley ed. 1899).

8. Duncan v. Louisiana, 391 U.S. 145, 156 (1968).

9. Frankfurter & Corcoran, "Federal Petty Offenses and the Constitutional Guaranty of Trial by Jury," 39 Harv. L.R. 917, 922 (1926).

10. 4 W. Blackstone, *Commentaries* 349 (Cooley ed. 1899).

11. R. Perry, ed., *Sources of Our Liberties,* 270 (1959).

12. 43 Britannica Great Books, ed., 2.

13. U.S. Const., Art. III, §2; Amend. VI.

14. Duncan v. Louisiana, 391 U.S. 145 (1968); Baldwin v. New York, 399 U.S. 66 (1970).

15. Thompson v. Utah, 170 U.S. 343 (1898); Patton v. United States, 281 U.S. 276, 288 (1930); Rules 23 (b) and 31 (a) of the Fed. R. Crim. Pro., 18 U.S.C.A.

16. District of Columbia v. Clawans, 300 U.S. 617 (1937); Rule 3(c) (1), Fed. R. Pro. Trial of Minor Offenses, 18 U.S.C.A.; United States v. Beard, 313 F. Supp. 844 (D. Minn. 1970). Probation for a period in excess of 6 months is permissible without a jury trial, Frank v. United States, 395 U.S. 147 (1969).

17. 18 U.S.C. §5033.

18. Rule 23(b), Fed. R. Crim. Pro., "Juries shall be of 12 . . ."

19. Williams v. Florida, 399 U.S. 78, 86-103 (1970).

20. Note 19 above, at 100; The decision has been criticized by Hans Zeisel, "And then there were none: the diminution of the federal jury," 38 U. of Chi. L.R. 710 (1971).

21. See concurring opinion of Powell, J. and dissenting opinion of Douglas, Brennan, Stewart and Marshall, J.J., in Apodaca v. Oregon, 40 LW 4528 (1972) at 4531, 4536, 4540 and 4541 which, collectively, indicate that the five Justices regard unanimity as a Sixth Amendment requirement; Thompson v. Utah, 170 U.S. 343 (1898); Patton v. United States, 281 U.S. 276, 288 (1930).

22. Rule 31(a), Fed. R. Crim. Pro.

23. Blackmun, J. Concurring in Apodaca v. Oregon, 40 LW 4528, 4531 (1972).

24. See Baldwin v. New York, 399 U.S. 66, 70-72 (1970).

25. Baldwin v. New York, 399 U.S. 66 (1970); Dyke v. Taylor Implement Mfg. Co., 391 U.S. 216 (1968).

26. Williams v. Florida, 399 U.S. 78, 86 (1970).

27. Johnson v. Louisiana, 40 LW 4524 (1972). For an anticipatory criticism see Zeisel, note 20 above.

28. McKeiver v. Pennsylvania, 403 U.S. 528 (1971); as a matter of fact the majority of states deny a jury trial in juvenile proceedings, Id. at 549-550; In Re Fucini, 44 Ill. 2nd 305 (1970).

29. Rule 23(a), Fed. R. Crim. Pro.

30. Singer v. United States, 380 U.S. 24 (1965).

31. People v. Spegal, 5 Ill.2nd 211 (1955).

32. Dranow v. United States, 325 F.2nd 481 (8th Cir. 1963), cert. den. 376 U.S. 912.

33. See Rosemon v. United States, 364 F.2nd 18 (9th Cir. 1966) cert. den. 386 U.S. 918.

34. See People v. Rodgers, 276 N.E.2nd 504 (4th Dist. Ill. App. Ct. 1971) rejecting argument that defendant should be advised of requirement of unanimity.

35. See notes 32, 33, and 34, above.

36. 18 U.S.C. §243, 1861 et seq.; Whites v. Georgia, 385 U.S. 545 (1967); Smith v. Texas, 311 U.S. 128 (1940); Norris v. Alabama, 294 U.S. 587 (1935).

37. Note 36, above; Alexander v. Louisiana,   U.S.   , 31 L.ed.2nd.

38. E.g., Irvin v. Dowd, 366 U.S. 717 (1961); Sheppard v. Maxwell, 384 U.S. 333. (1966); Groppi v. Wisconsin, 400 U.S. 505 (1971).

39. Witherspoon v. Illinois, 391 U.S. 510 (1968).

40. Swain v. Alabama, 380 U.S. 202 (1965).

41. Note 40, above.

42. Note 40, above; U.S. ex rel. Goldsby v. Harpole, 263 F.2nd 71 (5th Cir. 1959) cert. den. 361 U.S. 838; United States v. Pearson, 448 F.2nd 1207 (5th Cir. 1971).

43. Patton v. United States, 281 U.S. 276, 288 (1930); "The Right of the Judge to Comment on the Evidence," 6 F.R.D. 317 (1947); Kalven & Zeisel, *The American Jury* 420 (1966).

44. In Re Winship, 397 U.S. 358 (1970).

45. Allen v. United States, 164 U.S. 492 (1896).

46. See Standards Relating to Criminal Appeals, Commentary to §1.4 (A.B.A. 1970).

47. Duncan v. Louisiana, 391 U.S. 145, 156 (1968); but see United States v. Moylan, 417 F.2nd 1002 (4th Cir. 1969) rejecting argument that jury should be instructed as to power of nullification; compare, Van Dyke, "The Jury as a Political Institution," Center Mag. March 1970, pp. 17 et seq.

48. In the late 1930s and early 1940s psychologists and lawyers at Cornell University studied the jury under experimental conditions using students as subjects. See H. P. Weld and E. R. Danzig, "A study of the way in which a verdict is reached by a jury," 53 Amer. J.

Psych., 1940, pp. 518-536; reprinted in R. J. Simon (ed.), *The Sociology of Law,* San Francisco, 1968, pp. 83-93; also H. P. Weld and M. F. Roff, "A study in the formation of opinion based upon legal evidence," 51 Amer. J. Psych., 1938, pp. 609-628.

49. But not all regions were represented proportionately; the South for example was underrepresented. In addition, not all judges participated for the same period of time or for the same number of cases.

50. For a complete account of the judicial surveys see Harry Kalven, Jr. and Hans Zeisel, *The American Jury,* Boston, 1966.

51. Tables 1 and 2 do not contain the hung juries which comprised about 5.5 percent of all the cases.

52. Harry Kalven, Jr. "The dignity of the civil jury," 50 Virginia Law Review, 1964, pp. 1055-1075; reprinted in R. J. Simon (ed.) *The Sociology of Law,* San Francisco, 1968, p. 302.

53. Fred L. Strodtbeck was the director of the experimental section of the Jury Project. He designed the basic experimental plan.

54. A more detailed account of the experimental design and procedure may be found in Rita J. Simon, *The Jury and the Defense of Insanity,* Chapter 2, Boston, 1967.

55. Ibid, p. 175.

56. Jerome Frank, *Courts on Trial,* New York, 1963, p. 122.

57. The 56 percent was based on 30 juries who heard the housebreaking case; and the 13 percent was based on 68 juries who heard the incest case.

58. The Durham rule replaced the M'Naghten, right from wrong criterion, and established the criterion that if a person's criminal behavior was a product of his mental illness, he should not be held responsible for such behavior.

59. The jurors' opinions were polled after they had completed the deliberation. A brief definition of the M'Naghten and Durham rules were included in the questionnaire so that all jurors had the same basis for judgment.

60. See for example: F. L. Strodtbeck and R. D. Mann, "Sex role differentiation in the jury," Sociometry, 19, March, 1956, pp. 3-11; F. L. Strodtbeck, R. M. James and C. Hawkins, "Social status in jury deliberations," Amer. Sociol. Rev., XXII, 6, December, 1957, pp. 713-719; R. M. James, "Status and competency in jury deliberations," Amer. J. Sociol., LXIV, 6, May, 1959, pp. 563-570.

61. If participation in jury deliberations were apportioned equally, each juror would use 8-1/3 percent of the total time (8-1/3 X 12 = 100%).

62. The same type of data are available for 360 additional jurors with practically identical results.

63. Kalven and Zeisel, op. cit., p. 488.

64. Ibid., p. 488.

65. Ibid., p. 489.

66. David W. Moffat, "As jurors see a lawsuit," Oregon Law Review, 24, 1944-1945, pp. 199-207.

67. Dale Broeder, "The University of Chicago jury project," Nebraska Law Review, 38, 1959, pp. 744-760.

68. Harry Kalven, Jr., "The dignity of the civil jury," 50 Virginia Law Review, 1964; reprinted in Simon (ed.) *The Sociology of Law,* 1968, pp. 293-313. The three positions were: (1) On balance the jury system is thoroughly satisfactory; (2) The jury system has serious disadvantages which could be corrected and should be corrected if the system is to

remain useful; (3) The disadvantages of the jury system outweighs its advantages so much that its use should be sharply curtailed.

69. Op. cit., p. 310.

70. See notes 5 and 6.

71. In an article that appeared before the Supreme Court's decision on nonunanimous guilty verdicts, Hans Zeisel voiced concern about the implications of the decisions that the court *might* adopt. See Hans Zeisel, "And then there were none: the diminution of the federal jury," pp. 710-724.

Chapter 8

TRIAL, TESTIMONY, AND TRUTH

In all criminal prosecutions, the accused shall enjoy the right to . . . be confronted with the witnesses against him [and] to have compulsory process for obtaining witnesses in his favor

From the Sixth Amendment
to the U.S. Constitution

JAMES MARSHALL is a member of the New York bar. He was a member of the New York City Board of Education, and its president from 1938 to 1942. He has served for many years on the United States National Commission for UNESCO, and was a member of the U.S. delegation to UNESCO. He has taught at New York University and at the Boston University Human Relations Laboratory. Dr. Marshall is author of *Law and Psychology in Conflict* (1966), *Intention—In Law and Society* (1968), *Swords and Symbols: The Technique of Sovereignty* (1969) and numerous articles.

Chapter 8

TRIAL, TESTIMONY, AND TRUTH

JAMES MARSHALL

The basic right of the accused is to have a fair trial within the cultural definition of fairness of the forum. Under our Constitution we call this right due process of law or the equal protection of the laws, including a speedy and public trial by an impartial jury. Whatever the philosophical description of a fair trial may be, it is in fact a pragmatic construct resting in considerable measure on legal fictions or perhaps unverified hypotheses. There is experience but little empirical evidence to justify this pragmatic approach and while it is the common notion that a trial is to determine reality and do justice this is in the nature of a Platonic ideal which at best is a goal or norm against which to measure our concept of a fair trial.

I. ORAL TESTIMONY AND PERCEPTION

In most criminal cases evidence is essentially oral based on recall of what the witness perceived. To a lesser extent real evidence (a gun, merchandise, a scar) or written evidence (a memorandum, bookkeeping entries, other records) are introduced in evidence. These must, of course, be shown to be relevant and this is usually by means of oral evidence. Evidence is presented, under our Anglo-Saxon American system, through adversary proceedings. This we believe makes possible a fair trial by a process of challenge and interrogation to test the validity of perception and recall and reveal bias and perjury. Under the Sixth Amendment a fair trial entitles a defendant to confrontation of witnesses, and this is made obligatory on the states by the Fourteenth Amendment (Pointer v. Texas, 1965).

How reliable is evidence? How effective is this system in attaining truth and justice? And perhaps we should ask whether truth and justice are the only goals to be considered as validating a criminal trial.

The lore of ancient times as well as our contemporary experience has questioned the reliability of perception and the legal process. Simeon ben Shatach (first chapter, ninth citation) is quoted in the Talmud as warning "Be thorough in the examination of witnesses, and be heedful of your words, lest through your words the witnesses be led to testify falsely."

After his trial, just before he took the hemlock, Socrates (Plato, 1938: 99) in discussing the difficulty of knowing about life after death asked "Have sight and hearing truth in them? Are they not, as the poets are always telling us, inaccurate witnesses?" Since then many convicted men and numerous people found to be at fault and liable in civil suits have come to similar conclusions: the other side's witnesses, if they were not lying, were blind and deaf. The psychological sciences have described man's faulty perceptions and erratic memory, so that we have a considerable body of empirical evidence supporting Socrates' views (Kilpatrick, 1961; Marshall, 1966a: 5-81). And surely every lawyer and judge can give examples of the unreliability of witnesses and jurors as perceivers of reality.

We perceive in large measure what we expect to perceive and we expect what we have already experienced. Past experiences of successes and failure influence our perception of similar situations. This is pragmatic. Similarly we interpret— that is, we give meaning to what we perceive in terms of our experience. We make use of values that have demonstrated validity in similar transactions. We make bets and guesses on the basis of what has happened before (Kilpatrick and Cantril, 1961: 357-358). Thus the police may look to the style of a particular crime, recall that X has done this kind of crime before, that he is out of jail and so they pick him up. An example of this betting on experience is to be found in Rita James Simon's (1967: 154-160) study of *The Jury and the Defense of Insanity*. She found the jurors tended to measure insanity by experiences that they had had with mental illness in their families or among their friends or acquaintances.

Let me give a few examples of how experience may give meaning to phenomena. In a dark room the subjects were shown two moving dots, one large and one small. When the larger dot followed the smaller the subjects tended to describe the larger dot as chasing the smaller. When the larger dot preceded it was described as leading the smaller (Heider and Simmel, 1944: 254).

One of our most popular errors is the so-called moon illusion. The moon looks larger on the horizon than at its zenith. The reason is that on the horizon we are measuring it against the height of known objects, whereas in the heavens it cannot be related to any object of a size we have experienced (Rock and Kaufman, 1962).

If we see two lights in the dark, one bright and one dull or one large and one small, we tend to see the larger or brighter light as nearer than the duller or smaller (Kilpatrick and Ittelson, 1961). That is why the ancients assumed that the large stars were closer to the earth than the smaller ones. Our experience is that things that are closer look bigger and clearer too. Thus brightness and size may be cues to distance as they may be also cues to weight.

It is difficult even for trained persons to be accurate witnesses. Some years ago Kerensky, the former Premier of Russia, was lecturing in New York. A woman came on the stage and struck him. Eight experienced reporters from different newspapers gave eight different accounts of the event and seven or eight different versions of Kerensky's reaction to the occurrence (Hutchins and Slesinger, 1928).

In an experiment with air force personnel it was found that they were unable accurately to estimate the speed of a car moving at 12 miles an hour. The estimates ran from 10 to 50 miles an hour (American Society for Public Administration, 1959).

Furthermore, even unconsciously, our perception is subject to biases conditioned by experience. Hastorf and Cantril (1954), one at Dartmouth and the other at Princeton, showed their students a picture of a Dartmouth-Princeton football game which had been described as a particularly rough game. They asked their respective students to indicate which team had violated the rules or had been unnecessarily rough. As one might expect the Dartmouth men attributed most of the rule-breaking and roughness to the Princeton team and the Princeton men made the contrary attributions.

In an experiment conducted by Marshall and Mansson (1966) a few years ago at New York University, they showed students of two criminal law classes a picture. To some they assigned the role of witness for the prosecution and to others that of witness for the defense. They found that the witnesses for the prosecution had more accurate recall than those for the defense. They discovered, too, that those people who, on a test, were shown to be the more punitive, had better recall than the less punitive. However, in another experiment the latter correlation did not occur (Marshall et al., 1971).

In the selection of jurors an attorney will try to exclude persons whose interests and experience might bias him against the attorney's client or his case. Alice Padawer-Singer (1970) and Allen Barton conducted an experiment in selection of jurors. With permission of the court they used jurors from the regular jury panel. Some of them were exposed in advance to material damaging to the defendant's case and some were not. They found that those exposed tended to find guilt far more frequently than those not so exposed.

In our aural perception we also take cues from our past experience. We rarely hear every word or syllable that is spoken but from the context we guess what the word or sentence is. Few people have the capacity to recall a speech they have heard but they can reconstruct the substance and, on interrogation, may recognize what they heard. In effect they draw upon the bank of their experience. This process was described long ago by Thucydides (1934: 14) in his introduction to the *History of the Peloponnesian Wars*. He referred to the differences in the accounts of events by eye witnesses whether due to imperfect memory or partiality. He admitted to his own inability to carry in his memory word for word the speeches he heard and repeated. He said "[M] y habit has been to make the speakers say what was in my opinion demanded of them by the various occasions, of course adhering as closely as possible to the general sense of what they really said." In other words, taking the cues we fill in the gaps. We get the drift of the speaker and these cues give momentum to our memory. This is similar to the momentum that causes us to assume a car will continue at the same speed and in the same direction as we last saw it moving. Such fictions are, of course, pragmatic. They are necessary to effective daily living. However, they are hazardous bets if the precise words of a conversation (or the exact courses of two cars) have determining effects in a litigation. The element that we choose to repress, or what selection we make as the likeliest expectation for what we see or hear, will depend on what bet, or what selection, we make as the likeliest expectation for what we see or hear; and that too will, of course, be conditioned by past experience in similar situations (Ittelson, 1961).

This may result in wishful thinking and a witness may swear to a "truth" which he never heard. I remember a murder case in which a woman sitting on a window sill cleaning her windows three stories up testified that she had heard a conversation on a corner half a block away just before the murder occurred. Learning that the crime had been committed she evidently felt a sense of participation as a witness and "heard" what the occasion required.

In an experiment in which the subjects were exposed to the novel sound of a tornado, many of them heard it as a sound of an oncoming train which better conformed to their experience (Kilpatrick, 1961: 317).

Because we fill in gaps and because the fill is a composite of our experience, we hear selectively—just as we see selectively—what we expect or want to hear. Our perceptions may, therefore, be compared with values. Cook (1969: 217) said that "One way of looking at values is that they describe conditions which their holders desire in some degree to exist."

II. EFFECTS OF STRESS

Difficult as is accurate perception in normal situations, the inaccuracy tends to increase in conditions of danger and stress. They distort time and distance. The elapse of time is always difficult to perceive. In the experiment referred to above, our subjects' estimates of the length of a 42 second moving picture ranged from 1.5 to 3 minutes (Marshall, 1966a: 53). We are all familiar with the expression that time seems endless when one feels in danger. In other words, particularly under stress, we overestimate time. In danger we also tend to overrate distance (Goldstone et al., 1959; Behar and Bevar, 1961; Langer et al., 1961). Time and distance expand. Thus one must become skeptical of estimates of time and distance made by witnesses. It has been found, however, that moderate stress may improve performance while severe stress distorts (Munsterberg, 1923).

Thus one must question two of our legal rules, the dying declaration and the res gestae rule. It is assumed that when a man knows he is going to die and therefore will shortly face his maker, any statement he makes will be the truth and it will be admitted into evidence even though it is hearsay. But the stress of knowing he is about to die may cause him to make statements that are false. It may be his last chance to exploit paranoid tendencies.

The res gestae rule, also an exception to the hearsay rule, is that where a statement is made as part of a happening it is reliable. However, again, in the stress of a happening the statement may be completely unreliable. Sir Frederick Pollock (1941: 284-285) in his correspondence with Justice Holmes talked of "the damnable pretended doctrine of res gestae." He hoped that "some high authority would prick the bubble of verbiage: the unmeaning term merely fudges the truth that there is no universal formula for all kinds of relevancy."

Witnesses, particularly in cases played up by the mass media, may be influenced by the stress of public pressure. An important factor of public influence that is often overlooked, according to Morris (1957), is the general climate outside the courtroom or, for example, the tones and moods that prevail in the country. The public may appear as a possible threat. Some witnesses because of personality or status are better able to withstand threat than others.

III. SUGGESTIBILITY OF WITNESSES

This brings us to the matter of suggestibility. Witnesses are not autonomous. They are not independent of the field, that is, the litigation in which they participate. They are constantly interacting with other persons from the moment they make their first statement of the case to the time when they are dismissed as witnesses. Although a great deal of study has been made as to suggestibility of one person by another or by a group, little has been done in the field of recall and testimony. But every witness is affected by counsel, by the statements of other witnesses, by participation as a party or by his desire to be on the winning side. [1] Above all a witness is affected by his desire to appear credible to judge and jury—he dislikes to admit ignorance by answering "I don't know" (Wellman, 1923: 21).

The reasons why witnesses are affected by others are the same as those which cause all of us to be sensitive to what those, with whom we interact, think and feel. This is part of reality testing which we normally do during wakefulness. If we cease to do so, as Hilgard (1964: 19) says, "it is easy to drift into a hypnoidal state." This reality testing implies that "one is always on the verge of losing his grip on reality, of falling into error, or becoming disoriented." In each relationship, therefore, we keep asking, as we proceed from transaction to transaction, "How am I doing?" The answer generally sought is approbation but, on the other hand, it may sometimes be to be rejected and punished.

Witnesses may be subject to the dissonance between their inferences or their biases and reality. Consequently, if they can adjust their testimony in the direction that counsel indicates may be effective and other witnesses or parties indicate to be the "correct" testimony, this can relieve such dissonance. This can be restated in another way. Others can influence the expectations and consequently the recall (as well as perception) and behavior of a witness. In order to maintain his self-image an individual will tend to conform to the norms of those others if he does not have satisfying norms of his own. Thus, as Sherif (1936: 111, see also 96, 108) said, "Once the common norm is established, later separate individuals keep on perceiving it [and recalling it] in terms of the frame of reference which was once the norm of the group."

In considering the suggestibility of witnesses we should bear in mind that a large part of the population is subject to hypnotic influence. This does not mean that these people go through the usual stages of induction, trance, etc. or that they are equally suggestible. A large proportion of the population can be induced by counsel to follow his cues and perceive and recall events as he guides them (Spiegel, 1967: 364). Again, this does not mean that counsel is trying to hypnotize a witness or that a witness is conscious of any hypnotic effect. The phenomenon, however, is frequently present and is something that requires extended research.

IV. IDENTIFICATION OF ACCUSED

Nowhere has the problem of perception become more critical than in the identification of persons accused of crime. In the identification process witnesses are commonly asked to describe or recognize persons who may have been seen under stress and, frequently, only fleetingly. In such circumstances the phenomena of suggestibility by others and inference occur. We have too little empirical information concerning the process of identification and this gap in knowledge calls for thorough research.

Wall [2] (1965) has shown the numerous ways in which police and prosecuting attorneys, especially by means of the line-up, have used suggestibility in the identification of the accused. This is perhaps one of the most shocking sources of injustice in criminal cases. The Supreme Court has held that the identification is a "critical stage" of the criminal proceeding laden with the hazards of irreparable mistake and, therefore, under the Sixth Amendment the accused is entitled to the presence of a lawyer at a "line-up" (or its equivalent) (United States v. Wade, 1967; Stovall v. Denno, 1967).

Although the Sixth Amendment's requirement applies only if formal charges have been brought against the accused, line-ups or confrontations held prior to the bringing of formal charges may be challenged if they were "unnecessarily suggestive and conducive to irreparable, mistaken identification" under the Due Process clause of the Fifth and Fourteenth Amendments (United States v. Kirby, 1972: 4610). The question as to whether the Sixth Amendment entitles in-custody defendants to the presence of counsel at photographic identifications is still open (United States v. Ash, 1972, cert. granted, 1972; Contra, Reed v. Anderson, 1972).

Much of police tactic is suggestive, appealing to the mind or the emotions of the suspect. The atmosphere of police interrogation is calculated to obtain admissions or confessions. This is well documented by Inbau and Reid (1967).

An admirable article on confessions, describes their legal and psychological aspects and provides justification for Miranda v. Arizona (1966). As Edmund B. Driver (1968: 57), its author, states: "[W]hatever its deep roots may be, the urge to talk is almost certainly intensified by the host of fears generated by the situations and procedures of arrest and detention" (see also Foster, 1969). And this urge to talk accounts, too, for the willingness of prospective witnesses in a criminal case frequently to accept the cues of a prosecuting attorney before a trial especially when the prosecutor holds as a threatening weapon some illicit or suspicious behavior of the witness.

V. RECALL

As a result of what are known as the "Aussage" experiments[3] (Binet, 1905; Munsterberg, 1923; Stern, 1939; Stern, 1910; Cady, 1924; Marston, 1924; see also Snee and Lush, 1941; Fishman and Morris, 1957) in the early part of this century it has been assumed that accuracy of recall would decline substantially and the range of material reported increase with the specificity of interrogation and that leading questions would have a seductive effect and result in more inaccurate testimony. It has also been assumed that accuracy and completeness of testimony would be higher if interrogations were conducted in a supportive manner rather than in a challenging atmosphere.

An experiment conducted by Marshall et al. (1971) indicated that these hypotheses were wrong. They showed a moving picture with sound track to groups of up to four witnesses at one time (151 in all) and told them that they were witnesses and should give an account of what they had seen and heard and to tell the truth, the whole truth, and nothing but the truth, without conclusions. Each witness was taken separately into a room for interrogation and all interrogations were tape recorded. Witnesses were first asked to give a free, spontaneous report on what they had seen and heard. After that each of them was interrogated in one of four different ways. Half of each of these four groupings were interrogated supportively and half in a challenging manner. The questions and interventions by the interrogators were all prepared in advance.

One type of interrogation was with moderate guidance. In this form 12 general questions were asked, designed to cover all items that could have been observed in the film. Secondly, there was the high-guidance interrogation which was rather similar to direct examination in a courtroom. Thirdly, there was structured multiple-choice interrogation similar to that used in school and employment examinations, except that all the questions asked for *recognition* recall and *not* for reconstruction of the event. Finally, there was the structured leading type of question modeled on cross-examination conducted in courtrooms. In both the multiple-choice and leading interrogations the questions were directed sometimes toward true and sometimes toward false answers.

In the supportive atmosphere the interrogator tried to create a friendly atmosphere praising the quality of the free report and offering to help the witness remember more. In the challenging atmosphere the interrogator expressed disapproval of the free report because of its inadequacy and stated that he was going to see if, as a result of the interview, the witness could not do a better job.

At the end after completing the interrogations the witnesses were taken into another room and requested to fill in self-administered questionnaires designed to measure both their affective and cognitive reactions to the interrogations.

We found that atmosphere, whether supportive or challenging, had no important effect on either the accuracy or completeness of the testimony.

We also found that as interrogation became more specific there was a slight fall-off in accuracy—far less than earlier experiments had led us to expect—but a great increase in coverage. *The very act of interrogation and the type of questions asked markedly affected completeness but had very little effect on accuracy.* In other words, there was small trade-off between loss of accuracy and coverage. It was quite apparent from our study that increased specificity of interrogation has a beneficial overall effect on testimony.

In the spontaneous report and the medium and high guidance interrogations very few items were reported that were not in the picture (we call them absent items). In the two structured types of interrogation which specifically asked about items not in the film, some absent items were testified to but the accuracy of testimony about them was not greatly different from that about items present in the picture.

We divided the items also as to their legal relevance; that is, their relevance to possible suits that might have arisen out of the incidents in the picture. Except in the free report, legally relevant items were slightly less accurately reported than legally irrelevant items. But there was greater completeness in the coverage of legally relevant items.

We also divided the items in the picture as to their salience, that is, the likelihood of their being recalled, which we had pretested. We found that the greater the salience the greater was the accuracy of report and the increase in coverage. In other words, the more salient items were better remembered. As to the high-salience items, there was little difference as to accuracy and coverage resulting from different styles of interrogation. We believe that the failure of the early Aussage experimenters to consider salience caused them to come to different results than we did.

It should be noted, too, that the type of memory demanded of a witness is critical. When the memory called for is that of recognition, as in the case of multiple choice and leading questions, it tends to be more complete than when the interrogator is asking for a report or reconstruction of a happening (Luh, 1922).

We found two other interesting effects. Those of our witnesses who said that they had changed their testimony on interrogation from that given on their free, spontaneous statements, tended to be the more accurate witnesses. This would throw doubt on, if not make improper, the frequent statements by counsel derogating the capacity to recall or even the integrity of a witness because he changed his testimony.

We also found a trend to greater accuracy on the part of those witnesses who suspected that the interrogator was trying to induce them to lie or falsify their answers.

We must recognize the fact that our witnesses were not biased, that is, they did not have a case to make or support. Further research should be done with witnesses who are committed to one or another side of a case (see Marshall and Mansson, 1966: 135).

VI. INFERENCES

We are all subject to making inferences. Juries are permitted to make inferences but not witnesses, because what is sought in testimony is fact not inferences or conclusions, or guesses. Nevertheless, the probability is that all of us frequently state as fact what is in reality an inference or conclusion. On the witness stand we cannot divorce ourselves from our habitual way of behaving, for pragmatically we construct an inference or conclusion out of one bit of perception which we adulterate with our experience with similar phenomena. So in all innocence a witness will testify to inferences and conclusions as if they were fact and the court can not often be the wiser.

Inferences and conclusions are ways in which we fill the gaps in our perception. We make interpretations of those perceptions, we make pragmatic guesses. As Cantril and Bumstead (1960: 83) have said:

> On the basis of the significances we experience, we are constantly guessing that certain things we do will give us the value-qualities of experience we hope for. We try to repeat many types of activities because they show high promise of recapturing or maintaining certain qualities of experience that have already proved satisfying. Likewise we try to avoid those transactions which we believe will lead to a high degree of negative value-quality. . . .

We should bear in mind that inferences and conclusions are frequently necessary in order to achieve consistency within ourselves. As Zimbardo (1969: 239) said: One "must first convince his observing, critical self (who stands in for society) that his commitment follows *rationally* from an analysis of the stimulus conditions. . . . The psychological homeostasis posited by such a consistency principle is not an end in itself, but rather a means toward minimizing dependency on the environment and maximizing control over it."

VII. INTENT

Serious crimes involve the element of intent, of mens rea, the evil mind, malice aforethought. There are many legal and philosophic definitions of intent. When all is said and done, what ordinary folk mean when they say something was intended is that "It was done on purpose."

Even assuming that consciousness of intent is requisite, that there is purpose behind the act, this is not always what the court looks for as a fact. It may accept an inference of intent to justify a conclusion of intent. [4] For example, as Glanville L. Williams (1965: 26) has said: "To begin by requiring intention for a particular crime, and then to say that intention can be inferred from recklessness, is to cheat with words." In other words, it is a deceptive fiction to say, as the law does, that a man intends to do a wrongful act because he behaves recklessly, that is, without any intention to do the wrong at all.

It may be asked whether it is not fiction that the trial process in an atmosphere of courtroom conflict can determine what a man's intention was. With greater humility than we today exhibit, the courts of earlier times did not try to judge intent. Thus, in the days of Edward the IV, Judge Brian (quoted in Pollock and Maitland, 1911: 474-475) said: "The thought of man shall not be tried, for the devil himself knoweth not the thought of man." But Judea-Christian and Greek traditions have been too strong and the idea from Deuteronomy to Aristotle to St. Thomas has been that men are free to choose between good and evil and that if they behaved in a manner defined as evil it was the result of their own free will, their own wickedness. This is a norm accepted by our courts and is exemplified by Mr. Justice Jackson's opinion in Morisette v. United States (1952: U.S. at 250, S. Ct. at 243):

> The contention that injury can amount to a crime only when inflicted by intention is no provincial or transient notion. It is as universal and persistent in mature systems of law as belief in freedom of the human will and a consequent ability and duty of the normal individual to choose between good and evil.

Intent implies, therefore, that a choice must be made. If law is to be even-handed is it reasonable and just to assume that all men have the same choices available? The norms of law are not the norms of a whole society but of those in power. It has always been those who held the sovereign power who determined the norms of right and wrong in positive law, what is permissible and what forbidden to the population under penalty retribution. At the present time the norms we apply and on which our laws are based are primarily those of the middle class, the norms of the dominant culture of the state. Consequently the same choices may not be available to minority groups or people in great poverty and ignorance as to the lawmakers. Education may broaden the apparent choices available; but the poor, the immigrant, and those in very subordinate positions may have less education, certainly less education than the dominant culture of the country. Therefore, they may be less able to perceive the choices available to the lawmakers and law-enforcers. Once again experience and the suggestibility of one's culture or subculture may determine perception, in this instance perception of right and wrong, good and evil (Marshall, 1968: 26-121; Jacob. 1971).

Furthermore, people of the slum cultures and subcultures tend to be more motoric in their reactions to the situation than the middle class (Miller and Swanson, 1956: 146, 157). It may seem perfectly reasonable to them to use violence in a situation in which more highly educated or economically favored people would use argument or shrewd device (see, as an example, Herman Melville's story of "Billy Budd," 1961).

There are psychological reasons which may cause people to be unable to perceive choices or to act upon them. One can think of a continuum of behavior from pure accident to action with conscious intent, with purpose, as when a man in cold blood waylays another and assaults or slays him (Marshall, 1966b).

Between these extremes there are actions out of the unconscious, actions under stress, actions under hypnotic suggestions, actions arising out of interrelationships with others, that is from social suggestion, and finally actions where the consequences might have been foreseeable by that legal construct "the reasonable man." It is often difficult to draw the line between these different behaviors. How much of reflex action is unconsciously motivated? What are the unconscious drives that make some people succumb to hypnotism? What is the effect of stress in inducing psychological denial of reality and how does stress blind people to the reasonable consequences of their behavior (see Travers and Morris, 1961; compare Director of Public Prosecution v. Smith, 1960; Regina v. Smyth, 1957)?

Neurotic compulsion certainly does not permit freedom of choice. Dostoevsky's (1945) grim story about the gambler in "Notes From The Underground" illustrates this and there are, of course, numerous clinical and laboratory examples (Sarnoff, 1962; Alexander and Staub, 1962). Shoplifting, kleptomania, compulsive lying and betrayal, pyromania are generally the results of neurotic compulsions. Theft and robbery sometimes occur because of fetishism. These are compulsive acts, not free choices. The very power of judgment—that is, of problem-solving—which is inherent in formulating an intent will be absent. As Alexander and Staub (1956: 79) said, "The characteristic thing about the *neurotic criminal* is that he identifies himself only partly with the criminal act he commits."

Milgrim (1965) found that a large proportion of people tend to obey the commands of one whom they consider a legitimate authority even if this involves doing cruel acts. This is especially true when the authority figure is present and when the actor has no contact with and does not see the suffering of the persons he hurts.

Certainly the same choices are not available to all people, if indeed *any* choices are perceived in many circumstances.

VIII. THE TRIAL AS A WIN-LOSE GAME

Most lawyers will concede that perception and recall are not entirely accurate, that the situation and other persons may influence the witness and that the trial process itself is interlarded with fictions. But they hope to reduce error by adversary proceedings that test perception and recall and challenge the veracity of witnesses by a process of examination and cross-examination. And correction of error undoubtedly occurs, although we have no empirical data as to the frequency of occurrence. As a distinguished trial lawyer (Frank, 1969: 126) has said: "The law may or may not be a sure way of determining the truth, but it is surely the most awkward method ever devised."

There are, of course, rules to the game, some guaranteed by the Bill of Rights and the Fourteenth Amendment. Among those is the right to cross-examination, sustained by the Supreme Court in Pointer v. Texas (1965), Douglas v. Alabama (1965), and Namet v. United States (1963). Similarly guaranteed are the right to call witnesses (Washington v. Texas, 1967) and the right to inspect prior statements by witnesses for the prosecution in the possession of the prosecutor as a basis for cross-examination (Jencks v. United States, 1957). The rules of the game also prohibit the prosecutor (and presumably counsel for the accused) from using testimony known to him to be perjurious (Giles v. Maryland, 1967).

While adversary proceedings have the advantage of avoiding the pitfalls of unilateral dogmatism they do not necessarily winnow accurate perception. The trial itself as an adversary proceeding is a species of duel. This is what may create interest in the case on the part of jurors and it certainly gives excitement to theatrical and television reproductions of trials. But the goal of an adversary proceeding, whatever the parties may hope or believe, is not to find reality or justice. It is rather to outwit the opponent and to win.

This is not to suggest that adversary proceedings are evil. Probably they are far better in reaching a just conclusion than a judicial determination would be if parties were unable to present their cases. [5] But we must have no illusions that in this adversary process we are finding truth or even necessarily justice. It does serve, however, a social purpose of offering to litigants a legitimized channel for the expression of their hostility and thus acts as a stabilizer of society. There are exceptions, as in the case of automotive accidents where it has been found that the belief is that the impersonal insurance company was to pay in any event (Hunting and Neuwirth, 1962).

In a criminal proceeding prosecution may express public feeling that an offender must be punished, but it also is an attempt to protect society and a symbolic substitute for self-help and vendetta (Cardozo, 1930). The defendant in a criminal case has a chance to exculpate or justify himself and his chance to accomplish either will be greater before a neutral court than before some executive officer or board that acts as prosecutor and trier of fact.

While the adversary proceeding may serve to mediate controversy it is essentially a win-lose relationship, a zero-sum game. Though this may be a ritualized form of hostility reduction or hostility containment, in itself it is not creative. It does not provide a win-win relationship or what the game theorists call a variable-sum game. Essentially, a criminal trial is a punitive process. If society were less interested in punishing and more interested in reforming the offender the trial might be used not only to determine whether the accused committed the act, but also to obtain data on the basis of which the court might more readily judge how and to what extent the accused if guilty could be reformed or prevented from endangering society. It would not then be purely a win-lose transaction for the defendant or society.

IX. TRIERS OF FACT

In considering the trial we should bear in mind that the triers of fact, that is, judges and jurors, are subject to the similar limitations as are witnesses. As has been said, they are permitted to indulge in inferences and conclusions. But in other respects they are witnesses to witnesses. They perceive and recall just as witnesses do, basing their perception and recall as well as their inferences and conclusions on their own prior experience and expectations (see Simon, 1967).

What jurors perceive will also be related to their personalities.

The Authoritarians seemed prone to using subjective impressions of the character of the persons involved in the case that they had gleaned in some fashion from the evidence presented as the basis of their verdicts. . . . The

Anti-authoritarians tended to use the same kind of impressionistic evidence to conclude that even if the defendant were guilty as charged, it was not his fault but society's, because he had led a difficult life [Boehm, 1968: 746].

It has been found that the party which first makes its presentation has the greater opportunity for success. While the plaintiff is presenting its case the jurors are already in the process of opinion formation (Lund, 1925). This, of course, gives an advantage to the prosecution, an advantage further weighted where the prosecution also has the last word in summation.

But in spite of this and of the unreliability of testimony and the distortions implicit in the adversary system, the jury trial often acts as an instrument to legitimize leniency. The burden of proof in criminal cases tends to weight error in that direction. The anonymity of jury deliberations and the rules prohibiting judges from directing verdicts of guilt and overruling not-guilty verdicts probably tend to neutralize the weaknesses of the trial system (Winter, 1971). But not always, especially not in cases in which the public outcry for a victim, publicized through the mass media, biases the jurors (Padawer-Singer, 1970).

It is now established that one accused of crime is denied due process of law when a court is paralyzed by mob domination or the public has been so aroused that a fair verdict cannot be reached. Although the Supreme Court in 1915 in Frank v. Mangum, Holmes and Hughes dissenting, upheld the conviction of Leo M. Frank when a mob outside the courthouse was demanding that he be convicted of murder (it later lynched him) and threatened the jury, the court reversed itself in Moore v. Dempsey (1923: U.S. at 91, S. Ct. at 266), holding, in the words of Mr. Justice Holmes, that when "counsel, jury and judge were swept to the fatal end by an irresistible wave of public passion . . . neither perfection in the machinery for correction nor the possibility that the trial court and counsel saw no other way of avoiding an immediate outbreak of the mob can prevent this Court from securing to the petitioners their constitutional rights." And in the recent case of Connecticut v. Bobby Seale (see New York Times, May 26, 1971: 1, col. 5) the trial judge dismissed the indictment on the ground that a fair trial could not be secured.

The courts have protected the accused from the possible prejudicial effects of other events in the course of the trial. For example, where the judge learned from a juror that somebody had communicated with him and told him that he could profit by an acquittal and the judge discussed this with the FBI and the prosecution without the knowledge of defendant's counsel, the Supreme Court reversed the denial by the trial judge of defendant's request to determine the circumstances surrounding the incident and its effect on the jury (Remmer v.

United States, 1954). In Turner v. Louisiana (1965) the Supreme Court held that a defendant who had been convicted of murder had been denied his right to a fair trial by an impartial jury when the two deputy sheriffs who were key witnesses against him were in charge of the jury during the three-day trial and fraternized with them outside the court room during the performance of their duties.

The trend in the courts has been to make the fair trial as much a reality as possible and not merely a verbal statement of principle. It would, however, be idle to suppose that there are not frequent violations, that matters of impropriety do not enter into a trial and trickery does not occur. It might be said that the judicial heart is right, the judicial eye sometimes unseeing and the judicial hand frequently clumsy.

X. CONCLUSION

What we have in our trial system is an edifice built on fictions. It can only be justified if it serves a useful social purpose and if within the rules of the game it is fair. Fairness in the trial, that is, due process of law, equal protection of the laws, is the fundamental right of an accused. But social purpose cannot forever be acceptable if law and order are exalted over individual rights, if empirical study demonstrates the invalidity of the rules of the game, if it is pretended that fictions are realities or if no serious attempts are made to readjust the rules to empirical findings. For then fairness must come in question and social purpose become a corruption.

The social function served by our trial system cannot survive if there is a public sense abroad that the trial is a form of mystery play untouchable by reality, unreachable by justice.

NOTES

1. McCarty (1960: 213) describes a common practice:

It is very important in interviewing witnesses that the first impression be favorable. This is where suggestion comes in. Do you ask the witness what happened and let him tell the story? Not if you are experienced and know the psychology of approach. You start out and tell him what happened, giving your client's story and then go back and go over it item by item and have the witness verify it. In this way his memory will be refreshed from your standpoint and he will be more apt to make a good witness for your client.

A similar effect can be obtained by interviewing an uncertain witness in the presence of the party for whom he is to be called and other prospective witnesses whose positive statements will tend to influence the uncertain one. Whether by this process "his memory will be refreshed" or whether he is induced to accept the version of the others is questionable (see Sherif, 1936: 138; Asch, 1952).

2. See also Borchard (1932), especially Andrews case, pp. 1-6, Hess and Craig case, pp. 93-98; Frank and Frank (1957), especially Majczek and Marcinkiewicz case, pp. 17-30, Southerland and Mathis case, pp. 40-50, Mattice case, pp. 50-57.

3. Wigmore (1931: 530-556) discusses at length some of the Aussage experiments. It should be noted that since that time there has been a great improvement in research techniques including statistical analysis and use of computers. The Aussage experiments did not distinguish between recall expressed in narrative form and by recognition of items. Moreover, they ignored the salience of the items for which recollection was sought.

4. In some cases legal presumptions have been rejected where there is not "a rational connection between the fact proved and the fact presumed" (Tot v. United States, 1943: U.S. at 467, S. Ct. at 1245; Leary v. United States, 1969).

5. "Nonetheless, the legal system gives to the adversary proceedings an overblown value. The opposing system of direct inquiry by the court is given a bad name, the inquisitorial system, to ensure its demise and lawyers commonly place talismanic value on their traditional methods of inquiry" (Frank, 1969: 128). It may even be that the Continental system under which the judge takes the lead in examining witnesses may be more effective (but see Besnard, 1963). We have no empirical evidence on this matter. In any event, it would be unrealistic to assume that that system could replace the Anglo-American.

REFERENCES

Alexander, F. and H. Staub (1956) *The Criminal, the Judge and the Public.* New York: Free Press.

American Society for Public Administration (1959) Public Administration Bulletin 3, 12.

Asch, S. (1952) *Social Psychology.* New York: Prentice-Hall.

Behar, I. and W. Bevar (1961) "The perceived duration of auditory and visual intervals: cross model comparison and interaction." Amer. J. of Psychology 74, 1: 17-26.

Besnard, M. (1963) *The Trial of Marie Besnard.* New York: Farrar, Straus.

Binet, A. (1905) "La science du temoignange." L'Annee Psychological 11: 128-136.

Boehm, V. R. (1968) "Mr. prejudice, miss sympathy and the authoritarian personality: an application of psychological measuring techniques to the problem of jury bias." Wisconsin Law Rev. 1968, 3: 734-750.

Borchard, E. M. (1932) *Convicting the Innocent.* Garden City: Doubleday.

Cady, H. (1924) "On the psychology of testimony." Amer. J. of Psychology 35, 1: 110-112.

Cantril, H. and C. H. Bumstead (1960) *Reflections on the Human Venture.* New York: New York University Press.

Cardozo, B. N. (1930) *What Medicine Can Do For Law.* New York: Harper and Brothers.

Cook, S. W. (1969) "Motives in a conceptual analysis of attitude-related behavior," pp. 179-231 in W. Arnold and D. Levine (eds.) *Nebraska Symposium on Motivation.* Lincoln: University of Nebraska Press.

Director of Public Prosecution v. Smith (1960) 3 WL.R. 546, 3 A11 E.R. 161, 44 Cr. App. R. 261.

Dostoevsky, F. (1945) *The Short Novels of Dostoevsky*. New York: Dial Press.

Douglas v. Alabama (1965) 380 U.S. 417, 85 S.Ct. 1074.

Driver, E. D. (1968) "Confessions and the social psychology of coercion." Harvard Law Rev. 82, 1: 42-61.

Fishman, J. A. and R. E. Morris [eds.] (1957) "Witnesses and testimony at trials and hearings." J. of Social Issues 13, 2.

Foster, H. J., Jr. (1969) "Confessions and the station house syndrome." DePaul Law Rev. 18: 683-701.

Frank, J. P. (1969) *American Law: The Case for Radical Reform*. Toronto: Macmillan.

Frank, J. and B. Frank (1957) *Not Guilty*. New York: Doubleday.

Frank v. Mangum (1915) 237 U.S. 309, 35 S.Ct. 582.

Giles v. Maryland (1967) 386 U.S. 67, 87 S.Ct. 793.

Goldstone, S., W. K. Bordman and W. T. Lhamon (1959) "Intersensory comparisons of temporal judgments." J. of Experimental Psychology 57, 4: 243-248.

Hastorf, A. H. and H. Cantril (1954) "They saw a game: a case study." J. of Abnormal and Social Psychology 49, 1: 129-134.

Heider, F. and M. Simmel (1944) "An experimental study of apparent behavior." Amer. J. of Psychology 57, 2: 243-259.

Hilgard, E. R. (1964) "The motivational relevance of hypnosis," pp. 1-44 in D. Levine (ed.) *Nebraska Symposium on Motivation*. Lincoln: University of Nebraska Press.

Hunting, R. and G. S. Neuwirth (1962) *Who Sues in New York City?* New York: Columbia University Press.

Hutchins, R. and D. Slesinger (1928) "Some observations on the law of evidence." Columbia Law Rev. 28, 4: 432-440.

Inbau, F. and J. Reid (1967) *Criminal Interrogation and Confessions*. Baltimore: Williams & Wilkins.

Ittelson, W. H. (1961) "The constancies in visual perception," pp. 339-353 in F. P. Kilpatrick (ed.) *Explorations in Transactional Psychology*. New York: New York University Press.

Jacob, H. (1971) "Black and white perceptions of justice in the city." Law and Society Rev. 6, 1: 69-89.

Jencks v. United States (1957) 353 U.S. 657, 77 S.Ct. 1007.

Kilpatrick, F. P. [ed.] (1961) *Explorations in Transactional Psychology*. New York: New York University Press.

——— and H. Cantril (1961) "The constancies in social perception," pp. 354-365 in F. P. Kilpatrick (ed.) *Explorations in Transactional Psychology*. New York: New York University Press.

Kilpatrick, F. P. and W. H. Ittelson (1961) "The perception of movement," pp. 58-68 in F. P. Kilpatrick (ed.) *Explorations in Transactional Psychology*. New York: New York University Press.

Kirby v. Illinois (1972) 40 U.S.L.W. 4607 (U.S.).

Langer, J., S. Wapner and H. Werner (1961) "The effect of danger upon the experience of time." Amer. J. of Psychology 74, 1: 94-97.

Leary v. United States (1969) 395 U.S. 6, 89 S.Ct. 1532.

Luh, C. W. (1922) "The conditions of retention." Psych. Monographs 31, 3 (No. 142).

Lund, F. H. (1925) "The psychology of belief." J. of Abnormal and Social Psychology 20, 2: 174-196.

Marshall, J. (1968) *Intention in Law and Society.* New York: Funk & Wagnalls.
––– (1966a) *Law and Psychology in Conflict.* Indianapolis: Bobbs-Merrill.
––– (1966b) "Relation of the unconscious to intention." Virginia Law Rev. 52, 7: 1256-1282.
––– and H. Mansson (1966) "Punitiveness, recall and the police." J. of Research in Crime and Delinquency 1966 (July): 129-139.
Marshall, J., K. H. Marquis, and S. Oskamp (1971) "Effects of kinds of question and atmosphere of interrogation on accuracy and completeness of testimony." Harvard Law Rev. 84, 7: 1620-1643.
Marston, W. M. (1924) "Studies in testimony." J. of Criminal Law and Criminology 15: 5-31.
McCarty, D. G. (1960) *Psychology and the Law.* Englewood Cliffs, N.J.: Prentice-Hall.
Melville, H. (1961) *Billy Budd and the Piazza Tales.* New York: Dolphin Books.
Milgrim, S. (1965) "Some conditions of obedience and disobedience to authority." Human Relations 18, 1: 57-76.
Miller, D. R. and G. E. Swanson (1956) "The study of conflict," pp. 131-174 in M. R. Jones (ed.) *Nebraska Symposium on Motivation.* Lincoln: University of Nebraska Press.
Miranda v. Arizona (1966) 384 U.S. 436, 86 S.Ct. 1602.
Moore v. Dempsey (1923) 261 U.S. 86, 43 S.Ct. 265.
Morisette v. United States (1952) 342 U.S. 246, 72 S.Ct. 240.
Morris, R. E. (1957) "Witness performance under stress: a sociological approach." J. of Social Issues 13, 2: 17-22.
Munsterberg, H. (1923) *On The Witness Stand: Essays in Psychology and Crime.* New York: Doubleday, Page.
Namet v. United States (1963) 373 U.S. 179, 83 S.Ct. 1151.
New York Times (May 26, 1971): 1, col. 5.
Padawer-Singer, A. M. (1970) "Free press-fair trial." Paper presented at the Symposium on Psychological Research in Legal Settings of the American Psychological Association.
Plato (1938) *Phaedo* (Sir R. W. Livingstone, trans.) London: Oxford University Press.
Pointer v. Texas (1965) 380 U.S. 400, 85 S.Ct. 1065.
Pollock, F. (1941) *Holmes-Pollock Letters* (Vol. 2, M. Howe, ed.). Cambridge: Harvard University Press.
–––and F. W. Maitland (1911) *The History of English Law,* Vol. 2. Cambridge: Cambridge University Press.
Reed v. Anderson (1972) 40 U.S.L.W. 2736 (3rd Cir.).
Regina v. Smyth (1957) 92 C.L.R. 163.
Remmer v. United States (1954) 347 U.S. 227, 74 S.Ct. 450.
Rock, I. and L. Kaufman (1962) "The moon illusion." Science 136 (June 22): 1023.
Sarnoff, I. (1962) *Personality Dynamics and Development.* New York: John Wiley.
Sherif, M. (1936) *Psychology of Social Norms.* New York: Harper and Brothers.
Simeon Ben Shatach, *Talmud,* first Chapter, ninth citation, Tractate, Sayings of the Fathers.
Simon, R. J. (1967) *The Jury and the Defense of Insanity.* Boston: Little, Brown.
Snee, T. J. and D. E. Lush (1941) "Interaction of the narrative and interrogatory methods of obtaining testimony." J. of Psychology 11: 229-236.
Spiegel, H. (1967) "Hypnosis and invasion of privacy," pp. 355-364 in V. Lawyer and B. George, Jr. (eds.) *How to Defend a Criminal Case—From Arrest to Verdict.* Boston: American Trial Lawyers Association.

Stern, W. (1939) "Psychology of testimony." J. of Abnormal and Social Psychology 34, 1: 3-20.

——— (1910) "Abstracts of lectures on the psychology of testimony and on the study of individuality." Amer. J. of Psychology 21, 2: 270-282.

Stovall v. Denno (1967) 388 U.S. 293, 87 S.Ct. 1967.

Thucydides (1934) *The Complete Writings of Thucydides* (R. Crawley Translation). New York: Modern Library.

Tot v. United States (1943) 319 U.S. 463, 63 S.Ct. 1241.

Travers, J. L. and N. Morris (1961) "Imputed intent in murder, or Smith v. Smyth." Australian Law J. 35, (August 31): 154-176.

Turner v. Louisiana (1965) 379 U.S. 466, 85 S.Ct. 546.

United States v. Ash (1972) 40 U.S.L.W. 2568 (D.C. Cir.), cert. granted, 40 U.S.L.W. 3581 (U.S. June 12, 1972)

United States v. Wade (1967) 388 U.S. 218, 87 S.Ct. 1926.

Wall, P. (1965) *Eye-Witness Identification in Criminal Cases.* Springfield: C. C Thomas.

Washington v. Texas (1967) 388 U.S. 14, 87 S.Ct. 1920.

Wellman, F. L. (1923) *The Art of Cross-Examination.* New York: Macmillan.

Wigmore, J. H. (1931) *The Principles of Judicial Proof.* Boston: Little, Brown.

Williams, G. L. (1965) *The Mental Element in Crime.* Jerusalem: Magnes Press.

Winter, R. K. Jr. (1971) "The jury and the risk of non persuasion." Law and Society Rev. 5, 3: 335-344.

Zimbardo, P. G. (1969) "The human choice: individuation, reason and order versus deindividuation, impulse, and chaos," pp. 237-307 in W. Arnold and D. Levine (eds.) *Nebraska Symposium on Motivation.* Lincoln: University of Nebraska Press.

PART V.

POST-TRIAL

Chapter 9

THE SENTENCING AND CORRECTIONAL PROCESS

nor cruel and unusual punishments inflicted

From the Eighth Amendment
to the U.S. Constitution

ROBERT O. DAWSON received his A.B. at University of Missouri, 1960, his LL.B. at Washington University, 1963, and his S.J.D. at University of Wisconsin, 1969. He has taught at University of Wisconsin Law School, Washington University, and University of Texas, where he currently is Professor of Law. Dr. Dawson has been involved in Texas law revision, as well as work for the Joint Commission on Correctional Manpower and Training, American Bar Foundation Survey of the Administration of Criminal Justice in the United States, and University of Texas Criminal Justice Project, of which he was Director, 1969-1970. He authored *Sentencing: The Decision as to Type, Length, and Conditions of Sentence* (1969).

Chapter 9

THE SENTENCING AND CORRECTIONAL PROCESS

R O B E R T O. D A W S O N

Perhaps no segment of the criminal justice process has received as little attention from legal commentators as the correctional process. Doubtless, this is due in large part to the fact that until very recently convicted offenders had few, if any, legal rights that would affect the correctional process. Furthermore, although the correctional phase of criminal justice administration was studied and analyzed by behavioral scientists, they tended to concentrate on the quality (or lack thereof) of the product, rather than upon process itself. Thus, studies of the recidivism rates produced by various modes of correctional treatment abound, but with few exceptions behavioral scientists failed to describe and analyze what happens in the correctional process without regard to its possible impact upon the likelihood that the offender will commit crime again when released.

The purpose of this chapter is to analyze the correctional process as it exists today, concentrating not upon the formal legal aspects of the process but upon the realities of day-to-day administration.

The correctional process should be regarded as a system for making decisions about what to do with the convicted criminal offender. The decisions involve numerous public officials—prosecutors, trial judges, probation officers, prison officials, authorities exercising powers of executive clemency, parole boards, and parole officers. The process consists of a series of interrelated decisions about the offender, decisions that are based upon a variety of criteria, involve various decision-making authorities and may in some cases span a period of several years.

The key concept in the correctional process is discretion. Discretion in this context should be understood as the legal and practical freedom of a public official to make a choice that affects the convicted offender. But to say that discretion exists should not be understood to imply that it exists without controls and limits—indeed, a major part of the concern of this chapter is to identify those legal and extralegal controls and limits upon the discretion of correctional decision makers.

The correctional process can be analyzed in terms of major stages: the initial sentencing stage at which a trial judge decides whether to sentence the convicted offender to imprisonment or to select an alternative mode of sentencing; if an alternative is selected—normally a term on probation—what happens to the offender on probation and under what circumstances may probation be revoked; if the trial judge decides to sentence the offender to imprisonment what decisions does he make about the length of imprisonment; if the offender is sentenced to imprisonment what are his rights within a prison community; how is the decision made when to parole—release conditionally—the prison inmate; when the inmate is released on parole what happens to him during parole supervision and under what circumstances may parole be revoked and the offender returned to prison.

I. PRECONVICTION CORRECTIONS

The correctional process is normally conceived of as beginning with an adjudication of guilt of crime. However, there is a recent trend to initiate correctional treatment prior to conviction, and, indeed, with an expectation that the defendant will never be brought to trial. Such rehabilitative programs are based at least nominally upon the consent of the defendant. They are part of a broader trend in the administration of criminal justice toward the "diversion" of cases from the criminal justice process. Diversion reflects despair over the efficacy of the criminal process in controlling socially deviant behavior and also a recognition that the increasing volume of criminal cases requires disposition as early in the process as feasible in order to conserve the expenditure of limited enforcement resources. Thus, in many communities selected misdemeanor cases are not prosecuted but the case is continued and the defendant given correctional treatment with the expectation that, if it is successful, there will never be a criminal trial.

Similar programs have been in operation for years in the juvenile justice system. The juvenile justice process operates on the assumption that a court hearing is the step of last resort—only if the problem posed by the suspected offender cannot be solved by means short of court hearing is a formal hearing justified. Until recently, the criminal justice process operated on the opposite assumption—the normal way of handling criminal cases should be processing through adjudication and only in extraordinary cases should the case be terminated short of adjudication. It is that fundamental assumption about the way the process should respond to socially deviant behavior that is now undergoing change and the criminal process in this instance is borrowing an approach long used by the juvenile process, a nice contrast to the importation into the juvenile process of many of the legal rights of persons accused of crime. [1]

II. GUILTY PLEA BARGAINING AND SENTENCING

The correctional process cannot be understood without taking into account another aspect of the criminal process that occurs prior to conviction—the phenomenon of guilty plea bargaining. Plea bargaining is virtually universal and accounts for the fact that the vast majority—sometimes estimated as high as 90 percent—of criminal cases are disposed of by plea of guilty. In brief, plea bargaining is an agreement by the defendant to waive his right to trial and to jury trial in exchange for some sort of leniency in the disposition of his case. The leniency may involve a reduction in the seriousness of the offense charged, dismissal of some of the offenses charged, or a recommendation or promise by the prosecutor as to the sentence that will be imposed. [2]

No matter what form guilty plea bargaining takes, when it exists it effectively limits the discretion of the sentencing authority in disposing of the case. Thus, the interesting result is that perhaps the most important decision made about the correctional disposition of a criminal case occurs (1) prior to a determination of guilt, (2) by a defense attorney and a prosecuting attorney rather than a correctional official, and (3) without the detailed social study thought to be essential to proper correctional decision-making. Although guilty plea bargaining is less than a totally satisfactory system for making correctional decisions, one thing can be said in its favor: The existence of plea bargaining is a force that tends to reduce the harshness of criminal sentencing in the United States, and to that extent, is probably beneficial. In the usual criminal case, it is only within the limits imposed by the guilty plea bargain that the trial judge is able to exercise choice in the disposition of the case of a convicted criminal offender—plea bargaining imposes substantial limitations upon sentencing discretion.

III. THE PRESENTENCE INVESTIGATION AND REPORT

For years it has been believed by correctional leaders that the key to rational sentencing is to place before the decision maker sufficient information about the offender to enable him to choose the proper disposition from among the alternatives available. The basic information upon which sentencing is supposed to rest in most jurisdictions comes from the presentence report. The presentence report is a document prepared by a probation officer summarizing the result of an investigation into the circumstances of the offense and the background of the offender—his family situation, his education, his employment history, prior criminal offenses, his residential stability, military history, religious practices, medical status, and attitudes toward authority and his offense. [3] It is this document that is supposed to supply the sentencing authority, normally the trial court judge, with the information needed to make a rational sentencing decision.

Presentence reports are not used in every case. The trial judge usually has discretion whether to order a presentence investigation and report. Some trial judges rarely utilize these aids to sentencing, while other trial judges use them in virtually every case. Furthermore, in some communities the manpower—probation officers—necessary to conduct presentence investigations and prepare presentence reports is simply unavailable. When this situation exists or when the trial court fails to order a presentence investigation, then the sentencing decision is based upon the information given to the trial court in a sentencing hearing. The sentencing hearing is an informal proceeding at which the prosecutor may present testimony bearing upon the sentence to be imposed and the defendant may testify himself or may present witnesses—such as character witnesses—who he hopes will convince the court to give a favorable sentence to him.

When a presentence report is prepared, it is given to the trial court but is only sometimes given to the defendant. The United States Supreme Court in the case of Williams v. New York [4] held that the United States Constitution does not prohibit the use of presentence reports in the disposition of criminal cases. This decision has been widely interpreted—some argue misinterpreted [5]—to permit the trial court to consider information contained in the presentence report without disclosing that report to the defendant. Many trial judges do exactly that. Many other trial judges, however, in their discretion regularly permit the defendant to see the presentence report, give him an opportunity to comment upon its contents, and argue to the court that some information or statements contained in the report are misleading or simply not accurate. Probation officers frequently argue that the presentence report should not be disclosed to the defendant because (1) disclosure of the report to the defendant will dry up sources of confidential information that are essential to a full investigation and report, (2) disclosure will lead to extended court proceedings involving arguments about the accuracy of various statements made in the report, and (3) disclosure of the diagnostic statements made by the probation officer in the report will have an adverse effect upon the defendant's course of rehabilitation. The arguments on the other side of the controversy are that (1) disclosure is necessary to assure that the presentence report is accurate and fair in its presentation of the case, (2) that most of the information contained in the presentence report is obtained from sources that are in no sense confidential sources—most of the information in the report is in fact obtained from the defendant and from public records, such as police and prosecutor's file—and (3) that very little real diagnosis appears in the presentence report and therefore, there is very little likelihood of adversely affecting the course of treatment.[6]

The importance of the presentence report extends beyond the sentencing stage. If the defendant is put on probation the presentence report is used by the probation officer in supervising the offender and may also influence a trial judge at a later stage in deciding whether to revoke probation and sentence the offender to prison. If the offender is sentenced to prison, the presentence report is almost always sent to prison with him. In prison the presentence report is used to make various classification decisions about the offender—what kind of job, training, educational, recreational, and living opportunities he is to have within the prison community. The presentence report is also used by the parole board in deciding whether to release the inmate on parole, and if he is released on parole the presentence report is used by the parole officer in supervising him and, finally, may be used in revocation of parole. The presentence report is in fact the basic document in the correctional process and a well-prepared report will have a substantial impact upon the entire course of conduct of correctional officials with respect to that particular case.

Relatively little use is made of presentence psychiatric examinations in the criminal process. The resources for psychiatric examinations are in most communities quite limited, and there is always the problem with psychiatric examinations of the judge not understanding the language used by psychiatrists in their diagnosis of the offender. Psychiatric examinations are used in extraoridinary cases, cases of great seriousnesses, such as murder or rape or cases in which the defendant's behavior appears to be aberrant. When psychiatric examinations are conducted and psychiatric reports made as part of the sentencing process the same position about disclosure of those reports to the defendant is normally adopted by the trial judge as the position he takes with respect to the presentence report.[7]

IV. THE BASIC DECISION: IMPRISONMENT OR AN ALTERNATIVE

After all the information has been assembled, after the presentence report, psychiatric examination, testimony of character witnesses and other witnesses, and argumentation by prosecutor and defense attorney has been received by the trial court, he must then make a decision as to the disposition of the case.[8] This is easily the most important decision in the criminal process. In most situations, the law gives the trial judge discretion whether to impose a prison sentence or whether to choose an alternative to imprisonment—such as probation or a fine. This discretion is as a practical matter unreviewable, i.e. the trial judge's decision except in extraordinary cases is final.

It is difficult to generalize upon the factors or criteria that influence a trial judge to decide upon imprisonment or an alternative form of disposition, but studies have identified some of the factors that recur.[9] It is quite clear that the trial court is influenced by the defendant's criminal record, indeed there seems to be a tendency to impose progressively more severe sentences as the defendant reappears in court. Thus, the first time he is in court he might receive a fine, the second time probation, and the third time a prison sentence. Another factor of some importance is the family relationship of the defendant. If the defendant is married and supporting a family, trial judges are more reluctant to sentence him to imprisonment, because it results in deprivation of support for the family and perhaps in the family becoming welfare clients. Trial judges are also quite reluctant to sentence an extremely young person to imprisonment because of the belief that a prison environment is criminogenic for such persons. The seriousness of the offense is also of great importance: if the offense involves violence or personal injury the trial court is more likely to impose a prison sentence than if the offense is one against property. Community attitudes toward the offense are also significant—if the community is seriously upset about sexual offenses, particularly sexual offenses against children, a prison sentence is extremely likely to result, or if the community is particularly upset about narcotic or drug offenses, then the court is likely to respond by imposing a prison sentence in those situations. Other criteria are more specific and involve obtaining some benefit for the criminal justice system or for the victim of the offense that would be denied if the offender were sentenced to prison. Thus, the fact that the defendant has pleaded guilty makes it much more likely he will receive probation than if he was convicted following a plea of not guilty; this is done to encourage the disposition of criminal cases by plea of guilty. If the defendant has given valuable information to law enforcement he is more likely to receive probation in order to encourage defendants to cooperate with law enforcement agencies. If the defendant is willing and able to make restitution to the victim of a property offense he is very likely to be given probation, since a prison sentence would, in most instances, preclude the giving of restitution to the victim of the offense.

Fines are used most often in cases of lesser seriousness. They are, however, sometimes used in serious or felony cases. In Tate v. Short,[10] the United States Supreme Court greatly limited the ability of the trial courts to use fines as an alternative to a prison sentence when it held it is a violation of the federal constitution to imprison a criminal offender because of financial inability to pay a fine. Thus, the trial court no longer has the alternative of merely imposing a fine and leaving it up to the defendant to try to pay the fine, relying upon a system of laying out or working out the fine if the defendant is unable to come up with the money.

Other alternatives to imprisonment involve various combinations of penal sentence and community treatment, such as a term in the local jail followed by a period of probation or permitting the defendant to serve his sentence on weekends while he is during the week free to live at home and work at employment, and the commitment of persons addicted to narcotic drugs to various kinds of residential treatment programs.

V. SUPERVISION OF THE OFFENDER ON PROBATION

Probation supervision is intended to accomplish several objectives related to the prevention of further crime by the probationer and assisting him in living lawfully in the community. To some extent, the probation officer functions as a police officer, keeping the probationer under surveillance and receiving reports from police and other agencies about the probationer's conduct in the community. To some extent, the probation officer also marshalls the resources of the community to assist the probationer in adjusting to the community; for example, he may obtain employment, welfare, psychiatric counseling, family counseling or alcoholic treatment services for the probationer. To some extent, also, the probation officer may engage in a course of personal counseling with the probationer to attempt to change the probationer's attitudes toward himself, his family, authority, employment—attitudes thought to be related to the commission of crime.

A probation officer in the supervision process functions within the legal framework provided by conditions of probation. Although probation conditions vary from state to state and court to court the following are typical conditions imposed upon the conduct of probationers: pay the cost of prosecution, the

cost of probation, and make restitution as ordered by the court; obey all orders
of the probation officer; obtain the permission of the probation officer before
leaving the state or county, changing residence or employment, possessing or
applying for a license to operate a motor vehicle, getting married or filing for a
divorce or legal separation, engaging in any financial or other legal contract;
make every effort to obtain and hold a legitimate job and if discharged from
employment immediately report that fact to the probation officer; if arrested
immediately report that fact to the probation officer; support dependents;
abstain from use and consumption of all alcoholic beverages and not enter places
where such are sold or consumed; not associate with any person having a
criminal record or otherwise a bad reputation or with any other person with
whom the probation officer forbids association; comply with all municipal,
county, state and federal laws, ordinances and orders; conduct yourself in an
honorable manner as a good member of the community and not endanger in any
way the person, property right, dignity or morals of yourself or others; not
correspond either directly or through any other person with inmates of any
prison, jail, reformatory or other correctional institution, or visit such persons,
unless you have the permission of your probation officer and the superintendent
of the institution; not own, possess, use, sell, distribute or have under control
marijuana, narcotic drugs in any form without medical prescription, or firearms
or other deadly weapons; permit your probation officer to visit at your home
and place of employment at any time; waive extradition to this state from any
state or district in the union and not contest any effort to return to the United
States or this state; and follow any additional specific conditions imposed by the
court. [11]

It is obvious that even a person of saintly disposition would have difficulty
complying with all those restrictions upon his life. It must be even more obvious
that a person who has demonstrated an inability to conform to the criminal law
would find it impossible to comply with all those conditions. That is in fact the
case. There probably has never been a probationer who has fully complied with
all the conditions of probation and, furthermore, the great majority of
probationers violate probation to the knowledge of their supervising probation
officers. Yet the law permits revocation of probation and a prison sentence to be
imposed for a single violation of a single condition of probation. It is apparent,
however, that that does not occur—that probation conditions, like the criminal
laws, are not fully enforced. Violations are regularly excused and the probation
officer responds to probation condition violations by measures short of
revocation, by counseling, by imposing further restrictions on the probationer,
by increasing the number of contacts the probationer must make with the

officer, and sometimes by placing the probationer in jail for a short period of time. [12] The purpose of broad probation conditions, then, is not to obtain the revocation of every probation granted but rather to give the probation officer a broad and flexible legal tool with which to work with the probationer—a tool that is obviously subject to abuse in the hands of an incompetent or overworked or insensitive probation officer. [13]

One of the difficulties in probation supervision is the large caseloads carried by most supervising officers. It is not at all uncommon in the United States for a probation officer to have a caseload in excess of 150 probationers. When that occurs, about all the probation officer can do is to keep records of his cases: he becomes little more than an accountant and has very little time for even surveillance, much less for active personal counseling of his probationers.

There are increasing legal restrictions upon the discretion of the trial court to revoke probation. The United States Supreme Court in the case of Mempa v. Rhay[14] held that in a deferred sentencing proceeding, very similar to probation revocation, the defendant must be given a right to counsel and must have counsel appointed for him if he is indigent. This was a significant decision because it was the first to recognize federal due process rights in the probation revocation setting. Although it is not entirely clear to what extent the Mempa case limits probation revocation proceedings, most courts now assume that counsel must be provided for probation revocation. The prosecutor or probation officer usually has a burden of proving that the probationer violated at least one condition of his probation. However, as has been earlier indicated, that is not a terribly difficult task. The key to the revocation decision, then, is not whether probation lawfully can be revoked but whether the judge in his discretion should revoke probation. The kinds of considerations that influence the judge in deciding whether he should revoke probation when there has been proof of a violation are very similar to the considerations that sway the judge in deciding whether to put the defendant on probation in the first place. Although it impossible to generalize with complete accuracy, it does seem quite likely that it is a rare case in which probation is revoked without at least a strong belief by the trial court that the probationer has committed a felony offense while on probation. That is not to say that new felony charges would be brought against him in a court proceeding, or even that a violation of the felony statutes would be charged as a probation violation; technical violations, such as failure to report to the probation officer as directed, instead may be charged. However, the motive for revoking probation is almost invariably a new felony violation. [15]

VI. SELECTING THE LENGTH OF THE PRISON SENTENCE

If the trial judge elects to impose a prison sentence in lieu of probation or an alternative to imprisonment, he normally has discretion, within limits set by statute, to select the length of the prison sentence. Usually this involves selecting a maximum sentence, which determines the longest period of time the offender can be kept incarcerated. In addition, however, it frequently also involves selecting a minimum sentence or in some other way determining the period of time the offender must remain incarcerated until he is eligible for release in the discretion of the parole board. The criteria for selecting the prison sentence are basically the same as those used in the decision to grant or deny probation and in the decision to revoke probation. There is recent indication from the United States Supreme Court that it is not a violation of the Federal Constitution to give unreviewable discretion to a body such as a trial judge or a trial jury in the imposition of penal sanctions, even sanctions as severe as a penalty of death.[16] There are, however, some limitations on the process of selecting the prison sentence. In North Carolina v. Pearce,[17] the United States Supreme Court held that it was a violation of due process of law for a trial judge to impose a prison sentence that would permit an offender who had previously been sentenced and had secured the reversal of his sentence to serve a longer period of time than he could have served initially. The rationale was that this limitation upon otherwise free judicial sentencing discretion is necessary in order to permit the free exercise of the right to appeal or otherwise to challenge a conviction and sentence.

The length of the prison sentence is also affected by a number of devices that select out certain types of offenders for particularly long prison sentences. Examples of this are habitual offender statutes in which persons who have previously been convicted of crimes may receive an increase in the prison term, special prison sentences, normally indeterminate in duration, for persons convicted of certain kinds of sex offenses, and the possibility if the offender has been convicted of more than one offense of imposing the sentences consecutively, that is, adding up their lengths, instead of concurrently, that is, permitting the service of all the sentences at one time.

The actual time the offender spends in prison in felony cases, then, is a result of independent decisions made by two authorities—the trial court in selecting the prison sentence and the parole board in deciding within the limits imposed by the trial court when actually to release the offender. The system is intended to be a method of checks and balances in order to guard against placing too much discretion with either the sentencing judge or the parole board. However, in practice the checks and balances work in a rather haphazard fashion since there is very little, if any, reliable and regular communication between the trial judge and parole board. [18]

VII. APPELLATE REVIEW OF SENTENCING

A reform long advocated by students of the correctional process is to make available some method of reviewing the sentencing decisions of the trial judge. Appellate courts have traditionally taken the position that they lack power to review a sentence that is within the limits imposed by the legislature. However, in a steadily growing number of jurisdictions, now over twenty, the appellate courts have been given the power to review sentences. One of the reasons for that innovation is to permit the appellate court by the process of reviewing sentences and publishing their decisions to develop criteria for sentencing in the hope that more intelligent and consistent sentencing will result. Most observers of the process have concluded, however, that appellate review of sentencing does not accomplish this objective, perhaps because it is difficult if not impossible to articulate in this fashion the criteria that in fact influence the sentencing decision. It, nevertheless, remains true that appellate review of sentencing is important in order to correct the occasional excessive sentence, thereby permitting the offender to be released in a reasonable period of time. The availability of this remedy for excessively harsh sentences may also deter trial judges from imposing them in the first instance. [19]

VIII. RIGHTS OF PRISON INMATES

Despite increasing beliefs in recent years that absent extraordinary needs for community protection the criminal justice system should handle the convicted criminal offender by community programs of control and treatment, such as probation, imprisonment in state and federal penitentiaries and correctional institutions remains a major disposition for criminal cases. There are in the United States a wide variety of penal institutions. These range from institutions that are minimum in security, such as prison farms and modern open institutions, through those institutions in which security is medium, to institutions of very close custody, such as large-walled penitentiaries. It is important to consider internal as well as external security in the classification of penal institutions. Institutions that are nominally medium or minimum security in the sense of effort taken to prevent escape may still be maximum security in the sense of the extent of control and restriction on the daily life of prison inmates within the institution. Conversely, an institution that is nominally maximum in security in the efforts taken to prevent escape may be minimum security within the institution in that the inmates may be given relative freedom of movement within the institution. Institutions are also specialized in terms of the sex and age of the inmate they deal with, in terms of the programs and opportunities they offer, and in whether they are designed for inmates serving long sentences or relatively short sentences.

Upon admission to a penal system, an inmate is subjected to a process of study and classification. The end result of the process is to categorize the degree of security risk the inmate poses, thereby placing him in one of several kinds of institutions or giving him more or less freedom within an institution. He is also categorized in terms of the kind of work within the institution he can perform, such as farm work, factory work, institutional maintenance, or operating various service functions of the institution, such as laundry work or kitchen work. He is also classified in terms of his living arrangements, whether he will live in a relatively desirable wing or cell block of the institution, whether he will live in a dormitory or in a single or multicell. He is also classified in terms of the kind of improvement program he will receive, whether he will receive full- or part-time academic education, whether he will receive full- or part-time vocational training and, if so, what kind of training, and whether he will receive personal counseling services beyond that offered by the casework staff.

Most modern correctional institutions have in addition to the custodial, work supervision, vocational training, and educational staff, a staff of caseworkers whose job it is to conduct individual and group counseling. Casework loads tend to be high in correctional institutions and as a result there is tendency for the caseworker to function merely as a liaison man and interpreter of institutional rules and decisions to the inmates, rather than providing intensive personal counseling services. Thus, on most occasions on which an inmate would see his caseworker it would be in order to secure relief from some administrative regulation, for example, to add a person to a visiting or correspondence list or to find out when he will receive a parole hearing or the results of a parole hearing, or to request some specific change in his program from the caseworker, such as a change in employment or education or living arrangement. The caseworker, then, tends to be the person who arranges for changes in the institutional program for the inmate and does relatively little individual or group counseling in the typical correctional institution.

Until very recent years, prison inmates had few if any rights that would be recognized and enforced by the courts. The courts typically took with respect to internal prison matters what has been aptly described as a "hands off" attitude, that is to say, they took the position that matters of internal prison administration are to be decided with final authority by prison officials and that the court cannot "run the state's prison system." However, in very recent years courts have taken a more realistic attitude and have scrutinized prison practices to determine whether they comply with basic constitutional mandates. There is now developing a body of law defining the rights of prison inmates with respect to their keepers.

Historically, the first of these cases departing from the "hands off" attitude involved Black Muslim inmates. Prison officials were reluctant to recognize the Black Muslim religion and to permit freedom for its practice from fear that racial hatred and violence would result. The courts generally took a much more sympathetic view toward the Black Muslims and, applying the First Amendment to the United States Constitution, repeatedly compelled prison officials to permit Black Muslims with reasonable regulation to practice their religious beliefs in the prison community. [20]

Also in recent years courts have examined under the Eighth Amendment prohibition of cruel and unusual punishment various prison practices. The courts have declared some extreme forms of corporal punishment to violate the Eighth Amendment. [21] Courts have also scrutinized the physical conditions in solitary confinement—conditions such as lack of heat, lack of clothing, lack of nutritional diet, lack of sanitary facilities and supplies, and lack of medical supervision. In extreme cases the courts have prohibited the use of solitary confinement facilities that do not meet basic standards of humane treatment. [22]

Courts are also beginning to examine prison censorship. Traditionally prisons have imposed restrictions upon inmate mailing privileges, permitting inmates to correspond with only certain individuals and censoring all correspondence going into or out of the prison. If a letter did not meet ill-defined standards of propriety, it would be intercepted and returned to the sender. If the sender was a prison inmate he might well receive punishment for violating the prison regulations on correspondence. Prisons also limited newspapers and magazines that might be subscribed to by a prison inmate, permitting only "safe" publications to be received within the institution. In the series of recent cases, courts have struck down many of these prison regulations. The courts have been particularly sensitive about the prisons' reading and, in some cases, refusing to forward, letters from prisoners to courts, attorneys and public officials. Some courts have even said that all the prisons may do in examining correspondence of this type is to determine whether or not it contains contraband by various kinds of physical manipulation of the envelope but may not read legal correspondence, much less prevent its being forwarded to the addressee. [23]

The conditions in some prisons, lack of supervision by the staff, placing of official authority in the hands of vicious inmates, lack of physical security of one inmate from assault by another, and the deplorable physical conditions of the institutions, have led some courts to declare entire prisons or entire prison systems to be unconstitutional in violation of the Eighth Amendment prohibition of cruel and unusual punishment.[24] Although these rulings have not resulted in massive releases of prison inmates, there is some evidence that they have resulted in securing more funds for prisons from legislatures.

In the field of compulsory mental hospitalization several courts have recognized either a statutory or a constitutional right to treatment. The theory is that the only justification for compulsory mental hospitalization is to provide treatment for mental illness and that if the government fails to provide treatment, the patient is entitled to release. This same theory has been applied by some courts to create a right to treatment in the juvenile justice system.[25] There have been some suggestions in appellate cases that a similar right to treatment applies to imprisonment of the adult offender.[26] These are only suggestions, however, and the full development of a right to treatment in adult corrections, giving content to this vague concept must await future cases.

All prisons have disciplinary rules to govern the conduct of inmates and procedures and sanctions to respond to violations of those rules. Until very recently there were no legal requirements concerning the procedures that must be followed by prisons in the enforcement of disciplinary rules. Recent cases, however, suggest a vague contour of federal procedural due process limitations on the power of prisons to impose sanctions, such as solitary confinement or forfeiture of good time credit, for the violation of prison disciplinary rules. Some cases suggest merely that notice of the charges and a hearing is necessary. Other cases go further and suggest that a right to confront and cross-examine witnesses, a determination by an impartial tribunal, and the assistance of some person, such as a member of the prison staff or even an attorney, may be required by federal due process of law. Some cases have even gone so far as to suggest that there is a federal constitutional obligation upon prisons to reduce to writing the disciplinary rules that prevail within the institutions, rather than relying upon vague statements about the good conduct and filling in the details with case-by-case adjudication. This is an area of developing law that will continue to grow in the future.[27]

Adult prisoners not infrequently are faced with criminal charges filed against them by other jurisdictions. When an offender violates the law of more than one jurisdiction before he is apprehended and he is prosecuted and convicted and imprisoned by one jurisdiction, the other jurisdiction is very likely to file a detainer against him. A detainer is merely an informal device notifying the holding institution that the inmate is wanted in another jurisdiction. The holding institution as an informal matter of comity agrees to notify the other jurisdiction before the inmate is released and to give the other jurisdiction an opportunity to take the inmate into custody. Unfortunately, the detainer has other effects upon the inmate's prison program: the inmate may be denied the opportunity for parole because of the detainer; he may be classified as a security risk because of the detainer; and he may be denied opportunities in vocational training or educational programs because the institution is uncertain whether he will be released to the free world or imprisoned folowing his stay in the correctional institution. There are several kinds of detainers, depending upon the reason why the authority that lodged them wants custody of the inmate. The most frequent kind of detainer represents a criminal charge against the inmate that has not yet been tried, but there may be detainers from the federal government requesting custody of an inmate for deportation, and there may be detainers requesting custody of an inmate for purposes of probation or parole revocation. Up until recently, courts took the position that there was no obligation upon the authority that lodged the detainer to secure a speedy adjudication of the underlying charges. However, the United States Supreme Court held in Smith v. Hooey [28] that the fact that the inmate is in a different jurisdiction does not justify the authority that lodged a detainer to merely wait until he is released in order to give him a trial on the charges that the detainer represents. Now, at least upon request of an inmate, a detaining authority is obligated to either bring the inmate to the jurisdiction for a speedy trial or to dismiss the detainer and the charges. It has also been held that this right to a speedy determination, based upon the Sixth Amendment of the United States Constitution, applies to probation revocation. [29] As yet there has been no case law development that would apply the same right to a speedy determination to detainers based upon deportation orders or upon violation of parole.

A continuing problem of prison inmates is obtaining access to the judicial process in order to determine the legality of their custody. It was noted earlier that courts are now jealously guarding the right of inmates to correspond with the judiciary about the legality of their custody. The courts have held in effect that there is a federal constitutional right on the part of prison inmates of access to the courts. Prisons have been prohibited from screening petitions for writs of habeas corpus[30] on the ground that this interferes with the inmates' right of access to court. Recently the United States Supreme Court in the case of Johnson v. Avery [31] held that a prison may not prohibit one inmate from assisting another in the production of a petition for a writ of habeas corpus unless it provides reasonable alternatives to the services of a jailhouse lawyer.

Prisons have long sought to prohibit the functioning of jailhouse lawyers in the prison community but the Johnson v. Avery case limits their ability to do so to those situations in which they provide alternative means of legal assistance for inmates without legal training or for inmates who are in effect illiterate. It is not yet clear what "reasonable alternatives" means but it probably ultimately will be decided that it means the services of an attorney or at least of law students functioning as under the supervision of an attorney. A very recent United States Supreme Court case suggests that a prison is obligated to provide a law library to prison inmates without funds that is comparable to a law library that a prisoner with funds would be permitted under the receipt of literature regulation to purchase from publishers. [32] It is not yet clear exactly the extent of reach of this case. The future will hold developments in this area in the form of prison regulations limiting the amount of time an inmate may spend upon his legal work, prohibiting him from doing legal work when he is in solitary confinement, and requiring transcripts of various legal proceedings for use by an inmate in his petitions for writs of habeas corpus.

IX. RELEASE FROM PRISON ON PAROLE

Parole is the conditional release of an inmate under supervision. Most felony sentences in the United States are indeterminate—the trial judge selects the outer limits of the sentence but the date of actual release from prison is fixed by an administrative body, usually called a board of parole. Statutes typically impose requirements that an inmate must meet in order to become eligible for release on parole. These requirements are usually expressed in terms of serving a minimum sentence or serving a portion, such as one-fourth, one-third, or one-half the maximum sentence. When an inmate becomes eligible for parole he is normally given a parole hearing. A parole hearing is simply an appearance before the parole board, a member of the parole board, or a hearing examiner for the parole board for an interview. The hearing is very informal and normally other persons are not permitted to attend the interview. The parole board questions the inmate about his progress in prison and tries to determine whether he would be a good risk for release on parole or whether he should for other reasons be paroled. The criteria used by the board in deciding whether to grant parole are very similar to those employed by the trial judge in deciding whether to grant probation. The inmate is then informed of the decision and if he is granted parole he will be released. There is very little opportunity for review of a decision to deny parole. Courts still take the position that the matter is within the jurisdiction and discretion of the board of parole and they will not intervene except in cases in which the board fails to follow an express statutory requirement or acts in an arbitrary and capricious manner.[33] As a practical matter, then, the board's decision is final.

An increasing number of jurisdictions now require that every inmate released from prison be provided with parole supervision services. These laws, called mandatory release laws, require parole supervision from when the inmate has served his maximum sentence less good time credits until he has served full maximum sentence. Parole conditions, supervision and the possibility of revocation are normally the same for the mandatory releasee as for the parolee. The important distinction is that the person on mandatory release has attained that status by operation of law and has earlier been rejected for parole consideration by the parole board.

X. PAROLE SUPERVISION AND REVOCATION

The conditions of parole are almost identical to those of probation and the process of parole supervision is virtually identical to probation supervision. Where parole differs from probation is in the revocation proceedings. Probation revocation requires returning the case to court and proving of a probation condition violation. Parole revocation, on the other hand, is administrative and may or may not require an administrative hearing at which the parolee is informed of the conditions he has violated and is given an opportunity to respond to those charges. Recent court decisions have indicated that the U.S. Constitution may require some type of administrative hearing for parole revocation,[34] but it is not altogether clear what form that hearing must take and it is also not altogether clear what rights, such as the right to representation by an attorney, a parolee may have in the parole revocation process.

XI. MISDEMEANOR CORRECTIONS

Persons convicted of misdemeanors, offenses carrying punishment only by fine or confinement in a jail, are subjected to a correctional process that is a considerably truncated version of the felony correctional process. Normally the trial judge sentences the person convicted of a misdemeanor without the extended sentence hearing and without the presentence report that are commonly used in felony cases. The person sentenced for a misdemeanor who is imprisoned in a jail is usually given only very minimal classification attention, since the programs of local jails normally do not present diverse opportunities for inmates. Although one sentenced for a misdemeanor may be released from jail before he serves his full sentence as a result of receiving credit for good behavior, it is very unusual for release from service of misdemeanor sentences to be effected by parole. Most persons released from jail have served their full jail sentence and do not receive supervision following their term in jail. Although probation is increasingly being used for misdemeanants, the quality of supervision may be less than in felony cases because of the great number of misdemeanants who pass through the criminal justice system.

XII. DISABILITIES OF CONVICTION OF CRIME

The fact of conviction of a criminal offense, particularly of a felony offense, is of great significance to the offender even after he is released from the correctional process. Typically a felony conviction prohibits the offender from serving on a jury, from holding public office, and from voting. It may also prohibit him from entering certain professions, such as the medical profession, legal profession, or licensed occupations such as those of a barber or plumber. But beyond such formal legal disabilities, a record of a conviction of crime works considerable disadvantage for the offender on an informal level. Employers frequently ask whether the applicant for employment has been convicted of crime and may not hire him because of a conviction. Some educational institutions screen their applicants to determine whether they have been convicted of crime and may reject applicants because of a reported conviction. [35]

The formal legal disabilities of conviction of crime can be removed by operation of a statute or a pardon from the governor of the state in which the conviction occurred, but the informal disabilities of conviction of crime—the detrimental impact upon employment and educational opportunities—are not affected. Some states have statutes permitting the expungment or sealing of criminal records upon application by a person who is able to show that he has rehabilitated himself and that the record works a prejudicial effect upon him. Such records then may be removed from law enforcement files and either destroyed or kept in a sealed file in a court office, and the offender is permitted to state he has never been convicted of crime. [36] There is, of course, doubt as to the efficacy of sealing or expungment of criminal records since it is always possible for recollection of cases to be reported to employers or other persons or for all of the files not to be destroyed or sealed. Nevertheless, expungment or sealing is a worthwhile innovation.

N O T E S

1. The "criminalization" of the juvenile justice process has occurred as a result of a series of decisions by the United States Supreme Court beginning with In Re Gault, 387 U.S. 1 (1967).

2. The most comprehensive discussion of the guilty plea as a means of adjudicating criminal cases appears in D. Newman, *Conviction: The Determination of Guilt or Innocence Without Trial* (1966). See also Alschuler, "The Prosecutor's Role in Plea Bargaining," 36 U.Chi.L. Rev. 50 (1968).

3. For a discussion of the presentence report and the techniques used in presentence investigation, see R. Dawson, *Sentencing: The Decision as to Type, Length, and Conditions of Sentence,* 15-41 (1969).

4. 337 U.S. 241 (1949).

5. See S. Rubin et al., *The Law of Criminal Correction,* 98-101 (1963).

6. The issue of accuracy of presentence information is discussed in R. Dawson, note 3 at 56-65.

7. The use of psychiatric examinations as aids to sentencing is discussed in R. Dawson, note 3 at 41-51.

8. The jury makes the sentencing decision in some situations. Normally, the jury decides upon whether a person convicted of a capital offense will receive a sentence of death or a term in prison. In a few states, if the defendant was convicted in a trial by jury, the jury makes the sentencing decision. See American Bar Association Project on Minimum Standards for Criminal Justice, "Standards Relating to Sentencing Alternatives and Procedures," 43-48 (1968).

9. See R. Dawson, note 3 at 79-99; American Law Institute, Model Penal Code §7.01 (Proposed Official Draft, 1962).

10. 401 U.S. 395 (1971). See also Williams v. Illinois, 399 U.S. 235 (1970).

11. These are the probation conditions used by the New Mexico Board of Probation and Parole and appear fully in F. Miller, R. Dawson, G. Dix and R. Parnas, *Criminal Justice Administration and Related Processes,* 945-946 (1971).

12. See R. Dawson, note 3 at 164-168.

13. There is a limited, but developing, body of law placing legal limits upon the restrictions that can be imposed on probationers. See F. Miller et al., note 11 at 947-955.

14. 389 U.S. 128 (1967).

15. See R. Dawson, note 3 at 151-164.

16. See McGautha v. California, 402 U.S. 183 (1971).

17. 395 U.S. 711 (1969).

18. See R. Dawson, note 3 at 258-260.

19. Appellate review of sentencing is fully discussed in American Bar Association Project on Minimum Standards for Criminal Justice, "Standards Relating to Appellate Review of Sentences" (1968).

20. See Fulwood v. Clemmer, 206 F.Supp. 370 (D.D.C. 1962).

21. See Jackson v. Bishop, 404 F.2d 571 (8th Cir. 1968).

22. See Jordan v. Fitzharris, 257 F.Supp. 674 (N.D. Cal. 1966); Wright v. McMann, 387 F.2d 519 (2nd Cir. 1967).

23. See Note, "Prison Mail Censorship and the First Amendment," 81 Yale L.J. 87 (1971).

24. See Holt v. Sarver, 300 F.Supp. 825 (E.D.Ark. 1969); Holt v. Sarver II, 309 F.Supp. 362 (E.D.Ark. 1970).

25. See F. Cohen, *The Legal Challenge to Corrections,* 100-104 (1969).

26. See Holt v. Sarver II, 309 F.Supp. 362, 378-379 (E.D.Ark. 1970).

27. For a discussion of disciplinary procedures in two federal prisons, see Kraft, "Prison Disciplinary Practices and Procedures: Is Due Process Provided?" 47 N.D.L.Rev. 1 (1970).

28. 393 U.S. 374 (1969).

29. Fariss v. Tipps, 463 S.W.2d 176 (Tex.Sup.Ct. 1971).

30. Ex parte Hull, 312 U.S. 546 (1941).

31. 393 U.S. 483 (1969).

32. Gilmore v. Lynch, 319 F.Supp. 105 (N.D.Cal. 1970) affirmed sub nom. Younger v. Gilmore, 92 S.Ct. 250 (1971).

33. See, e.g., Menechino v. Oswald, 430 F.2d 403 (2nd Cir. 1970).

34. See, e.g., Alverez v. Turner, 422 F.2d 214 (10th Cir. 1970).

35. See F. Cohen, *The Legal Challenge to Corrections,* 82-87 (1969).

36. Gough, "The Expungment of Adjudication Records of Juvenile and Adult Offenders: A Problem of Status," 1966 Wash.U.L.Q. 147; Kogan & Loughery, "Sealing and Expungment of Criminal Records—The Big Lie," 61 J. of Crim.L., C & PS 378 (1970).

THE NEW BROOM: THE FEDERALIZATION OF DOUBLE JEOPARDY

nor shall any person subject for the same offense to be twice put in jeopardy of life or limb

From the Fifth Amendment
to the U.S. Constitution

JAY A. SIGLER received his B.A. magna cum laude from Rutgers
University, 1954, his J.D. 1957 and M.A. 1960, and his Ph.D. 1962, all at
the same institution. He has taught at Kent State University, University of
Vermont, and at Rutgers, where he is currently Assistant Dean, College of
Arts and Sciences. He is author of *An Introduction to the Legal System*
(1968), *Double Jeopardy* (1969), *The Conservative Tradition in American
Thought* (1969), *Problems in Public Law* (1970), *The Growth of American
Government* (in preparation), and *Civil Rights Policy* (in preparation), as
well as numerous articles in sociology and law journals.

Chapter 10

THE NEW BROOM: THE FEDERALIZATION OF
DOUBLE JEOPARDY

J A Y   A.   S I G L E R

I. DOUBLE JEOPARDY BEFORE 1970

The rules concerning the scope and import of the concept of double jeopardy are undergoing massive tension in America. The Supreme Court has undertaken the gruelling intellectual task of separating the various strands of policy considerations which underlie the doctrine, a task which has previously baffled the judges of most federal and state courts. In doing this the court has attempted to introduce symmetry and rationality into a protection which was "in a state of considerable confusion."[1] At the same time the Court has had to develop some new directions in double jeopardy policy which suggest that the future will hold more reforms in future terms of the Court. The changes in the Court brought about by President Nixon's appointments do not seem likely to reverse the gradual unfolding of a new national double jeopardy policy.

The attitudes of legal writers concerning the significance of double jeopardy has varied greatly over the years. Throughout the nineteenth century when the American version of double jeopardy was being developed in the states and at the federal level there was great optimism about it and a glorification of its historical roots.[2] By the 1920s and 1930s many critics averred that the original purposes of the doctrine had disappeared because the risks of the defendant in criminal cases had been sharply reduced.[3] Improved trial procedure and the unlikelihood of governmental tyranny have, according to this attitude, obviated many of the problems which gave rise to original double jeopardy policy.

Basically, the critics feel that the accused is already armed with enough defenses against judicial and administrative arbitrariness, and that the society should be protected against those who might "jeopardize the public."[4] This chapter is written in the belief that double jeopardy is an important part of the civil liberties of Americans. The various policies which it supports are not, in my view, adequately met by the many changes in criminal procedures introduced in the twentieth century. On the contrary, the rapid increase in the number of crimes as defined by modern statutes and the rise in the incidence of arrests both have led to a greater need for the protection today than was present in the last century. While it is true the death penalty is no longer a great hazard for those accused of crime, and it is also true that limbs are no longer removed from the bodies of offenders, the psychological, social, economic and political damage created by repeated prosecution is a real concern of the criminal justice system. The basic policy needs today are at least as great as they were in 1873 when the Supreme Court announced that:

> once acquitted or convicted of a crime for his conduct in a particular transaction, a defendant should be able to consider the matter closed and plan his life ahead without the threat of subsequent prosecution and possible imprisonment.[5]

Authors rarely have the satisfaction of having their dreams come true. Yet, in 1966 I wrote an article calling for the incorporation of the double jeopardy clause into the "due process clause" of the Constitution. Coupled with this was a prediction that if this were done "states will be forced to consider the total body of federal double jeopardy policy."[6] That prediction has proven true in Benton v. Maryland. At least, it now appears that the Supreme Court has not only incorporated double jeopardy as a protection available for every accused person against state prosecutions, it has also changed the direction of double jeopardy policy in many states. In some, double jeopardy has become federalized.

The outcome of Benton v. Maryland was easy to foresee. The modern march towards incorporating much of the Bill of Rights into the Constitution began, as dissenting Justice Harlan pointed out, in 1961, with the decision in Mapp. v. Ohio.[7] Harlan argued that the due process clause of the Fourteenth Amendment did not incorporate or take over the double jeopardy clause of the Fifth Amendment. He reminded the court of the constitutional wisdom of Palko

v. Connecticut,[8] a well-established 1937 case which set the basic meaning of due process as a "fundamental . . . principle of justice."[9]

In spite of the fact that the Supreme Court had ruled in 1937 that double jeopardy was not required by due process, in 1959 they were willing to do so. The Supreme Court justified this shift by rejecting the approach of Palko on the issue of the fundamental quality of double jeopardy. The Court argued that the right was, indeed, fundamental and traceable back to Greek and Roman times, as well as the common law of England. They cited the Sigler book for this proposition[10] although Sigler pointed out that a full double jeopardy rule had emerged prior to the eighteenth century, yet, it is evident that the court did regard double jeopardy as a very important constitutional right, and by its ruling served notice of an intention to spell out the dimensions of that right. As the Court concluded: "like the right to trial by jury, it (double jeopardy) is clearly fundamental to the American scheme of justice."[11]

Only Harlan and Stewart dissented. Their grounds for dissent were the same as their earlier dissents in cases involving the incorporation of many other rights mentioned in the Fifth, Sixth, and Eighth Amendments. It seems unlikely that their dissents are sufficient to turn the tide at some near future date, especially since the resignation of Justice Harlan. Double jeopardy is now a national protection available against state and federal actions, and probably will remain so for a long time to come.

II. THE 1970 CASES

A. Collateral Estoppel

In the wake of the Benton case the Supreme Court began the process of revising federal double jeopardy and systematizing state double jeopardy policy. Probably the most important case was Ashe v. Swenson[12] in which the Court held that double jeopardy requires that a criminal defendant acquitted of a crime be able to invoke the doctrine of collateral estoppel in a later trial. This principle, which has often been invoked in civil cases as a means of preventing repetitious litigation can be best reduced to the following formula:

> Where a question of fact essential to the judgment is actually litigated and determined by a valid and final judgment, the determination is conclusive between the parties in a subsequent action on a different cause of action. . . .[13]

This precept had not been applied consistently in federal courts, yet the Supreme Court chose to elevate it to the dignity of a constitutional requirement.

Federal courts had vied collateral estoppel as part of the general rulemaking power of the Supreme Court over the federal court system.[14] It is interesting to note that in a 1961 circuit court decision, Judge Friendly did give great weight to the fairness inherent in the collateral estoppel principle.[15]

In spite of this rather uncertain foundation, and in spite of the various evidentiary tests applied in federal courts in similar double jeopardy issues the Supreme Court took the bold step of making collateral estoppel a constitutional principle. To reach this conclusion the Supreme Court had to reverse its important 1958 decision in Hoag v. New Jersey,[16] in which it rejected a claim of collateral estoppel. According to the Court the question presented in 1958 was possible "fundamental unfairness" as part of the Fourteenth Amendment due process requirement. But because of the decision of the Benton case the question had changed from whether collateral estoppel is a requirement of due process in general to whether it is a part of the double jeopardy guarantee.

Apparently the Supreme Court was willing to redefine double jeopardy for all courts in the nation, not just the state courts. The Court cited a 1948 case as the basis of its collateral estoppel adoption,[17] but claimed that the doctrine had existed for 50 years in the federal courts.[18] The Court seems to have accepted as a ground for its argument a well known 1960 Harvard Law Review Article which is quoted in the majority opinion.[19]

The effect of the Ashe decision is to reduce the scope of the authority of criminal juries. Collateral estoppel applied to criminal cases allows appellate courts to determine the true meaning and scope of a jury verdict in order to determine the double jeopardy significance of the first prosecution. As the Court said, quoting the law review article, the real question is "whether a rational jury could have grounded its verdict upon an issue other than that which the defendant seeks to foreclose from consideration."[20]

In view of the many inconsistent tests previously created by federal and state courts to determine the scope of an earlier verdict when double jeopardy is pleaded in a later prosecution the Ashe case represents a major step towards uniformity and simplicity. Collateral estoppel is by no means a panacea. An appellate court must still decide what issues were "necessarily determined" by a prior acquittal. The test places a heavy burden upon appellate courts to search the trial record for the import of an acquittal, but at least the appellate tribunals will rest their opinions on facts in the record rather than upon abstract arbitrary rules.

Ashe v. Swenson also succeeded in making double jeopardy "fully retroactive."[21] This ruling, which was made in passing, invites further double jeopardy claims, and many cases have come to the Court which arose before Benton.

B. Dual Jurisdictions (State and City)

Many commentators predicted that the Supreme Court would overturn several long-standing double jeopardy precedents involving separate prosecutions brought by the state and federal governments. So far this view seems unfounded. In Waller v. Florida the Court barred a city reprosecution which followed a state prosecution on the ground that a city is part of the same sovereignty as a state. Cities are creatures of the state legislatures and the same act cannot be separately prosecuted by two arms of the same sovereign power. Chief Justice Burger, who wrote the majority opinion emphasized that the second prosecution was based on the same acts as were involved in the violation of the two city ordinances. The Burger opinion was careful to avoid any implication that separate federal and state prosecutions would fall under a double jeopardy prohibition, and the principle of "dual sovereignty" seems to this writer still to permit dual prosecutions.[22] Benton did not change this aspect of double jeopardy policy.

C. Greater and Lesser Offenses

Price v. Georgia,[23] another 1970 case, does show a change from previous rulings as a result of Benton. The power of a state to retry an accused for murder after an earlier verdict of voluntary manslaughter was denied because of the application of the federal case law to a situation which had been tolerated prior to Benton. The Supreme Court stated that a 1910 case which had permitted this kind of reprosecution[24] was overruled by Benton v. Maryland retroactively. The federal rule was held to cover the situation. As a result the fact that defendant has successfully appealed from a judgment precluded a new trial for a greater offense for a more serious charge growing out of the same facts. The defendant could be retried for the same offense or a lesser one because of the federal principle of "continuing jeopardy" but he could not be retried for murder.

D. Mistrials

The most hotly disputed double jeopardy case after Benton was United States v. Jorn[26] in which the Court was split over the meaning of the "manifest necessity" doctrine in double jeopardy law. In brief, the question revolved around the issue of whether a trial judge's declaration of a mistrial could be found so improper as to bar a new trial. Obviously, the issue touched upon a sensitive judicial nerve. Furthermore, the "manifest necessity" doctrine is in disarray in the state and federal courts. "Manifest necessity" is a rule created as an exception to the general rule that a defendant is in jeopardy at a certain point (usually with the impaneling of a jury) in the conduct of a trial. Generally, once jeopardy has "attached," the defendant cannot be tried again for the same offense. Then, a "person has been in jeopardy when he is regularly charged with a crime before a tribunal properly organized and competent to try him."[27] "Manifest necessity" creates the exception which softens the effect of the defendant-prone general rule.

The Jorn case does not involve state courts, but by virtue of Benton, its ruling will probably apply to the states. The gist of the case is to deny the absolute authority of the trial judge to declare mistrials. The trial judge will be deemed to have abused his discretion if he fails to "recognize that lack of preparedness by the Government to continue the trial discreetly implicates policies underpinning both the double jeopardy provision and the double jeopardy guarantee."[28] The Supreme Court is prepared to disturb the judgments of trial judges in early dismissal of criminal cases in the name of double jeopardy.

III. RECENT STATE CASES

The full effects of Benton v. Maryland have not yet been felt in the states. Since most double jeopardy claims arise in state cases the real meaning of the concept is still subject to considerable variation among the states. A handful of state cases can be examined out of the mass in order to sense the future development of the concept. Furthermore, the extent to which state courts are adapting to the Benton case can also be perceived.

A. Dual Jurisdictions (Federal and State)

State v. Fletcher,[29] an Ohio case decided almost immediately after Benton discloses some very interesting features. Benton did not reach the question "whether the federal prescription against double jeopardy prevents a state prosecution following a federal acquittal or conviction."[30] That question was presented squarely in State v. Fletcher because of an attempt by the state of Ohio to prosecute one Michael Fletcher and one Willie Walker after the two defendants had been jointly charged for bank robbery in the federal jurisdiction for the Northern District of Ohio. The state charges were based upon the same claimed criminal act.

Judge Day, writing the decision of the Court of Appeals for Cuyahoga County, Ohio decided this important issue in favor of the defendant's double jeopardy claims, thus brushing aside certain well established federal precedents. Judge Day felt that Benton suggested that these precedents were no longer controlling, even though they were not directly involved in that decision. He seemed to feel that the Supreme Court would eventually overrule these earlier precedents[31] because the Palko case, an even more fundamental precedent, had been partly overturned in Benton. The dual sovereignty argument was rejected by Judge Day as a matter of Ohio constitutional law, in interpreting the Ohio constitutional provision, which is quite similar to the federal clause. This language was interpreted to preclude successive federal-state prosecution:

> The evils that policy was meant to proscribe are not improved because the state and federal sovereignties combine to generate them. It would be incongruous to allow a basic constitutional policy of a state, determined as an aspect of its sovereignty, to be frustrated by a consequence of the duality which allows that sovereignty to exist. Furthermore, it would be both inconsistent and ironic to use that federalism, which is justified in the name of protecting freedom, to obliterate a fundamental right.[32]

At this moment in time the Supreme Court has not moved as far as Judge Day predicted it would. These are many good reasons for agreeing with Judge Day,[33] but he seems to have been well ahead of the Supreme Court. Federalism does not seem to be threatened by a denial to one level of government of the power to prosecute an individual for an offense growing out of precisely the same prohibited conduct. The fact that national interests are not endangered by this expension of the double jeopardy principle is evidenced by the fact that after the Supreme Court, in 1959, handed down a decision which allowed federal prosecution in the wake of state prosecution the United States Attorney General announced a policy that no federal prosecution would follow a state trial for the same act except in unusual circumstances and then only with his express approval.[34]

B. Defendant Appealing

Some state courts are not as ready to receive the message of Benton and its successors. In Walsh v. Commonwealth,[35] the Supreme Judicial Court of Massachusetts handed down a narrow, technical decision which seems to misunderstand the point of the Supreme Court's recent double jeopardy assertions. The case involved a defendant who pleaded guilty to three indictments for armed robbery. Walsh was sentenced on each indictment for a term of five to ten years, the sentences to run concurrently. When he was informed of his statutory right to appeal, Walsh elected to do so. His appeal resulted in a dismissal of two indictments and an amended sentence for the third, which increased the sentence to a term of eight to twelve years. Then Walsh petitioned the Supreme Judicial Court, asserting that his double jeopardy rights had been violated by the increase in sentence.

The petitioner relied upon North Carolina v. Pearce[36] a companion case to

Benton v. Maryland. In Pearce there was a new trial and a new conviction with a greater sentence following an appeal. This was held by the Supreme Court to be barred by double jeopardy. The facts in Walsh are distinguishable from Pearce and from Price v. Georgia, the 1970 case covering a similar point. The review which the Massachusetts statute provided was for the sentence only, not the verdict.[37] The Supreme Judicial Court seemed to rely upon this distinction (they did not expressly make it) in denying the double jeopardy claim. Pearce rested upon the narrow ground that whenever a court resentences a criminal defendant it must affirmatively state its grounds and rationale for an increased sentence. Thus, the concept favored was that:

> Due process of law . . . required that *vindictiveness* against a defendant for having successfully attacked his first connection must play *no part* in the sentence he receives after retrial.[38]

The Supreme Judicial Court of Massachusetts noted that the Massachusetts statute provides that the same judge who imposes the original sentence may not sit upon its review.[39] This, the court suggested, would largely eliminate the element of vindictiveness. The court went on to cite statistics which showed that over a fourteen-year span only 2.07 percent of the total appeals resulted in an increased sentence.

That the Massachusetts tribunal have taken too narrow a view of the law seems evident after examining Price v. Georgia,[40] the Supreme Court ruling decided later in the same year as the Walsh case. It appears that the Price case touches only the question of reprosecution but the principle of continuing jeopardy which is applied there may preclude a greater resentencing as well. The matter is distinguishable and the Walsh court could be correct. A 1970 denial of certiorari[41] may have been relied upon by the Supreme Judicial Court of Massachusetts in reaching its conclusions.

C. Higher State Standards, Juveniles, and Waiver

Several interesting double jeopardy cases have arisen in state courts which deserve brief comment because of their general significance. The Nebraska Supreme Court, for example, has held that the double jeopardy requirements of the federal and state constitutions do not prevent the state from fixing higher standards by statute or even by judicial decision.[42] This sensible ruling recognizes that Benton only set a floor for double jeopardy standards. A California appellate court has held that a statute which permits a hearing to determine whether a juvenile comes within a court's jurisdiction as a juvenile is not unconstitutional for double jeopardy reasons because it permits the transfer of a juvenile for trial as an adult.[43] This issue is likely to reach the Supreme

Court at some time soon, and the California ruling seems sound. A final example of an important future problem is the question of an intentional or unintentional waiver of double jeopardy. Is the right subject to waiver? Most state courts are ready to imply a waiver from other acts or omissions of a defendant.[44] This matter needs clarification, because excessive use of implied waiver could undercut the significance of double jeopardy policy.

IV. THE NEAR FUTURE

There are a number of issues which remain unresolved in double jeopardy policy development. The decisions since Benton V. Maryland show that the Supreme Court and other courts are ready to reconstruct the character of criminal policy in the double jeopardy area. It is heartening to see that the impetus of Benton has been creative and forward-looking. Out of the need for uniformity which was generated by the 1969 decision has come a careful examination of the several competing, confusing policies which have grown up around the country since the inception of the double jeopardy concept. Courts seem willing to look below the surface of comfortable formulae to the genuine social issues which are at stake. The process is now in motion which would, in the long run, recognize that the term "double jeopardy" covers a number of different policy issues, each of which requires a separate set of policy considerations.

A. Same Offense

Perhaps the most difficult issue is that of the scope of the impact of the criminal trial. The word "same offense" in the federal and state constitutions does not yet have a settled meaning, but until it does unfairness and inequality of treatment of defendants will continue. Until this point in time courts have taken a mechanical view of the problem, without due consideration of the ultimate policy issue. There are a number of so-called "tests" for double jeopardy which are still applied to define the meaning of the "same offense" phrase.

The most popular, and the narrowest test, is the "same evidence" rule which was adopted from English common law. This rule, which is very favorable to the prosecution, is based upon the premise that: "unless the (first) indictment were such as the prisoner might have been convicted by proof of the facts contained in the second indictment, an acquittal on the first indictment can be no bar to the second."[45] This test would limit the protection of double jeopardy to the language of the offense charged in the indictment, not to other offenses which the prosecution might later charge. Obviously, this test almost makes mockery of the double jeopardy clause since it leaves the defendant at the mercy of the prosecution in situations which happen to violate several different portions of the substantive criminal law. Yet the test is still applied in many states.[46] The test has also been read to apply to multiple punishments, although the policy considerations are very different.[47]

The Supreme Court has avoided this basic problem thus far, although it was presented to them in Ashe v. Swenson,[48] as Justices Brennan, Douglas, and Marshall perceived in criticizing the application of the principle of collateral estoppel. These jurists contended that the time was ripe to apply another test for the meaning of the "same offense" phrase. They stated:

> The double jeopardy clause requires the prosecution . . . to join at one trial all the charges which grew out of a single criminal act, occurrence, episode, or transaction. This "same transaction" test of "same offense" not only enforces the ancient prohibition against vexatious multiple prosecutions embodied in the Double Jeopardy Clause, but also responds as well to the increasingly widespread recognition that the consolidation in one law suit of all issues arising out of a single transaction or occurrence best promotes justice, economy, and convenience.[49]

The concurring Justices reminded the Court that the same tests for double jeopardy ought to apply in state and federal courts after the Benton case. Indeed, the "same transaction" test had been applied in many federal courts prior to Ashe, but after that decision, lower federal courts may drift towards a use of the collateral estoppel rubric, a most unfortunate development.[50]

Collateral estoppel is a much less satisfactory principle for the defendant than the "same transaction" rule. It requires the defendant to show that an earlier trial *necessarily* decided facts which are at issue in a later trial. As a practical matter it may frequently be hard to determine just what facts a criminal jury intended to decide in reaching a verdict. This uncertainty about the significance of the criminal verdict places an undue burden upon the defendant who claims double jeopardy and upon a court which must evaluate the claim.[51] The "same transaction" test is neater, cleaner, and it places the burden for proving the legitimacy of a second prosecution where it objectively belongs, on the prosecutor. Obviously the Supreme Court majority is not yet ready to move very far in favor of a defendant-oriented interpretation of the meaning of the "same offense," but the logic of the problem favors the proponents of the "same evidence." The Model Penal Code[52] and an American Bar Association study[53] reject the "same evidence" test for successive prosecution cases, and their work carries some weight in the courts. It is likely that the "same transaction" test will prevail in multiple prosecution cases.

B. Federalism

A second area of double jeopardy policy is the significance to be given to federalism in the enforcement of substantive criminal law. For years each sovereign in American federalism—the state and the federal government—has been able to make separate prosecutions for criminal offenses, even though the evidence to support the prosecution might be identical. The leading Supreme Court case dealing with this doctrine of "dual sovereigns" supports this practice in the interest of the federal principle.[54] Waller v. Florida[55] the 1970 case mentioned above seems at first glance to challenge the "dual sovereign" doctrine, but close inspection of the language discloses no threat to the doctrine.

State courts have generally rejected the view that the dual sovereign doctrine was ended by the Benton case.[56] The Supreme Court had not yet clearly indicated the current status of the doctrine, but some inferences can be drawn from recent actions. In 1971 the Court denied certiorari to a case which seemed to present a clear test of the dual sovereign doctrine, although the courts below had relied upon it.[57] Consequently, we can anticipate no change of policy in the near future, although the theoretical underpinnings of this doctrine are extremely flimsy.[58] The doctrine is eventually going to be overthrown, if only because of the inconsistency which it creates between the impact of federalism and the rules of international law in the criminal field.[59]

The central confusion in double jeopardy law is, however, still beyond the reach of judicial decision-making. The myriad criminal statutes of state legislatures and of the federal Congress still pour out of these bodies adding to the possibility of multiple incrimination, as each new statute tends to overlap and duplicate some provision of an earlier act. Obviously, a broad legislative reconsideration of criminal law policy will solve the basic problems of double jeopardy. Only in that way can the social policy which double jeopardy is intended to treat be adequately managed. In the absence of a legislative pruning of the criminal law, procedural rules compelling the prosecution to join all possible charges in one trial can make inroads into the core idea of double jeopardy which is to protect individuals from repeated risks of prosecution and punishment, while assuring the public protection by a full presentation of its case against an accused through the efforts of a thoroughly prepared prosecutor.

V. THE LONGER VIEW

Many of the problems encountered in double jeopardy law concern the discretion accorded to American prosecutors at the state and federal level to institute criminal charges according to their own personal views of public policy. Legal reform groups, aware of this situation, have called for various procedural methods to compel prosecutors to make choices which are now generally available to them without restriction. The Model Penal Code states, for example, that "a defendant shall not be subject to separate trials for multiple offenses based on the same conduct or arising from the same criminal episode, if such offenses are known to the appropriate prosecuting officer at the time of the commencement of the first trial and are within the jurisdiction of a single court."[59] However, another section authorizes a court "on application of the prosecuting attorney or the defendant" to "order any such charge to be tried separately, if it is satisfied that justice so requires."[60] This substitution of judicial discretion for prosecutorial discretion indicates the pervasive distrust of prosecutors which has arisen throughout the elite circles of the legal profession.

The ABA Minimum Standards for Criminal Justice exhibits the same distrustful attitude towards prosecutors. The ABA proposal would allow defendants to make motions which would compel joinder of related offenses "which should be granted unless the court determines that because the prosecuting attorney does not have sufficient evidence . . . or for some other reasons the ends of justice would be defeated if the motion were granted."[61] Our most progressive rules on these matters, the Federal Rules of Criminal Procedure, do provide for permissive joinder of offenses which "are of the same or similar character or are based on the same act or transaction."[62] However, the same preference for judicial discretion is apparent in those rules, so that joinder is a matter of judicial choice, not of right.[63]

The Supreme Court, too, is deeply concerned with prosecutorial abuse of the criminal process. No doubt this feeling is a powerful force in the emergence of a more meaningful double jeopardy protection. Justice Brennan is most sensitive to prosecutorial abuses in double jeopardy areas, which accounts for his adoption of the same transaction test. As of this writing the majority of the Court is not prepared to address this issue directly, nor has it come to grips with the problems of multiple charges or multiple sentencing, both of which are not even considered within the ambit of the double jeopardy concept. It will be interesting to see whether the Court will be able to continue to present double jeopardy in the light of possible prosecutorial abuse, when the deeper policy matters touch upon the very character of the criminal justice system, and the interacting roles of the legislatures, prosecutors, and judges, all of whom are actors in the double jeopardy drama.

It is undoubtedly true that prosecutors have vast discretionary power. Probably, some checks upon this authority are needed to curb abuses.[64] Even so, increased judicial discretion is not a completely satisfactory answer. To transfer a situation from the prosecutor's desk drawer to the judge's chambers may not ultimately provide defendants with greater rights, or clarify the policy which double jeopardy is meant to serve. Only a reconsideration of the criminal statutes themselves and the sanctions which they provide will eliminate the root causes of double jeopardy problems. The largest number of double jeopardy situations are caused by poor legislative drafting because of the failure of most criminal statutes to state clearly what should be the allowable unit of prosecution or to refer to other similar, criminal law provisions. The need for a comprehensive criminal code is readily apparent. Simplification of the criminal laws and modernization of the criminal justice system are the best cures for double jeopardy dilemmas. Perhaps the need for double jeopardy will diminish as the laws and procedures improve. Right now double jeopardy is a protection against a system in decay so as to protect accused persons from repeated exposure to an ineffective process.

Chief Justice Burger and former Attorney General Mitchell have been outspoken in favor of a streamlined criminal justice system.[65] The various procedural reforms they have favored would have the effect of speeding along the pace of criminal trials, especially at the appellate level. There is little doubt that the efficient and expeditious management of criminal procedure are desirable goals, but one can hope that the values which appellate review and double jeopardy represent are more important. There seems to be no need to sacrifice the right to appeal and the double jeopardy rights of accused persons to the drive for a more streamlined criminal justice system.[66]

NOTES

1. D. Fellman, *The Defendant's Rights,* 202 1958).
2. See Payne, "The Doctrine of Previous Jeopardy," 62 Cent L.J. 295 (1906).
3. See Cowley, "Former Jeopardy," 35 Yale L.J. 678 (1926) and Slovenko, "The Law on Double Jeopardy," 30 Tul. L. Rev. 428 (1955) which is the best recent expression of this view.
4. 14 U. Pitt. L. Rev. 538, 589 (1953).
5. Ex parte Lange, 85 U.S. 163, 166 (1873).
6. Sigler, "Double Jeopardy Policy," 19 Vand. L. Rev. 375 (1966).
7. 367 U.S. 643. Harlan's dissent is in Benton v. Maryland, 395 U.S. 784, 808 (1969).
8. 309 U.S. 319 (1937).
9. Id., at 810.
10. 395 U.S. 784, 795. J. Sigler, *Double Jeopardy: The Development of a Legal and Social Policy,* 34-37 (1959). Sigler argued that "history has given American law a double jeopardy concept as a part of its most fundamental principles," but also stated that "the

conflicting needs of society and the individual which are inherent in double jeopardy must be resolved by each generation." Sigler called for the overruling of Palko in the interest of a uniform national double jeopardy policy. Id., at 50.

11. 395 U.S. 784, 796.

12. 397 U.S. 436 (1970).

13. "Restatement of Judgments," see GF (1) (1942).

14. See McNabb v. United States, 318 U.S. 433 (1943).

15. United States v. Kramer, 28a F.2d 909 (2d Cir., 1961).

16. 356 U.S. 464.

17. Sealfon v. United States, 332 U.S. 575 (1948).

18. The Court cited United States v. Oppenheimer, 242 U.S. 85 (1916) which actually was based upon another, narrower, principle of res judicata.

19. Mayers & Yarbrough, "Bis Vexari: New Trials and Successive Prosecutions," 74 Harv. L. Rev. 1, 38-39 (1960).

20. 397 U.S. 436 at 444.

21. 397 U.S. 436, footnote 1.

22. United States v. Lanza, 260 U.S. 377 (1922); Barkus v. Illinois, 359, U.S. 121 (1959); Abbate v. United States, 359 U.S. 187 (1959).

23. 398 U.S. 323 (1970).

24. Brantley v. State, 217 U.S. 284 (1910) which affirmed, Brantley v. State, 132 Ga. 573, 64 S.E. 676 (1909).

25. Green v. United States, 355 U.S. 184 (1957).

26. 400 U.S. 470 (1970).

27. Kepner v. United States, 195 U.S. 100, 128 (1904).

28. 400 U.S. 470 at 473 (1970).

29. 22 Ohio App. 2d 83 (1970).

30. Id., at 92.

31. United States v. Lanza, 260 U.S. 377 (1922); Barkus v. Illinois, 359 U.S. 121 (1959); Abbate v. United States, 359 U.S. 187 (1959).

32. Fletcher v. State, 22 Ohio App. 2d 83, 99 (1970).

33. See Pontikes, "Dual Sovereignty and Double Jeopardy: A Critique of Barkus v. Illinois and Abbate v. United States," 14 Case W. Res. L. Rev. 700 (1963) and Note, "Double Prosecution by State and Federal Governments: Another Exercise in Federalism," 80 Harv. L. Rev. 1538 (1967).

34. 27 U.S.L.W. 2509 (1959).

35.   Mass.   , 260 N.E. 2d 911 (1970).

36. 395 U.S. 711 (1969).

37. Mass. Gen Laws ch. 278 & 288 (Supp. 1970).

38. 395 U.S. at 725.

39. Mass. Gen. Laws ch. 278, & 28A (Supp. 1970).

40. 398 U.S. 323 (1970).

41. In Moon v. Maryland, 398 U.S. 319 (1970) the defendant received an increased sentence after retrial and conviction. First certiorari was granted, but it was subsequently denied in a per curiam decision in which the fact that defendant's counsel did not allege vindictiveness seemed to have been the basis of a judgment that certiorari had been improvidently granted.

42. State v. Pope, 106 Neb. 489; 1R N.W. 2d 395 (1971).

43. People v. Brown, 13 C.A. 3d 876, 91 Cal. Rptr. 904 (1970).

44. People v. Smith, 13 C.A. 3d 897, 91 Cal. Rptr. 786 (Cal. App., 1970) waiver from failure to invoke the defense at the trial level; People v. Walker, 184 N.W. 2d 142 (Mich. App. 1970)–waiver from entry of guilty plea after a bargain with the prosecutor; City of Minot v. Knudson, 184 N.W. 2d 58 (N.D., 1971)– wavier implied from motion to quash complaint.

45. The King v. Vandercomb & Abbott, 169 Eng. Rep. 455, 461, 2 Leach CC 708, 720 (1796).

46. See Johnson v. Commonwealth, 201 Ky. 314, 256 S.W. 388 (1923) which allowed the possibility of separate prosecutions for each of 75 poker hands in the course of one illegal gambling session.

47. See Bigelow, "Former Conviction and Former Acquittal," 11 Rutgers L. Rev. 487 (1957) and Horack, "The Multiple Consequences of a Single Criminal Act," 21 Minn. L. Rev. 805 (1937).

48. 397 U.S. 436 (1970).

49. 397 U.S. 436, 448 (1970).

50. In United States v. Fusco, 427 F. 2d 361 (7th Cir. 1970) decided shortly after Ashe the court could have applied the "same transaction" test but seemed to defer to the Supreme Court by applying collateral estoppel instead.

51. Comment, "Res Judicata in Successive Criminal Prosecutions: Hing v. State of New Jersey and a Proposal," 25 Brooklyn L. Rev. 33 (1959).

52. Section 1.08 (2), Model Penal Code, Commentary (Tent. Draft No. 5) 31 (1956) and Section 1.10 Model Penal Code Commentary (Tent. Draft No. 5) 61 (1956).

53. ABA Minimum Standards for Criminal Justice, Joinder and Severance, Sec. A 1.3 (Tent. Draft 1967) (approved by ABA House of Delegates, August 1968).

54. Bartkus v. Illinois, 359 U.S. 121 (1959) and Abbate v. United States, 359 U.S. 187 (1959) are the latest expressions of this view.

55. 397 U.S. 387 (1970).

56. See Melville v. State, 10 Md. App. 118, 125-126, 268 A2d 497, 501 (1970); Bankston v. State, 236 So. 2d 757, 758 (Miss. 1970); Common. v. Mills, 217 Pa. Super. 269, 269 A.2d 322, 323 (1970); State ex rel. Cullen v. Ceci 45 Wis. 2d 432, 457, 137 N.W. 2d 175, 187 (1970). See also State v. Cooper, 54 N.J. 330, 255 A 2d 232, 235 (1969), cert. denied, 396 U.S. 1021 (1970).

57. No. 70-287, Jacks v. N.J., 40 USLW 3147-48 (1971).

58. Grant, "Successive Prosecutions by State and Nation: Common Law and British Empire Comparisons," 4 UCLA Rev. 1 (1956).

59. Model Penal Code, Sec. 1.07(2) (Proposed Official Draft 1962).

60. Model Penal Code, Sec. 1.07(3) (Proposed Official Draft 1962).

61. ABA Minimum Standards for Criminal Justice, Joinder and Severance, Sec. 1.1, 1.3 (App. Draft, 1968).

62. Fed. R. Crim. 8 (a).

63. Fed. R. Crim. 13 provides that "the court may order two or more indictments or informations to be tried together if the offenses . . . could have been joined in a single indictment or information," while Rule 14 allows severance of offenses if either the prosecution or the defense would be prejudiced by joinder or if justice otherwise requires it."

64. See K. Culp, *Discretionary Justice,* 209 (1969).

65. Chief Justice Burger's best statement appears at 57 A.B.A.J. 855 (1971) and Mitchell's at 55 Judicature 203 (1971).

66. See Price v. Georgia, supra. note 23 which seems to expand the double jeopardy privilege to a new category of appeals.

INDEX OF CASES

Abbate v. United States, 296 (notes 22, 31, 33), 297 (note 54)
Ackies v. Purdy, 180
Adams v. New York, 56 (note 73)
Adams v. Williams, 54 (note 28)
Alexander v. Louisiana, 231 (note 37)
Allen v. United States, 231 (note 44)
Alston v. United States, 74
Alverez v. Turner, 280 (note 34)
Anders v. California, 157
Anderson v. Heinze, 162
Apodaca v. Oregon, 230 (note 6), 231 (note 21)
Argersinger v. Hamlin, 150, 151, 169, 170 (note 15)
Ashe v. Swenson, 285, 286, 292
Ashworth v. United States, 171 (note 61)
Austin v. State, 173 (note 85)

Baldwin v. New York, 150, 230 (note 14), 231 (notes 24, 25)
Bandy v. United States, 199
Banks v. United States, 184
Bankston v. State, 297 (note 56)
Barkus v. Illinois, 296 (notes 22, 31, 33), 297 (note 54)
Beal v. Turner, 172 (note 65)
Beck v. Washington, 130
Beecher v. Alabama, 104 (note 109)
Bellamy v. Justices, 200, 201 (note 2)
Benton v. Maryland, 284-292, 295 (note 7)
Berger v. New York, 40, 43
Betts v. Brady, 149, 150, 158, 161, 165
Bishop v. Brurly, 171 (note 60)
Bivens v. Six Unknown Named Agents of the Federal Bureau of Narcotics, 56
    (notes 67, 71)
Blackburn v. Alabama, 66, 67, 68
Boles v. Stevenson, 100 (note 59)
Boyd v. United States, 48
Bram v. United States, 65, 71
Brantley v. State, 296 (note 24)
Brewer v. Bennett, 172 (note 82)
Broguglio v. New York, 172 (note 65)
Brown v. Allen, 173 (note 91)
Brown v. Mississippi, 66
Burns v. Wilson, 100 (note 31)
Butler v. Crumlish, 200 (note 1)

Cahey v. Mazurkiewicz, 55 (note 32)
California v. Stewart, 99 (note 2)

Camara v. Municipal Court, 56 (note 58)
Carlson v. Landon, 192
Carter v. State, 173 (note 85)
Catenzaro v. New York, 100 (note 59)
Chambers v. Florida, 66, 68
Chambers v. Maroney, 54 (note 9)
Chapman v. California, 170 (note 28)
Chimel v. California, 54 (note 19)
Clewis v. Texas, 104 (notes 108, 109)
Coates v. Cincinnati, 136
Coleman v. Alabama, 153, 170 (note 33)
Collins v. Commonwealth, 171 (note 57)
Collins v. Walker, 131
Colson v. Smith, 131
Combs v. La Vallee, 172 (note 75)
Commonwealth v. Bennett, 90
Commonwealth v. Hoffman, 173 (note 85)
Commonwealth v. Johnson, 172 (note 76)
Commonwealth v. McCloskey, 80
Commonwealth v. Mills, 297 (note 56)
Commonwealth v. Mitchell, 173 (note 85)
Commonwealth v. Tinson, 160
Commonwealth v. Ware, 90
Connally v. General Construction Company, 136
Connecticut v. Seale, 251
Coolidge v. New Hampshire, 54 (note 19), 55 (note 34), 56 (note 69)
Coppedge v. United States, 155, 156, 162, 163
Costello v. United States, 130
Covington v. Coparo, 192
Cullen v. Ceci, 297 (note 56)
Culumbe v. Connecticut, 67

Darwin v. Connecticut, 104 (note 109)
Dash v. Mitchell, 190, 204 (note 19)
Davis v. North Carolina, 72
Davis v. United States, 54 (note 8)
DeVita v. New Jersey, 100 (note 31)
Del Hoyo v. New York, 100 (note 59)
Dennis v. United States, 123
Dillion v. United States, 172 (note 82)
Director of Public Prosecution v. Smith, 248
District of Columbia v. Clawans, 230 (note 16)
Douglas v. Alabama, 249
Doughty v. Maxwell, 70
Douglas v. California, 156, 157, 158, 162, 163
Dombrowski v. Pfister, 137
Dranow v. United States, 231 (note 32)

Duncan v. Louisiana, 230 (notes 1, 8, 14), 231 (note 47)
Dunn v. California, 172 (note 65)

Earnest v. Willingham, 160, 172 (note 65)
Elkins v. United States, 81, 105 (note 143), 106 (note 171)
Ellis v. United States, 155, 156
Erving v. Sigler, 107 (note 198)
Escobedo v. Illinois, 61, 70, 72, 73, 80, 85, 86, 101 (note 73)
Escoe v. Zerbst, 159
Evalt v. United States, 104 (note 104)

Fariss v. Tipps, 280 (note 29)
Fay v. Noia, 69, 70, 161
Fernandez v. United States, 180
Fikes v. Alabama, 67, 104 (note 108)
Fleming v. Tate, 172 (note 65)
Fletcher v. State, 296 (note 32)
Frank v. Mangum, 251
Frank v. Maryland, 56 (note 57)
Frank v. United States, 230 (note 16)
Frazier v. Cupp, 55 (note 30)
Fredericks v. Reinche, 171 (note 51)
Fredericksen v. United States, 103 (note 104)
Fulwood v. Clemmer, 279 (note 20)

Gaines v. United States, 204 (note 21)
Gaither v. United States, 128
Gessner v. United States, 102 (note 84)
Gideon v. Wainwright, 69, 70, 150, 154, 158, 161, 163, 199
Giles v. Maryland, 249
Gilmore v. Lynch, 280 (note 32)
Go-Bart Importing Company v. United States, 54 (note 11)
Gockley v. Myers, 80
Goldberg v. Kelley, 192
Goldman v. United States, 55 (note 38)
Goldsby v. Harpole, 231 (note 42)
Goldsby v. United States, 125
Gomino v. Maroney, 101 (note 59)
Gonzalez v. Warden, 199
Gouled v. United States, 55 (note 44)
Government of Virgin Islands v. Williams, 90
Green v. United States, 296 (note 25)
Greene v. McElroy, 192
Greenwald v. Wisconsin, 104 (note 109)
Greenwell v. United States, 74

Griffin v. Illinois, 156, 163, 172 (note 64), 199
Grillo v. New Jersey, 100 (note 31)
Grooms v. United States, 106 (note 186)
Groppi v. Wisconsin, 231 (note 38)

Hamilton v. Alabama, 153, 158, 170 (note 11)
Hamilton v. Love, 197
Hampton v. State of Oklahoma, 162, 172 (note 82)
Harper v. State, 173 (note 85)
Harris v. New York, 91, 93, 107 (note 191)
Harris v. South Carolina, 100 (note 29)
Harris v. Texas, 100 (note 59)
Harris v. United States, 54 (note 6)
Haynes v. Washington, 69, 70
Heryford v. Parker, 173 (note 94)
Hewett v. North Carolina, 158, 171 (notes 61, 63)
Hoag v. New Jersey, 286
Hoffa v. United States, 55 (note 51)
Holden v. United States, 171 (note 60)
Holt v. Sarver, 197, 280 (notes 24, 26)
Huff v. United States, 107 (note 203)
Hurtado v. California, 122
Hyser v. Reed, 159, 172 (note 65)

In Re Dionisio, 124
In Re Gault, 163, 192, 279 (note 1)
In Re Nash, 171 (note 51)
In Re Smith, 171 (note 50)
Irvin v. Dowd, 231 (note 38)

Jacks v. New Jersey, 297 (note 57)
Jackson v. Bishop, 279 (note 21)
Jackson v. Denno, 70, 80, 93, 101 (note 61), 107 (note 198)
Jencks v. United States, 249
Jenkins v. Delaware, 77
Jenkins v. McKeithen, 192
Jenks v. McMann, 173 (note 85)
Jennings v. Superior Court, 170 (note 27)
Johnson v. Avery, 275, 276
Johnson v. Commonwealth, 297 (note 46)
Johnson v. Louisiana, 230 (note 6), 231 (note 27)
Johnson v. New Jersey, 72, 73
Johnson v. Stucker, 172 (note 65)
Johnson v. United States, 103 (note 104), 155, 156, 160
Johnson v. Zerbst, 149, 155, 165

Jones v. River, 160, 172 (note 65)
Jones v. United States, 102 (note 104), 155
Jordan v. Fitzharris, 279 (note 22)

Kadis v. United States, 140 (note 12)
Kastigar v. United States, 107 (note 202)
Katz v. United States, 40, 55 (note 31), 57 (note 88)
Kemp v. Pate, 103 (note 104)
Kepner v. United States, 296 (note 27)
Ker v. California, 47, 48
Killough v. United States, 103 (note 104)
King v. Vandercomb and Abbott, 297 (note 45)
Kingsley International Pictures Corporation v. Board of Regents, 100 (note 32)
Kuhn v. Russell, 103 (note 104)

Lankford v. Gelston, 56 (note 61)
Lanza v. United States, 55 (note 43)
Lanzetta v. New Jersey, 136
Larson v. Bennett, 172 (note 82)
Lathan v. New York, 101 (note 59)
Lawn v. United States, 123
Leary v. United States, 253 (note 4)
Leathers v. United States, 184
Lee v. United States, 41
Lego v. Twomey, 93, 94, 107 (note 197)
Lewis v. United States, 55 (note 50)
London v. Pardon Parole Commission, 172 (notes 65, 71)
Lopez v. Texas, 101 (note 59)
Lopez v. United States, 41
Lynumn v. Illinois, 69

McConnell v. Rhay, 158
McCray v. Illinois, 55 (note 52)
McDonald v. Board of Election Commissioners, 200 (note 1)
McGautha v. California, 279 (note 16)
McKeiver v. Pennsylvania, 231 (note 28)
McLaughlin v. State, 171 (note 51)
McNabb v. United States, 65, 73, 74, 80, 103 (note 104), 296 (note 14)
McNerlin v. Denno, 100 (note 59)
Mallory v. United States, 65, 66, 73, 74, 80, 81, 82, 89, 90, 91, 103 (note 104)
Malloy v. Hogan, 70, 72
Mapp v. Ohio, 46-51, 56 (note 76), 57 (note 79), 92, 127, 150, 284
Marron v. United States, 54 (note 11)
Martin v. Fay, 103 (note 104)
Martinez v. Patterson, 172 (note 66)

Massachusetts v. Hornig, 130
Massiah v. United States, 55 (note 49), 70, 73, 75, 101 (note 73)
Mathis v. United States, 77
Mayers v. Yarbrough, 296 (note 19)
Melville v. State, 297 (note 56)
Mempa v. Rhay, 157-160, 171 (note 58), 269
Menechino v. Oswald, 172 (note 65), 280 (note 33)
Menechino v. Warden, 172 (note 77)
Minot v. Knudson, 297 (note 44)
Miranda v. Arizona, 37, 38, 52, 54 (note 27), 61, 62, 71-74, 76-80, 84-93, 99
     (note 1), 102 (note 104), 105 (note 151), 106 (notes 168, 169, 191), 173
     (note 96)
Moon v. Maryland, 296 (note 41)
Moore v. Dempsey, 251
Morisette v. United States, 247
Murphy v. Waterfront Commission of New York Harbor, 70, 140 (note 3)
Muschette v. United States, 100 (note 59)

Namet v. United States, 249
Nardone v. United States, 55 (note 37)
Nelson v. United States, 204 (note 21)
New Jersey v. Russo, 101 (note 77), 107 (note 211)
Nichols v. State, 173 (note 85)
North Carolina v. Pearce, 270, 289, 290

Oister v. Pennsylvania, 101 (note 59)
Oklahoma Press Publishing Company v. Walling, 123
Olmstead v. United States, 39, 40, 55 (note 35), 57 (note 89)
Orozco v. Texas, 77
Owen v. Arizona, 100 (note 59)
Oyler v. Bales, 130

Palko v. Connecticut, 284, 285, 289
Palmer v. City of Euclid, 136
Palmigrano v. Travisero, 197
Patton v. United States, 230 (note 15), 231 (note 43)
Payne v. Arkansas, 67
Pea v. United States, 100 (note 59)
People v. Allen, 77
People v. Arrighini, 107 (note 207)
People v. Bonino, 100 (notes 47, 50)
People v. Brown, 297 (note 43)
People v. Cahan, 81, 82, 83, 106 (note 171)
People v. Defore, 56 (note 64)
People v. Donovan, 76

People v. Dorado, 73, 84, 85, 105 (note 151), 106 (note 168, 169)
People v. Faila, 76
People v. Friedlander, 76
People v. Gray, 130
People v. Hamilton, 103 (note 104)
People v. Howell, 124
People v. Huntley, 70, 71, 84, 101 (notes 61, 63)
People v. Lego, 107 (note 198)
People v. Meyer, 75
People v. Novo, 102 (note 104)
People v. Rodgers, 231 (note 34)
People v. Ruppert, 79, 80, 104 (note 120)
People v. Sanders, 157
People v. Shipman, 163
People v. Smith, 297 (note 44)
People v. Spegal, 231 (note 31)
People v. Taylor, 76
People v. Walker, 297 (note 44)
People v. Ware, 106 (note 180)
People v. Waterman, 75
People v. Whisenant, 90
Perry v. Williard, 171 (note 61)
Peters v. Hobby, 192
Pittsburgh Plate Glass v. United States, 123
Pointer v. Texas, 238, 249
Powell v. Alabama, 148
Price v. Georgia, 287, 290, 298 (note 66)
Pyles v. United States, 102 (note 83)

Reck v. Pate, 67, 68
Reed v. Anderson, 243
Regina v. Smyth, 248
Reinke v. United States, 106 (note 182)
Remmer v. United States, 251-252
Riddell v. Rhay, 92
Riffle v. Thorne, 171 (note 60)
Rigney v. Hendrick, 200 (note 1)
Rivera v. McKendrick, 80
Roach v. Bennett, 162, 173 (note 85)
Robinson v. California, 203 (note 16)
Robinson v. Cox, 172 (note 65)
Rogers v. Richmond, 67, 68
Rose v. Haskins, 172 (note 65, 71)
Rosemon v. United States, 231 (note 33)
Rudolph v. Alabama, 101 (note 61)
Rudolph v. Holman, 101 (note 61)
Russell v. United States, 128

Russo v. New Jersey, 98
Russo v. New York, 73

Sammons v. United States, 171 (note 60)
Sanders v. United States, 161
Sarno v. Illinois Crime Investigating Commission, 107 (note 202)
Schlib v. Kuebel, 204 (note 22)
Schmerber v. California, 55 (note 45)
Schwartzberg v. United States Board of Parole, 160, 172 (note 65)
Sciortino v. Zampano, 125
Sealfon v. United States, 296 (note 17)
Seals v. United States, 103 (note 104)
Senk v. Pennsylvania, 101 (note 59)
Shakur v. Commissioner of Corrections, 199
Sheer v. United States, 106 (note 182)
Sheppard v. Maxwell, 231 (note 38)
Sherman v. United States, 132, 133
Sibron v. New York, 36, 37, 52
Silverman v. United States, 55 (note 39)
Sims v. Georgia, 104 (note 109)
Singer v. United States, 231 (note 30)
Smith v. Hooey, 275
Smith v. O'Grady, 127
Smith v. Texas, 231 (note 36)
Smith v. Yeager, 80, 104 (note 118)
Snyder v. Massachusetts, 127
Sorrells v. United States, 132
Spano v. New York, 67
Specht v. Patterson, 192
Spriggs v. United States, 74
Stack v. Boyle, 178, 179, 180, 199
State v. Burke, 101 (note 61)
State v. Cooper, 297 (note 56)
State v. Fletcher, 288
State v. Myers, 102 (note 80)
State v. Pope, 296 (note 42)
State v. Randolph, 102 (note 83)
State v. Seymour, 171 (note 61)
Stave v. Garner, 173 (note 85)
Stein v. New York, 100 (note 31)
Stidham v. Swenson, 79, 107 (note 198)
Stirone v. United States, 128
Stoner v. California, 55 (note 33)
Stovall v. Denno, 243
Swain v. Alabama, 231 (note 40)

Tate v. Short, 199, 267
Taylor v. Director, 173 (note 85)
Terry v. Ohio, 36, 37, 54 (note 28)
Thompson v. Utah, 230 (note 15)
Tot v. United States, 253 (note 4)
Townsend v. Burke, 157, 158, 161
Townsend v. Sain, 161, 162
Turner v. Louisiana, 252
Turner v. Pennsylvania, 100 (note 29)
Two Guys from Harrison-Allentown v. McGinley, 130

Ullmann v. United States, 99 (note 1)
United States ex rel v. Mancusi, 79
United States v. Allen, 184
United States v. Arcuri, 124
United States v. Ash, 243
United States v. Barber, 90
United States v. Beard, 230 (note 16)
United States v. Bozza, 104 (note 105)
United States v. Cavalcante, 128
United States v. Cox, 123, 140 (note 4)
United States v. Cranston, 106 (note 191)
United States v. Curry, 103 (note 104)
United States v. Elliott, 131
United States v. Ewell, 140 (note 13)
United States v. Funk, 125
United States v. Fusco, 297 (note 50)
United States v. Gilbert, 180
United States v. Greenberg, 140 (note 12)
United States v. Harrison, 184
United States v. Hartsell, 171 (note 60)
United States v. Halbert, 91
United States v. Jorn, 287
United States v. Kirby, 243
United States v. Kramer, 296 (note 15)
United States v. Lanza, 296 (notes 22, 31)
United States v. Lefkowitz, 54 (note 11)
United States v. Marion, 113, 136
United States v. Middleton, 102 (note 104)
United States v. Oppenheimer, 296 (note 18)
United States v. Rabinowitz, 54 (note 5)
United States v. Robinson, 91
United States v. Schipani, 90
United States v. Smith, 106 (note 190)
United States v. Stevens, 106 (note 190)
United States v. United States District Court for Eastern District of Michigan, 56
    (note 56)
United States v. Wade, 170 (note 33), 243

United States v. Winter, 122
United States v. Youngblood, 123

Vauss v. United States, 184, 201 (note 3)
Veney v. United States, 103 (note 104)
Vignera v. United States, 99 (note 2)
Vorhauer v. State, 103 (note 104)

Waller v. Florida, 287, 293
Walsh v. Commonwealth, 289
Wansley v. Wilkerson, 192
Warden v. Hayden, 40
Washington v. Texas, 249
Wassenfeld v. Wilkins, 62, 172 (note 84)
Watts v. Indiana, 62, 100 (note 29)
Wayne County Jail Inmates v. Wayne County Board of Commissioners, 197
Weeks v. United States, 46, 47, 48
West v. United States, 123
Westover v. United States, 99 (note 2)
White v. Maryland, 153
White v. United States, 41
Whites v. Georgia, 231 (note 36)
Wilbanks v. State, 173 (note 85)
Williams v. Fay, 102 (note 89)
Williams v. Florida, 230 (notes 3, 5, 19), 231 (note 26)
Williams v. Illinois, 199, 279 (note 10)
Williams v. La Vallee, 173 (note 85)
Williams v. New York, 264
Williams v. Patterson, 172 (note 65)
Willner v. Committee on Character and Fitness, 192
Witherspoon v. Illinois, 231 (note 39)
Wolf v. Colorado, 47
Wong Sun v. United States, 101 (note 73)
Wright v. McMann, 279 (note 22)
Wyman v. James, 56 (note 60)

Yick Wo v. Hopkins, 130
Younger v. Gilmore, 280 (note 32)
Younger v. Harris, 137

Zicarelli v. New Jersey State Commission of Investigation, 107 (note 202)
Zap v. United States, 54 (note 8)

INDEX OF NAMES

Abrams, 141 (note 15)
Acheson, David C., 80
Alexander, F., 248, 249
Alexander, Paul, 87, 88, 106 (note 167)
Almog, Zvi, 79
Alschuler, 279 (note 2)
Amsterdam, A., 230 (note 2)
Ares, C., 19, 21, 201 (note 2)
Arnold, 120
Asch, S., 253 (note 1)

Barrett, Edward L., Jr., 64, 99 (note 16)
Bartels, John R., 79
Barton, A., 240
Bartlett, 130
Bazelon, David L., 74, 105 (note 149), 184
Beaney, William, 16, 23 (note 1d), 169 (notes 2, 3), 170 (notes 7, 12)
Bedau, H., 19
Behar, I., 241
Bellamy, 178
Bentham, 96, 97
Berry, 131
Besnard, M., 253 (note 5)
Bevar, W., 241
Bickel, 131
Bigelow, 297 (note 47)
Binet, A., 244
Birzon, 122
Black, 31, 66, 77, 99 (note 1), 156, 165
Blackmun, 33, 48
Boehm, V. R., 251
Borchard, E. M., 253 (note 1)
Brandeis, 29, 39, 53
Brennan, J., 70, 91, 92, 93, 107 (note 191), 292, 294
Brian, 247
Broeder, D., 21, 101 (note 73), 227
Brown, Edmund G., 83, 105 (note 143)
Buckley, William F., Jr., 79, 80
Bullock, H., 21
Bumstead, C. H., 246
Burdick, Quentin N., 90
Burger, 33, 48, 64, 79, 80, 93, 94, 95, 150, 153, 287, 295, 298 (note 65)
Byrne, Brendan T., 85

Cady, H., 244
Calkins, 123
Cantril, H., 238, 246
Cardozo, B. N., 46, 250
Castro, Fidel, 76
Chambliss, William, 16, 22
Charles II, 94
Choper, Jesse, 16
Christian, Almeric L., 90
Clark, 31, 62, 73
Clark, Ramsay, 80
Cohen, F., 280 (notes 25, 35)
Cook, S. W., 241
Covell, Howard, 81
Cowley, 295 (note 3)
Cromwell, Oliver, 94

Davey, J. P., 57 (note 85)
Davis, Kenneth C., 141 (note 15)
Dawson, Robert O., 16, 23 (note 1h), 279 (notes 2, 6, 7, 9, 11, 12, 15, 18)
Day, 288, 289
Dershowitz, 107 (note 191)
Dix, G., 279 (note 11)
Dodd, Thomas J., 90
Donnelly, 133
Dostoevsky, F., 248
Douglas, 31, 32, 37, 64, 91, 92, 93, 99 (note 1), 199, 292
Driver, E. B., 243

Edward IV, 247
Edwards, George, 85
Elsen, 101 (note 73)
Ervin, S., 181, 182, 189, 196
Ely, 107 (note 191)
Enker, 101 (note 73)

Fahy, Charles, 74, 91
Fellman, D., 16, 21, 169 (note 2), 295 (note 1)
Fletcher, C., 23 (note 3)
Fong, Hiram L., 90
Fishman, J. A., 244
Foote, C., 178, 180, 201 (note 2)
Fortas, Abe, 22, 33, 80
Foster, H. J., Jr., 243

Frank, Jerome N., 69
Frank, J. P., 221, 249, 253 (note 5)
Frankfurter, Felix, 31, 48, 67, 68
Freed, D. J., 177, 181, 185, 201 (note 2)
Friendly, 286
Fuld, C. J., 107 (191)
Fuller, 131

Gasch, Oliver, 82, 105 (note 141)
Gessner, George J., 74, 75
Gibbons, John J., 79, 80
Gillers, Stephen, 16
Gillies, 170 (note 10)
Girard, 122
Goldfarb, 201 (note 2)
Goldstone, S. W., 241
Gough, 280 (note 36)
Graff, Selma, 75
Graham, 126
Green, E., 23 (note 4)
Gremillion, Jack P.F., 86
Grosscup, Peter S., 99 (note 1)
Guevara, Ernesto Che, 76

Hall, L. Y., 126, 140 (note 9)
Harlan, 31, 32, 33, 41, 48, 62, 73, 93, 230 (note 3), 284, 285, 295 (note 7)
Hart, Philip A., 90
Hastorf, A. H., 239
Haynsworth, C., 171 (note 62)
Heider, F., 239
Heinz, J., 22
Herman, 106 (note 169)
Hickey, 139
Hilgard, E. R., 243
Hoffa, James, 41
Hofstadter, Samuel H., 107 (note 212), 108 (note 212)
Holmes, 55 (note 36), 241, 251
Hruska, Roman L., 80, 192
Hughes, 251
Hunting, R., 250
Hutchins, R., 239

Inbau, F., 106 (note 170), 243
Israel, Jerold, 84, 105 (note 144), 140 (note 9)
Ittelson, W. H., 239, 240

Jackson, 62, 157, 173 (note 91), 247
Jacob, H., 171 (note 59), 248
James, H., 170 (note 18)
Jardine, David, 94, 107 (note 201)
Johnson, Lyndon B., 75
Junker, 170 (note 20)

Kalven, H., 19, 219, 220, 227, 228, 229, 231 (note 43), 232, (notes 50, 52, 63,
    68)
Kamisar, Yale, 16, 81, 105 (notes 138, 139, 140, 149), 140 (note 9), 149, 170
    (note 8)
Kanowitz, M., 21
Kaplan, 139
Karlen, Delmar, 16, 23 (1e), 121, 128
Katz, M., 56 (note 76)
Katzenbach, 105 (note 149)
Kaufman, L, 239
Kennedy, Edward M., 90
Kennedy, R., 182
Kerensky, Premier, 239
Kilpatrick, F. P., 238, 240
Kleindienst, R., 193
Kogan, 280 (note 36)
Konvitz, M., 21
Koota, Aaron E., 86
Kraft, 280 (note 27)

La Fave, W., 16, 56 (note 59), 140 (note 9)
Landynski, Jacob, 16, 23 (note 1a)
Langer, J., 241
Layton, John B., 80
Lefstein, N., 23 (note 3), 173 (note 93)
Letivin, 126
Levitan, Shirley R., 107 (note 212), 108 (note 212)
Lewin, N., 55 (note 52)
Lockhart, William, 16
Long, Edward V., 90
Loughery, 280 (note 36)
Luh, C. W., 245
Lund, F. H., 251
Lush, D. E., 244

McCarthy, 201 (note 2)
McCarty, D. G., 252 (note 1)
McClellan, John J., 80

McIntyre, Donald M., Jr., 23 (note 2), 56 (note 77)
Maitland, F. W., 247
Mann, S. E., 98
Mansson, 239, 246
Marshall, 91, 93, 158, 238, 241, 244, 246
Marshall, J. K., 16, 23 (note 1g), 248
Marshall, P., 16
Marston, W. M., 244
Martin, G., 20
Medalie, Richard J., 16, 23 (note 4), 87, 88, 106 (note 167)
Melville, H., 248
Miller, D. R., 248
Miller, F., 16, 116, 124, 130, 135, 137-140 (notes 6, 7, 8, 9), 279 (notes 11, 13)
Miller, M., 230 (note 2)
Milner, Neal A., 16, 105 (note 163), 106 (note 166)
Mitchell, J. N., 44, 295
Mitchell, M., Jr., 192
Moore, Leonard P., 76, 77, 180
Morris, N., 248
Morris, R. E., 241, 244
Munsterberg, H., 241, 244
Murphy, 67
Murray, Robert, 81

Nagel, S. S., 20, 21, 22, 23 (note 4), 56 (note 76)
Navarro, J., 19
Neuwirth, G. S., 250
Newman, D., 174 (note 105), 279 (note 2)
Nixon, 283

Oaks, Dallin H., 50, 51, 56 (note 78), 57 (notes 80, 82, 83)
Orfield, 122

Packer, 121
Padawer-Singer, A., 240, 251
Parnas, R., 279 (note 11)
Payne, 295 (note 2)
Piersante, Vincent W., 84, 105 (note 149)
Plato, 238
Pollock, F., 241, 247
Powell, 33, 150

Randall, 105 (note 144)
Rankin, A., 18, 178, 201 (note 2)
Rehnquist, 33, 150

Reid, J., 106 (note 170), 243
Remington, 116, 124
Ritz, 101 (note 73)
Roberts, 149
Robinson, Cyril D., 16, 87, 88, 106 (note 168)
Roche, J., 21
Rock, I., 239
Rogge, O. John, 16, 23 (note 1b), 99 (notes 1, 8, 11)
Rotenberg, D. L., 56 (note 77), 133
Rubin, S., 139, 279 (note 5)
Rutledge, 67

Sachs, 201 (note 2)
Sage Publications, 105 (notes 159, 163), 106 (note 166)
Sarnoff, I., 248
Scott, Hugh, 80, 128
Segal, B., 230 (note 2)
Seidman, Robert, 16, 22
Shapiro, J. Irwin, 76
Sharma, 171 (note 59)
Shawcross, Lord, 81, 97, 98, 104 (note 134), 107 (note 209)
Sherif, M., 242, 253 (note 1)
Sherry, 123
Sigler, J., 16, 23 (note 1i), 285, 295 (notes 6, 10)
Silverstein, L., 16, 23 (note 3), 99 (note 15), 152, 165, 170 (note 24), 173 (note 98), 174 (note 104), 179
Simmel, M., 239
Simon, R. J., 16, 23 (note 1f), 238, 250
Skolnick, J. H., 56 (note 77), 135
Slesinger, D., 239
Smith, Edgar H., 78, 79, 80, 201 (note 2)
Snee, T. J., 244
Sobel, Nathan R., 77, 78, 83
Spiegel, H., 242
Sprague, Richard, 85
Stapleton, V., 23 (note 3), 173 (note 93)
Staub, H., 248, 249
Steele, Jr., 170 (note 25)
Stephen, James, 97
Stern, W., 244
Stewart, 62, 81, 285
Stouffer, S., 22
Strodtbeck, F. L., 232 (note 53)
Sturz, H., 201 (note 2)
Subin, 137
Sutherland, 149
Swanson, G. E., 248

Taylor, T., 19, 54 (note 17)
Teitelbaum, 173 (note 93)
Thucydides, 240
Tiffany, L. P., 56 (note 77)
Traynor, 163
Travers, J. L., 248
Tydings, Jos. D., 90

Van Pelt, Robert, 90
Vinson, 67
Von Moltke, 170 (note 10)

Wahl, 201 (note 2)
Wald, Patricia, 16, 23 (note 1c), 177, 181, 201 (note 2)
Wall, P., 243
Walsh, 290
Warren, Earl, 33, 48, 61, 66, 67, 68, 71, 72, 77, 79, 83, 91, 94, 95, 98, 99 (note 1), 105 (note 144), 106 (note 169), 155, 156, 161, 169
Wasby, Stephen, 23 (note 2)
Weinstein, Jack B., 90
Weintraub, 98
Wellman, F. L., 242
Wenger, D., 23 (note 3)
White, 61, 65, 153, 154
Wigmore, J. H., 46, 65, 96, 97, 99 (notes 19, 20), 107 (notes 205, 208), 253 (note 3)
Williams, G. R. 247
Williams, S. T., 75
Wingo, 127
Winter, R. K., Jr., 158, 171 (note 62), 251
Wright, J. S., 74, 103 (note 104)

Younger, Evelle J., 84, 85, 105 (note 151), 121

Zeisel, H., 19, 219, 220, 227, 228, 230 (note 20), 231 (note 43), 232 (notes 50, 63), 233 (note 71)
Zeitz, Leonard, 87, 88, 106 (note 167)
Zielinski, Virginia, 78
Zimbardo, P. G., 246
Zion, 105 (notes 152, 153, 156)

SUBJECT INDEX

Accusation, right of, 19, 20, 23, 113-44
abuses categorized, 114, 120
abuses discussed:
inappropriate application of criminal law, 136-37
insufficient evidence, 121-29
selective prosecution, 129-35
overview of procedures, 114-21
for juvenile offenses, 114
major and minor offenses contrasted, 114
for minor non-traffic violations, 116-17
for minor traffic violations, 116
notice required, 113
prosecutor, role of in, 115
Accusatorial method; see Adversary system
Administrators, 22
Adversary system, 18, 61-62, 69, 70, 72, 95, 147-48, 237-38, 253
purposes served by, 249-50
as zero-sum game, 250
Arraignment, 124
Arrest, 18, 23
after a stop-and-frisk, 37
pursuant to a search, 35-36
Arrest Warrants; see Warrants

Bail, right to, 18-19, 21, 23, 124, 152, 177-205; see also Bondsmen; Preventive detention
constitutionality of, 199-200
efforts to reform, 180-88
legislative action, 181-83
opposition to, 184
Vera Foundation studies, 181, 188
functions of, 177-78
future alternatives, 195-200
setting of, 178-80, 183, 199-200
Bench trials, 19
Bondsmen 177, 181

Canadian law, 37
Capital punishment, 19
Chimel rule, 33-34
Collateral estoppel; see estoppel
Confessions, 18, 21, 23, 61-108; see also Self-incrimination, privilege against
in absence of counsel 62, 71-77
applicability of fourteenth amendment due process requirements to, 66-71
in Communist nations, 95
decisions on under the Burger court, 91-95
effects of exclusionary rulings on, 80-89
effect of Omnibus Crime Act of 1968 on, 89-91
involuntary, 65-71

in multi-defendant trials, 76-77
post-Miranda cases on, 77-80
repudiation of during trial, 61, 65, 72, 74
rules governing admission:
in federal prosecutions, 61, 65-66
in state prosecutions, 61, 66-71
use of to impeach a defendant's testimony, 91-93
voluntariness, proof of, 70-71, 93-94
Confrontation, right of, 19
Correctional process; see also Probation; Sentencing
components of, 261-62
discretion in, 262
effect of plea bargaining on, 263
for misdemeanors, 277-78
treatment prior to conviction, 262-63
Counsel, right to, 17, 20, 21, 23, 61, 147-74
at arraignment, 153-54
before arraignment, 76, 152
cost of providing, 168
at detention hearings, 190
during arrest, 77
in federal appellate proceedings, 154-56, 162
in felony cases, 150
in grand jury proceedings, 122, 152-53
at habeas corpus evidentiary hearings, 161-63
history of, 148-50
after indictment, 70
before indictment, 75-76
in juvenile and other commitment proceedings, 163-64
at line-ups, 243
methods of providing for indigents:
assigned counsel system, 166-67
mixed private-public system, 166, 168
public defender system, 167-68
volunteer defender system, 166, 167
in misdemeanor cases, 150-51
at parole revocation hearings, 277
at photographic identifications, 243
during police interrogation, 62, 71-77
at post-conviction proceedings, 157-61
at preliminary hearings, 126, 153
by prisoners, 275-76
prospective application of, 77
in deferred sentencing proceedings, 269
in state appellate proceedings, 156-57, 162
in tax investigations, 77
at trial, 154
waiver of, 148, 164-66
when waiving a jury trial, 214
Cross-examination, right to, 249

Delay in arraignment, 66, 74
Deportation, 275
Desuetude, 131-32
Detainer, 274-75
Discovery, pre-trial, 128-29
Discretion; see Prosecutorial discretion
Double jeopardy, 19, 23, 283-98
  in appellate proceedings, 287
  application of, 297
  and dual jurisdictions, 287, 293
  effect on defendant appeals, 289-90
  effect on jury verdicts, 286
  effect on state courts, 288-91
  and federalism, 287, 289, 293
  as a fundamental right, 285
  incorporation of into due process clause of
    fourteenth amendment, 284
  and mistrials, 287-88
  and principle of collateral estoppel,
    285-86, 292
  tests used to determine, 291-92
Due process:
  and double jeopardy, 285
  in fifth amendment, 127, 136, 243
  in fourteenth amendment, 66-71, 127,
    136, 162, 212, 213, 243
  and jury trials, 251
  meaning of, 285
  in prison discipline, 274
  in probation setting, 269
  in searches and seizures, 47
  in setting prison sentences, 270
Dying declaration, 241

Eavesdropping, electronic and mechanical;
    see Searches and seizures
Eighth amendment, 189, 190, 191
  bail provision of, 178
  cruel and unusual punishment provision
    of, 273, 274
Entrapment, 132-35
Equal protection of fourteenth amendment,
    163, 197
Estoppel, collateral, 285-86; see also Double
    jeopardy
Evidence, types of, 237-38; see also Witnesses
Exclusionary rule; see Searches and seizures

Fifth amendment; see also Self-
    incrimination, privilege against
  double jeopardy, 284
First amendment, 273
Formal accusation; see Accusation, right of
Fourteenth amendment, 162, 212, 238
  due process clause of, 66-71, 213, 284,
    286
  equal protection clause of, 197
Fourth amendment; see also Privacy, right
    of; Searches and seizures

clauses of discussed, 30, 33, 35
origins of, 30
U.S. Supreme Court interpretations of,
    30-35
waiver of, 38
Free press, 136-37

Grand juries, 119
  and admissability of evidence, 123
  composition of, 121-22
  counsel, right of before, 152-53
  discriminatory selection of, 130-31
  indictment by, 21
  influence of prosecutor on, 123
  judicial control over, 123-24
  secrecy of, 122-23
Guilty pleas, 61-65, 151
  in federal courts, 63-64
  in state courts, 64

Habeas corpus, writs of, 149, 161-63,
    275-76
Huntley hearings, 70-71

Immunity, 119
Imprisonment, 20, 271-76
Indictment, 62, 119, 121, 127
Information, 119, 121, 127
Inquisitional system, 61-62, 66-67, 69, 70,
    96-98, 253
Intent; see also Witnesses
  effects of culture on definition of, 247-49
  and freedom of choice, 248-49
  in law, 247

Jail; see Imprisonment
Judges 21, 22, 43-44, 119, 218-20, 228-29,
    250-51, 261, 265, 266, 270-71, 276,
    288, 294
Juries and Jurors, 23, 135, 250-52
  criminal, 286
  effect of order on presentation of informa-
    tion on, 251
  empirical research on:
    characteristics of jurors, 224-25
    comparing bench and jury trials, 218-20
    decision-making by, 225-28
    evaluating expert testimony, 221-22
    reaction of jurors to jury service, 228-29
    using experimental juries, 220-24, 240
  representation of blacks on, 22
Jury trial, right to, 20, 21, 19, 237
  effect of pretrial publicity on, 215-16
  effect of public opinion on, 251
  number of jurors required for:
    in federal courts, 212-13
    in state courts, 212-13
  prejudicial events during, 251-52
  purpose of, 214

and selection of jurors, 214-17, 240
  when required, 211-12
Juveniles, 20, 114, 274

Legislators, 22

Mallory Rule; see McNabb-Mallory ex-
  clusionary rule
McNabb-Mallory exclusionary rule, 65-66,
  73-77, 89-91
Mens rea; see Intent
Miranda warnings, 37, 38, 52, 71-89
Motions to suppress, 127

Narcotics, 34
Negroes, 20, 22
Nolle prosequi, 119
Notice of charges, right of, 19, 113
    application to states, 127
    and pre-trial discovery, 128-29
    in prison disciplinary actions, 274
  reform needed, 128-29
  requirement of, 127-28
  rules for, 128-29

Overbreadth principle, 136-37

Pardon, power to, 278
Parole, 275, 276-77; see also Probation
  compared to probation, 277
  and misdemeanors, 278
  parole hearings, 277
  revocation of, 277
Parole Boards 261, 270-71, 276-77
Parole hearings, 276
Parole officers, 261
Plea bargaining, 62, 87, 119, 128, 135, 151,
  165, 263
Police, 18, 20, 29, 30, 31, 32, 33, 34, 35,
  36, 37, 39, 46-49, 49-53, 67, 72,
  117-18
Preliminary hearing, 124, 125-27, 153
  contrasted with grand jury proceedings,
    126
  evaluation of, 125-26
  purpose of, 125
  ways to improve, 126-27
Presentment, 121
Pressure groups, 22
Pretrial release; see Bail
Preventive detention, 37, 189-200
  constitutionality of 189-93, 198
  District of Columbia legislation on, 189,
    193
  problems of, 193-95
Prison officials, 261
Prisoners:
  classification of, 272
  effect of detainers on, 275

effects of prison record on future of, 278
  rights of, 272
Prisons:
  censorship of mail in, 273
  conditions in, 273
  counsel, right to in, 275-76
  disciplinary rules in, 274
  and eighth amendment, 273-74
  practice of religion in, 273
Privacy, right to, 38, 39-53; see also
  Searches and seizures
Privilege against self-incrimination; see Self-
  incrimination, privilege against
Probable cause, 135, 153
  to arrest, 32
  general definition, 30, 36
  to search, 32-33
  to stop-and-frisk, 37
Probation; see also Parole
  compared to parole, 277
  conditions of, 267-69
  effect of felony violation on, 269
  revocations of, 268-69, 270, 275
Probation officers, 261, 264, 267-69
Prosecutorial discretion, 113, 114, 135-37,
  294
  in decision to charge, 135
  proving abuse of, 130
  types of, 118-19
  ways of controlling, 120-21
Prosecutors; 18, 62, 72, 80, 261, 264,
  293-94; see also Prosecutorial discretion
  constraints on policy-making by, 137-39
  at federal level, 115-16
  and police 118
  role of, in accusation, 115-22
  at state and local level, 115

Rights of the accused:
  behavioral research on, 18-19, 23
  causal forces behind, 19-23
  defined, 15
  differential recognition of, 20-21
    and characteristics of decision-makers,
      21
    toward the disadvantaged, 20
    and industrialization, 20-21
    toward juveniles, 20
    and nature of crime, 21
    and nature of victim, 20-21
    toward women, 20
  earlier literature on, 16
  effects of, 17-19
  effects of education on, 20, 22-23
  expansion of, 21-23
  from first court appearance to trial,
    109-205; see also Accusation, right of;
    Counsel, right to; Bail, right of; Notice,
    right of

in law and action, 16
overview, effects and causes, 15-24
post-trial, 261-98; see also Correctional
    process; Double jeopardy; Parole;
    Prisons; Prisoners; Probation; Sentenc-
    ing
prior to first court appearance, 25-108; see
    also Searches and seizures; Confessions;
    Self-incrimination, privilege against
and societal affluence, 22-23
summarized, 15
at trial, 207-56; see also Jury trials; Bench
    trials; Trials; Witnesses; Cross-
    examination
Reasonable doubt standard, 191
Res gestae rule, 241
Right to silence; see Self-incrimination,
    privilege against
Riots, 22

Searches and seizures, 18, 29-57; see also
    Probable cause
administrative searches, 44-45
without an arrest warrant, 35-36
Chimel Rule on, 33-34, 35
compared with the use of informers, 41-42
by consent, 38
evolution of Supreme Court doctrines on,
    33-35
exclusionary rule on, 18, 22, 29, 42,
    46-53, 127
compared with practices in other coun-
    tries, 46
empirical evaluations of compliance
    with, 49-53
in federal prosecutions, 46-48
to ensure police compliance, 48-49
in state prosecutions, 46-48
of a home, 32-33, 35, 38
mere evidence rule, 40
in minor offenses, 34
of moving vehicles, 32, 34-35
mechanical eavesdropping and wire-
    tapping, 29, 39-44
in narcotics cases, 34
and national security eavesdropping, 44
by participant monitoring, 41-42
particularity requirement, 30, 40
plain sight rule, 35
on probable cause alone, 32, 35
regulation of under Omnibus Crime Act of
    1968, 42-44
requirements for and limitations on stop-
    and-frisks, 36-38
by third parties, 39-40
without a search warrant, 29, 32-35
types of, 31
incident to valid arrest, 32, 33
views of Supreme Court justices on, 31-32
warrant requirements for, 32-33, 40
Search warrants; see Warrants

Seizure; see Searches and seizures
Self-incrimination, privilege against 23, 49,
    61-108; see also Confessions
before grand juries, 122
as basis for inadmissability of involuntary
    confessions, 65-66, 70
extension of to state prosecutions, 66-71,
    72-73
during police interrogation, 71-77
and granting of immunity from prosecu-
    tion, 119
under the required records doctrine, 98
during a stop-and-frisk, 37
Sentencing; see also Correctional process;
    Probation
    appellate review of, 271
    decision to imprison:
    alternatives to, 267
    factors affective, 266-267
    determining length of sentences,
    270-71
    expungement of from records, 278
    presentence investigation, 264
    presentence report, 264-65
    psychiatric examinations, 265
    sentencing hearings, 264
    Sixth amendment 113, 191-92, 238,
    243, 275; see also Counsel, right of;
    Habeas Corpus, writs of; Notice, right
    of
Spike mike, 39-40
State's attorney; see Prosecutors
Stop-and-frisk; see Searches and seizures
Summons, 117

Testimony, 23; see also Witnesses
Treatment, right to, 274
Trial; see also Bench trials, Jury trial, right
    to; Adversary system
    right to confront witnesses at, 238
    and detainers, 275
    right to, by jury, 211-33
True bill, 123

Vagueness doctrine, 136

Warrants:
    arrest, 35, 117, 124
    general warrant, 30
    search warrant, 30
Wiretapping; see Searches and seizures
Witnesses; see also Evidence; Intent
    effects on of different methods of
    interrogation, 244-46
    in identification proceedings, 243-44
    influence of public pressure on, 241
    perjurious testimony by, 249
    reliability of perceptions of, 238-41
    right to call and question at trial, 19
    in sentencing hearings, 264
Women, 20

DATE DUE

RESERVE OC 28 76			
JE 2 '77			
MY 7 '79			
JUN 9 1980			
OCT 1 9 1981			
JAN 2 5 1982			
MAR 8 1982			
JUL 1 2 1982			
DEC 5 1983			
MAY 2 3 '88			
APR 2 8 '90			
AUG 4 '91			
MAY 31 '92			
			PRINTED IN U.S.A.